(Map: The Theatre of War in North America — geographic labels include) LABRADOR, Little Esquimaux, QUEBEC, GULF of St. LAURENCE, NOVA SCOTIA, NEW FOUND LAND, C. BRETON I., Nova Scotia Fishing Banks, Great Bank of Newfoundland, Gaspesia, Fundy Bay, Annapolis Royal, C. Cod, OCEAN, Longitude West from London, Longitude West from Ferro.

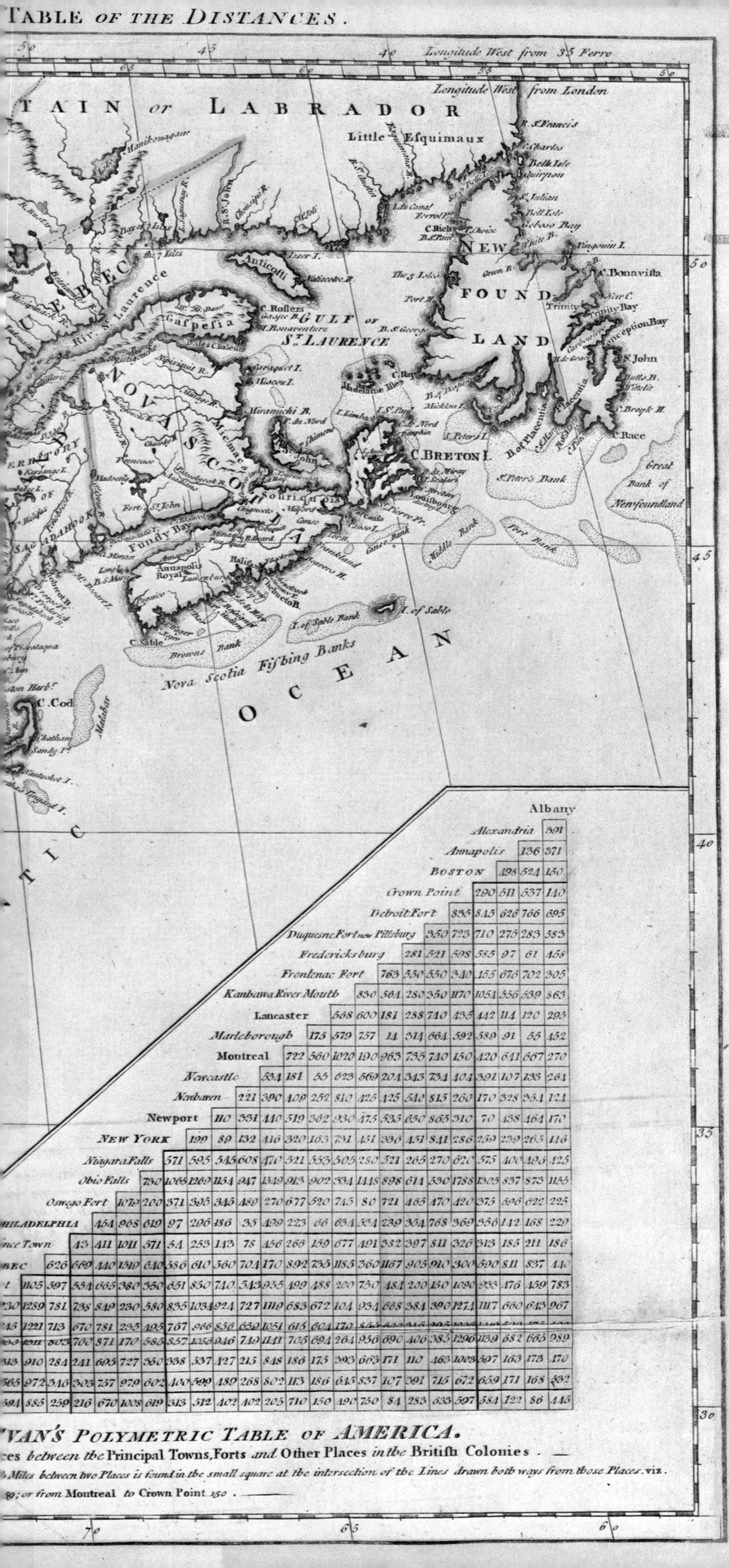

The Theatre of War in North America

¶ This map was published in early 1776 and sold in the streets of London for one shilling. It had text printed below the map which described the colonies in detail. The colonies listed were Newfoundland, Quebec, Nova-Scotia, New England, New York, New Jersey, Pennsylvania, Maryland, Virginia, North and South Carolina, Georgia, and East and West Florida. ¶ The table of distances emphasized the expanse of the area covered by the colonies. The 586 miles shown in the table between Philadelphia and Quebec was farther than the entire north-south length of Great Britain.

The Theatre of War in North America, with the Roads and A Table of the Distances. London, R. Sayer & J. Bennett, March 20, 1776. (16″ x 20″)

The map is repeated on the back endsheet with an overlay locating the fifty basic maps of the Atlas.

Distance Table (Evan's Polymetric Table of America)

	Albany																				
Alexandria	391																				
Annapolis	136	371																			
BOSTON	498	524	150																		
Crown Point	290	511	537	110																	
Detroit Fort	895	845	625	766	695																
Duquesne Fort now Pittsburg	350	723	710	275	283	583															
Fredericksburg	281	521	508	585	97	61	458														
Frontenac Fort	763	550	550	340	155	676	702	305													
Kanhawa River Mouth	850	564	280	350	1170	1051	556	539	863												
Lancaster	568	600	181	288	710	435	442	114	120	295											
Marleborough	175	579	757	14	314	664	592	389	91	55	452										
Montreal	722	560	1020	190	963	735	740	150	420	641	567	270									
Newcastle	584	181	55	623	569	204	343	731	404	391	107	133	261								
Newhaven	221	390	409	252	810	425	425	510	815	260	170	328	354	121							
Newport	110	331	410	519	362	930	475	535	650	865	310	70	438	464	170						
NEW YORK	190	89	132	416	320	163	731	451	336	451	841	286	259	239	265	116					
Niagara Falls	571	595	545	608	470	521	553	305	280	521	265	270	620	575	400	493	425				
Ohio Falls	750	1065	1269	1154	947	1349	913	902	334	1148	898	614	530	1788	1305	837	873	1155			
Oswego Fort	1079	200	371	395	345	489	270	677	520	745	80	721	465	470	420	375	396	622	225		
PHILADELPHIA	454	968	619	97	296	186	35	499	223	66	634	334	239	334	768	369	956	142	168	229	
Prince Town	43	411	1011	571	54	253	143	78	456	266	159	677	491	382	397	811	326	313	185	211	186
QUEBEC	626	669	440	1519	640	586	610	560	704	170	892	735	1185	360	1167	905	910	300	590	811	837

(Additional rows of figures continue below, with row labels trimmed off the page.)

EVAN'S POLYMETRIC TABLE OF AMERICA.

...ces between the Principal Towns, Forts and Other Places in the British Colonies.

...e Miles between two Places is found in the small square at the intersection of the Lines drawn both ways from those Places. viz.

...; or from Montreal to Crown Point 150.

Atlas of the
AMERICAN REVOLUTION

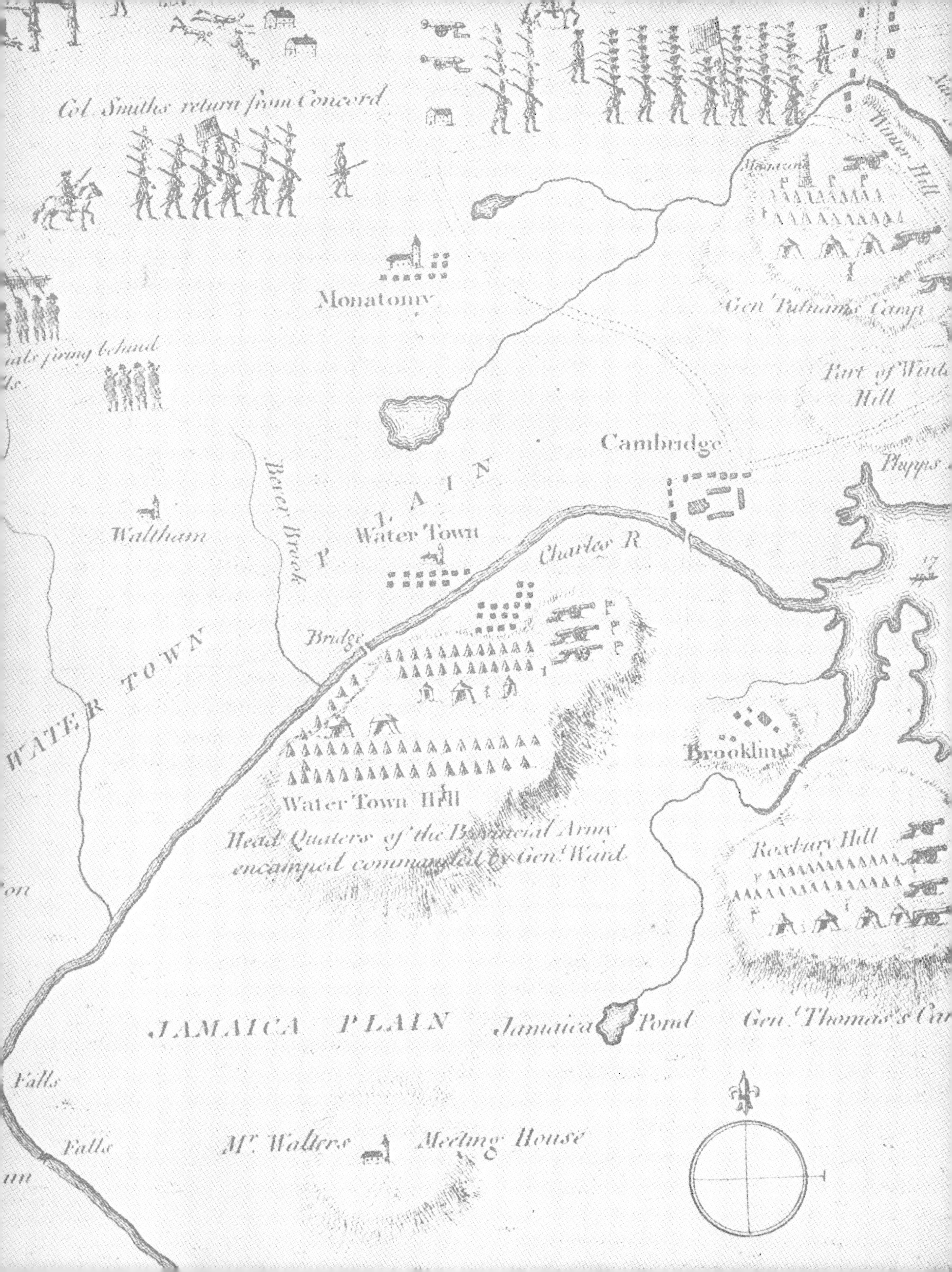

Col. Smiths return from Concord

Monatomy

ials firing behind
ds

Waltham

Bever Brook

P L A I N

Water Town

WATER TOWN

Bridge

Charles R.

Water Town Hill

Head Quaters of the Provincial Army
encamped commanded by Gen! Ward

JAMAICA PLAIN   Jamaica Pond

Falls

Falls   Mr. Walters   Meeting House

Winter Hill

Magazine

Gen! Putnams Camp

Part of Winter
Hill

Cambridge

Phipps

Brookline

Roxbury Hill

Gen! Thomas's Ca

17

Atlas of the
AMERICAN
REVOLUTION

Map selection and commentary by Kenneth Nebenzahl
Narrative text by Don Higginbotham

RAND McNALLY & COMPANY
Chicago • New York • San Francisco

PHOTO CREDITS

Acknowledgment is made to the following sources for use of the photographs in this atlas on the pages listed:

22-23 Library of Congress/24 Yale University Art Gallery/25 Yale University Art Gallery/26 Gilbert Stuart, *John Adams,* National Gallery of Art, Washington, D.C., Gift of Mrs. Robert Homans; New York Public Library, Astor, Lenox and Tilden Foundation/27 Fort Ticonderoga Library; John Trumbull, *John Jay,* Yale University Art Gallery/28 Mount Vernon Ladies Association; Independence National Historical Park Collection; Independence National Historical Park Collection/31 Library of Congress/32 Courtesy, Patrick Henry Memorial Foundation, Inc., Red Hill Shrine, Charlotte County, Va.; Library of Congress; New York Public Library/33 Library of Congress/34 Worcester Art Museum/35 The Granger Collection; Library of Congress/36 Concord Antiquarian Society; American Antiquarian Society/38 Concord Antiquarian Society; Independence National Historical Park Collection; Connecticut Historical Society/39 Picture Collection, New York Public Library/42 Courtesy, The Mariners Museum, Newport News, Va./54 Library of Congress; Courtesy, Washington and Lee University; John Trumbull, *Battle of Bunker Hill,* Yale University Art Gallery/64 Independence National Historical Park Collection; Collection of Mrs. Harriet Moseley Bodley, Newburyport, Mass. (Photo by David F. Lawlor)/65 Courtesy, The Mariners Museum, Newport News, Va.; Historical Society of Pennsylvania; Courtesy, Chicago Historical Society/68-69 Library of Congress/ 70 Colonial Williamsburg Collection, Williamsburg, Va./71 New York Public Library, Astor, Lenox and Tilden Foundations/72 Courtesy, Fort Ticonderoga/73 Courtesy, The Mariners Museum, Newport News, Va.; Concord Antiquarian Society/75 American Antiquarian Society; Mount Vernon Ladies Association/76 Historical Society of Pennsylvania/77 Library of Congress/78 Guilford Courthouse National Military Park (Photo by Dave Nicholson); Sanborn Studio; Courtesy, Chicago Historical Society/81 Bequest of Charles Allen Munn, 1924, Metropolitan Museum of Art; Library of Congress/82 Minute Man National Historical Park Project; Ewing Galloway/83 New York Public Library; Courtesy, The Mariners Museum, Newport News, Va./101 Courtesy, Museum of Fine Arts, Boston, Gift of Owners of Boston Museum/107 Library of Congress/111 Courtesy, The Mariners Museum, Newport News, Va.; Saratoga National Historical Park/130 Chase Manhattan Bank Museum of Moneys of the World; Historical Society of Pennsylvania; Valley Forge Historical Society/131 Historical Society of Pennsylvania/136-137 Library of Congress/139 Massachusetts Magazine, 1793 (William L. Clemens Library)/141 American Antiquarian Society/143 Kennedy Galleries; Museum of Early Southern Decorative Arts/144 Library of Congress/145 Library of Congress; Spencer Collection, New York Public Library/146 Index of American Design/147 The Filson Club/147 New York Public Library; Library of Congress/148 Indiana Historical Department; Library of Congress/149 Eastern National Park Association; Chicago Historical Society; Courtesy, The Mariners Museum, Newport News, Va./150 Library of Congress/151 United States Naval Academy Museum (Photo by Stu Whelan)/164 Library of Congress/185 Library of Congress/189 Library of Congress/190 Rembrandt Peale, *Washington Before Yorktown,* In the Collection of the Corcoran Gallery of Art, Gift of Mount Vernon Ladies Association; John Trumbull, *Surrender of Lord Cornwallis,* Yale University Art Gallery/191 Library of Congress/192-193 Library of Congress/195 Historical Society of Pennsylvania/199 Bequest of Charles Allen Munn, 1924, Metropolitan Museum of Art/200 Courtesy, Museum of Fine Arts, Boston, Bequest of Robert C. Winthrop; Courtesy, Henry DuPont Winterthur Museum/201 Rare Book Division, New York Public Library/202 Library of Congress/ 203 New York Public Library

Contents

BEHIND THE LINES
Pages 138-145

THE FRINGES: LAND AND SEA
Pages 146-161

Acknowledgments

One of the unique features of this atlas is that the publisher was able to work directly from the often priceless original engravings. This allowed the maps illustrated here to have been reproduced without the intermediary steps of reduction and enlargement that working from photographic film transparencies would have required. The fidelity of these reproductions was thus made possible. The cooperation and generosity of the owners or custodians of the original maps enabled us to present 200-year-old maps in a way seldom seen by the public. The source of each original is indicated beside the map.

Many people have aided significantly in the compilation and production of this atlas and it is a privilege to recognize them here. Mr. Robert W. Karrow, Jr., Curator of Maps of The Newberry Library, was my research associate for *The Bibliography of Contemporary Printed Maps of The American Revolutionary War*, forthcoming from The University of Chicago Press. During the compilation of the bibliography, in which we worked together, Mr. Karrow made numerous contributions to the atlas. Also at The Newberry Library, Dr. David Woodward, Program Director of The Hermon Dunlap Smith Center for the History of Cartography; Dr. Barbara Bartz Petchnik, Cartographic Editor, *Atlas of Early American History;* the library's director, Dr. Lawrence W. Towner; and many others of the staff have been of great assistance. Mr. Howard H. Peckham, Director, and Mr. Douglas W. Marshall, Curator of Maps, of The William L. Clements Library, The University of Michigan; Dr. Walter W. Ristow, Chief, and Mr. Andrew M. Modelski, of The Library of Congress Geography and Map Division; Mr. Thomas R. Adams, Director, and Miss Jeanette Black of The John Carter Brown Library, Brown University; Mrs. Elizabeth E. Roth of The New York Public Library; Mr. James Gregory of The New-York Historical Society; Mr. Alexander O. Vietor, Sterling Memorial Library, Yale University; General Edmund C. R. Lasher; Dr. Seymour Schwartz; and Mr. Isadore M. Scott have all helped in various important ways.

Professor Higginbotham has contributed a text setting the stage, giving the background, and analyzing the results of the American Revolution, which compliments the maps themselves and their descriptions. His narrative has been described by a leading historian as brilliant.

Mr. Paul T. Tiddens of Rand McNally and Company has served effectively and tirelessly as liaison between the publisher and the editor and has made many important contributions.

My wife, Jocelyn Spitz Nebenzahl, has worked with me on this atlas and the associated bibliographical project for the past four years. Her continual inspiration and critical arrangement of time enabled the completion of both publications.

Kenneth Nebenzahl
Chicago, 1974

Introduction

A<small>T THE TIME</small> of the American Revolution, instant dissemination of news from remote battle scenes, as we are accustomed to today, was of course unknown. Telephones to connect the combat zone with headquarters; wire services to keep the world in touch with the day's events; cameras to record views of the battle; and immediate television transmission around the world by satellite, with the ability to virtually transform the viewer into a participant—all these are techniques of a later era. However, the English people were just as keenly interested in the war in America as people are today in events taking place elsewhere on the globe because chances were great that they had kith and kin involved in the struggle. Maps helped them to understand and visualize the military engagements between His Majesty's forces and the rebels across the sea. As Lloyd Brown, one of the most respected historians of cartography, wrote some forty years ago, "Pictorial news about the war was limited almost entirely to maps, and as source material on the Revolution these are of the utmost importance."

The maps and battle plans that make up this *Atlas of the American Revolution* record specific military and naval activities, from the first confrontation at Lexington and Concord to the British surrender at Yorktown. The actions shown range geographically from Quebec to Savannah and from the coast of Maine to the Mississippi. Also included are battle maps of significant engagements in the West Indies and a plan of the epic siege of Gibraltar—two areas of the world where the war spread beyond the American continental boundaries. In addition to this graphic coverage of the War of Independence, the Atlas includes street plans of the principal cities of eighteenth century North America and regional maps for overall orientation.

The unusually excellent and interesting maps seen here have been carefully selected, based on their content, rarity, and quality of engraving. Each map was engraved from a drawing made by an eyewitness, and they were all originally published during the period of the events they depict. They are arranged chronologically by area in accordance with the way the fighting progressed. The Flowchart (pages 19–21) summarizes the actions by location and time.

Most of the maps included were engraved and published in London. The best surveyors and cartographers in America at the time were British military engineers. The British had more facilities available for mapmaking, and they had a larger audience—several of the maps appeared in more than one edition, an indication that they were avidly sought not only by the government and the military but by the public as well. In some cases the same plate was reworked several times to revise the location of the troops as movements progressed. Maps from the "Theatre of War in America" represented a substantial business for the London map trade.

It is amazing how promptly many of these graphic interpretations of the military activities were produced. Some of the maps published in London, over 3,000 miles from the scene of battle, appeared in print just a month after the action, despite the fact that merely crossing the Atlantic could take from four to twelve weeks. Also included are some examples of maps that were produced later in the apologias of John Burgoyne, Banastre Tarleton, John Graves Simcoe, and other British commanders attempting to justify their performances in view of the often disappointing results.

The maps produced represented the publishers' sense of demand at the time. Thus, the most important events were usually the most adequately mapped. We can only speculate as to why elaborate maps were produced of some minor engagements. For instance, a detailed plan of the minor skirmish at "Spencer's Ordinary" appeared in Colonel John Simcoe's *A Journal of the Operation of the Queen's Rangers* (1787). On the other hand, no map was published in the eighteenth century of two important battles in South Carolina, King's Mountain and Cowpens, although these were the most important American victories in the South until Yorktown. If British publishers understandably did not trouble themselves to produce engravings of these reverses, even though there are examples of other occasions when they did so, it is regrettable that no one in Philadelphia or Boston published a map of either of these events.

The science of military topographical engineering, and the art of mapmaking based upon it, had been developed to a very high degree by 1775. Viewing the maps, charts, and plans in this Atlas makes it possible to visualize the events somewhat as they appeared to the eighteenth century public. The map commentary is written to tell the general story of each map and what it shows, but there is much left for the reader to discover as he studies the map.

The outcome of the War of Independence surprised the watching world. Many time-honored beliefs were suddenly dissolved. Not only did a rag-tag, ill-equipped army of civilians emerge as the victor, but the aristocrats and professional soldiers whom they defeated lost the first colonial revolution of modern history. Imperialism was far from dead throughout the world, but its armor was seriously cracked.

The next few generations were to see most of the Western Hemisphere gain independence from the European powers. While Asia and Africa had to wait until this century to break the bonds of colonialism, the significant beginning was made when the Declaration of Independence was issued and the ensuing contest won.

Independence from the crown was not a pressing issue at the onset. This was made clear at the time of Lexington and Concord — numerous opportunities existed for reconciliation. However, what had begun as rectifiable administrative grievances between the colonies and the home government developed, through unskilled handling, into the first great call to freedom by people governed from afar.

The *Atlas of the American Revolution* will give another dimension to the many accounts, interpretations, and reinterpretations of the war that are being prepared during this decade of the Bicentennial Commemoration of Independence and the establishment of the United States of America.

Regional Maps

The Seat of War in the Northern Colonies

¶ Originally published in *The American Military Pocket Atlas* issued in 1776 to British officers fighting in America, this and the two maps which follow reflect the standard view of the geography of America held by people at the outbreak of the Revolution. ¶ Considerable emphasis was placed on mapping the banks in the Atlantic as they affected the important fishing industry. Halifax, Nova Scotia, is shown. It was to this port that the British army and navy proceeded after the evacuation of Boston and before the invasion of New York. ¶ In this delineation the province of New York extends eastward to the Connecticut River, including all of what later became Vermont. The strategic St. Lawrence Valley is emphasized, as is the waterway from Quebec via Lake Champlain into the heart of New York. ¶ Within the limits of this map may be found the locations of the actions listed on the Chronological Flow chart for the New England, Northern, and Middle Atlantic Theaters.

SHOWN ON PAGES 12—13
A General Map of the Northern British Colonies in America. Which comprehends the Province of Quebec, the Government of Newfoundland, Nova-Scotia, New-England and New-York. From the Maps Published by the Admiralty and Board of Trade, Regulated by the Astronomic and Trigonometric Observations of Major Holland, and Corrected from Governor Pownall's Late Map 1776. London, Sayer & Bennett, 14 August 1776 (19" x 26")

The Seat of War in the Middle British Colonies

¶ The central arena of the conflict is shown here on a larger scale than the previous map. The coastline from the mouth of the Chesapeake to Narragansett Bay is carefully delineated, and considerable detail appears westward as far as what is now Indiana. The inset focuses on the "Illinois Country"— the western Great Lakes region north of the Ohio River. Fort Detroit is shown from where the British governor Hamilton unsuccessfully attempted to hold this farthest western frontier region against George Rogers Clark and his small force of Virginia militiamen. ¶ The considerable detail included on this map enables the viewer to follow most of the continental campaigns of the war, excepting New England, Quebec, and the deep South. Although more accurate in the coastal areas than in the interior, as was generally the case with maps of the eighteenth century, a good idea of the relationship between the Appalachian Mountains and coastal colonies is indicated, as is a reasonably accurate conception of the Ohio River valley.

SHOWN ON PAGES 14—15
A General Map of the Middle British Colonies in America. Containing Virginia, Maryland, the Delaware Counties, Pennsylvania and New Jersey. With the addition of New York, and of the Greatest Part of New England, as also of the Bordering Parts of the Province of Quebec, improved from several Surveys made after the late War, and Corrected from Governor Pownall's Late Map 1776. London, Sayer & Bennett, 15 October 1776 (19" x 26")

London, Printed for Robt. Sayer & Jno. Bennett, Map & Sea Chart Se

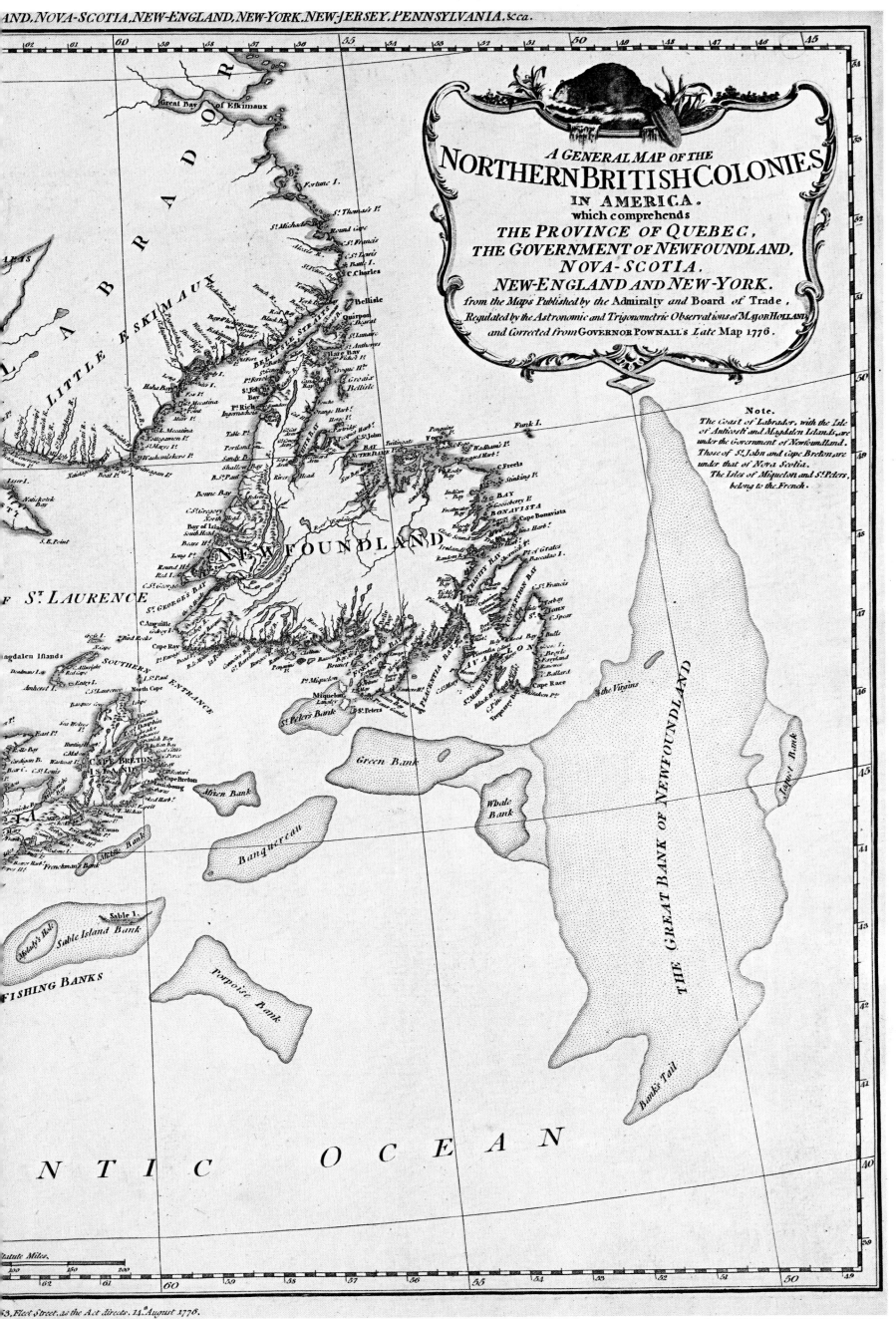

A GENERAL MAP OF THE

NORTHERN BRITISH COLONIES

IN AMERICA.
which comprehends
THE PROVINCE OF QUEBEC,
THE GOVERNMENT OF NEWFOUNDLAND,
NOVA-SCOTIA.
NEW-ENGLAND AND NEW-YORK.
from the Maps Published by the Admiralty and Board of Trade,
Regulated by the Astronomic and Trigonometric Observations of MAJOR HOLLAND
and Corrected from GOVERNOR POWNALL's Late Map 1776.

Note.
The Coast of Labrador, with the Isle
of Anticosti and Magdalen Islands, are
under the Government of Newfoundland.
Those of St John and Cape Breton are
under that of Nova Scotia.
The Isles of Miquelon and St Peters,
belong to the French.

LABRADOR

Great Bay of Eskimaux

LITTLE ESKIMAUX

NEWFOUNDLAND

F ST. LAURENCE

SOUTHERN ENTRANCE

Magdalen Islands

CAPE BRETON ISLAND

AVALON

BAY BONAVISTA

Cape Bonavista

TRINITY BAY

CONCEPTION BAY

PLACENTIA BAY

FORTUNE BAY

Cape Race

St Peters Bank

Green Bank

Whale Bank

Misen Bank

Banquereau

THE GREAT BANK OF NEWFOUNDLAND

Jaquet Bank

Sable I.

Middle Bank

Melady's Hole

Sable Island Bank

FISHING BANKS

Porpoise Bank

Banks Tail

ATLANTIC OCEAN

Statute Miles

53, Fleet Street, as the Act directs. 14 August 1776.

13

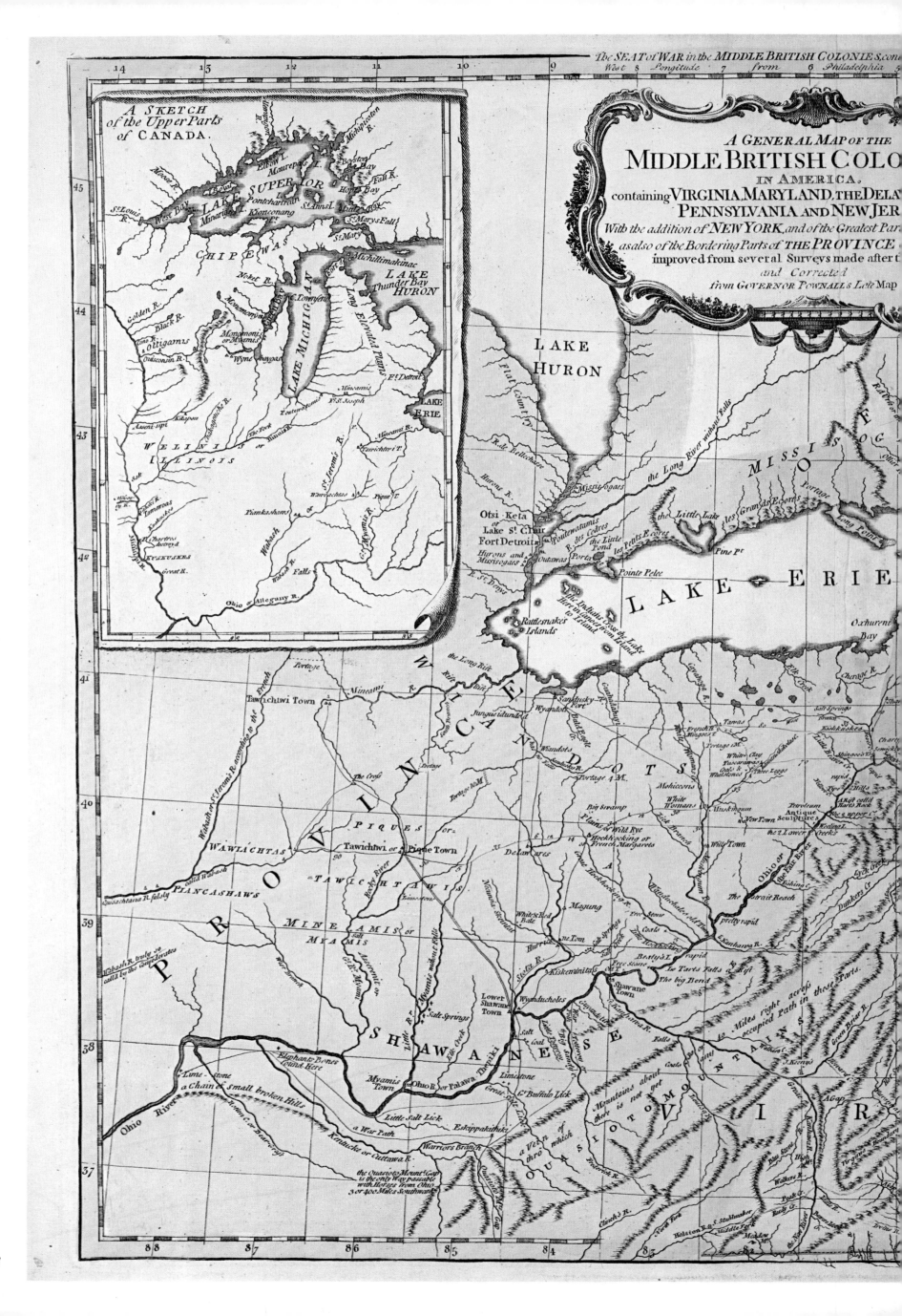

A SKETCH
of the Upper Parts
of CANADA.

LAKE SUPERIOR

CHIPEWAS

LAKE MICHIGAN

LAKE
HURON
Thunder Bay

Ft Detroit
LAKE
ERIE

WELINIS
or
ILLINOIS

Ohio or Allegany R.

A GENERAL MAP OF THE
MIDDLE BRITISH COLO
IN AMERICA,
containing VIRGINIA, MARYLAND, the DELA
PENNSYLVANIA AND NEW JER
With the addition of NEW YORK, and of the Greatest Par
as also of the Bordering Parts of THE PROVINCE
improved from several Surveys made after t
and Corrected
from GOVERNOR POWNALL's Late Map

LAKE
HURON

MISS
OG

Otsi-Keta
or Lake St Clair
Fort Detroit

Hurons and
Mussisogaes

LAKE   ERIE

Oxhurent
Bay

Rattlesnake's
Islands

W I C A N D O T S

Tawichtwi Town   Mineami

Sandusky
Fort
Wyandots

Wyandots

P R O V I N C E

PIQUES or

Tawichtwi or   Pique Town

WAWIACHTAS

TAWICHTAWIS

PIANCASHAWS

MINE AMIS or
MYAMIS

Delawares

Muskingum

Ohio or

SHAWANESE

Lower
Shawane
Town

Shawane
Town

The big Bend

Ohio River

Myamis
Town   Ohio River Palawa Theepi

Elephants Bones
found Here

a Chain of small broken Hills

Lime-stone

S
I
O
T
O   M O U N T A I N S

V I R

Kentucke or Cuttawa R.

Warriors Branch

IRGINIA MARYLAND, THE DELAWARE COUNTIES, &c.

CANADA

QUEBEC

LAKE ONTARIO

NEW ENGLAND

NEW HAMPSHIRE

MASSACHUSETS BAY

PENNSYLVANIA

NEW YORK

NEW JERSEY

MARYLAND

DELAWARE COUNTIES

VIRGINIA

NORTH CAROLINA

ATLANTIC OCEAN

LONG ISLAND

CHESAPEAK BAY

DELAWARE BAY

London: Printed for R. Sayer & J. Bennett, Map, Chart & Printsellers, Nº 53, Fleet Street, as the Act directs, 25 Octr. 1775.

British Statute Miles 69½ to a Degree.

West Longitude from London

15

GULF OF MEXICO

LOUISIANA

WEST FLORIDA

EAST FLORIDA

GEORGIA

SOUTH

CHICKASAWS

CHOCTAWS

NAHCHEES

CHEROKEES

THE CREEK COUNTRY

THE MUSKOHGE NATION

BAY OF APALACHE

BAY OF TAMPA

CHATHAM BAY
Formerly
Bay of Juan Ponce de Leon

RICHMOND BAY

PLAN OF
CHARLESTOWN.

References
a. State House
b. Church
c. Beef Market
d. Watch House
e. St. Philips Church
f. Exchange
g. Work House

PLAN OF
ST. AUGUSTINE.

References
a. Fort St. Mark
b. Governor's House
c. Parade
d. a Church
e. Guard House
f. Parish Church
g. Franciscan Fryars
h. Dutch Church

A GENERAL MAP OF THE
SOUTHERN BRITISH COLONIES,
IN AMERICA,
comprehending
NORTH AND SOUTH CAROLINA,
GEORGIA,
EAST AND WEST FLORIDA,
with the NEIGHBOURING INDIAN COUNTRIES.
From the Modern Surveys of
Engineer de Brahm, Capt. Collet, Mouzon & Others;
and from the Large Hydrographical Survey of the Coasts
of East and West Florida.
By B. ROMANS.
1776.

The Seat of War in the Southern British Colonies

¶ The Carolinas, Georgia, and the Floridas are shown here with the territory that extended westward through the Indian countries to Louisiana. The complex Appalachian Mountains, with the Blue Ridge in the foreground, form a backdrop for the settlements inland of the port cities such as Savannah and Charleston, which flourished on the coast. It was out of the Cherokee country to the west that the "over mountain men" came to give the British their first serious defeat in the South at King's Mountain in the Camden district of South Carolina. ¶ From northern Georgia to southern Virginia during the years 1778 to 1781, many bloody engagements took place. The British under Cornwallis, Tarleton, and Rawdon fought against the Americans, led initially by Lincoln who was succeeded by Gates and finally by Greene. ¶ New Orleans was the base from which the Spanish governor, Galvez, launched his successful campaigns against Mobile and then Pensacola. These were significant victories which helped the Spanish to gain possession of both east and west Florida at the peace negotiations.

A General Map of the Southern British Colonies, in America. Comprehending North and South Carolina, Georgia, East and West Florida, with the Neighbouring Indian Countries. From the Modern Surveys of Engineer de Brahm, Capt. Collet, Mouzon & Others, and from the Large Hydrographical Survey of the Coasts of East and West Florida. By B. Romans. 1776. London, Sayer & Bennett, 15 October 1776 (19½" x 25")

THE REVOLUTIONARY WAR

1777

INVASION OF NEW YORK
Crown Point—Burgoyne's March
June 27, 1777
*Ticonderoga
July 2, 1777
Skenesboro
July 6, 1777
*Hubbardton
July 7, 1777
*Bennington
August 6, 1777
*1st battle of Saratoga
September 19, 1777
Brown's raid on Ticonderoga
September 24, 1777
*Clinton expedition
October 6, 1777
*2nd battle of Saratoga
October 7, 1777
*Burgoyne's surrender at Saratoga
October 17, 1777
St. Leger departs Montreal
June 23, 1777
Oswego
July 25, 1777
Fort Stanwix
August 2, 1777
Oriskany
August 6, 1777
Arnold's march
August 10, 1777
St. Leger's retreat
August 23, 1777

* NIAGARA-MOHAWK FRONTIER
British/Tory/Indian raids
1775-1777

*Princeton
January 3, 1777
Washington at Morristown
January 1777
Peekskill
March 23, 1777
Danbury
April 23, 1777
Howe opens Philadelphia campaign
August 28, 1777
*Brandywine
September 11, 1777
*Paoli (Trudruffrin)
September 21, 1777
*Occupation of Philadelphia
October 4, 1777
*Germantown
October 4, 1777
*Delaware River forts
October 10-November 21, 1777
Washington at Valley Forge
December 1777-June 1778

WESTERN FRONTIER
Wheeling raid
September 1, 1777

American Flag Resolution
June 14, 1777
Articles of Confederation adopted
November 15, 1777
Conway Cabal
October 28, 1777—January 1, 1778

1778

*American army & French fleet
at Rhode Island
July 29, 1778
*Battle of Rhode Island
August 29, 1778

Springfield
May 1778
Wyoming "Massacre"
July 3, 1778
*Cherry Valley "Massacre"
November 11, 1778

British leave Philadelphia
June 8, 1778
*Monmouth—last major battle in the north
June 29, 1778
Clinton in New York
July 5, 1778
Washington at White Plains
July 1778
*Stoney Point
July 16, 1778

British at Savannah
December 29, 1778

Nassau
January 27, 1778
British at Bermuda
November 2, 1778
*St. Lucia
December 12, 1778

George Rogers Clark to Falls of Ohio
June 26, 1778
*Kaskaskia
July 4, 1778
*Cahokia & Vincennes surrender
July 1778

Steuben at Valley Forge
February 1778
French Alliance
May 4, 1778

1779

*Penobscot
July 25, 1779

Sullivan's campaign
May-November 1779
Brodhead's expedition
August-September 1779
Tioga
August 1779
Newtown
August 29, 1779
Genesee
September 14, 1779
Sullivan returns to Wyoming
September 30, 1779

Augusta, Georgia
January 29, 1779
Beaufort, South Carolina
February 3, 1779
Portsmouth-Norfolk, Virginia
May 11, 1779
Charleston
May 11, 1779
*Savannah
October 9, 1779
Clinton to Charleston
December 26, 1779

St. Vincent
June 16, 1779
*Grenada
July 4, 1779

Spain enters war
June 1779
*Gibraltar siege
July 6, 1779—February 6, 1783
John Paul Jones' "Bonhomme Richard"
defeats "Serapis"
September 23, 1779

CHRONOLOGICAL FLOWCHART OF

1775   1776

	1775	1776
NORTHERN THEATER	**NEW ENGLAND** *Lexington & Concord *April 19, 1775* *Bunker Hill *June 17, 1775* **AMERICAN INVASION OF CANADA** Fort Ticonderoga *May 10, 1775* St. Johns-Chambly-Montreal *November 13, 1775* Arnold's march to Quebec *September 13, 1775* *Defeat at Quebec *December 31, 1775*	Dorchester Heights *March 2, 1776* *Evacuation of Boston *March 17, 1776* Retreat to Ticonderoga *June 8, 1776* *Valcour Island *October 11, 1776*
MIDDLE ATLANTIC THEATER		*New York—Howe at Staten Island *July 3, 1776* *Long Island *August 27, 1776* Harlem Heights *September 16, 1776* Throg's Point *October 12, 1776* *White Plains *October 28, 1776* *Fort Washington & Fort Lee *November 16-20, 1776* *Trenton, New Jersey *December 26, 1776*
SOUTHERN THEATER	Reedy River *November 22, 1775*	Clinton from Boston to Charleston *January 20, 1776* Moore's Creek bridge *February 27, 1776* Rendezvous off Cape Fear *May 31, 1776* *Attack on Sullivan's Island *June 28, 1776* British return to New York *July 21, 1776*
THE FRINGES		**WEST INDIES** Nassau *March 3, 4, 1776*
HISTORIC EVENTS	Patrick Henry, "liberty or death" *March 23, 1775* Paul Revere's ride *April 18, 1775* Second Continental Congress—Philadelphia *May 10, 1775* Howe, Burgoyne & Clinton at Boston with reinforcements *May 25, 1775* Washington Commander-in-Chief *June 15, 1775*	Gage succeeded by Howe *October 10, 1776* Paine's *Common Sense* *January 10, 1776* Declaration of Independence *July 4, 1776* First issue of Paine's *The Crisis* *December 19, 1776*

p in the Atlas

The Chronological Flowchart

The major battles and other important events have been indicated on the chart to give a three-page overview of the American Revolution. They have been plotted to show clearly where and when each action took place. The general trend of the war which started in the North and moved to the South is obvious.

At first the British hoped to quell the revolt in the North, but when this failed they tried to become firmly established in the Middle Atlantic Colonies. Similarly, attacks were launched in the South in an attempt to gain a firm foothold there.

*Ma

1780

1781

1782

British/Tory/Indian raids
March-April 1780

Mohawk Valley ravaged
April-June 1781
Johnstown
October 25, 1781

Springfield—Elizabethtown
June 7-23, 1780

Cowpens
January 17, 1781
*Guilford Courthouse
March 15, 1781
Chesapeake Bay battle
March 17, 1781
Hobkirk's Hill
April 25, 1781
*Petersburg
April 25, 1781
Charlottesville
June 4, 1781
The Peninsula—Yorktown
Cornwallis at Yorktown
August 22, 1781
DeGrasse reaches the Chesapeake
August 26, 1781
*Chesapeake Capes naval battle
September 5, 1781
Barras reaches the Chesapeake
September 10, 1781
Americans, French leave Williamsburg
September 28, 1781
Siege of Yorktown begins
September 29, 1781
*Bombardment begins
October 9, 1781
*Surrender of Cornwallis
October 19, 1781
Clinton arrives, return to New York
October 29, 1781

Clinton at Savannah
January 30, 1780
Siege of Charleston
March-May 1780
Camden
August 16, 1780
Augusta
September 14, 1780
Charlotte
September 26, 1780
King's Mountain
October 7, 1780

Cape St. Vincent
January 16, 1780
British embark for Nicaragua
February 3, 1780

Spanish take Bahamas
May 1782

Spanish hold St. Louis
May 26, 1780
Chillicothe (Little Miami River)
August 6, 1780

St. Eustasius
February 3, 1781

Gnadenhuetten massacre
March 1782
Fort Hunter (Wheeling)
September 11, 1782
Chillicothe
November 10, 1782

Lochry's defeat by Joseph Brant
August 24, 1781

Rochambeau army at Newport
July 1780
Benedict Arnold treason
September 23, 1780
Major Andre executed
October 2, 1780

Mutiny of Pennsylvania Line
January 1, 1781
Mutiny of New Jersey troops
January 23, 1781
Port Praia, Cape Verde Isles
April 16, 1781

Preliminary Treaty
November 30, 1782

On September 19 and 20, 1776, four days after Washington had withdrawn the colonial troops from Manhattan Island, a furious fire swept New York, destroying nearly 500 buildings in the area between Broadway and the Hudson River. General Howe and his British troops had occupied the city following Washington's withdrawal, and were preparing to use it as a winter base. John Jay, Nathanael Greene, and others had advised Washington to put the city to the torch rather than to leave it to the enemy; but the Continental Congress voted "no" to the idea when Washington queried them by letter. To this day, the origin of the fire, which leveled one-fourth of the city, remains a mystery.

Why the Revolution?

THE AMERICAN NATION was born in revolution and war. The world continues to feel the shock waves from those stirring events of the eighteenth century. For the American experience, from that time forward, has inspired men all over the globe to become the masters of their own destiny. In older countries, people have risen up to restructure their governments so as to throw off monarchy and other forms of special privilege. In underdeveloped lands, the inhabitants have cast down the yoke of colonialism to establish freedom and independence. Indeed, never was the story of the American Revolution more timely than it is today, and not merely because we are on the eve of the bicentennial of independence, although assuredly our 200th birthday is a most appropriate moment to take stock of where we have been and where we are going. Equally important is the fact that the post-World War II years have witnessed more revolutionary ferment than any other time since the Age of Enlightenment, when upheavals rocked France, Latin America, and other countries, on the heels of the American War of Independence. During this past quarter of a century the birth of the "Third World" nations—mostly in Africa and Asia—has more than doubled the number of national states in existence. Our own revolution, like contemporary struggles, was an anticolonial movement in the name of liberty, and the connection has been acknowledged by such widely diverse architects of revolution as Nehru of India, Sukarno of Indonesia, and Ho Chi Minh of North Vietnam.

How did it all begin? How did the thirteen North American English colonies happen to revolt and gain their independence? The schism in the British Empire began very late in the history of the English settlements. In 1763, just a dozen years before the guns of Lexington, the mother country was at the peak of her power and prestige. She had just defeated France and Spain in the Seven Years' War (or the French and Indian War, as it was known in America), stripping them of key New World possessions. Now Britannia ruled not only the waves but the entire eastern third of North America as well, from the Atlantic to the Mississippi, from the ice-clogged waters of Hudson's Bay to the scorching beaches of southern Florida.

At that time no colonial Americans wished to cut loose from the moorings of this mighty empire, which seemed to rival ancient Rome in its territorial expansiveness and to offer its subjects countless blessings and liberties. Moreover, it was widely believed that British political and cultural institutions were superior to all others. The settlement following the "Glorious Revolution" of 1688 had supposedly created the kind of political balance that promised the best guarantee for the preservation of the rights and privileges embodied in the British constitution, a balance consisting of the king, lords, and commons assembled in Parliament. Literary accomplishments were thought to be the equal of political advances in what Englishmen referred to as their "Augustan Age," whose leading lights were Addison, Defoe, Pope, Steele, and Swift. Nor did the economic front pale in comparison. An increasing volume of foreign trade and a heightened pace of domestic production led Britain's competitors to fear that she would ultimately far exceed them in power and riches.

The future looked bright, not grim, for the colonists under the British flag, the crosses of St. George and St. Andrew. They considered all these traditions and accomplishments as much a part of their heritage as that of Englishmen at home. Even with the restrictions imposed upon their external trade by the navigation laws, or perhaps because of them, they had prospered by their direct intercourse with England and other parts of the empire, and they had a real vested interest in continuing their economic connection with the island kingdom. Wealthy colonials imitated the life-styles of the mother country. They imported furniture, clothing, books, and artwork from London. Southern planters planned their houses and gardens in conformity with those of English country gentlemen. Would-be lawyers began their legal training with Coke and Blackstone. Merchants developed close ties with English exporters and London countinghouses.

John Hancock presided over the Second Continental Congress and was the first to sign the Declaration of Independence. Signing was not completed for fifty-five days.

In other ways we can see that colonial America thrived within the empire; that its people were not confined and cramped in their efforts to expand and prosper. More than a million and a half colonists lived along the Atlantic seaboard from the Maine district of Massachusetts to the Altamaha River in Georgia; and their numbers were doubling every quarter of a century—"multiplying like rattlesnakes," as Benjamin Franklin expressed it. England's expulsion of France from Canada and the Ohio Valley in 1763 meant that, despite British opposition expressed in the Proclamation of 1763, the tide of western settlement would surge through the land and water gaps in the Appalachian chain, that before another generation passed a human sea of traders, trappers, and farmers would move as far west as the Mississippi Valley.

Agriculture and related occupations were the predominant means of livelihood in the provinces. The Americans exported grain and flour from the middle colonies; lumber, masts, and fish from New England; rice, indigo, tobacco, and naval stores from the southern colonies. Indirectly, at least, traders and trappers lived off the land; their furs and deerskins were loaded on many a ship that crossed the Atlantic. The typical American, sooner or later, owned his own farm, for land was usually cheap and wages were high. Periods of white servitude—in return for the ocean passage from Europe—were relatively short, and such contracts or indentures normally carried little in the way of a permanent social stigma. Less fortunate were those half a million or more persons (by 1775) in permanent bondage, African Blacks, whose sweat and toil went toward the enrichment of their white masters. Slavery, of course, is associated with the plantation system of the South, but the "peculiar institution" existed everywhere; outside of that region black bondsmen were particularly visible in New York and New Jersey. But if slaves were not confined by sectional limits, neither were the landed aristocrats. The Livingstons, Schuylers, and Van Rensselaers of New York were not unlike the Carrolls of Maryland, the Carters of Virginia, the Johnstons of North Carolina, and the Manigaults of South Carolina in the accumulation of vast estates.

Not every colonial American was a son of the soil. By the standards of the day, America could boast of as many as five urban centers—Philadelphia, Boston, New York, Charleston, and Newport; and a sixth, Baltimore, was soon to have that status. The key men in the cities were merchants, a class with the aggregate influence of today's banking, mercantile, manufacturing, and shipping interests. In one way or another, all the urban dwellers—the artisans, the shopkeepers, the dockyard laborers, the seamen, even the prostitutes (of whom there were many)—depended upon the Hancocks of Boston, the Morrises of Philadelphia, the Laurens of Charleston, and the Habershams of Savannah; for without the multifarious activities of these princes of trade, New York, Charleston, and the rest would have declined and stagnated.

These and smaller "cities in the wilderness" exercised an influence far beyond their number and their size. They acted as a filter for thought from the outside—from the world of Europe. Just as they received the attitudes and concepts that made up their British inheritance, so, too, did they drink in new ideas from the continent in the realm of politics, literature, and science. These influences—associated with the Age of Enlightenment—helped breed everywhere a fresh, critical spirit in regard to the nature of man, his institutions, and his total environment.

The newspapers and colleges in the cities and towns served as disseminators of thought and culture. By 1764, there were twenty-three newspapers in the colonies; by 1775, thirty-seven. Letters to the printer from rural areas indicate an expanding circulation. These "publick gazettes" passed from hand to hand, occupied space on tavern walls, and generated myriad topics for discussion. Simultaneously, the colleges—there were three in 1701, nine in 1769—broadened their influence, spreading the new learning and attracting students from ever-widening regions; James Madison of Virginia, for example, matriculated at the College of New Jersey (now Princeton). Unlike today, however, the bulk of original inquiry and investigation occurred outside institutional walls. The most productive advances were in science, which in the eighteenth century was considered to be a branch of philosophy. In Boston, Cotton Mather and Zabdiel Boylston proved the value of inoculation against smallpox. In New York, Cadwallader Colden wrote on yellow fever, diphtheria, light, color, and gravitation. In Charleston, Alexander Garden, in whose honor the gardenia was named, sent unusually accurate descriptions of the flora of the New World to the great Swedish naturalist Carl Linnaeus. In Philadelphia, David Rittenhouse built the first American orrery, a mechanical model of the motions of the solar system. It was yet another Philadelphian, Benjamin Franklin, who best of all exemplified the Enlightenment spirit, a man whose genius for science and invention brought him high achievement in all he undertook.

America, nevertheless, scarcely shed its colonial status in science, to say nothing of literature and the arts. Indeed, America would remain culturally dependent on Europe until well after the birth of the United States. Even if the western shores of the Atlantic spawned no Newton in

John Adams was many men—patriot, statesman, signer of the Declaration of Independence, vice-president under Washington, and second president of the United States. Many of the colonials continued to practice the occupations they had learned in Europe, as this fish peddler and his wife.

*The Declaration of Independence was first
publicly proclaimed in Philadelphia on
July 8, 1776, then read to Washington
and his troops in New York City the
next day. John Jay, among its signers,
later served as the first chief justice
of the Supreme Court.*

Philadelphia's American Philosophical Society, no Shakespeare on the
banks of Maryland's Avon River, no Milton in puritan New England; if
no American novel had yet made its appearance, if no American painter
had at this time gained acclaim, it is still true that the colonists were a
rapidly maturing people. Nowhere else in the world were there such
economic opportunities because of high wages and cheap land, along with
the total absence of legal privileges reserved for a few, and other vestiges
of caste systems. American men were—except for the Blacks in bondage—
the freest people in the world.

Already, too, they were showing signs of excelling in politics and state-
craft, areas in which—a few short years later—they were to make notable
contributions to all mankind. Whether convening at small administrative
centers like Williamsburg or New Bern or at "metropolitan" trading places
like Boston or Charleston, the popularly elected lower houses of assembly
served as a nurturing ground for political leadership, where George Washington, Thomas Jefferson, James Wilson, John Dickinson, John Jay, John
Adams, and almost the entire galaxy of the Revolution's luminaries first
met the challenges and responsibilities of public service.

Inclusive rather than exclusive, the political systems of the colonies
functioned at different levels. Homegrown elites composed of men of
wealth and education and with important family connections occupied
most of the seats in the Massachusetts House of Representatives, Virginia
House of Burgesses, and South Carolina Commons House of Assembly.
But the middle and lower orders were also involved in the process, since
the great majority of free white males eventually owned sufficient property
to meet voting requirements. If they customarily elected their "betters"
to represent them in the colonial capitals, they demanded responsible
government in return, and they usually received it. Furthermore, many
local offices were diffused throughout a broad spectrum of the colonial
male population.

By the mid-eighteenth century there were additional safeguards against any narrow group enhancing itself at the expense of all others. The social ladder was short but shaky in a boom era, and the thousands of newcomers who arrived each year demanded parity with the older elements, not the subordinate status they had known in Europe. In the area of religious organization the established churches—the Anglican in the South, the Congregational in most of New England—had to compromise with the religious pluralism of early America, extending rights to the Baptists, Presbyterians, Lutherans, and so on. All these pressures likewise made it necessary to assimilate new and diverse groups into the political apparatus. Conflicts there were; sometimes between elites such as the Livingston and De Lancey clans in New York, the merchants of Newport and Providence in Rhode Island; sometimes between east and west, such as the tidewater-low country planters and the backcountry settlers in the Carolinas. But the capacity of the normal processes of government to heal fissures in the body politic seems to have been improving as the eighteenth century wore on.

But if the Americans were so experienced in the management of their internal affairs, so prosperous in agriculture and commerce, so mature after a century and a half of development, could it not be argued that they felt confident of easily severing their umbilical cord to the mother country and entering the family of nations? After all, with the removal of France, the hated Catholic enemy, from their northern frontiers in 1763, the colonists' need for English protection would no longer loom large in their thinking. And, one might add, was there not an emerging American nationalism by then? No doubt the colonists were getting to know each other better across provincial boundaries. They read each other's newspapers, dispatched ships to each other's ports, educated their sons at each

The hilt of George Washington's sword—a detail from the Peale portrait of Washington. Benjamin Franklin, almost seventy years old at the start of the Revolution, was a leading citizen in the colonies. Philadelphia was a flourishing colonial port nearly 100 miles up the Delaware River from the Atlantic Ocean.

other's schools. To be sure, these phenomena—together with the growth of colonial professions in law, medicine, and finance—were ingredients for the viability of an autonomous society. Yet nationalism was embryonic at best. In spite of changes springing from the New World environment, the life and institutions of the parent state always provided the central focus for colonial culture. If the word "American" was coming into usage, albeit slowly, the average man would have described his nationality as English or British or, less likely, Virginian or Pennsylvanian. If the growth and development of British America had been spectacular in the eighteenth

century, it still had been predominantly intracolonial rather than intercolonial.

There are two means of demonstrating that the colonists were far
removed from notions of union and independence. First is to look ahead
and observe the slow, torturous course of establishing a real political nation
between the Declaration of Independence in 1776 and the ratification of
the Federal Constitution in 1788, notwithstanding the pressures and in-
centives to consolidate in order to win a war for survival against a powerful
foe. Second, and more immediate, is to underscore the friction and lack of
cooperation between the colonies prior to 1763. Most of the provinces had
known disputes with their neighbors over boundaries, land policies, and
Indian relations that had engendered serious hostilities and rivalries.
When the colonists sought to make common cause against their French and
Indian enemies during the imperial wars of the eighteenth century, intercolonial ventures usually broke down because of these rivalries, because
of fear of leaving one's own colony stripped of adequate protection, or
because of suspicions that one assembly would be asked to contribute
more than others. Such local fears contributed to the scuttling of Franklin's
1754 Albany Plan of Union, which would have created a Grand Council
with permanent authority over taxation, defense, westward expansion,
and Indian diplomacy. Ten years later such provincialism continued to
prevail, prompting Massachusetts's James Otis to complain that "were
the colonies left to themselves tomorrow, America would be a mere shambles
of blood and confusion."

All the same, there was a potentially explosive area of confrontation
between Britain and America: it existed in the mother-child metaphor
that both Englishmen and colonials employed to describe their relationship, in the British stress upon American subordination and obedience,
in the colonists' emphasis upon London's obligation to protect their right
to a wide slice of autonomy based on freedoms guaranteed in the British
constitution to citizens of the empire everywhere. Ironically, some of the
very things that wedded the colonists to the mother country—especially
their being able to dominate their internal political structures and to
flourish economically—were seen in the island kingdom as a sign that the
provinces were gradually slipping away, were in time going to renounce
their dependence. Britons did not believe that pragmatic benefits and
deep-seated bonds of loyalty and affection would continue to bind the
American spokes to the wheel of empire indefinitely.

As long as these English conceptions were only somewhat dimly perceived, were not crystallized into new restrictive policies, no serious threat
existed to imperial solidarity. But crystallize they did, beginning in the
late 1740s, when certain London officials concluded that rather than the
accommodation that had marked the years of Sir Robert Walpole as first
minister (1723–1742), confrontation offered the surest means of holding
the maturing child in his proper subordinate relationship to his parent.
Between 1748 and 1756 the Board of Trade, which had played the primary
supervisory role in colonial relations since 1696, launched a movement to
bolster royal control over the colonies by urging crown-appointed governors to stand up to the assemblies in various ways. Since these measures
dealt with local issues in each colony, they elicited no broad-gauged or
collective response throughout America. Besides, British reform spurts
were almost wholly unsuccessful and were abandoned not only because
of their failure but also because of a desire to court colonial cooperation

in supplying men and provisions in the French and Indian War. Yet the very failure of piecemeal, ad hoc endeavors actually served to convince officialdom at Whitehall that more comprehensive, across-the-board regimentation was imperative.

Not that the American Revolution would have been inevitable in a decade or two. Governments often reverse themselves, and the British ministries in the eighteenth century, a series of shifting coalitions in the absence of a modern party system, were too fluid and unstable to develop a consistent program and adhere to it over a prolonged period of time. British-American relations during the French and Indian War, however, brought into focus the differences in views, for the conflict threw the colonies and England together in the closest working relationship they had ever experienced. The order and control that Britain considered essential to achieve victory aroused unrest among colonials schooled in holding their own reins. Local militia officers resented taking orders from inferior-ranking regular officers, who scarcely hid their condescending view of provincial fighters. When British generals dictated to American assemblies on raising men and military stores, the colonial legislators considered them as great a threat to their constitutional position as the crown's governors had been. Occasional schemes to quarter redcoats in private homes against the will of the citizenry aroused an old legal issue of the Stuart period.

The Americans felt they had contributed impressively to the final triumph over France. They had put five times as many men in the field as they had contributed in any previous colonial war, and they had reinforced the Royal Navy's rolls by 18,000 seamen. As renewed British patriotism surged through their veins, the colonists envisioned for themselves an expanded role in the empire, one of near equality in all respects with the mother country. English thought, on the other hand, turned in the opposite direction. The war confirmed the evolving notion of tightening the controls over the transmarine dominions, "to keep down," in the words of North Carolina's Governor Arthur Dobbs, "the rising Spirit of Independency."

It was fair, up to a point, for Britain to ask more of Americans, for she had run up a heavy debt and a sizable tax burden in a series of wars fought in part, at least, in defense of the colonies; fought, too—and this fact Englishmen rarely honestly admitted—for reasons of smashing French power worldwide and establishing her supremacy in Europe. The question for the historian is whether Britain went about securing her objectives in the right way, recognizing at the same time the sensitivity of her maturing subjects, who were no longer children in the sense that they had once been.

The answer is an unequivocal "no." The colonists were never consulted except individually or through unofficial channels, and only then in the most superficial or insincere ways. Furthermore, as a matter of tactics, London attempted too much too quickly. Even before the termination of the French and Indian War, beginning as early as 1759, when Britain sensed victory and colonial contributions became less vital, there were straws in the wind—minor British-colonial clashes over disallowance of popular assembly-passed measures, over writs of assistance empowering the king's customs officials to break into homes and stores, and over judicial tenure in the colonial courts. These provocative developments were soon followed by decisions to keep a standing army of nearly 7,000 men in the colonies; to temporarily forbid western settlement—the Proclamation of 1763—beyond the Appalachian divide; to eliminate provincial paper money as legal tender; to beef up the customs service; and to strengthen the vice-admiralty courts, whose jurisdiction covered the navigation laws. How much of an imperial disturbance were these events capable of producing? To say the least, they created a current of unrest, varying in intensity from colony to colony; when almost simultaneously combined with Parliament's placing revenue-producing taxes on America in 1764–65, the result was a veritable explosion.

It would be impossible to say who in London fathered the thought of England's taxing the colonies, for the idea was clearly in the air during the final Anglo-French war, and it was inseparably tied to the notion that these subsequent revenues should be employed for paying as much as

News of the new taxes traveled fast in places like Philadelphia's High Street.

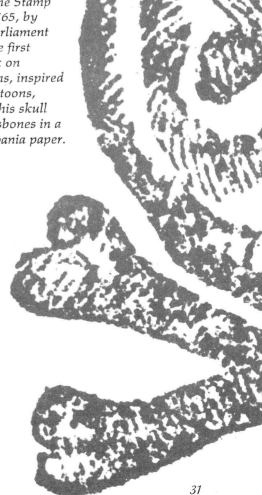

Feelings ran high in Boston following the tea party in the harbor. Within a month, John Malcolm, the Tory tax collector, was tarred and feathered. Earlier, the Stamp Act of 1765, by which Parliament levied the first direct tax on Americans, inspired bitter cartoons, such as this skull and crossbones in a Pennsylvania paper.

possible of the cost of maintaining the new postwar military establishment in America. It should be emphasized, however, that the redcoats were not there for the purpose of cramming objectionable British laws down colonial throats, but rather to regulate the fur trade and enforce the Proclamation of 1763. Despite the momentum to tap the American pocketbook, William Pitt and the Duke of Newcastle, two longtime friends of the colonies, might have successfully resisted this pressure had they retained high posts in the government; but both were gone in 1763, when George Grenville, the first minister and an acknowledged financial expert, decided to follow through on obtaining an American revenue. Parliament complied, although several Americans in London and a few members of Parliament—notably Colonel Isaac Barré, a one-eyed veteran of James Wolfe's recent victory at Quebec—warned that the colonists would resist.

First in 1764 came the Sugar Act, which revised an earlier Molasses Act, a trade measure, cutting the duty on imported foreign molasses from sixpence a gallon to threepence. But whereas the original law had been almost entirely ignored, the Sugar Act was to be rigorously enforced.

*In August 1764 the
Sons of Liberty,
protesting the Stamp Act,
burned the stamps and
court records in the
streets of Boston. The
stamps were printed on
paper to be fixed on
taxed goods.*

*After the adoption of the Stamp Act
of 1765, Patrick Henry rose in
Virginia's House of Burgesses to
deliver his famous "if this be
treason, make the most of it"
speech.*

More important and more disturbing to the colonists was the fact that the preamble to the Sugar Act changed the nature of the measure from one of regulating commerce to one of creating a revenue; it was, in short, now a tax. The next year Grenville obtained from Parliament the so-called Stamp Act, which provided for placing taxes on all legal documents and on almanacs, newspapers, playing cards, and dice. A few weeks later the first minister secured a third bill, the Quartering Act; a form of indirect taxation, it called upon American legislatures to assist English troops passing through any of the colonies by supplying them with temporary housing, firewood, candles, and an assortment of provisions.

The Grenville program aroused indignation and anger throughout the colonies. Americans believed it to be one of the main principles of the British constitution that Englishmen—in England, in Virginia, in New York, or anywhere else—could be taxed only by their own direct representatives. The colonists knew that Parliament itself had battled against the efforts in the seventeenth century of the Stuart kings to raise monies on their own. The issue was a major part of what the Glorious Revolution of 1688 had been all about, as the colonists knew from their reading of English history, especially John Locke's famous *Second Treatise on Government* (1690). Americans were also concerned about the ministry's method of enforcing these new laws. Alleged violators of the Sugar and Stamp measures were to be tried in juryless vice-admiralty courts, which placed the burden of proof on the defendant.

Whatever their individual views of the welter of British laws and regulations imposed since 1759, the Americans focused their defense on the constitutional issue of taxation. They agreed that it posed the gravest threat to their freedom as individuals. As Locke had pointed out, the power to tax was the power to take a man's property. If property gave man a stake in society, including the opportunity to vote, his liberty could scarcely exist if his pocket was tapped without his consent, either in person or by his representative. Quite predictably, the popularly elected lower houses of assembly led the fight. They, too, were in danger: of losing their

A favorite form of protest in England and the colonies in the eighteenth century was the burning of effigies. King George III and his Hessian mercenaries were most frequently consigned to the flames in New England.

positions of dominance over the internal affairs of the colonies, particularly their previously exclusive authority to tax, the bedrock of their existence. The assemblies, in essence, had become little parliaments.

If the legislatures directed the American response, those legislators who stood out were mostly lawyers, men best equipped to explain and defend constitutional rights. A profession that had risen rapidly in influence and prestige in the mid-eighteenth century (to some extent overshadowing the clergy, a field that initially had attracted the finest colonial minds), its ranks included in this period such articulate spokesmen of the American position as James Otis, Daniel Dulany, Patrick Henry, John Dickinson, Thomas Jefferson, John Adams, James Wilson, and James Iredell.

In 1766, Parliament retreated by reducing the Sugar Act to the level of a trade duty and by repealing the Stamp Act—not because English politicians bought the constitutional arguments expressed in countless

American pamphlets and legislative petitions, but chiefly because of damage to the island's economy by retaliatory colonial boycotts of British goods. The year 1767 saw a second parliamentary attempt to tap America's resources. This time the taxes, recommended by Chancellor of the Exchequer Charles Townshend, were solely of an external nature: sums to be collected at the ports on incoming lead, tea, paper, paint, and glass. But the purpose of these Townshend duties was not, like the old navigation laws, to regulate trade in the interest of the empire; like the Stamp Act, their purpose was revenue. This time the money would go not only for the upkeep of the troops, but also for something that seemed to the colonials to be far more sinister. There was a new kind of threat to their legislatures since Townshend revenues might be used to pay the salaries of royal officials who had previously received their incomes from the American assemblies, thus reducing the influence that these American political bodies could wield over the crown men in their midst. That same year still another blow aimed at a single legislature, New York's, was seen as a menace to the very existence of all the assemblies. Parliament in effect suspended the New York assembly for its failure to give sufficient aid to redcoats quartered there, yet another departure in British policy toward America. Finally, 1767 marked Townshend's reorganization of the customs service in America, establishing its headquarters in Boston, where such friction arose between collectors and townspeople that regiments of regulars were sent to the city.

Three years later an uneasy calm had once again settled over the empire. But only after American resistance, mainly reprisals against English trade, had brought about the repeal of all the Townshend taxes except the one on tea, whose retention was designed to show that Parliament maintained the right to tax America and indeed might do so again. Only after a compromise had restored the New York assembly to its full powers without compromising its integrity. And only after the redcoats had been pulled out of Massachusetts following the death of several people in the "Boston Massacre."

It is possible for us to look back and see a kind of lull, or interim, in the imperial crisis between 1770 and 1773, a time when the British government, with Lord Frederick North now as first minister, had an opportunity to regain American goodwill by altering the general outlines of its recent colonial policies and by removing certain specific irritants. Since they did not do so, the stage was set—in a continuing atmosphere of suspicion and mistrust—for fresh trouble. The East India Company was in financial distress, and Parliament, rather than finding inoffensive ways to assist it, not only did not repeal the Townshend tax on tea, but passed the Tea Act of 1773, which allowed the company to economize by selling its dutied brew directly to American retailers. If most historians feel that the ministry sought only to bail out the hard-pressed mercantile giant, Americans saw a plot to get them to drink huge quantities of the presumably less expensive but taxed drink, thereby undermining their constitutional objection to taxes and thus making themselves vulnerable to still another round of revenue-raising schemes in Parliament. When word reached America that initial shipments were bound for Boston, New York, Philadelphia, and Charleston, local pressures forced the consignees at all these ports save Boston to resign their commissions or remain passive. In the New England metropolis, however, Governor Thomas Hutchinson, smarting from rebuffs at the hands of Samuel Adams and other patriot leaders,

Incident between the redcoats and townspeople in 1770 culminated in the Boston Massacre, in which soldiers killed five colonists. This picture was printed and distributed by Paul Revere.

backed the consignees (two of whom were his sons and a third, his nephew) and insisted that the cargo vessels remain in the harbor.

The predictable outcome of this impasse—the "Boston Tea Party"—brought another explosion, from which the empire never recovered. In retaliation for the destruction of the tea (340 chests containing 90,000 pounds of Bohea leaves worth £10,000 sterling), Parliament hit Massa-

Bostonians, disguised as Mohawk Indians, dumped 342 chests of tea into the harbor during the Boston Tea Party in 1773. Earlier, in North Carolina, Governor William Tryon executed seven Regulators, a protest group.

chusetts with the hardest blows any colony had ever known—closing the port of Boston, altering town and provincial government, permitting accused royal governmental officials and functionaries to be tried in Britain, and providing for the billeting of troops in Boston.

Parliament called them the Coercive Acts. To Americans, they were "Intolerable Acts," and they refused to sit back and watch a sister colony suffer what might well happen later to the rest of them. During the past decade of controversy they had, while denying the constitutionality of specific laws and regulations, sought Britain's return to the practical, working relationship that had cemented the empire before the French and Indian War. That was a kind of federalism, a political system in which governmental powers are separated and distributed among different governments—in this case in London and in the colonies, each with its own sphere of operation and jurisdiction. But by 1774 it was painfully transparent to Americans that Parliament would never admit limits to its reach. The colonists concluded that they would have to deny that body any authority over them whatsoever, even in the areas of trade and diplomacy, if they were to remain within the empire with their rights and liberties intact.

Simultaneously, in the First Continental Congress—a gathering of delegates from twelve colonies at Philadelphia in September 1774—and throughout America, men were arriving at a bold new conception of the empire almost identical to the modern British commonwealth of nations, seeing the colonies in the status that today belongs to Canada, Australia, and New Zealand. The penetrating legal minds of Jefferson, Adams, Wilson, and Iredell were locating precedents from the early seventeenth century and in the relationship between England and Scotland prior to the Act of Union in 1707 for their contention that Parliament's overlordship did not pass beyond the coasts of the British Isles. Consequently, Americans felt that they were linked to the mother country only through the person of the king. Iredell described this commonwealth idea as "the cordial union of many distant people, descended from the same ancestors

. . . zealous in their attachment to each other, under the influence of one common sovereign, and by the participation of a common interest, mutually contributing to the prosperity of the whole."

Withal, the Americans would still have accepted sensible compromises. Though technically free of Parliament, many colonials favored continued adherence to English legislation that was drafted in the best interest of all sections of the empire. Given the intransigence of ministry and Parliament, Americans quite logically appealed to the king himself for acceptance of the commonwealth theory or a similar solution in the direction of greater American autonomy. George III, of the House of Hanover, has come down through the pages of chauvinistic histories as a corpulent, heavy-lidded, red-faced tyrant, singled out by Jefferson in the Declaration of Independence as the source of most of America's ills. A most conventional man, George loved honesty, barley water, and his mother; practiced fidelity to his deep Christian faith and to his homely German wife who bore him numerous progeny. If in fact he was no despot, he did solidly back Parliament throughout the Anglo-American controversy; and in 1774–75 he turned a deaf ear on American pleas that he step between his contending subjects and calm the imperial waters.

As the colonists saw themselves spurned by Parliament and king, as they saw the return of the scarlet legions to Boston—3,500 men by early 1775—many became increasingly convinced that a conspiracy existed on the part of politicians in England to rape them of all liberty and thus reduce them to the condition of slavery. Indeed, it seems that—as important as were Enlightenment ideas in adding a liberal coloration to colonial thought, as crucial as were the constitutional theories of Locke's generation in grounding Americans in their legal heritage—there was still another

British troops landed in Boston in 1768 and camped on the Commons. This picture of the harbor during the landing is from an engraving by Paul Revere.

cluster of ideas that uniquely lent themselves to a conspiracy theory of British behavior.

Emerging from the political conflicts in England in the seventeenth century and carried forward by a knot of radical Whig writers, known as "commonwealthmen," these beliefs had at their core the fear that liberty was always a fragile reed, eternally threatened by the corrupting influences that were inevitably at work on men who held power. Notwithstanding the virtues of mixed or balanced government in England, it was only through constant vigilance against vice, indifference, and moral decay that the distinct elements of government could be kept separate and the integrity of the British constitution be preserved.

Much of this literature found its way to the colonies, where—living amidst unsettled conditions, fearing Catholic plots, and experiencing continuing factional strife with royal governors and their placemen—the Americans found that it took on an immediacy unknown to most eighteenth century Englishmen. Now, in the context of the imperial rupture, these writings appeared to explain much that, at a distance of 3,000 miles, was otherwise inexplicable—the constant pressure of new taxes and unprecedented regulations and laws, culminating in the assault on Massachusetts. The British government, or so it was thought, had fallen into the hands of irresponsible, self-seeking politicians intent on enriching England at the expense of her colonies, whose enslavement was essential to complete their sinister designs.

Was there a true basis for this fear of a conspiracy? Not in the sense that a clandestine combination of power-drunk London ministers and legislators were out to destroy political liberty in order to gnaw away the economic heart of a prostrate America. Yet since 1748 there had been an unmistakable trend in London to tighten the controls of empire in ways that cut insensitively and at times cynically across a century and a half of American political and constitutional development. And in 1775 there was no relief in sight, least of all from George III, who now for the first time came out in favor of the use of armed force if the colonists refused to knuckle under. Unbeknown to the Hanoverian, his days as the king of the Americans were fleeting.

*George III was most
conventional, and not the
despot he was pictured.
But in events leading to
the Revolution, he backed
Parliament and ignored
American pleas. As a
result, respect for the
king gradually lessened
in the colonies.*

The First Year
1775-1776

This lantern delivered the signal that sent Paul Revere to rouse the countryside as British troops headed for Concord to destroy arms cached there. Next day, the first shots of the Revolution were fired at Lexington when the minutemen met the advancing redcoats.

JUST AS LORD NORTH, head of the ministry, and his cabinet colleagues miscalculated in 1774 in assuming that the other colonies would not rally to the support of Massachusetts with boycotts and petitions, so, too, he and his London cronies grossly erred in thinking that Americans would not fight if necessary to preserve their freedom. In a sense, one can understand these mistakes, for the colonists had scarcely cooperated effectively with each other in the war against the French, and provincial soldiers had often given a poor accounting of themselves. Yet the threat from England proved to be a powerful catalyst in bringing Americans together. Moreover, if colonial soldiers had been less than heroic in performing with redcoats in the past, they were capable of improving their performance when fighting under their own officers in a cause that vitally concerned them.

For the most part, Americans owned guns, and they knew how to use them. Whatever its limitations, a militia system, composed of almost all men between the ages of sixteen and sixty, existed in every colony. In time of peace the militia laws customarily fell into neglect, and the periodic drills were forgotten about or were mainly social events. But in 1774–75, the statutes were revitalized. Throughout Massachusetts companies paraded and practiced maneuvers on village greens, exercises soon repeated at scores of towns and county courthouses in the middle and southern colonies.

As royal government ground to a halt throughout the colonies, as extralegal congresses (the old assemblies), county committees, and town conventions took control of affairs, General Thomas Gage, British commander in chief in America, wrote pessimistic letters to London. It might take as many as 20,000 regulars to subdue New England alone, he warned, and the Yankees would be backed in the field by their southern brethren. If Gage's words went unheeded at Whitehall, this does not mean that the cabinet was eager to spill Massachusetts blood; but if it came to blows, Lord North and company were confident that Gage's 3,500 stalwarts were sufficient for the task. They were so sure that—in a letter marked "Secret" —they instructed their American commander, quartered in Boston, to take tougher measures. He was to arrest the principal Massachusetts troublemakers, and he was to employ the army in still other ways to subdue the Bay colony. More realistic than hard-lined politicians 3,000 miles away, Gage made no effort to secure arrests, although one of the most common errors in our historical literature is that he tried unsuccessfully to take Samuel Adams and John Hancock into custody. Gage, however, on the night of April 18, did decide to send a column of regulars, under Lieutenant Colonel Francis Smith and Major John Pitcairn, to confiscate the powder and other stores at Concord belonging to the Massachusetts Provincial Congress.

Crossing the Charles River in boats instead of marching over Boston Neck, Smith had no sooner begun his sixteen-mile march when the tolling of bells and the flashes of signal guns told him that his errand was no secret. For several days the Boston patriots had known of the mission, if not the date. When the embarkation started, William Dawes and Paul Revere, dispatch riders for the Boston Committee of Safety of the Provincial Congress, had hastened from the city and spread the word as far as Lexington. Fearing trouble, Smith sent back for reinforcements, and he ordered Pitcairn with six companies to push ahead rapidly to control the bridges over the Concord River. At Lexington, Pitcairn saw on the village green a local minuteman company of militia, commanded by Captain John Parker, forty-five years old, a veteran of the French and Indian War. Probably this demonstration was only symbolic, because the minutemen were scarcely capable of contesting Pitcairn's passage. Actually, the militiamen were some distance from the Concord road, and it was the British officer who precipitated a showdown. When Pitcairn approached and ordered them to disperse, they fell back, and a musket flashed. British or American, deliberate or accidental? No one knows. Then British muskets erupted again and again, and by the time the severely embarrassed Pitcairn silenced them, eight Americans were dead and ten wounded. Smith arrived on the scene, re-formed the British troops, and they marched on to Concord. (*See Map 1*)

Word of the bloodshed spread like wildfire. Thanks to a Concord physician, Dr. Samuel Prescott, the local citizens were already aware that the redcoats were coming. (Revere, the famous silversmith-engraver, had been captured just beyond Lexington by an enemy patrol. Dawes had escaped and returned to Boston.) Concord's two militia companies withdrew across the river to await reinforcements from other communities that had been alerted, and the British column occupied the village at about eight o'clock in the morning. Since the patriots had been able to hide much of their military equipment, Smith's mission turned out to be less than a great achievement; but it had blown up a storm over rural Massachusetts, as he could see from the steadily growing swarm of angry men beyond the river.

At noon, following the skirmish at the North Bridge, Smith, now very apprehensive, set out on his march back through the low, winding hills to Boston. Bunched together, the regulars formed a crimson mass as the militiamen hit them from both sides and rear. There were no volleys from formation or fixed-position fighting in the European manner on the part of their American assailants, who fired from behind trees, rocks, and stone fences bordering sections of the road. To British veterans of flat-surfaced German battlefields, it was a cowardly way to fight, but few of

MAP 1. ¶ The nineteenth of April 1775 is the day the War of Independence began. From the signing of the Treaty of Paris in 1763, which ended the Seven Years' War, colonial agitation against the policies of the crown and Parliament had grown to a feverish pitch. The Boston Massacre in 1770 and the Boston Tea Party in 1773 were among the events that warned of greater troubles to come. ¶ When the Massachusetts Provisional Congress was established in Concord and began accumulating guns and ammunition, the die seemed to have been cast. General Gage sent a corps of grenadiers and light infantry to Concord to destroy the military stores. At Lexington Captain Parker and a group of local minutemen stood on the village green, and as they began to fall back, as ordered by the British, a shot was heard. ¶ There are, of course, conflicting contemporary accounts of exactly what happened at Lexington and Concord on the nineteenth of April 1775. The differences reflect the respective prejudices of the Loyalist-Tory and the patriot-rebel. Even today no one can answer with certainty two questions: Who fired first? And, was the "shot heard 'round the world" deliberate or accidental? ¶ De Costa's map is the first graphic document to depict the actions at Lexington and Concord. It is the only map issued at the time to show the marches of British forces and sites of the major skirmishes. It primitively depicts the provincials firing from behind walls, and the British troops under Lieutenant Colonel Smith and Lord Percy retreating to Boston. ¶ Although this map was published after the Battle of Bunker Hill and even included references to that battle (see References 12 and 13), it was obviously designed to dramatize the Lexington and Concord affair. The first map devoted to the Bunker Hill battle was published three days later than this map in London by William Faden.

SHOWN ON FOLLOWING PAGE
A Plan of the Town and Harbour of Boston, and the Country adjacent with the Road from Boston to Concord Shewing the Place of the late Engagement between the King's Troops & the Provincials, together with the several Encampments of both Armies in & about Boston.... By I. De Costa. Engraved by C. Hall. London, I. De Costa, July 29, 1775. (14½" x 19¼")

This Amos Doolittle engraving shows colonial militiamen defending Concord's North Bridge from the British. The British were harassed all the way to Boston.

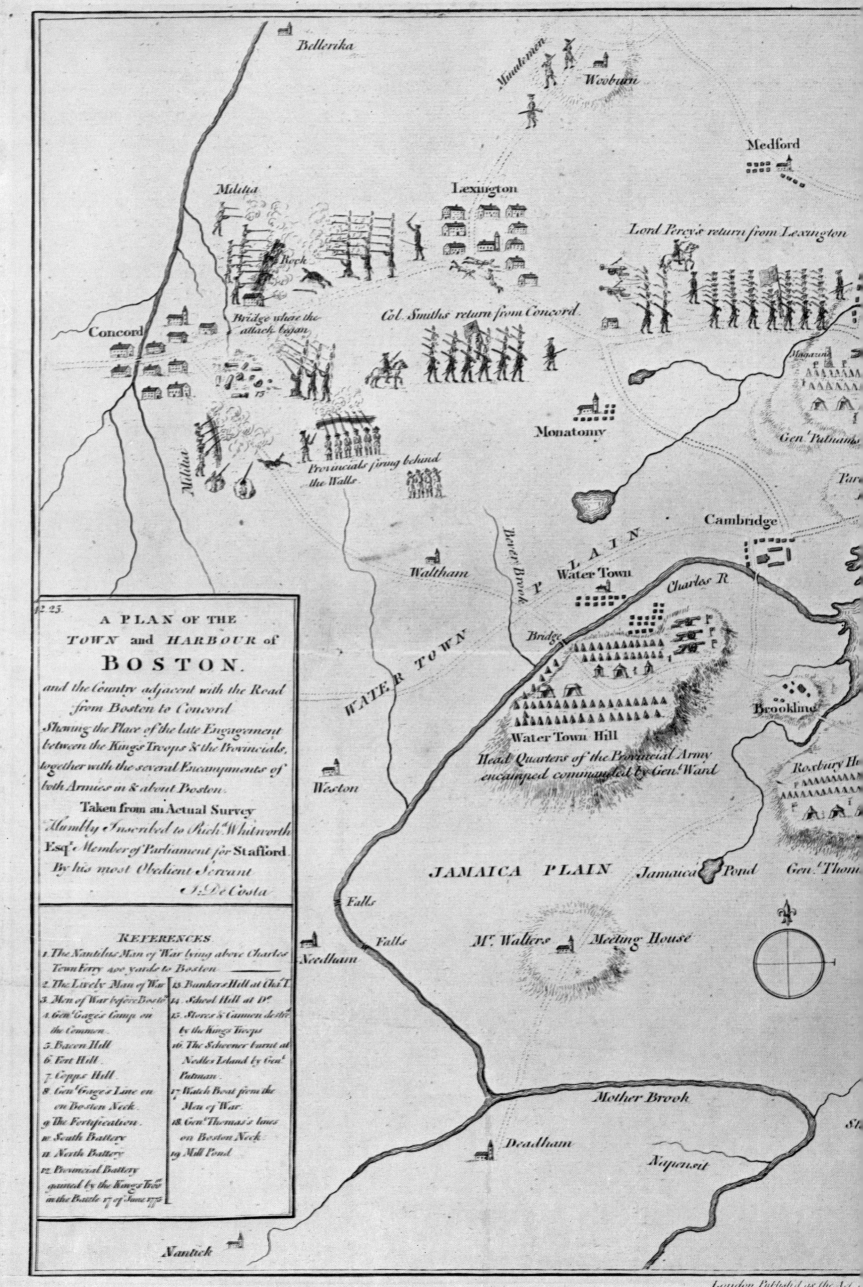

Bellerika

Minutemen

Wooburn

Medford

Militia

Lexington

Lord Percy's return from Lexington

Rock

Col. Smiths return from Concord

Concord

Magazine

Bridge where the
attack began

Gen.ˡ Putnams

Militia

Provincials firing behind
the Walls

Monatomy

Cambridge

Waltham

Water Town

Beaver Brook

P L A I N

Charles R.

W A T E R   T O W N

Bridge

Brookling

Water Town Hill

Head Quarters of the Provincial Army
encamped commanded by Gen.ˡ Ward

Roxbury Hd

Weston

p. 25.

A PLAN OF THE
TOWN and HARBOUR of
BOSTON.

and the Country adjacent with the Road
from Boston to Concord
Shewing the Place of the late Engagement
between the Kings Troops & the Provincials,
together with the several Encampments of
both Armies in & about Boston.

Taken from an Actual Survey
Humbly Inscribed to Rich.ᵈ Whitworth
Esq.ʳ Member of Parliament for Stafford.
By his most Obedient Servant
J. De Costa

JAMAICA PLAIN

Jamaica Pond

Gen.ˡ Thom

Falls

REFERENCES
1. The Nantilus Man of War lying above Charles
Town Ferry 400 yards to Boston.
2. The Lively Man of War
3. Men of War before Boston
4. Gen.ˡ Gages Camp on
the Common.
5. Bacon Hill
6. Fort Hill
7. Copps Hill
8. Gen.ˡ Gage's Line on
on Boston Neck.
9. The Fortification.
10. South Battery
11. North Battery
12. Provincial Battery
gained by the Kings Troo
in the Battle 17 of June 1775

13. Bunkers Hill at Chl.ˢ T
14. School Hill at D.ᵒ
15. Stores & Cannon destr.
by the Kings Troops
16. The Schooner burnt at
Nodles Island by Gen.ˡ
Putnam.
17. Watch Boat from the
Men of War.
18. Gen.ˡ Thomas's lines
on Boston Neck.
19. Mill Pond

Falls

M.ʳ Walters

Meeting House

Needham

Mother Brook

Deadham

Napeusit

Sto

Nantick

London Published as the Act

40

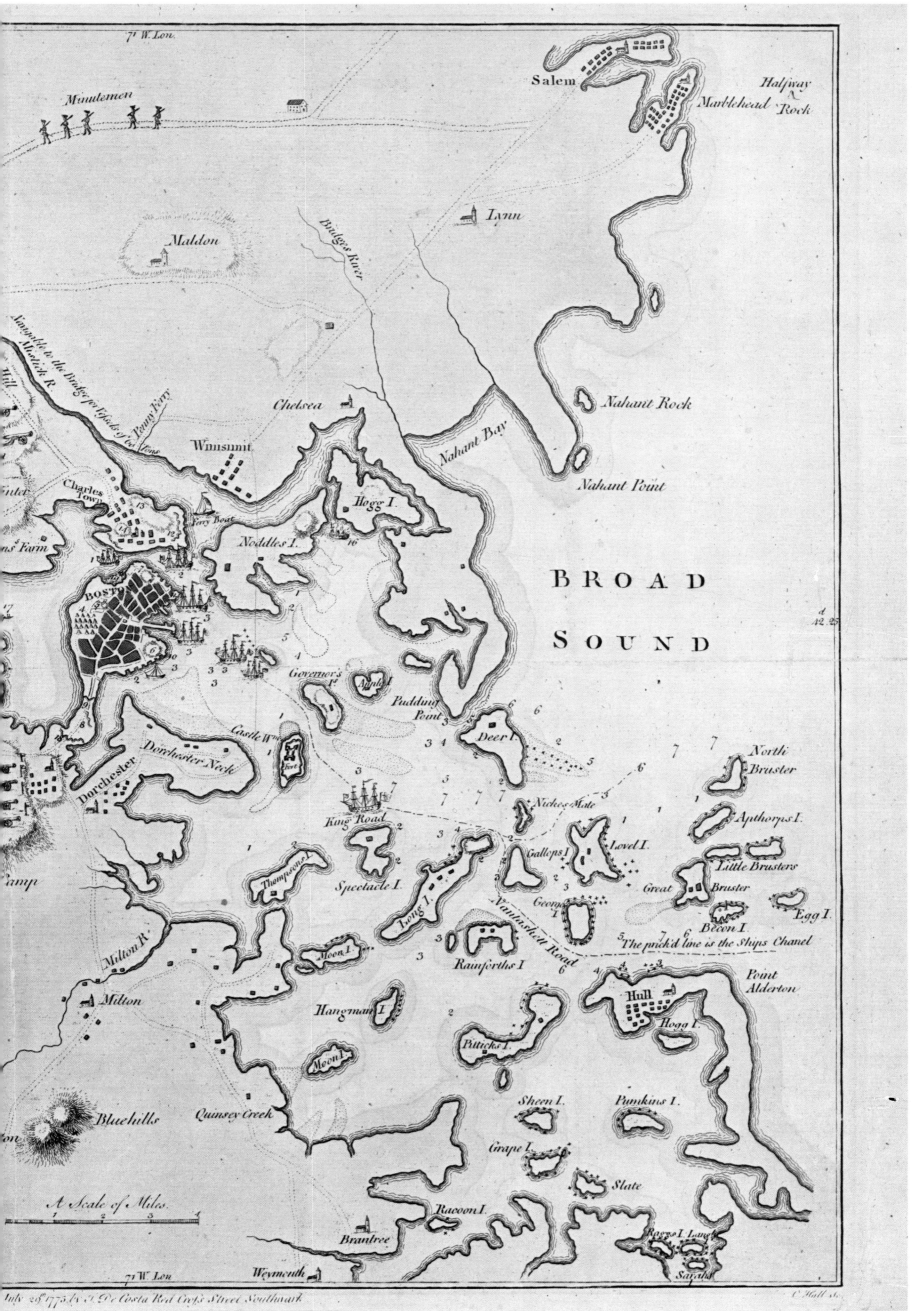

A Scale of Miles.

July 29 1775 by I. De Costa Red Cross Street Southwark.

C Hall Sc.

MAP 1. Reproduced from the permanent collections of The Library of Congress Geography and Map Division

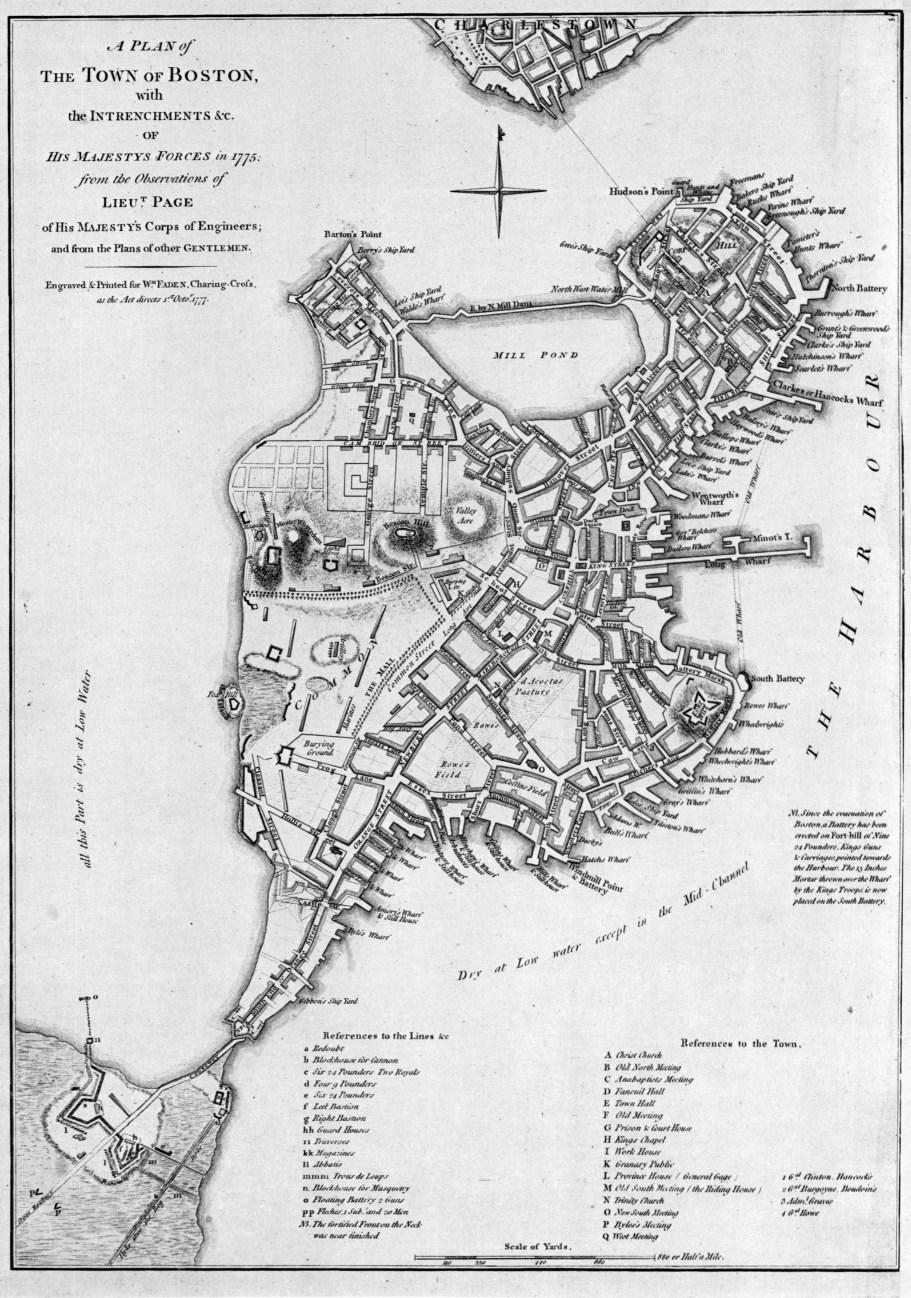

A PLAN of
THE TOWN OF BOSTON,
with
the INTRENCHMENTS &c.
OF
HIS MAJESTYS FORCES in 1775:
from the Observations of
LIEUT. PAGE
of His MAJESTYS Corps of Engineers;
and from the Plans of other GENTLEMEN.

Engraved & Printed for Wm. FADEN, Charing-Cross,
as the Act directs 1st Octor. 1777.

CHARLESTOWN

Hudson's Point

Barton's Point

MILL POND

THE HARBOUR

N.B. Since the evacuation of Boston, a Battery has been erected on Fort-hill of Nine 24 Pounders, Kings Guns & Carriages, pointed towards the Harbour. The 13 Inches Mortar thrown over the Wharf by the Kings Troops, is now placed on the South Battery.

all this Part is dry at Low Water

Dry at Low water except in the Mid-Channel

References to the Lines &c
a Redoubt
b Blockhouse for Cannon
c Six 24 Pounders Two Royals
d Four 9 Pounders
e Six 24 Pounders
f Left Bastion
g Right Bastion
hh Guard Houses
11 Traverses
kk Magazines
ll Abbatis
mmm Trous de Loups
n Blockhouse for Musquetry
o Floating Battery 2 Guns
pp Fleches, 1 Sub. and 20 Men
N.B. The fortified Front on the Neck was near finished

References to the Town.
A Christ Church
B Old North Meeting
C Anabaptists Meeting
D Faneuil Hall
E Town Hall
F Old Meeting
G Prison & Court House
H Kings Chapel
I Work House
K Granary Public
L Province House (General Gage)
M Old South Meeting (the Riding House)
N Trinity Church
O New South Meeting
P Byles's Meeting
Q West Meeting

1 6d. Clinton, Hancocks
2 6d. Burgoyne, Boudoins
3 Adml. Graves
4 6d. Howe

Scale of Yards.

them would have lived long enough to complain if Smith's reeling command had not been rescued near Lexington by a 900-man reinforcement under Lord Hugh Percy.

Even so, the British found it was still touch and go. The Americans kept coming and coming. To Ensign Henry de Berniere, it appeared that "there could not be less than 5,000" of them. But if the British were disorganized, so were the Americans, who had no real opportunity to coordinate their various militia contingents. For Smith and Percy their bloody ordeal ended at Charlestown, where, under an umbrella of darkness and Royal Navy vessels, their exhausted troops were ferried to Boston. If the British defeat—73 killed, 174 wounded, and 26 missing, as opposed to 95 total patriot losses—redounded to the discredit of General Gage, it was also, in a fashion, a vindication of his contention that he lacked sufficient muscle to subdue New England in war.

Unfortunately for Gage, fifty-six years old and a veteran of twenty years' American service, conditions became even worse. The motley throng that had nearly wiped out the Concord expedition now took up positions ringing Boston. The Massachusetts Provincial Congress recruited a volunteer force from the militia, and placed it under Brigadier General Artemas Ward, an old veteran of the French and Indian War of limited energy and ability. The congress appealed to the surrounding colonies for help, and their appeal was soon answered. Rhode Island dispatched a brigade headed by young Nathanael Greene, soon to be a rising star. Connecticut troops came in under Brigadier Generals Joseph Spencer and Israel Putnam, the latter a colorful Indian fighter. New Hampshire's contingent arrived under Colonel John Stark, a hardheaded, unpredictable man. And for Gage there was more bad news. On May 10, 1775, the small garrison at Fort Ticonderoga, guarding the juncture of Lake George and Lake Champlain in upper New York, had surrendered to a tall, leather-lunged Vermonter, Ethan Allen ("in the name of the great Jehovah and the Continental Congress"), and a chunky Connecticut ex-merchant, Benedict Arnold. Allen, leader of the so-called Green Mountain Boys, successfully dispatched some of these untamed frontier spirits under his crony Seth Warner to seize Crown Point, some miles north of "Old Ty." Gage also learned that patriots were confiscating powder and reducing to helplessness or expelling their royal and proprietary governors.

On May 9, 1775, Ethan Allen and Benedict Arnold led a force across Lake Champlain and early the following morning captured Fort Ticonderoga in at battle that was virtually bloodless.

MAP 2. ¶ Lieutenant Thomas Hyde Page, undoubtedly following the earlier survey of Captain John Montresor, drew this map of Boston, the most informative record available at the time of the Revolution. The original manuscript, which survives in the Library of Congress, was prepared in 1775 during the early days of the siege of Boston, when the city was surrounded by minutemen from the nearby colonies. Young Page, who had won King George's gold medal as a cadet at Woolwich a few years earlier, was severely wounded at Bunker Hill. Returned home as an invalid immediately after the battle, he later became a famous engineer in England and Ireland. In 1783 he was knighted and elected a Fellow of the Royal Society. ¶ William Faden, the leading British map publisher of his time, produced many beautifully engraved battle plans during the war. Frequently these maps were offered for sale in London for a shilling or two just a few weeks after the action took place — scarcely longer than it took to cross the ocean. Although Page was back in England shortly after the Battle of Bunker Hill, Faden did not publish this map until October 1777. Perhaps the details of the troop encampments were considered too sensitive for publication until after the British evacuation of Boston. ¶ No map of the period shows in greater detail the old city at the time of the siege.

SHOWN ON OPPOSITE PAGE
A Plan of the Town of Boston, with the Intrenchments &c. of His Majesty's Forces in 1775.... By T. H. Page. London, Wm. Faden, Oct. 1, 1777. (17¾" x 12¼")

The First Formal Confrontation

MAP 3. ¶ In its primitive simplicity this early engraved plan gives a clear picture of the relationship between Boston, Charlestown, and Bunker Hill. Among the important features pictured are the British landing places at the east end of Charlestown; the Cobbs Hill battery at the north end of Boston, with its eight 24-pound guns; and the position of the British warships. It was these cannon and the ships' guns which set Charlestown on fire. ¶ A most interesting accompaniment, printed on the same sheet, is the text of General Burgoyne's letter written from Boston on June 25, 1775, to his nephew Lord Stanley. Burgoyne's explanation of the original British plan to take Dorchester Heights to the south of Boston, which was thwarted by the American fortification of Bunker Hill, is most enlightening. His letter indicates that General Gage and his staff were aware that the heights of both the Charlestown and Dorchester peninsulas had to be controlled in order to hold Boston. Burgoyne, always with a flair for dramatics, describes the action at Bunker Hill as if he were observing a grand tournament.

SHOWN ON FOLLOWING PAGE
A Plan of the Battle on Bunkers Hill. Fought on the 17th of June 1775. By an Officer on the Spot. London, R. Sayer & J. Bennett, Nov. 27, 1775. (13¾" x 13¾")

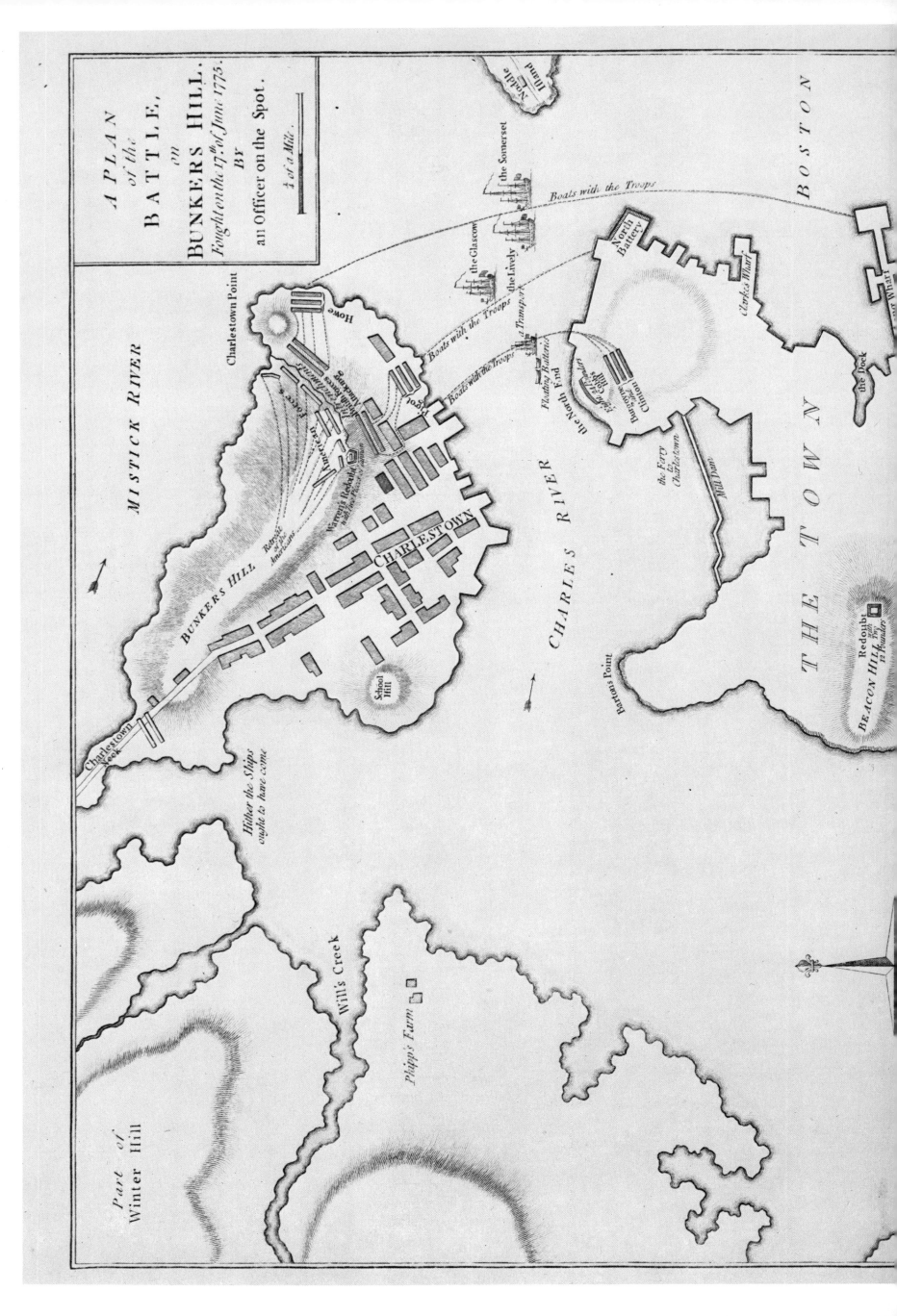

A PLAN of the BATTLE, on BUNKERS HILL. Fought on the 17.th of June 1775. By an Officer on the Spot.

¼ of a Mile.

MISTICK RIVER

Charlestown Point

Charlestown Neck

Part of Winter Hill

BUNKERS HILL

Retreat of the Americans

Warrens Redoubt and the Post made

School Hill

CHARLESTOWN

America's Force

Virginia's Force

Connecticut's Force

Howe

Hither the Ships ought to have come

Will's Creek

Phipp's Farm

Nuttle Island

the Somerset

the Glascow

the Lively

Boats with the Troops

Boats with the Troops

a Transport

Boats with the Troops

the North End

Floating Battery

North Battery

Clark's Wharf

Boats with the Troops

Clinton

CHARLES RIVER

Barton's Point

the Ferry to Charlestown

Mill Dam

BOSTON

THE TOWN

the Dock

Wharf

BEACON HILL

Redoubt with 12 Pounders

Boats with the Troops

44

CHARLES

A floating Battery and an Armed Transport to defend the Entrance of Charles River

RIVER or Charles River

HARBOUR

South Battery

the Fort with some Field Pieces

Windmill Point

THE COMMON

Fox's Hill

BOSTON

Batteries

Battery

the Neck

Redoubt and four 12 Pounders

London. Printed for R. Sayer & J. Bennett N.º 53 in Fleet Street, as the Act directs 27 Nov. 1775.

The following Description of the Action near Boston, on the 17th of June, is taken from a Letter written by General Burgoyne to his Nephew Lord Stanley.

"*Boston, June 25, 1775.*

"BOSTON is a peninsula, joined to the main land only by a narrow neck, which on the first troubles Gen. Gage fortified; arms of the sea, and the harbour, surround the rest: on the other side one of these arms, to the North, is Charles-Town (or rather was, for it is now rubbish), and over it a large hill, which is also, like Boston, a peninsula: to the South of the town is a still larger scope of land, containing three hills, joining also to the main by a tongue of land, and called Dorchester Neck: the heights as above described, both North and South, (in the soldier's phrase) command the town, that is, give an opportunity of erecting batteries above any that you can make against them, and consequently are much more advantageous. It was absolutely necessary we should make ourselves masters of these heights, and we proposed to begin with Dorchester, because from particular situation of batteries and shipping (too long to describe, and unintelligible to you if I did) it would evidently be effected without any considerable loss: every thing was accordingly disposed; my two colleagues and myself (who, by the bye, have never differed in one jot of military sentiment) had, in concert with Gen. Gage, formed the plan: Howe was to land the transports on one point, Clinton in the center, and I was to cannonade from the Causeway, or the Neck; each to take advantage of circumstances: the operations must have been very easy; this was to have been executed on the 18th. On the 17th, at dawn of day, we found the enemy had pushed intrenchments with great diligence, during the night, on the heights of Charles-Town, and we evidently saw that every hour gave them fresh strength; it therefore became necessary to alter our plan, and attack on that side. Howe, as second in command, was detached with about 2000 men, and landed on the outward side of the peninsula, covered with shipping, without opposition; he was to advance from thence up the hill which

was over Charles-Town, where the strength of the enemy lay; he had under him Brigadier-General Pigot: Clinton and myself took our stand (for we had not any fixed post) in a large battery directly opposite to Charles-Town, and commanding it, and also reaching to the heights above it, and thereby facilitating Howe's attack. Howe's disposition was exceeding soldier-like; in my opinion it was perfect. As his first arm advanced up the hill, they met with a thousand impediments from strong fences, and were much exposed. They were also exceedingly hurt by musquetry from Charles-Town, though Clinton and I did not perceive it, till Howe sent us word by a boat, and desired us to set fire to the town, which was immediately done. We threw a parcel of shells, and the whole was instantly in flames. Our battery afterwards kept an inceffant fire on the heights: it was seconded by a number of frigates, floating batteries, and one ship of the line.

"And now ensued one of the greatest scenes of war that can be conceived: if we look to the height, Howe's corps ascending the hill in the face of entrenchments, and in a very disadvantageous ground, was much engaged; and to the left the enemy pouring in fresh troops by thousands, over the land; and in the arm of the sea our ships and floating batteries cannonading them: strait before us a large and a noble town in one great blaze; the church steeples, being of timber, were great pyramids of fire above the rest; behind us the church steeples and heights of our own camp covered with spectators of the rest of our army which was not engaged; the hills round the country covered with spectators; the enemy all anxious suspence; the roar of cannon, mortars, and musquetry; the crush of churches, ships upon the stocks, and whole streets falling together in ruin, to fill the ear; the storm of the redoubts, with the objects above described, to fill the eye; and the reflection that perhaps a defeat was a final loss to the British empire in America, to fill the mind; made the whole a picture

and a complication of horror and importance beyond any thing that ever came to my lot to be witness to. I much lament Tom's* absence:—it was a fight for a young soldier that the longest service may not furnish again; and had he been with me he would likewise have been out of danger; for, except two cannon balls that went an hundred yards over our heads, we were not on any part of the direction of the enemy's shot. A moment of the day was critical: Howe's left were staggered; two battalions had been sent to reinforce them, but we perceived them on the beach seeming in embarrassment what way to march; Clinton, then next for business, took the part, without waiting for orders, to throw himself into a boat to head them; he arrived in time to be of service, the day ended with glory, and the success was most important, considering the ascendancy it gave the regular troops; but the loss was uncommon in officers for the numbers engaged,

"Howe was untouched, but his aid-de-camp Sherwin was killed; Jordan, a friend of Howe's, who came, *engage du cœur*, to see the campaign, (a ship-mate of ours on board the Cerberus, and who acted as aid-de-camp) is badly wounded. Pigot was unhurt, but he behaved like a hero. You will see the list of the loss. Poor Col. Abercrombie, who commanded the grenadiers, died yesterday of his wounds. Capt. Addison, our poor old friend, who arrived but the day before, and was to have dined with me on the day of the action, was also killed; his son was upon the field at the time. Major Mitchell is but very slightly hurt; he is out already; young Chetwynd's wound is also slight. Lord Percy's regiment has suffered the most, and behaved the best; his Lordship himself was not in the action:—Lord Roden behaved to a charm; his name is established for life."

* His nephew, the Hon. Tho. Stanley, Esq; (and brother to Lord Stanley), who is gone a volunteer to Boston, in his Majesty's service.

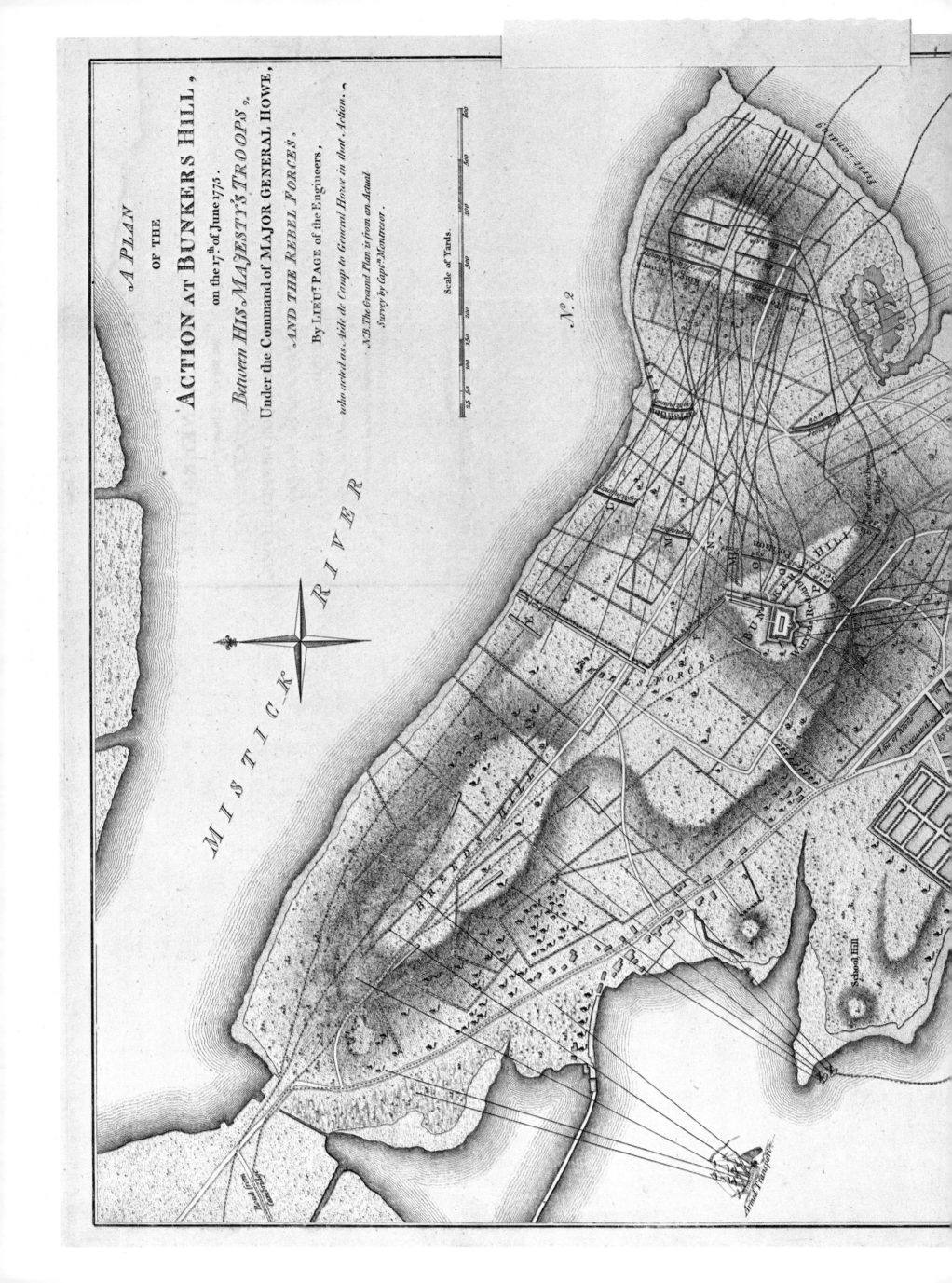

A PLAN
OF THE
ACTION AT BUNKERS HILL,
on the 17.th of June 1775.

Between HIS MAJESTY'S TROOPS,
Under the Command of MAJOR GENERAL HOWE,
AND THE REBEL FORCES.

By LIEU.t PAGE of the Engineers,

who acted as Aide de Camp to General Howe in that Action.

N.B. The Ground Plan is from an Actual
Survey by Capt.n Montresor.

Scale of Yards.
25 50 100 150 200 300 400 500 600

MISTICK RIVER

No. 2

Road from Cambridge

Armd. Transports

School Hill

MAP 4. Reproduced from the collection of The Newberry Library

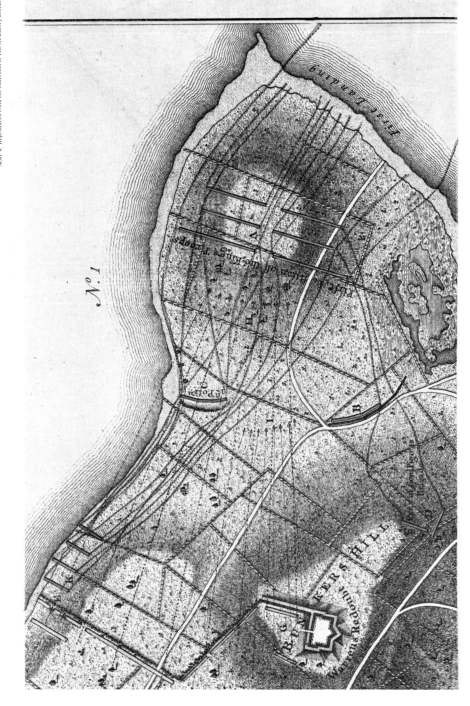

Nº 1

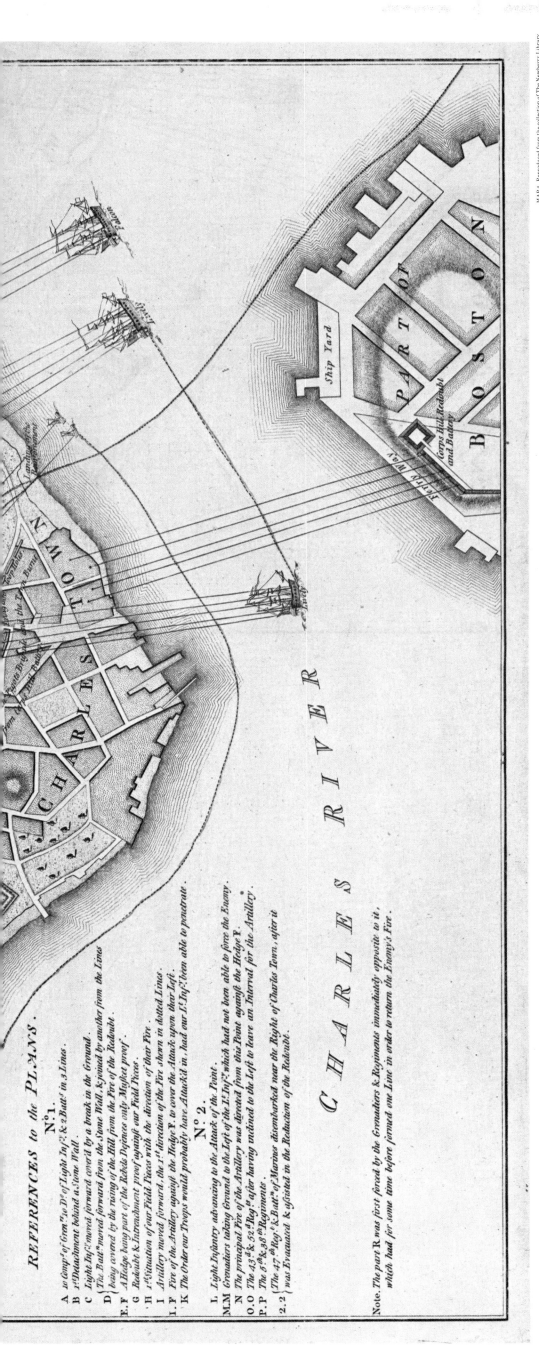

SHIP YARD

P A R T   O F   B O S T O N

Corps Hill Redoubt and Battery

ROYAL WAY

C H A R L E S T O N

C H A R L E S   R I V E R

REFERENCES to the PLANS.

Nº 1.

A *1st Comp.ies of Gren.rs 1st & D.rs of Light Inf.try 2d & 2 Batt.ns in 3 Lines.*
B *1st Detachment behind a Stone Wall.*
C *Light Inf.try moved forward cover'd by a break in the Ground.*
D *The Batt.ns moved forward from the Stone Wall, & joined by another from the Lines.*
E, F *being cover'd by the rising of the Hill from the Fire of the Redoubt.*
F *A Hedge being part of the Rebels Defence only Musket proof.*
G *Redoubt & Intreachment proof against our Field Pieces.*
H *1st situation of our Field Pieces with the direction of their Fire.*
I *Artillery moved forward, the 1st direction of the Fire shewn in dotted Lines.*
I, P *Fire of the Artillery against the Hedge F, to cover the Attack upon their Left.*
K *The Order our Troops would probably have Attack'd in, had our L. Inf.try been able to penetrate.*

Nº 2.

L *Light Infantry advancing to the Attack of the Point.*
M, M *Grenadiers taking Ground to the Left of the 1st Inf.try which had not been able to force the Enemy.*
N *The principal Fire of the Artillery was directed from this Point against the Hedge F.*
O, O *The 43.d & 52.d Reg.ts after having inclined to the Left to leave an Interval for the Artillery.*
P, P *The 5.th & 38.th Regiments.*
2, 2 *{The 47.th Reg.t & Batt.n of Marines disembarked near the Right of Charles Town, after it was Evacuated & visited on the Reduction of the Redoubt.*

Note. The part R was first forced by the Grenadiers & Regiments immediately opposite to it, which had for some time before formed one Line in order to return the Enemy's Fire.

British Military Victory: Patriot Morale-Builder

MAP 4. ¶ This is the most precise and detailed plan of the Battle of Bunker Hill, despite the fact that the names of Bunker Hill and Breed's Hill are transposed on this map, a minor detail that has been the source of great controversy through the years. Lieutenant Page, a participant at the Bunker Hill battle, drew the map from personal observation. The overlay (No. 1)* enables one to see the deployment of the British troops and their maneuvers as planned for the first phase; the main map (No. 2) shows the final movements and positions. ¶ This carefully prepared document illustrates the first major conflict of the two armies, during which the Americans proved they could stand and fight against a large force of British regulars. Both sides fought with great valor. Before they ran out of ammunition, the inexperienced militiamen fired disciplined volleys which twice turned back General Howe's best units. On their third assault, the redcoats swept the battlefield. As shown on the map, British artillery and naval support were crucial factors.

A Plan of the Action at Bunkers Hill, on the 17th of June 1775. Between His Majesty's Troops, Under the Command of Major General Howe, and the Rebel Forces. By T. H. Page after John Montresor. London, Wm. Faden, n.d. (19¼" x 17")

* The overlay appears at the end of the atlas for those who wish to hinge it to the main map as it was originally issued.

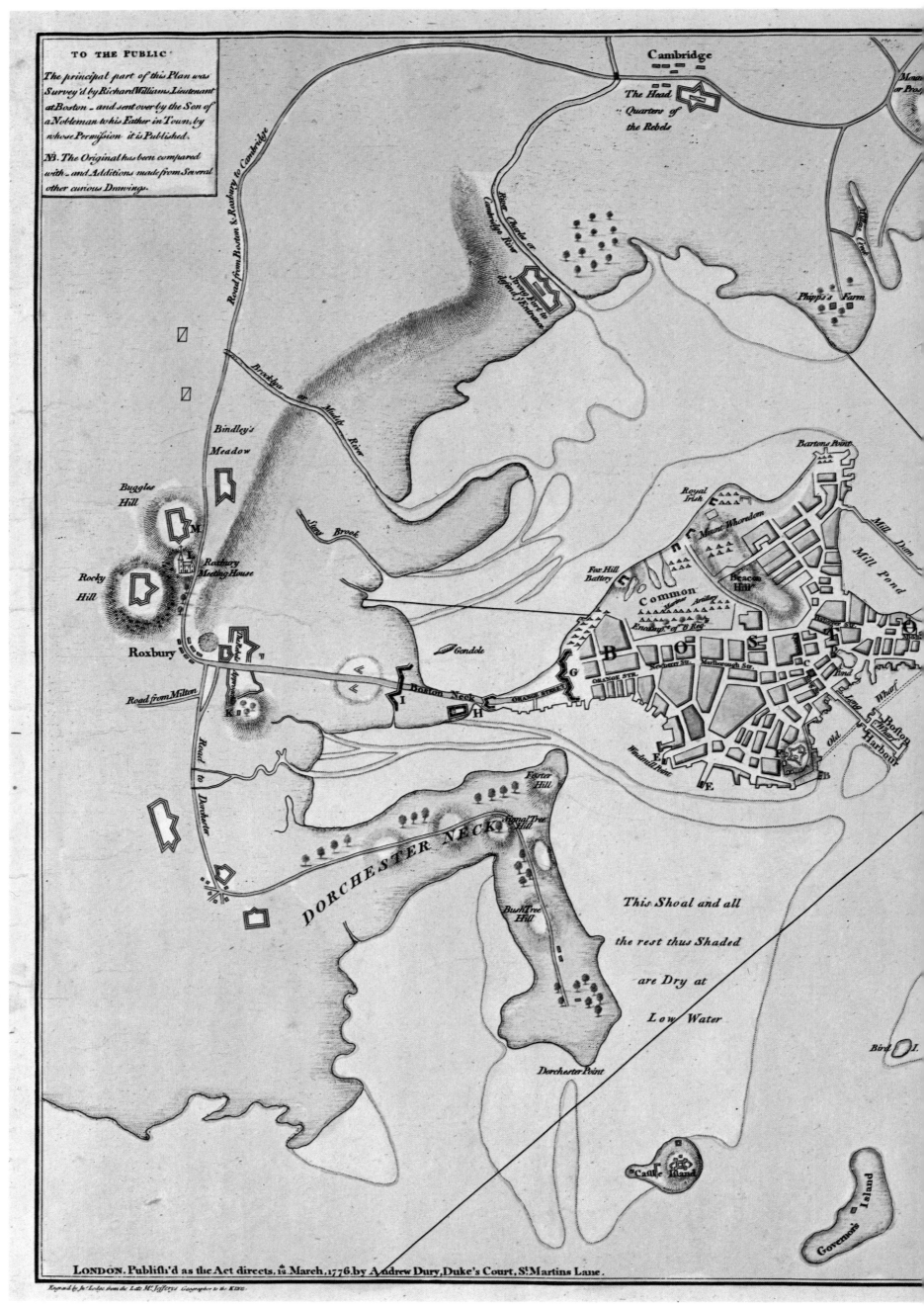

TO THE PUBLIC

The principal part of this Plan was
Survey'd by Richard Williams, Lieutenant
at Boston _ and sent over by the Son of
a Nobleman to his Father in Town, by
whose Permission it is Published.

NB. The Original has been compared
with _ and Additions made from Several
other curious Drawings.

Cambridge

The Head
Quarters of
the Rebels

Phipps's Farm

Road from Boston & Roxbury to Cambridge

River Charles or
Cambridge River

Ferry Port to defend Entrance

Brookelys or Muddy River

Bindley's
Meadow

Stony Brook

Buggles
Hill

M

Rocky
Hill

Roxbury
Meeting House

Roxbury

Road from Milton

K

Road to Dorchester

Gondole

Bartons Point

Royal
Irish

Mount Whoredom

Beacon
Hill

Fox Hill
Battery

Common

Marine Artillery

Encampmt of B Regt

Mill Dam

Mill Pond

BOSTON

Newbery Str.

Marlborough Str.

Orange Str.

Boston Neck

H

I

G

Newtery Str.

C

Pond

Old Long Wharf

Boston
Harbour

E

Windmill Point

Foster
Hill

DORCHESTER NECK

Ronal Tree
Hill

Bush Tree
Hill

This Shoal and all

the rest thus Shaded

are Dry at

Low Water

Bird I.

Dorchester Point

Castle Island

Governor's Island

LONDON. Publish'd as the Act directs, 1st March, 1776. by Andrew Dury, Duke's Court, St Martins Lane.

Engraved by Jno Lodge from the Late Mr Jefferys Geographer to the KING.

A PLAN
OF
BOSTON,
and its ENVIRONS.
shewing the true SITUATION *of*
HIS MAJESTY'S ARMY.
AND ALSO THOSE OF THE
REBELS.
Drawn by an Engineer at Boston. Oct.ʳ 1775.

Middle Hill

Plough'd Hill

Winter Hill

Moulds River

Charles Town Neck

Lines & Redoubts thrown up by our Troops after y Victory on y 17 June 1775.

Penny Ferry

Gondoles

Gen.ˡ Howe's Camp

Artillery

BUNKERS HILL

Redoubt taken from y Rebels by Gen. Howe

Dragoons

A Pond

Marines

Charlestown Point

Troops Landed 17 June under General Howe

North End

Dock Yard

Road to Marble Head & Salem

Winnisimmet Ferry

REFERENCE.

A { Corpse Hill, a Battery of 8 Pieces of Cannon, Mortars, &c.&c. Erected to favour the Troops Landing on y 17ᵗʰ June &, to set Fire to Charles Town

B { North & South Batteries, built by the Province for the defence of y Harbour, they are in a ruinous State

C. Town Hall

D. Faneuil Hall

E. Two Batteries Erected on Wharfs against Dorchester Neck

F. Fort Hill a proper Place for constructing a Citadel

G. Fortification now constructing for the immediate defence of the Town

H. A Block House & a Strong Batteries pointing on part of Dorchester Neck

I. Lines to defend the Boston Neck

K { A Hill from whence the Enemy annoy y Centrie & Officers with small Arms, but seldom do any Execution

L { Roxbury Meeting-House, upon a Hill from whence y Enemy often Fire Cannon into the Lines

M { A Strong Post of the Enemy, Fortified in appearance with great Judgment, & much Elevated, from whence with a 24 Pounder they can just reach the Lines

EXPLANATION.

The Works shaded Green shew those constructed by His Majesty's Troops

The Works shaded Yellow shew those thrown up by the Rebels, as they appear from Boston

Williams's House burnt by y Rebels

NODDLES ISLAND

HOG ISLAND

Yards or Half a Mile

49

Principal Port
of the Continent

MAP 5. ¶ Ironically published in London one week before the British evacuated Boston and sailed for Halifax, this map clearly reveals the situation of the siege of Boston by the Continental army nine months after Washington assumed command. ¶ Unable to be shown, of course, is the fact that the Americans just one week earlier had occupied and fortified the heights of Dorchester Neck. This skillfully executed, dramatic move rendered the British position untenable and caused Sir William Howe to pull his army out of Boston. Never again was Massachusetts to be occupied by British soldiers, except on the Maine coast (see Map 36). With an army of 11,000 men, and with full control of Boston and the Charlestown peninsula, Bunker Hill, and Breed's Hill, it is difficult to understand why the British failed to fortify Dorchester Heights themselves, and thus make Boston virtually impregnable. ¶ In October 1775 Richard Williams, a talented young lieutenant, drew the map from which this engraving was made. Williams's regimental records indicate that he was on the sick list at Boston in January 1776. He returned to England in May and died later that year. ¶ The same firm that published this map issued the fine plans of New York and Philadelphia which also appear in this atlas.

SHOWN ON PRECEDING PAGE
A Plan of Boston, and its Environs, shewing the true Situation of His Majesty's Army. And also those of the Rebels. By Richard Williams. Engraved by Jno. Lodge. London, Andrew Dury, March 12, 1776. (18" x 25½")

Currently the momentum was with the rebels, whose ranks had soared to as many as 17,000 men, extending in an arc around Boston from shore to shore, from Dorchester to Charlestown. Yet Gage, victim of London overconfidence, was expected to do something, to boost the morale of the crown's blockaded forces, and to strike a blow that would knock the wind out of the sails of the rebellion. Reinforcements arrived from England, along with moral support in the form of three major generals—William Howe, Henry Clinton, and John Burgoyne—sent to arouse Gage from his reputed lethargy or timidity. Howe, a dark-complexioned man, was in his middle forties, as was the short, paunchy Clinton, the two generals being some eight years younger than the vivacious, gregarious Burgoyne, master of both boudoir and drawing room. A "triumvirate of reputation" was Burgoyne's manner of describing them, and without doubt they were; Burgoyne and Clinton were experienced in continental warfare in Germany; Howe, a subordinate of the great Wolfe, had been schooled in American fighting in the 1750s.

These confident newcomers, all destined to have their military careers severely tarnished in America, shared the opinion that Gage had been timorous, and they did not hide their sentiments from the officers in Boston or from their superiors in London. They launched, at this opening stage of the war, the endemic backbiting and carping that would ultimately all but consume the British command structure in America. They demanded action: the seizure of the outlying heights of Dorchester and Charlestown, which, if fortified, would allow either army to enfilade the other's positions. Gage went along with the proposal, but that secret was kept no better than had been the plan to march on Concord, and General Artemas Ward responded by sending Colonel William Prescott down the Charlestown peninsula with 1,200 men to dig in on Bunker Hill. After a hurried conference, Prescott and several others decided to continue on to a lower elevation, Breed's Hill, which lay closer to the city.

At dawn on June 17 the British discovered that a redoubt (forty yards square with dirt thrown up to form a breastwork) had been constructed on Breed's Hill during the previous night. Dorchester Heights was now forgotten as Gage and his star-studded advisers laid preparations for a frontal assault on Breed's Hill at high tide. As the regulars began to cross in rowboats, Prescott, a balding, tough-minded provincial officer, made ready his position on Breed's Hill. To cover his left flank, he extended his lines down the hill to the edge of the Mystic River. He received two additional regiments from Ward, and he was joined by Dr. Joseph Warren, president of the Massachusetts Provincial Congress, who desired to fight as a volunteer. (*See Map 3*)

As Howe, commanding the operation, began his advance in midafternoon, Boston rooftops sagged under the weight of scores of Loyalists and British onlookers anticipating a glorious drama in which disciplined redcoats would sweep forward to the crest of Breed's Hill, there to make short work with their bayonets of the ill-trained, ragamuffin New England farmers. With Howe, a fearless officer, leading his own right wing, and Brigadier General Robert Pigot directing his left, the long scarlet lines, to the cadence of drums, set forth—through the tall grass, over fence after fence. On and on they came, their occasional harmless, unanswered volleys sending up clouds of acrid smoke. All was still in the redoubt until the enemy came within fifty yards, effective musket range. Then Prescott shouted "Fire!" and a sheet of flame seemed to engulf Pigot's front, tearing gaping holes in his line; a second blast from the redoubt rolled the British left back down the hill. (*See Map 4*)

Howe's own column, marching along the beach in the hope of turning the American left, fared no better than Pigot's as Israel Putnam's men unloosed a deadly barrage from behind a rail fence, their muskets spraying not only bullets but rusty nails and pieces of glass as well. Though Howe, too, withdrew, he refused to let British arms succumb to provincial marksmen for a second time in two months, but another thrust up the hill fared as badly as the first. Seasoned British regiments, hardened and battle-tested from Fontenoy to Quebec, broke and ran like raw recruits.

To Gage, Burgoyne, and Clinton, it was incredible, unbelievable, and they hastened another regiment across the water, and then another. On the British right, a renewed British surge resulted only in the loss of every single member of Howe's personal staff. Howe, whatever his shortcomings, knew no personal fear, but he was badly shaken by what seemingly could never have happened. He resolved to send his redcoats up the hill again, but this time they would virtually ignore the lower American positions and concentrate on the redoubt, and they would drop their packs to the ground to quicken their pace. Again they came, and again the Americans waited. With the king's legions just twenty yards away, New England muskets spoke again—and the carnage was frightful; but it was the final time. The Americans were out of ammunition and, at last, those glistening steel British bayonets swarmed over the parapet. Dr. Warren fell, so did thirty others. In the smoke, dust, and confusion, Prescott and many of his men escaped, their retreat continuing over Bunker Hill and across Charlestown Neck to the safety of the main American lines.

At Breed's Hill—or the Battle of Bunker Hill, as it is mistakenly known—American casualties in all categories numbered 397, whereas British losses were the heaviest of the eight-year war: 226 dead and 828 wounded, more than 40 percent of the almost 2,500 troops in action. Were these the Americans that Sir Jeffery Amherst had recently described in Parliament as incapable of offering combat against even small numbers of regulars? Were they the same Americans that Lord Sandwich, before that same body, had said would run at "the very sound of cannon . . . as fast as their feet would carry them"? Perhaps the effectiveness of American fighting men remained to be measured, but this much was clear. Neither Howe nor any other British general in the American war would ever take the rebels so lightly again as to violate a standard maxim of eighteenth-century warfare: namely, that expensive, highly trained professional armies were not to be squandered in costly head-on assaults; that instead the feint, the parry, and the flanking movement were the preferred methods of dislodging one's foe. Indeed, had Howe followed traditional strategy (and Clinton's advice), he would have landed part of his force at Charlestown Neck so as to squeeze Prescott's command from both ends of the peninsula.

If the Massachusetts Provincial Congress could take justifiable pride in the heroic performance of its men, the colony's leaders were sobered by the realization that poor coordination between Ward and Prescott and a shortage of powder and lead had contributed to Howe's eventually carrying the day. The provincial congress was scarcely prepared to direct a war, even to the point of synchronizing all of New England's efforts. One week before Bunker Hill, on June 10, John Adams had proposed to the Second Continental Congress, in session since May 10 at the State

Quebec
Fights Off Invaders

MAP 6. ¶ Early in the war, the Continental Congress hoped for a quick military victory in Canada to add a "14th colony" to the cause. Late in the summer of 1775, after Ethan Allen's capture of Fort Ticonderoga, General Richard Montgomery led 1,200 troops north to Canada. By November 13 he had overcome the posts of St. Johns and Chambly and walked into Montreal. ¶ Benedict Arnold, who had been at Ticonderoga with Allen, meanwhile was embarking on his justly famous and heroic march to Quebec. Starting from Cambridge in September with 1,100 men, he underestimated the inhospitable terrain and weather which lay ahead, along the Kennebec-Chaudiere River route. Only the first phase of their ordeal was over when they reached the "Heights of Abraham" on November 15. Although the strength of both armies had been so depleted that they could field only about 1,000 men after Arnold and Montgomery joined forces on December 2, the Americans attempted to storm the fortified city, whose defenders outnumbered them two to one. ¶ The heroic action failed completely. Montgomery, one of the patriots' best young generals, was killed; Arnold was badly wounded; Dan Morgan and his Virginia riflemen were captured after fighting their way well into the Lower Town. It was Sir Guy Carleton's leadership, during this engagement and for the ensuing three years, that saved Canada for the crown. ¶ The map clearly shows the plan of the fortified city and its defenses, as well as the surrounding topography. Arnold's positions before the attack are indicated on the "Heights of Abraham," as are the place ("L" near *Cap Diamant*) where Montgomery's assault began and "M" at "Lowertown") the disastrous "Saut de Matelot," which Arnold and Morgan were long to remember. Locations of the meaningless April siege guns are also shown to the west of the city and across the *River St. Laurence.*

SHOWN ON FOLLOWING PAGE
Plan of the City and Environs of Quebec, with its Siege and Blockade by the Americans, from the 8th of December 1775 to the 13th of May 1776. Engraved by Wm. Faden. London, Wm. Faden, Sept. 12, 1776. (17¾" x 24½")

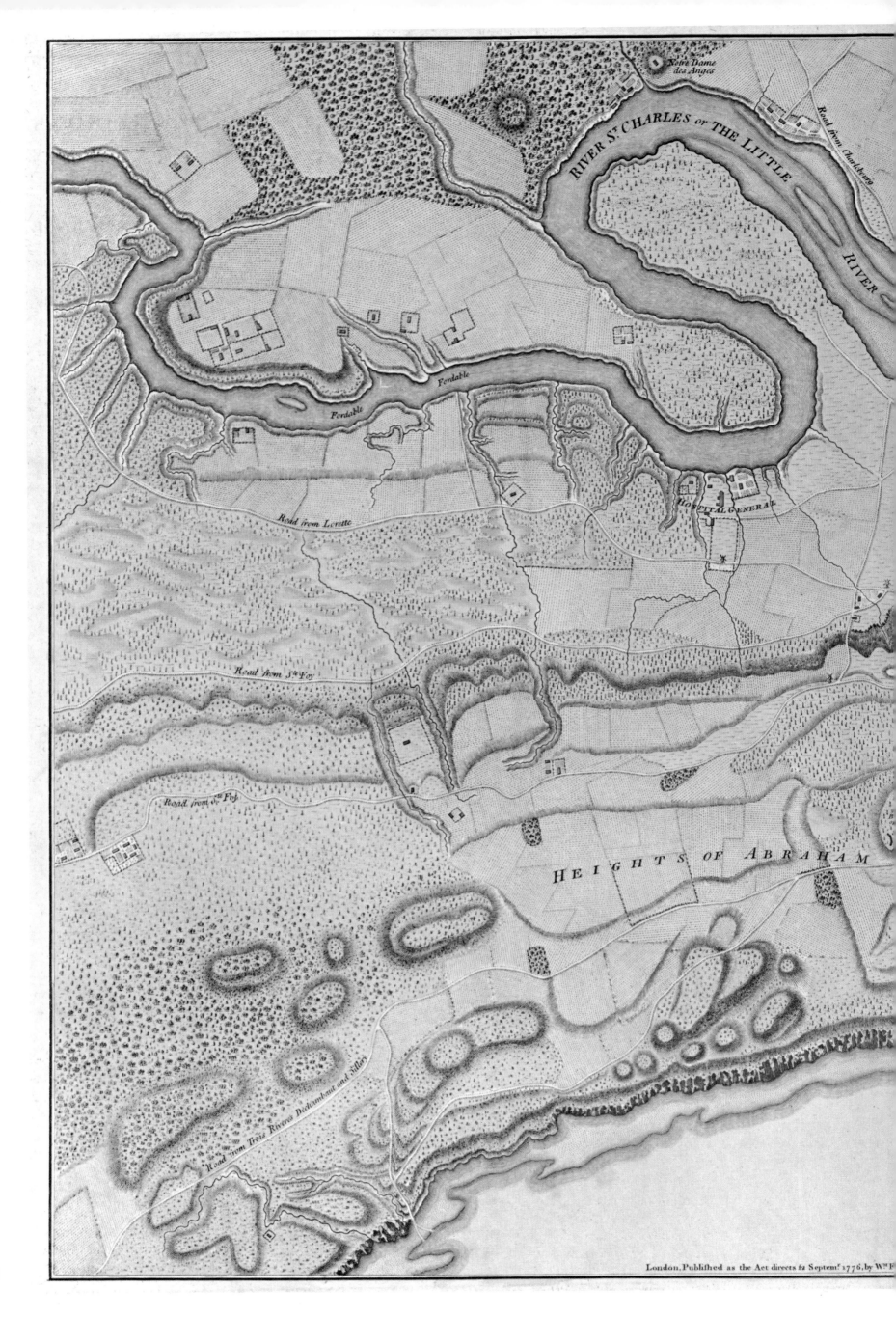

Notre Dame
des Anges

RIVER St. CHARLES or THE LITTLE

Road from Charlsbourg

RIVER

Fordable

Fordable

Fordable

Road from Lorette

HOSPITAL GENERAL

Road from St. Foy

Road from St. Foy

HEIGHTS OF ABRAHAM

Road from Trois Rivers Dechambaut and Sillery

London, Published as the Act directs 12 Septemr. 1776, by Wm. F.

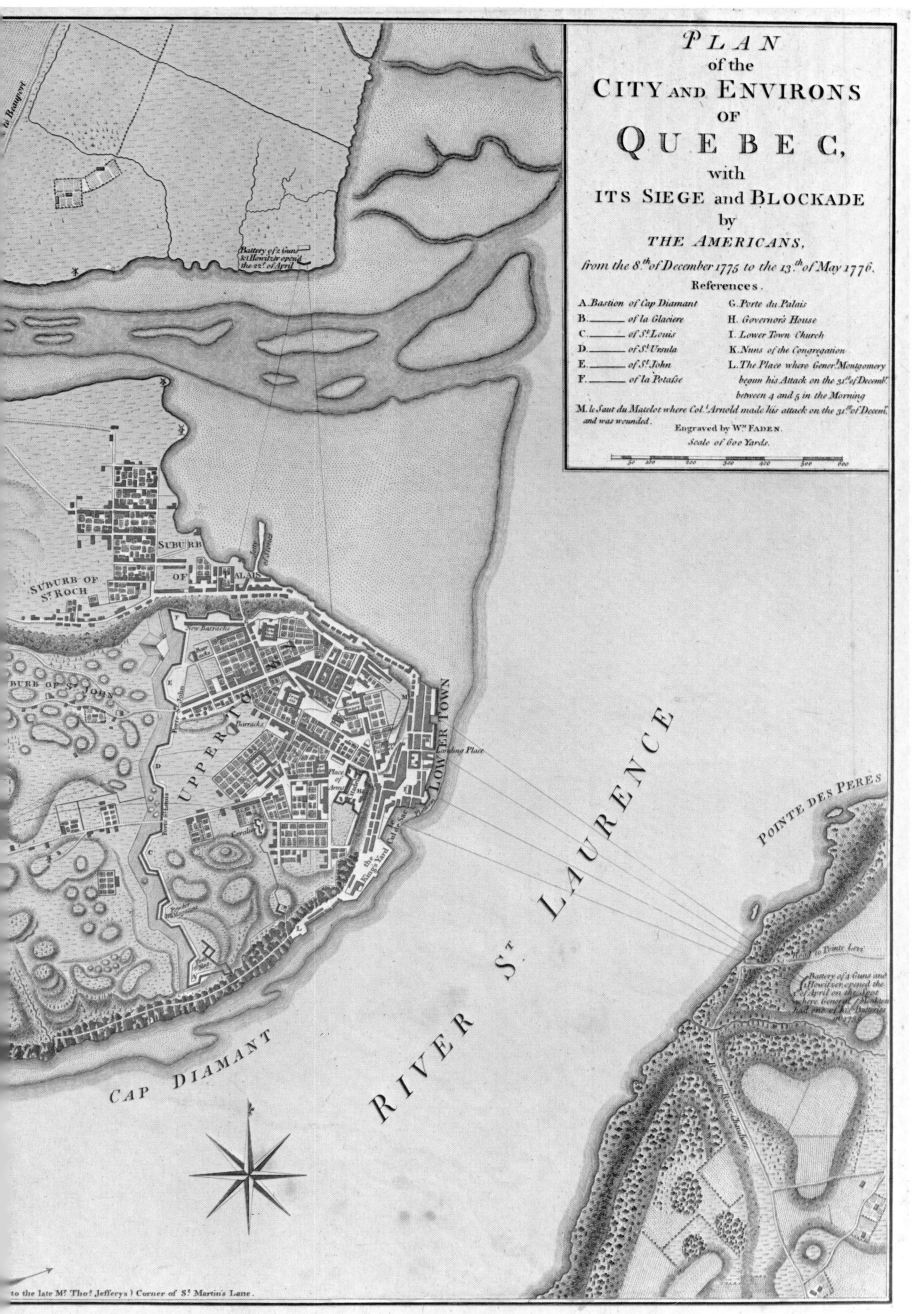

PLAN
of the
CITY AND ENVIRONS
OF
QUEBEC,
with
ITS SIEGE and BLOCKADE
by
THE AMERICANS,
from the 8.th of December 1775 to the 13.th of May 1776.

References.

A. Bastion of Cap Diamant
B. ———— of la Glaciere
C. ———— of S.t Louis
D. ———— of S.t Ursula
E. ———— of S.t John
F. ———— of la Potasse

G. Porte du Palais
H. Governor's House
I. Lower Town Church
K. Nuns of the Congregation
L. The Place where Gener.l Montgomery
begun his Attack on the 31.t of Decemb.r
between 4 and 5 in the Morning

M. le Saut du Matelot where Col.l Arnold made his attack on the 31.st of Decem.r
and was wounded.

Engraved by W.m FADEN.

Scale of 600 Yards.

SUBURB OF S.t ROCH

SUBURB OF ALAIS

BURB OF S.t JOHN

UPPER TOWN

LOWER TOWN

CAP DIAMANT

RIVER S.t LAURENCE

POINTE DES PERES

Battery of 2 Guns
& 1 Howitzer open'd
the 22.d of April

Battery of 4 Guns and
1 Howitzer open'd the
of April on the Spot
where General M. where
had one of his Batteries

to the late M.r Tho.s Jefferys) Corner of S.t Martin's Lane.

I. B. Forrest made this engraving of John Hancock; Charles Willson Peale did the portrait of Washington in his Regimental uniform. Breed's Hill, where the American forces were gathered and which was the actual site of the Battle of Bunker Hill.

House in Philadelphia, that it adopt the troops besieging Boston, making them the army of the united colonies, and that it call for the colonies to the southward to contribute men to that army. That step was revolutionary in itself, for the Second Continental Congress (which was arranged by the First Congress) had been chosen before the outbreak of hostilities and had no legal authority to conduct a war in the name of thirteen colonies. Yet its chieftains did not hesitate. Composed of America's most-distinguished men—Hancock, the Adamses of Massachusetts, Franklin of Pennsylvania, Washington and Jefferson of Virginia, the Rutledges of South Carolina, among others—the Congress was confident it could bank on the support of the people back home. On June 14 the Congress resolved to raise six companies from Pennsylvania, Maryland, and Virginia to join the New England militiamen ringing Boston.

Although British arms were driving the thirteen colonies together, their union, new and untested, continued to reveal some of the sectional suspicions and rivalries of the colonial decades. The maneuvering involved in the appointment of a commander in chief of the army is a prime example. Some felt that New Englanders had been too assertive, that it would be desirable to give the plum to a man from another region, to pass over Artemas Ward and also Hancock, who allegedly coveted the post; and, in the interest of intercolonial harmony, John Adams and a number of other Yankee congressmen agreed.

Scarcely the "Father of His Country" at this stage in history, George Washington nevertheless became the obvious and unanimous choice of Congress. A former colonial lawmaker and a member of the Continental

Congress, he was known and trusted by the members as a man who would be steadfastly wedded to the time-honored British-American principle of civil control of the military. From populous and influential Virginia, he would help swing the southern provinces behind a war effort that had been almost solely New England's up to that point. Possessed of wealth and social station, he would lend dignity to a cause that was described in Britain as under the domination of wild-eyed New England radicals. At first glance, his military background appears to have been highly inadequate, chiefly confined to commanding Virginia's western defenses during a crucial span

Plan of the Town of Boston with the Attack on BUNKERS-HILL in the Peninsula of CHARLESTOWN. the 17th of June 1775.

Clinton's Target: Capital of the South

MAP 7. ¶ Action in the Revolutionary War often proceeded at an amazingly unhurried pace. For example, in October of 1775 Lord Dartmouth instructed General Howe in Boston to move against the Carolinas. The theory was that many Tories in the South could be aroused by a moderate-sized invasion and the presence of a British fleet to form a combined army that could hold the southern provinces for the crown. ¶ Howe gave the assignment to Clinton on January 6, 1776. With a few ships and some 1,500 troops, Clinton sailed from Boston for the mouth of the Cape Fear River in North Carolina. Here he was to rendezvous with Commodore Sir Peter Parker's fleet and an army under Lord Cornwallis sailing from Cork in December of 1775. Although Clinton, proceeding leisurely to the meeting point, arrived at Cape Fear on March 12, the "Irish Fleet" did not begin to appear until April 18, and the last of their ships did not arrive until May 31! Even then, four more weeks were to pass before the attack. ¶ In the meantime, Congress had anticipated that Charleston, the commercial and cultural capital of the South, would be the target for such a thrust. At the beginning of January the defenses were ordered strengthened, and more troops, Continentals and militia, were sent there. Fort Sullivan was begun in January and was still unfinished at the time of battle. Unquestionably Charleston would have been more vulnerable had the invasion not consumed half a year in getting under way. ¶ On this sea chart can be seen the whole of Charleston Harbor and the outer islands. Sir Henry Clinton selected Long Island, to the northeast of Sullivan's Island, to disembark his army unopposed. Clinton apparently planned to cross to the mainland and circle around behind Sullivan's Island to cut off the garrison's retreat. The army was never engaged. Their maps showed a ford to the mainland eighteen inches deep at low tide, while in fact, seven feet was the shallowest these waters became. Thus Clinton was merely a spectator at this major British defeat.

SHOWN ON FOLLOWING PAGE
An Exact Plan of Charles-Town-Bar and Harbour. From an Actual Survey. With the Attack of Fort Sulivan, on the 28th of June 1776. By His Majesty's Squadron, Commanded by Sir Peter Parker. London, Robt. Sayer & Jno. Bennett, Aug. 31, 1776. (20" x 27½")

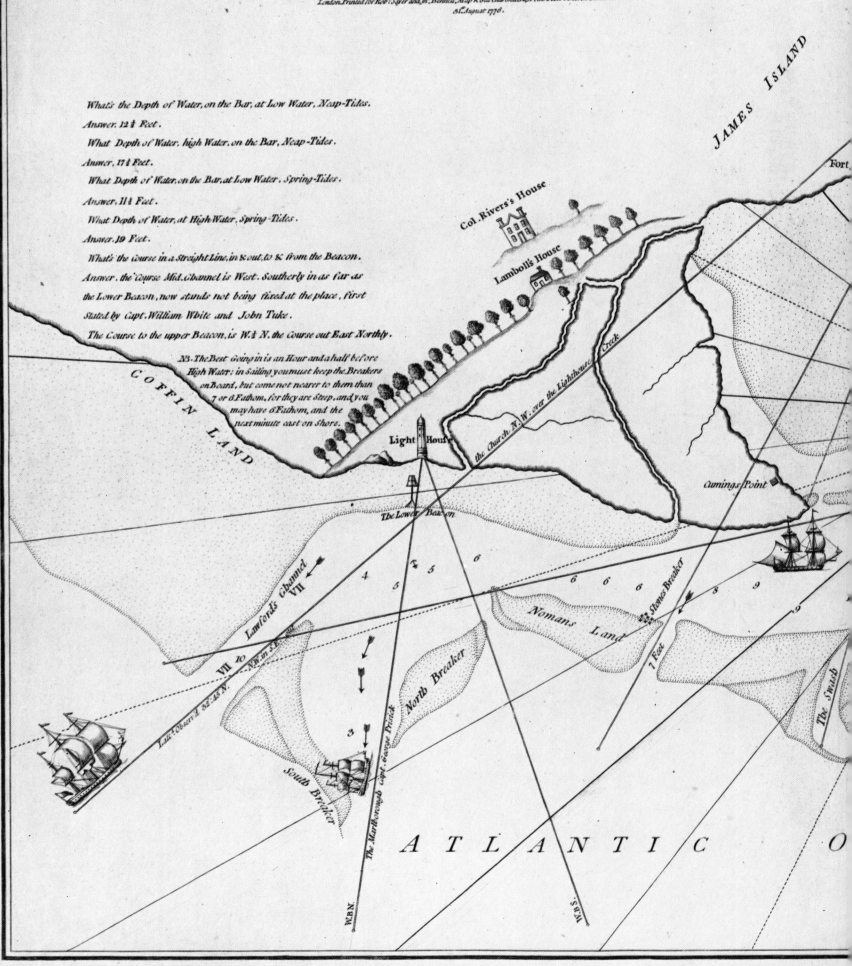

AN
EXACT PLAN
of
CHARLES-TOWN-BAR and HARBOUR.
From an Actual Survey.

With the Attack of FORT SULIVAN, on the 28.th of June 1776, BY HIS MAJESTY'S SQUADRON,
Commanded by Sir Peter Parker.
A Scale of three English Miles, Half a Mile to an Inch.

London, Printed for Robt. Sayer and Jno. Bennett, Map & Sea Chartsellers, No. 53 Fleet Street, as the Act directs.
31.st August 1776.

What's the Depth of Water, on the Bar, at Low Water, Neap-Tides.

Answer. 12¾ Feet.

What Depth of Water, high Water, on the Bar, Neap-Tides.

Answer. 17¾ Feet.

What Depth of Water, on the Bar, at Low Water, Spring-Tides.

Answer. 11¾ Feet.

What Depth of Water, at High Water, Spring-Tides.

Answer. 19 Feet.

What's the Course in a Streight Line, in & out, to & from the Beacon.

Answer. the Course Mid-Channel is West. Southerly in as far as
the Lower Beacon, now stands not being fixed at the place, first
Stated by Capt. William White and John Tuke.

The Course to the upper Beacon, is W.¼ N. the Course out East Northly.

N3. The Best Going in is an Hour and a half before
High Water: in Sailing you must keep the Breakers
on Board, but come not nearer to them than
7 or 6 Fathom, for they are Steep, and you
may have 6 Fathom, and the
next minute cast on Shore.

JAMES ISLAND

Fort

Col. Rivers's House

Lamboll's House

the Church, N.W. over the Lighthouse Creek

Cumings Point

Light House

The Lower Beacon

COFFIN LAND

Lanfords Channel
VII

4   5   6

6   6   6

The Stono Breaker

7 Fat.

Nomans Land

VII 10

N.W. on S. ½ E.

Lat.e Observd 32.45 N.

North Breaker

The Swash

3

The Marlborough Capt. George Frissele

South Breaker

ATLANTIC   O

W.N.

W.b.S.

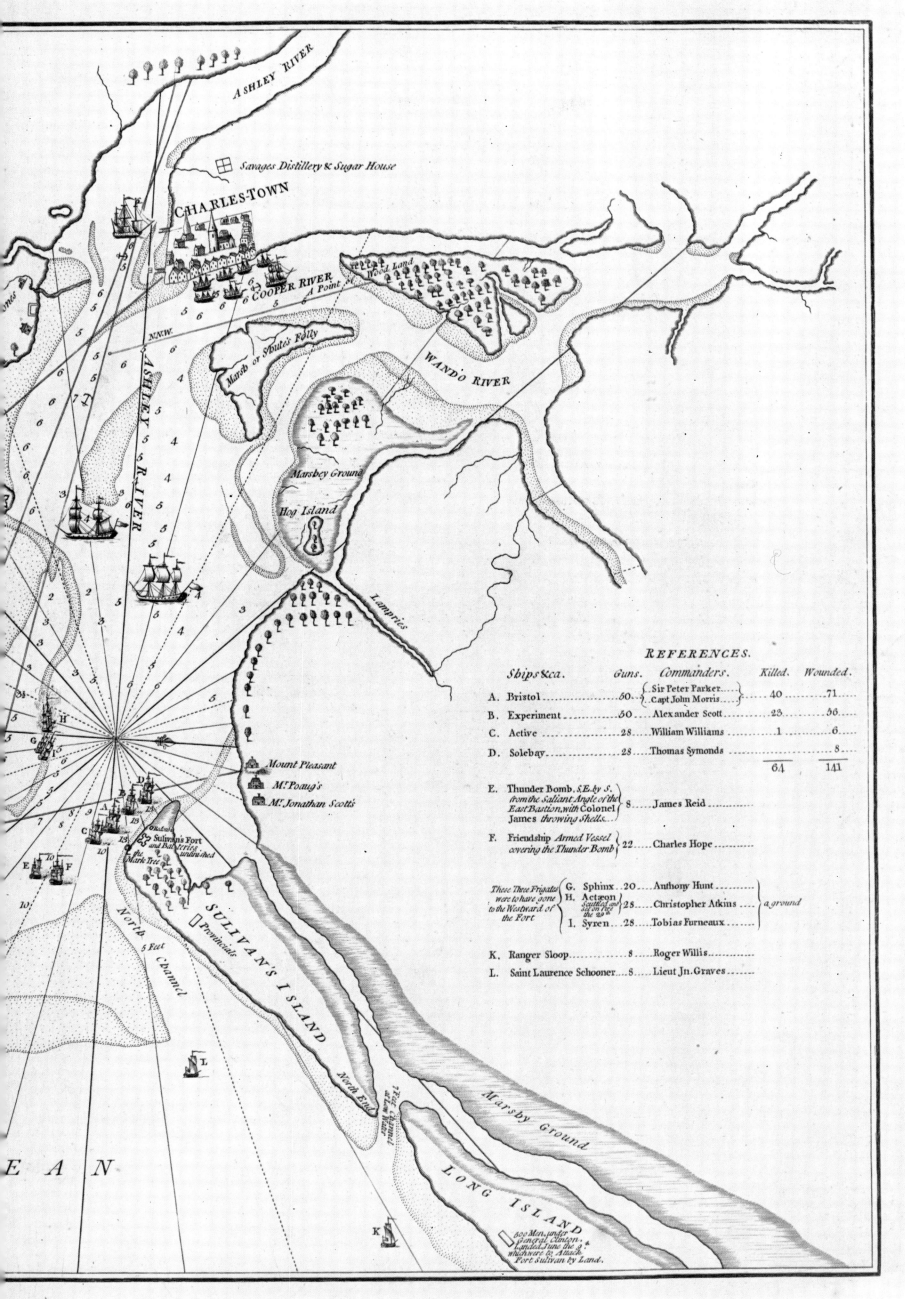

ASHLEY RIVER

□ Savages Distillery & Sugar House

CHARLES-TOWN

COOPER RIVER

A Point

Wood Land

N.N.W.

ASHLEY RIVER

March or Shute's Folly

WANDO RIVER

Marshy Ground

Hog Island

Lampries

Mount Pleasant

Mr Poaug's

Mr Jonathan Scotts

North Channel

5 Feet

SULIVAN'S ISLAND

Provincials

the Oak Tree

Sulivan's Fort and Batteries unfinished

North End

The Channel at Low Water

Marshy Ground

LONG ISLAND

500 Men under General Clinton Landed June the 9th which were to Attack Fort Sulivan by Land.

EAN

REFERENCES.

Ships &ca.	Guns.	Commanders.	Killed.	Wounded.
A. Bristol	50	Sir Peter Parker / Capt John Morris	40	71
B. Experiment	50	Alexander Scott	23	56
C. Active	28	William Williams	1	6
D. Solebay	28	Thomas Symonds		8
			64	141
E. Thunder Bomb. S.E. by S. from the Saliant Angle of the East Bastion, with Colonel James throwing Shells.	8	James Reid		
F. Friendship Armed Vessel covering the Thunder Bomb	22	Charles Hope		
These Three Frigates were to have gone to the Westward of the Fort G. Sphinx	20	Anthony Hunt		
H. Actæon Scuttled and set on Fire the 29th	28	Christopher Atkins	a ground	
I. Syren	28	Tobias Furneaux		
K. Ranger Sloop	8	Roger Willis		
L. Saint Laurence Schooner	8	Lieut Jn. Graves		

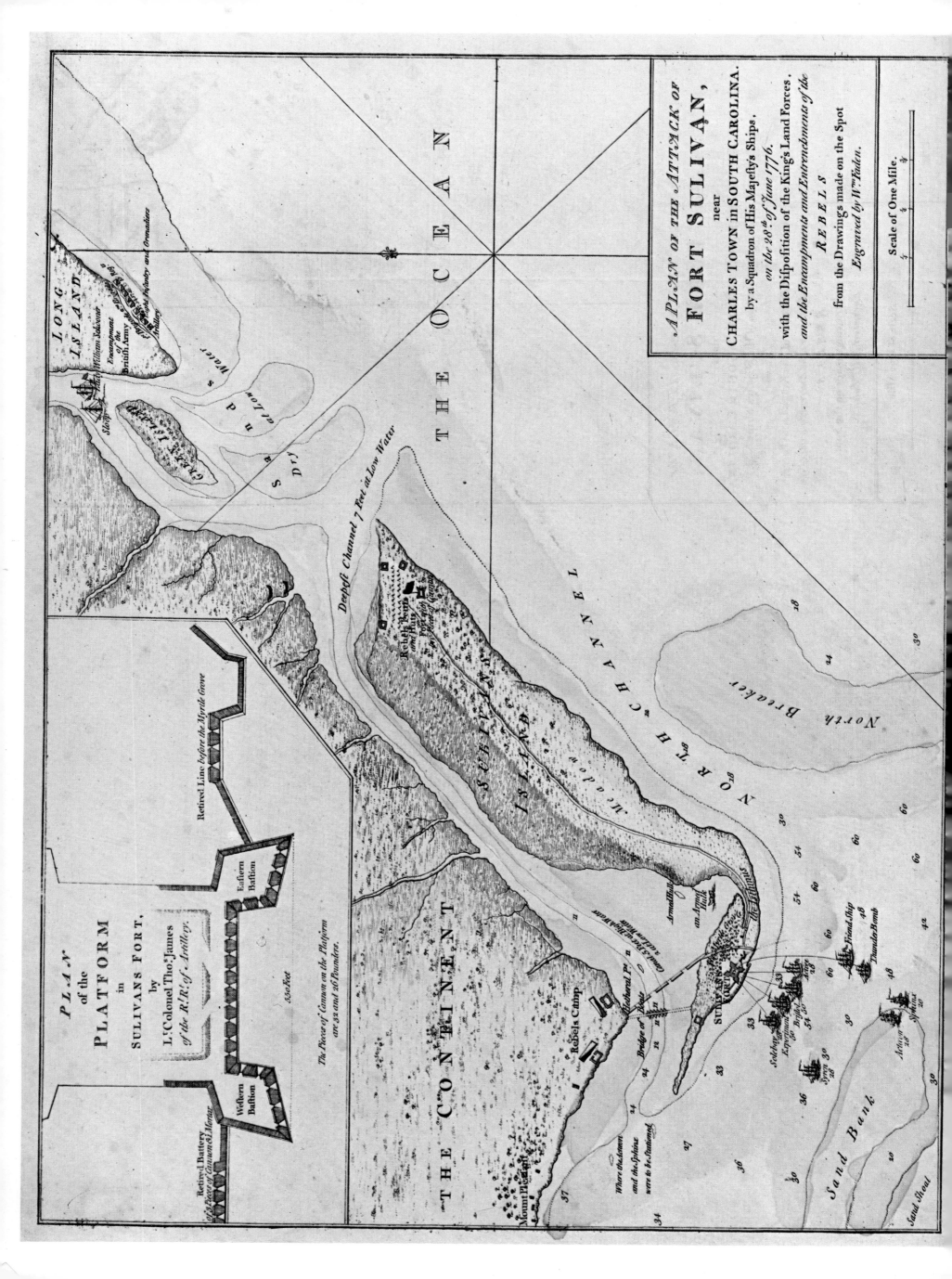

A PLAN OF THE ATTACK OF
FORT SULIVAN,
near
CHARLES TOWN in SOUTH CAROLINA.
by a Squadron of His Majesty's Ships.
on the 28th of June 1776.
with the Disposition of the King's Land Forces.
and the Encampments and Entrenchments of the
REBELS
from the Drawings made on the Spot
Engraved by Wm Faden.

Scale of One Mile.

PLAN
of the
PLATFORM
in
SULIVAN'S FORT.
by
Lt Colonel Thos James
of the R.Rt. of Artilley.

Retired Battery
of 4 Pieces of Cannon & Mortar.

Western Bastion

Eastern Bastion

Retired Line before the Myrtle Grove

630 Feet

The Pieces of Cannon on the Platform
are 32 and 26 Pounders.

LONG ISLAND

Encampment
of the
British Army

Light Infantry and Grenadiers
Artillery

Sloop

GREEN ISLAND

Dry Sands at Low Water

THE OCEAN

Deepest Channel 7 Feet at Low Water

Rebels Neuts
and Fury
Fort with
wooden Canon

SULIVANS ISLAND

NORTH CHANNEL

North Breaker

Sand Bank

Sand Shoal

THE CONTINENT

Mount Pleasant

Where the detour
and the Spluine
were to be Stationed.

Rebels Camp

Bridge of Boats

Richmond Pt.

Armed Hulk

The Isthmus

Myrtle Grove

Sulivans

Solebay

Experiment

Active

Sphinx

Bristol

Syren

Friendship

Thunder Bomb

LIST of his Majesty's Squadron commanded by Commodore Sir PETER PARKER, Knt. &c. on the Expedition against *Fort Sulivan* in *South Carolina*.

Ships.		Guns.	Commanders.
Briſtol	- - -	50	{Commodore Sir *Peter Parker*, Knt. Capt. *John Morris*.
Experiment	- - -	50	*Alexander Scott*.
Active	- - -	28	*William Williams*.
Solebay	- - -	28	*Thomas Symons*.
Actæon	- - -	28	*Chriſtopher Atkins*.
Syren	- - -	28	*Tobias Furneaux*.
Sphynx	- - -	20	*Anthony Hunt*.
Friendſhip arm'd veſſel	- - -	28	*Charles Hope*.
Ranger ſloop	- - -	8	*Roger Wils*.
Thunder bomb	- - -	8	*James Reid*.
St. Lawrence ſchooner			Lieut. *John Graves*.

The following Account of the Attack of FORT SULIVAN *is extracted from the Letters of Commodore Sir* PETER PARKER, *Knt. and Lieut. General* CLINTON, *to the Lords of the Admiralty.*

THE Commanders on the American ſtation deeming it expedient to make an attempt on Charles-Town in South Carolina, the fleet ſailed from Cape Fear on the 1ſt of June, and on the 4th anchored off Charles Town Bar. The 5th founded the Bar, and laid down buoys preparatory to the intended entrance of the harbour. The 7th all the frigates and moſt of the tranſports got over the Bar into Five-Fathom Hole. The 9th General *Clinton* landed on Long-Iſland with about four or five hundred men. The 10th the Briſtol got over the Bar with ſome difficulty. The 15th the Commodore gave the Captains of the ſquadron his arrangement for the attack of the batteries on Sulivan's Iſland, and the next day he acquainted General *Clinton* that the ſhips were ready. The General fixed on the 23d for their joint attack, but the wind proving unfavourable prevented its taking effect. The 25th the Experiment arrived, and next day came over the Bar, when a new arrangement was made for the attack. The 28th, at half an hour after nine in the morning, General *Clinton* was informed by ſignal that the ſquadron was going on the attack. At half an hour after ten the ſignal was made to weigh; and about a quarter after eleven the Briſtol, Experiment, Active and Solebay, brought up againſt the fort. The Thunder Bomb, covered by the Friendſhip armed veſſel, brought the faliant Angle of the eaſt baſtion to bear N. W. by N. and Colonel *Jams* threw ſeveral ſhells a little before and during the engagement in a very good direction. The Sphynx, Actæon, and Syren were to have been to the weſtward, to prevent fire ſhips or other veſſels from annoying the ſhips engaged, to enfilade the works, and, if the rebels ſhould be driven from them, to cut off their retreat, if poſſible. This laſt ſervice was not performed, owing to the ignorance of the pilot, who ran the three frigates aground. The Sphynx and Syren got off in a few hours, but the Actæon remained faſt till the next morning, when the Captain and Officers thought proper to ſcuttle and ſet her on fire.

A Court-martial was ordered on the Captain, Officers, and Company, of the Actæon, and they were honourably acquitted. During the time of the ſquadron being a-breaſt of the fort, which was near ten hours, a briſk fire was kept up by the ſhips, with intervals, and they had the ſatisfaction, after being engaged two hours, to oblige the rebels to ſlacken their fire very much. Large parties were drove ſeveral times out of the fort, which were replaced by others from the main. About half an hour after three, a confiderable reinforcement from Mount Pleaſant hung a man on a tree at the back of the fort, and it was imagined that the ſame party ran away about an hour after, for the fort was then totally ſilenced, and evacuated for near one hour and an half; but the rebels finding that the army could not take poſſeſſion, about ſix o'clock a con-

ſiderable body of people re-entered the fort, and renewed the firing from two or three guns, the reſt being, we ſuppoſe, diſmounted. About nine o'clock, it being very dark, great part of our ammunition expended, the people fatigued, the tide of ebb almoſt done, no proſpect from the Eaſtward, and no poſſibility of their being of any further ſervice, the Commodore ordered the ſhips to withdraw to their former moorings.

General *Clinton* landed his troops on Long-Iſland, which had been repreſented to him as communicating with Sulivan's Iſland by a Ford, paſſable at low water; but he found the channel which was reported to have been eighteen inches deep, to be ſeven feet deep; which circumſtance rendered it impoſſible for the army to give that aſſiſtance to the fleet in the attack made upon the fortreſs, that the General intended. In the courſe of the attack, the Briſtol had the whole of her mizen and half her main maſt ſhot away, and was twice on fire; the Experiment, Capt. Scott, was almoſt unrig'd, which with the Briſtol had ſeveral ſhot through their ſides, and their colours ſhot in pieces; the Sphynx had her bowſprit ſhot away, and the whole fleet received conſiderable damage.

					Number of Men killed	and wounded.
The Briſtol, Commodore's ſhip	-	-	-	-	40	71
The Experiment	-	-	-	-	23	56
The Active	-	-	-	-	1	6
The Solebay	-	-	-	-		8

Not one man who was quartered at the beginning of the action on the Briſtol's quarter-deck eſcaped being killed or wounded. Captain Morris loſt his right arm, and received other wounds, and is ſince dead; the maſter was wounded in his right arm, but will recover the uſe of it; the Commodore received ſeveral contuſions at different times, but none of them were dangerous. Lord William Campbell, a Volunteer on board the Briſtol, who accepted of the direction of ſome guns on the lower gun deck, received a contuſion on his left ſide, but did not prove of much conſequence. Capt. Scott, of the Experiment, loſt his left arm, and was otherwiſe ſo much wounded, that it is feared he will not recover.—Lieut. Pike of the Active was killed.

When it was known that the ſquadron had many men too weak to come to quarters, almoſt all the ſeamen belonging to the tranſports offered their ſervice with a truly Britiſh ſpirit, upwards of fifty were accepted to ſupply the place of the ſick. The maſters of many of the tranſports attended with their boats during the attack, particularly Mr. Chambers, the maſter of the Mercury.

LONDON: Printed and Sold by WILLIAM FADEN, Succeſſor to the late Mr. THOMAS JEFFERYS, Geographer to the KING, the Corner of *St. Martin's-Lane, Charing-Croſs.*

Heroic Colonel Moultrie's Surprise for the Royal Navy

MAP 8. ¶ William Faden's plan, the earliest to appear, differs significantly from the Sayer and Bennett sea chart of the harbor shown in the previous plate. This is particularly evident in the area between Sullivan's Island, which made up the bulk of the defense of Charleston, and Long Island where Clinton had landed with his troops. ¶ The fort on the southwestern end of Sullivan's Island was still incomplete when Parker's fleet began its bombardment. Charlestonian William Moultrie, later to be a Continental major general and two-term governor of South Carolina, supervised the fort's construction. He had great confidence in its ability to withstand assault from the sea, although it was crudely built of palmetto logs. (As yet, the fort was totally unprotected on the land side.) Those logs, which appeared so vincible to the British, took everything that a heavy bombardment from ten ships could deliver. The cannonade kept up by the defenders took a tremendous toll of men and ships of the Royal Navy, as Commodore Parker's letter of explanation, printed with the plan, reveals. After being driven off, Parker's fleet eventually picked up Clinton's army and limped back to New York. ¶ Since Charleston in 1776 was a conspicuous British failure, it is surprising that several editions of this plan and text were published in London. A direct copy was even engraved and issued in Philadelphia during the British occupation in 1777.

SHOWN ON PRECEDING PAGE
A Plan of the Attack of Fort Sulivan, near Charles Town in South Carolina. By a Squadron of His Majesty's Ships, on the 28th of June 1776. With the Disposition of the King's Land Forces, and the Encampments and Entrenchments of the Rebels. Engraved by Wm. Faden. London, Wm. Faden, Aug. 10, 1776. (11" x 15")

(1755–58) of the French and Indian War. Yet his problems of securing supplies, raising men, combating desertion, and dealing with a superintending legislative organ were a microcosm of many of his manifold problems in the Revolution. Coupled with this was his growing insight in coping with such strengths and weaknesses as part-time soldiers, the mixing of militia and regulars, and the deep-rooted provincialism that was intracolonial as well as intercolonial.

Fortunately for Washington, military theory—elementary at best—underwent no marked change in the interim between Virginia command and American command. Mistakes he would make, but he rarely repeated the same error. Solid and judicious rather than brilliant and innovative, he was a determined fighter, no McClellan-type who found endless excuses to avoid battle. However, he did see that his main task was to hold his army together, because for many—in the absence of traditional symbols of nationalism—the Continental army was the most visible sign of the Revolution and American union. As a man and as a soldier, he showed the capacity to grow; his vision of America became continental rather than sectional, and his army in time earned the grudging respect of many of its opponents.

Politics also combined with military experience in the selection of Washington's chief subordinates, four major generals who ranked in seniority as follows: Ward, "a fat old gentlemen" better qualified as a "church-warden," an obvious sop to Massachusetts for that colony's leaders being bypassed for the top post; Charles Lee, a tall, thin, ugly British veteran, noted for his biting tongue and unkempt appearance, but withal an able soldier of keen intelligence; Philip Schuyler, a leading patriot if not a very experienced soldier, of New York, an influential colony that urged the appointment of one of its sons to high rank; and Israel Putnam, a veteran fighter but a man of limited talent as a tactician, whose choice was a kind of payoff to Connecticut for its substantial contributions, present and future. Sons of New England also dominated the list of freshly appointed brigadier generals: Seth Pomeroy, William Heath, and John Thomas of Massachusetts; David Wooster and Joseph Spencer of Connecticut; John Sullivan of New Hampshire; and Nathanael Greene of Rhode Island. The eighth brigadier, one of the best, was Richard Montgomery of New York. The adjutant general, chosen at this time, was Horatio Gates, who, like Lee and Montgomery, was an ex-British officer; the trio gave the new army at least a small degree of sorely needed professional experience, since almost all the other officers had seen duty only in their colonial militias.

The first week of July found Washington and his new lieutenants in Cambridge, Massachusetts, where the Virginian assumed command—according to dubious tradition—under the "Washington elm." It took his initial weeks to bring order out of confusion: to exact a precise count of men, muskets, tents, and clothing; to instill discipline in the independent-minded New England husbandmen and the companies of recently arrived, high-spirited backwoods riflemen from Virginia, Maryland, and Pennsylvania; to ease rivalries in this peculiar coalition war, where jealousies were not restricted to contention between Yankees and southerners over the respective merits of muskets and rifles, but likewise extended to Connecticut's wanting no Massachusetts men in its regiments, to the Bay colony's displeasure over mixing Rhode Islanders with its own troops. All of these tasks were to be more or less repeated each year, because each year the army, in substantial measure, had to be recruited anew, owing to desertions, expiring enlistments, and other vicissitudes of the struggle. So it was that after months of careful, painstaking labor, Washington confronted the crisis of having most of his men go home in December. What was to be the annual year-end trauma was relieved, as it would be later, by the arrival of the militia. This time they were contingents from Massachusetts and New Hampshire who filled the lines as Washington slowly recruited a new Continental army for 1776, an army—including irregulars—that had grown to 14,000 when the Boston siege ended.

Meanwhile, the British within the city had their own adversities, although their positions were virtually unassailable as long as Washington lacked heavy cannon. On October 10 General Thomas Gage took ship for England, succeeded by William Howe as supreme commander. Food shortages resulted from the activities of New England privateers ("George Washington's navy"), which picked off Boston-bound transports, and even those that did arrive safely all too often carried supplies unfit for consumption because of spoilage in passage or because of the irresponsibility of contractors in England. Scurvy and severe diarrhea were commonplace, and, to compound matters, smallpox spread and fuel became scarce.

Then came more trouble. American Colonel Henry Knox sledded eastward the British cannon captured at Fort Ticonderoga, and on the night of March 4, 1776, Washington placed them atop Dorchester Heights. Now the city was quite untenable for the British army, and the small fleet of Admiral Molyneaux Shuldham was also within the range of Knox's long pieces. At first Howe proposed to hurl his redcoats up Dorchester Heights; but bad weather caused him to delay his operation. He abandoned the project and prepared to evacuate the city. Howe had earlier concluded that New York was the most strategic point from which to crack the rebellion, so his decision to evacuate Boston immediately was only a matter of stepping up his timetable. For the time being, however, he withdrew to Halifax in Nova Scotia to prepare his army and to await reinforcements.

If the first sustained campaign of the war had terminated in favor of the Americans, who expelled the main British army from the thirteen colonies, a second campaign that had begun in the summer of 1775 was approaching a different conclusion; this time the outcome favored the mother country. Canada, from the beginning, had political and military importance for the patriots. If the French inhabitants, who had been British subjects only since 1763, would join the rebellion, so much the better. (The French in Canada actually showed little interest in either side.) In any case, it was feared that Canada in British hands would be a staging area for an invasion of the thirteen colonies.

Aware of the threat, Congress appointed General Schuyler head of the newly established Northern Department, subsequently defined as embracing "Albany, Ticonderoga, Fort Stanwix, and their dependencies." His orders were to invade Canada before Britain had time to station a powerful army there. Although General Guy Carleton, governor of Quebec, had fewer than 1,000 regulars to defend his position, Schuyler faced substantial problems (underestimated by many Americans) in his campaign, especially in collecting the huge quantities of stores and in raising the troops necessary to hold such a vast area. It is not easy at this point to tell how much of the criticism heaped upon Schuyler for his slowness to launch the attack is justified. He does not seem to have been a forceful field officer, and he was plagued at this time with ill health. Ultimately, command of the army that departed from Fort Ticonderoga in late August and headed

Long-Disputed Crucial Waterway

MAP 9. ¶ This is the best known Revolutionary-period map of that ancient arena of conflict, Lake Champlain and Lake George. The key link in the natural highway between the St. Lawrence and Hudson rivers, Lake Champlain was the gateway from the north into the heart of New York. It also served as the entrance from Canada to New England's western frontier, the Connecticut Valley. ¶ It was in 1609 that the French explorer and mapmaker Samuel de Champlain first visited the lake later named for him. Long before, this had been a contested no-man's-land between the Iroquois Indians of New York and the Algonquin and Huron Indians of Canada. The prehistoric antipathy of the Hurons and Iroquois was exploited by the French and English during the colonial period. The French allied with the Canadian Indians and the British with the Iroquois. There were battles in this theater throughout the seventeenth and eighteenth centuries, terminating in 1759, when the British under General Amherst finally took both Fort Ticonderoga and Crown Point. ¶ In 1775 Ethan Allen captured Ticonderoga and opened the way for an American invasion of Canada. After General Carleton held Quebec, the Americans retreated to Ticonderoga in 1776. Carleton followed, but Benedict Arnold bought enough time at Valcour Island to hold off the British that year. ¶ The major expedition of Burgoyne from Canada in 1777 followed the same route. When the British and Hessians surrounded old Fort Ticonderoga, St. Clair withdrew the Continental garrison, setting the stage for the first Battle of Saratoga. ¶ This map was first published in August of 1776. The revised map shown here was issued later, perhaps in November. It contains notes and references to the Battle of Valcour Island on October 11 of the same year.

SHOWN ON FOLLOWING PAGE
A Survey of Lake Champlain, including Lake George, Crown Point and St. John....By Wm. Brassier. London, Robt. Sayer & Jno. Bennett, Aug. 5, 1776 (i.e., after Nov. 1776). (26½" x 19¾")

In: The American Military Pocket Atlas. *London, Sayer & Bennett, 1776*

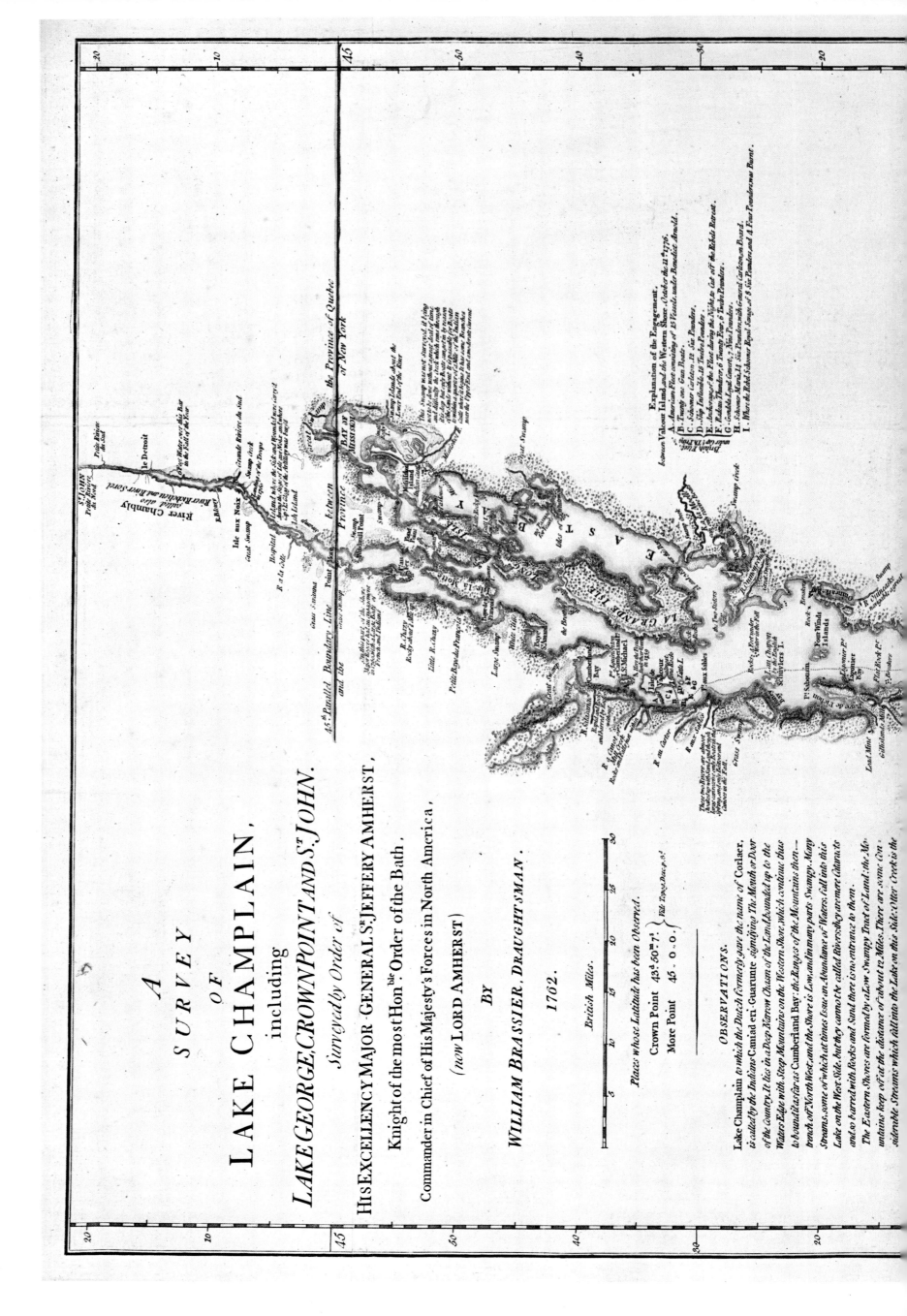

A
SURVEY
OF
LAKE CHAMPLAIN,
including
LAKE GEORGE, CROWN POINT AND S.ᵗ JOHN.
Surveyed by Order of
His Excellency Major-General S.ᵗ JEFFERY AMHERST,
Knight of the most Hon.ᵇˡᵉ Order of the Bath.
Commander in Chief of His Majesty's Forces in North America,
(now LORD AMHERST)
By
WILLIAM BRASSIER, DRAUGHT·SMAN.
1762.

British Miles.

Places whose Latitude has been Observed.

Crown Point 43.ᵈ 50.ᵐ 7.ˢ } Vid. Topog. Desc. p. 54.
More Point   45 · 0 · 0 ·

OBSERVATIONS.

Lake Champlain, to which the Dutch formerly gave the name of Corlaer, is called by the Indians Caniad-eri-Guarunte, signifying The Mouth or Door of the Country. It lies in a Deep Narrow Chasm of the Land, bounded up to the Waters Edge with Steep Mountains on the Western Shore, which continue thus to bound it as far as Cumberland Bay: the Ranges of the Mountains then trench off North West, and the Shore is Low, and in many parts Swampy. Many Streams, some of which at times Issue an Abundance of Waters, fall into this Lake on the West Side, but they cannot be called Rivers, they are mere Drains, as also barred with Rocks and Sand there is no entrance to them.

The Eastern Shores are formed by a Low Swampy Tract of Land: the Mountains keep off at the distance of about 12 Miles. There are some Considerable Streams which fall into the Lake on this Side: Otter Creek is the

Explanation of the Engagement,
between Valcour Island and the Western Shore, October the 11ᵗʰ 1776.

A. American Fleet consisting of 15 Vessels under Benedict Arnold.
B. Twenty one Gun Boats.
C. Schooner Carleton, 12 Six Pounders.
D. Ship Inflexible, 18 Twelve Pounders.
E. Anchorage of the Fleet during the Night to cut off the Rebels Retreat.
F. Rebels Thunderer, 6 Twenty Four, 6 Twelve Pounders.
G. Gondola Loyal Convert, 7 Nine Pounders.
H. Schooner Maria, 14 Six Pounders, with General Carleton on Board.
I. Where the Rebel Schooner Royal Savage of 8 Six Pounders and 4 Four Pounders Burnt.

62

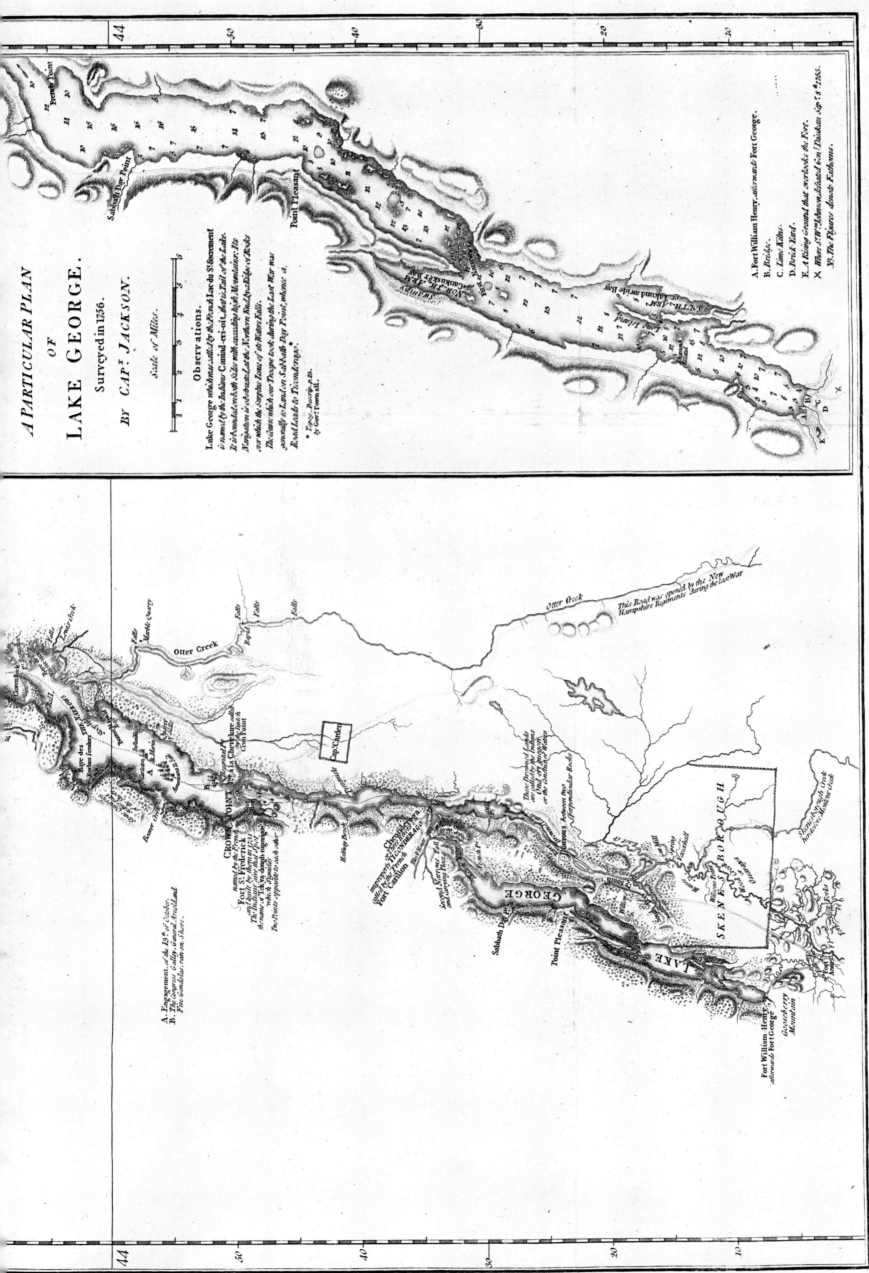

A PARTICULAR PLAN
OF
LAKE GEORGE.

Surveyed in 1756.

BY CAPT JACKSON.

Scale of Miles.

Observations.

Lake George which intersects the French Lac du St. Sacrement is named by the Indians Canid-eri-oit, that is Tail of the Lake. It is bounded on both Sides with ascending high Mountains. Its Navigation is obstructed at the Northern End by a Ridge of Rocks over which the Surplus Issue of its Waters falls.

The place which our Troops took during the Last War was generally at Landon Sabbath Day Point, whence it Road Leads to Ticonderoga.

*Topog. Descrip. p.25. by Gov.' Pownall.

A. Fort William Henry, afterwards Fort George.
B. Bridge.
C. Lime Kilns.
D. Brick Yard.
E. A Rising Ground that overlooks the Fort.
X. Where S.' W.' Johnson defeated Bar.' Dieskau, Sep.' 8.' 1755.
W. The Figures denote Fathoms.

A. Engagement of the 13.' of October.
B. The deserted Valley, General Amherst and Five Gondolas seen on Shore.

London, Printed for R.' Sayer & Iº. Bennett, Map & Iº. Chart sellers Nº 53 Fleet Street, as the Act directs, Aug.' 15.' 1776.

northward toward Montreal fell to Richard Montgomery, a fine young officer, while Schuyler remained behind to nurse himself back to good health and send forward supplies. At Fort St. John's on the Sorel River, Carleton's subordinate, Major Charles Preston, delayed Montgomery's advance for fifty-five days before the American general's siege operations reduced that post. Eager to make up for lost time and fearing a Canadian winter, Montgomery pressed forward and on November 13 occupied Montreal as Carleton fled eastward to Quebec City.

Washington, meanwhile, had acted independently of Congress in dispatching an expedition of 1,100 men from his own camp to invade Canada by way of the Maine wilderness. Commanded by Colonel Benedict Arnold, who was ably assisted by Captain Daniel Morgan, a powerfully built Virginia backwoodsman, the column had traversed the torturous 350-mile trail of snow-covered swamps, roaring streams, and exhausting portages in six weeks, finally reaching the St. Lawrence River at a point opposite the city of Quebec on November 8. Five days later Arnold crossed the river, and on December 3 he and Montgomery united upstream in preparation for an assault on the walled city that sits high atop a rocky promontory. It became a case of the feeble attacking the feeble—Montgomery and Arnold, their armies having unraveled at the seams through deaths, sickness, desertions, and expiring enlistments, were reduced to 950 men; Carleton, with an odd assortment of English civilians, French Canadian militia, sailors, Loyalists, and a sprinkling of redcoats, had a total of 1,800 men to defend the city. (*See Map 6*)

Hoping to push into the Lower Town, which ran along the river's edge, and then ascend into the Upper Town, the Americans attacked

Thomas Jefferson, a great statesman and diplomat but not a soldier, authored the Declaration of Independence. General Thomas E. Gage commanded the British troops in America until October 1775 when General William Howe took over.

under cover of a blinding snowstorm on December 30. Except for ill luck they might have succeeded; Montgomery was killed at the outset, and shortly afterward Arnold was wounded and carried from the field. Their men were driven off, leaving half their number killed or captured. Despite Congress's hastening additional units northward, the Canadian invasion collapsed. That frozen region was too distant from American bases, too expansive to be held in view of logistical and manpower problems that existed. The meager American forces still managed to maintain a siege of the city throughout the winter, but when royal troops arrived from England in the spring of 1776, the Americans retreated through Montreal and down to Lake Champlain. By July, they were once again at Ticonderoga, and Canada was forever lost to them.

At the same time, however, the thirteen colonies were to be forever lost to England. Neither Parliament nor king had shown any positive signs of desiring a reconciliation. The closest step was Lord North's Conciliatory Resolution (February 1775), which proposed to omit parliamentary taxation of any colonies that would agree to taxing themselves "their proportion to the common defence." How much that might be was never indicated, and the resolution was mute on other issues contained in the Coercive Acts, just as it ignored the declarations and concerns of the Continental Congress. Parliament further called into question its good faith in passing the Prohibitory Act (November 1775), authorizing a complete naval blockade of the colonies, the seizure of all American goods on the high seas, and the forcible enlistment of seamen on provincial vessels in the Royal Navy. That same fall Britain sowed a harvest of hatred in America by employing foreign mercenaries—the so-called Hessians in American history books—from *six* German principalities to fight against her American cousins: Hesse-Cassel, Brunswick, Hesse-Hanau, Anspach-Bayreuth, Waldeck, and Anhalt-Zerbst. These principalities eventually furnished over 30,000 men to the British army in return for sterling, a traffic in human flesh that outraged such Enlightenment intellectuals in fragmented Germany as Goethe, Schiller, and Schubart. There were other indications, too, that Britain was increasing the tempo of the struggle, particularly the burning of Falmouth in Maine by a naval party in late 1775, the efforts of Governor Dunmore of Virginia to enlist slaves and

Indians, and the campaign of Governor Martin of North Carolina to raise the Loyalists of that colony in conjunction with a British fleet that was to raid the southern coastline.

Even so, sentiment in Congress for independence crystallized slowly. There was no hint of that desire in the legislators' "Declaration of the Causes and Necessities of Taking Up Arms" (July 1775), which in fact expressly renounced "ambitious designs of separating from Great Britain, and establishing independent states." In response to the legislators' "Olive

In the spring of 1776, the Americans
lifted their siege of Quebec.
The previous spring, Ethan Allen had taken
Fort Ticonderoga "in the name of the great
Jehovah and the Continental Congress."
Photo courtesy Chicago Historical Society.
A month later, June 1775,
patriots dug in to fight on Breed's Hill.

Branch Petition'' (July 1775), asking the king to intercede in their behalf, the ministry unofficially passed back the word that there would be no answer, that neither the king nor the ministry would ever treat with the ''illegal'' Continental Congress. More meaningful an answer was a royal proclamation (August 1775) declaring America in a state of ''open and avowed rebellion.'' In such an atmosphere, the Americans' fear of a London conspiracy to rob them of their liberties (discussed in the previous chapter) became all the more real; and the Americans gradually concluded that there was simply no relief to be had anywhere in England.

Independence would surely have come before long without Thomas Paine's widely read and brilliantly devastating pamphlet ''Common Sense,'' which appeared anonymously in January 1776; but Paine's persuasive discourse on the evils of monarchy in general and George III's rule in particular helped to bring the subject of a final severing of the imperial ties out into the open. Men in the army and in Congress agreed with Paine that foreign military assistance was imperative, but that Americans could scarcely attract cash and weapons from England's inveterate enemies, France and Spain, as long as the war was fought within the British family; only the prospect of irreparably weakening England by the permanent loss of her colonies would induce the Bourbon princes of Europe to stick their necks out. The spring of 1776 saw Congress authorize privateering against British vessels, vote to disarm the Loyalists, place an embargo on exports to Britain and the West Indies, and declare American trade open to all the world except Britain.

Just as the Continental Congress was behaving more and more like an independent national government, so, too, were the colonies increasingly acting like independent states. The South Carolina Provincial Congress drafted a republican constitution, and the Rhode Island Provincial Congress withdrew an act making allegiance to the king compulsory. North Carolina authorized and Virginia required their delegates in Congress to vote for independence. But when Richard Henry Lee of Virginia introduced on June 7, 1776, a resolution for independence, an American confederation, and ''measures for forming foreign Alliances,'' the reluctant rebels in the middle colonies urged delay so that public opinion in their region might be won over to the idea. The majority gave them nearly a month, and then on July 2, Congress agreed to Lee's motion by a vote of 12–0, the divided New York delegation abstaining.

Thomas Jefferson, thirty-three years old, a moderately shy, redheaded Virginian, was assigned the principal role—with secondary support from Franklin and John Adams—in drafting a document to explain and justify the final severing of the imperial connection. Couched in general phrases as well as in specific grievances against the king and his servants, the Declaration of Independence was designed to appeal to men everywhere, to lift the dozen-year dispute out of an imperial context and to place it within the philosophical and intellectual framework of the Enlightenment. Certainly, as Jefferson readily conceded in after years, his document said nothing new, and it owed much to John Locke. But never had such ideas been said so well: that ''all men are created equal,'' that the origin of government rests in the consent of the governed, that government must protect the natural rights of the people, that government should be altered or abolished if it fails to fulfill these obligations. If Locke had immortalized this body of thought for eighteenth century Europe and America, Jefferson was to immortalize it for the world.

MAP 10. ¶ Before his shocking treason, Benedict Arnold distinguished himself as a forceful and effective military leader at Ticonderoga, on the march to Quebec, in the Mohawk Valley, and at Saratoga. His finest hour had come, however, as an ad hoc admiral on Lake Champlain in the first naval battle of the Revolutionary War. ¶ After the failure of the American invasion of Canada, followed by the retreat from Quebec, General Carleton counterattacked, intending to strike through Lake Champlain to Albany and join forces with General Howe on the Hudson. Carleton organized his expedition at St. Johns, where he assembled a strong fleet. Reinforcements brought the British strength to 16,000 men. ¶ Hoping to stop Carleton on Lake Champlain, Arnold devised an audacious plan of building ships from standing timber. He actually had ten craft afloat before Carleton arrived with his armada. The fierce delaying action fought by Arnold and his men stopped the British. Because of the approaching winter, Carleton was forced to abandon his plan and return to Canada. It is generally conceded that had the British reached Albany that winter the American Revolution could have collapsed altogether. ¶ This battle plan accurately depicts the movements of the two squadrons. The opponents may be seen in the narrow channel between Valcour Island and the New York shore, where Arnold decided to fight. The map also shows the line that the American survivors followed silently under cover of fog during the night, after the initial blistering action. ¶ Interestingly, there was an earlier issue of this map that carried the name of Sir Guy Carleton in the title where Captain Pringle's name appears in the issue illustrated here. It is possible the first indications were that Valcour Island was an important British victory. The substitution of Pringle's name would seem to suggest that Carleton or a supporter reconsidered and arranged the change.

SHOWN ON OPPOSITE PAGE
The Attack and Defeat of the American Fleet under Benedict Arnold, by the King's Fleet Commanded by Captn. Thos. Pringle, upon Lake Champlain. The 11th of October, 1776. London, Wm. Faden, Dec. 3, 1776. (10¼" x 16½")

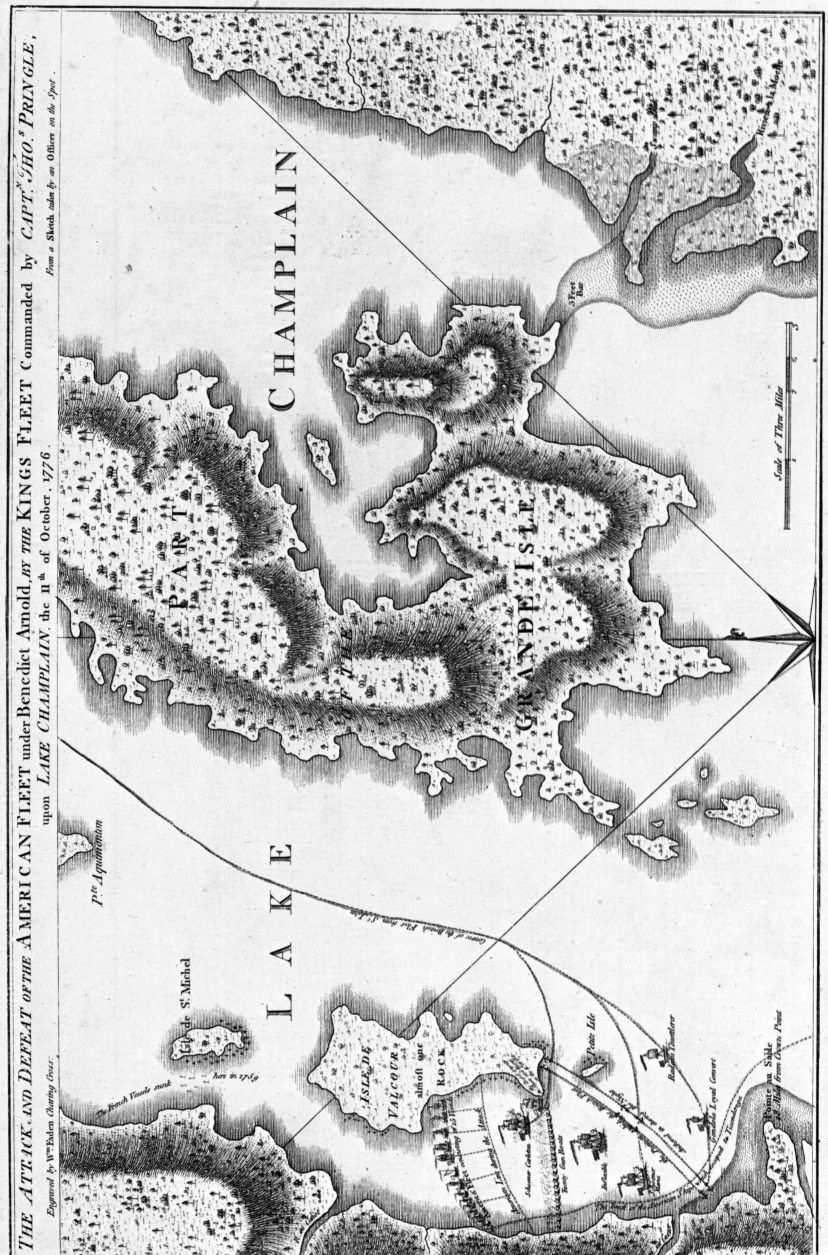

THE ATTACK AND DEFEAT OF THE AMERICAN FLEET under Benedict Arnold, BY THE KINGS FLEET Commanded by CAPT.N THO.S PRINGLE,
upon LAKE CHAMPLAIN, the 11th of October, 1776.

Engraved by Wm. Faden Charing Cross.

From a Sketch taken by an Officer on the Spot.

CHAMPLAIN

PART

GRANDE ISLE

LAKE

3 Feet Bar

P.te Aquamentam

Isle de St. Michel

The French Vessels sunk here in 1759

Isle de VALCOUR

almost one ROCK

Petite Isle

Scale of Three Miles

London, Publish'd (according to Act of Parliament) Dec.r 3.d 1776 by Wm.Faden (Successor to the late M.r Jefferys) Geographer to the King) Charing Cross.

New Market, South Second Street,
Philadelphia was only two blocks
from the wharf area on the
Delaware River. The city was the
first to be planned in America
with parallel consecutively
numbered streets; cross streets
were named for trees. It is truly
an American city in layout.

The Combatants

Unable to find sympathetic ears in Parliament, the Americans appealed to King George III himself, bringing to him a vision of colonial membership in a commonwealth. The king refused to interfere.

At the conclusion of the War of Independence Washington remarked that the patriots' victory carried all the signs of fiction. He predicted that succeeding generations of historians would encounter great difficulty in explaining the outcome. Until well into the twentieth century, however, chroniclers of the war tended to come up with simplistic and largely erroneous explanations. For the most part, British writers maintained that the mother country blew opportunity after opportunity to crush the rebellion. Only the incompetence of the North ministry and the stupidity of the king's generals and admirals could account for the rebels achieving their independence. Such nineteenth century American patrician scholars as George Bancroft saw the hand of God operating at crucial moments on the side of the Continental army. Or they depicted Washington as a military genius "bolder than Hannibal, wiser than Caesar, more prudent than Adolphus, more resourceful than Frederick, more sagacious than Napoleon."

Turgid and high flown in the manner of the last century's popular nonfiction, the war literature pictured bold and fearless patriots rushing from their fields and shops and hurling back the invading hordes sent by George III. These trends in historical writing are understandable, for America, a new nation, needed its pantheon of warriors who had performed glorious deeds. Growing American nationalism combined with the emerging romantic movement in America made the Revolution an epic and dramatic event.

The twentieth century saw new currents of historical orientation, a backlash to seeing the Revolution through patriotic glasses, which now classified the struggle for independence as something decidedly less than glorious. Sophisticated, college-educated Americans steeped in economic determinism, Sigmund Freud, and Henry Mencken did not object to learning that the American Revolution would have collapsed without French aid, that an embarrassingly high number of Americans had in fact been Loyalists, that Washington committed serious battlefield mistakes, and that militia and short-term enlistees were useless.

Many fine new books appearing since World War II have tended to alter dramatically the bold-colored stereotypes on both sides of the historical argument over the Revolutionary War. British leaders were not as inadequate as they were once described, nor was their task a simple one. And if the Americans were not all heroes, neither were their efforts as feeble or as lucky or as dependent on French support as they were said to have been.

The British war machinery was centered in London, where the king acted as a kind of cheerleader for his ministers rather than as one who planned campaigns and directed the movement of regiments and ships. Most of all, George needed to push Lord North, a good political manager, but a dull, methodical man. No William Pitt, he was scarcely equipped to inspire the country or galvanize the wheels of government as the Great Commoner had done in the Seven Years' War. Therefore, military preparations then became increasingly a collective enterprise of the cabinet. After plans were concluded, it was the responsibility of the secretary of state for the American Department to follow through—to issue "timely orders to the Treasury, Admiralty, Ordnance and Commander-in-Chief of the Army on these heads, so that every necessary preparation can be made." Since divided authorities and overlapping jurisdictions characterized government in Hanoverian England, it was no easy matter to assemble the mountains of supplies, equipment, and ordnance required to conduct a war across the Atlantic. If at any time a well-provisioned force was readied on schedule with transports and naval escort, it reflected the energizing influence of the American secretary.

Since that official came closest to being the director of the American war, George III wished to fill that post in 1775 with a man of energy and military background combined with a desire to deal sternly with the revolting provinces. His appointee, sixty years of age, Lord George Germain, was such a man. Yet Germain had certain serious liabilities—a biting tongue, a quick temper, and an aloofness that made it hard for subordinates and even cabinet equals to work with him. He no more than North could play a unifying and symbolic role in the fashion of Pitt.

The army, from which Germain had once been dismissed for cowardice in battle (probably unfairly), stood at approximately 50,000 men in 1775, and although it grew considerably thereafter, it was never possible to send all of it to North America, nor could all the regiments in the New World be concentrated against the rabble in arms, for there were garrisons in the Floridas and the West Indies that had to be maintained against the chance of attacks by the French and Spanish.

The redcoat in the ranks was a good soldier. This is not to say that he was influenced by ideological considerations. He lived in a day when common soldiers in Europe have been described as "prepolitical." He was taught to fight for his king and in response to commands. Sternly disciplined and trained, he may have responded something like a robot, but he took pride in his unit. His pay was poor, and his promotion from the rank and file would have been almost unheard of. His background was likely that of a criminal who accepted military service as an alternative to prison, or that of a ne'er-do-well who chose the soldier's hard life over the misery of near starvation, or that of a country boy—in William Hogarth's painting—beguiled by the gin of a recruiting officer into enlisting for a period of time at the king's pleasure. Not every regiment, of course, projected such a dismal profile. Sylvia Frey has recently qualified our picture, at least for a number of units that included Scottish Highlanders, Irish volunteers, and foot guards. They were fairly responsible little people in economic trouble, a goodly portion of them ex-weavers displaced from their jobs by a decline in the textile industry. Yet confronted by the demands of the American war, Parliament lowered whatever standards that existed in recruitment by authorizing the impressment of all men not lawfully employed ("able bodied loose idle and disorderly persons"), the enlistment of Roman Catholics, and the relaxing of physical standards to take in sixteen-year-old boys and fifty-year-old men, provided they were at least five feet three inches tall.

The infantry regiment was the backbone of the land service, which had little cavalry and which considered artillery mainly as a supporting arm of its foot soldiers. Regiments contained about 475 men, divided into ten companies, including one each of grenadiers and light infantry, the cream of the unit. The soldier advanced into battle with his "brown Bess," a smoothbore flintlock musket from which a bayonet protruded fourteen inches. To load his weapon, the redcoat extracted a cartridge from a small box attached to his belt or connected to his shoulder strap, broke open the paper cylinder, and poured a thimbleful of the powder into the firing pan above the trigger. The remainder of the cartridge—powder, paper, and a lead ball—he inserted in the barrel and rammed down with a long, thin

Recruits for the British army were taken largely from the ranks of the unemployed. In America, recruits were enticed with the promise of "good and handsome clothing" and a twelve-dollar bounty for signing up.

rod. As was the case at Bunker Hill, soldiers usually moved in rows two or three deep, drums beating and fifes shrilling, firing in unison at a fixed level rather than taking individual aim. The standard rule (which Howe had violated on that occasion) was to come as close to the enemy as possible before each line unleashed its volley, to be followed by a bayonet charge into the presumably disorganized ranks of the opponents. And British troops were unexcelled in Europe in the combined volley-bayonet tactics. Many who had fought in America or Germany in the French and Indian War were still in the army, graying veterans in their forties and occasionally older. In fact, some regiments contained a majority of men over thirty, with ten or more years in the service.

It was this bayonet charge, always preceded by a loud "hurrah," that not infrequently terrorized unsteady American recruits more than anything else, and it was perhaps the chief reason for the success of British arms on American battlefields in the Revolution. There were times when the redcoat had no alternative to his bayonet, for the flintlock was often unreliable. When the soldier fired the brown Bess into the wind, the flame from the touchhole (after flint struck steel igniting the powder) could sear his face. If the weapon was not carefully protected in rainy weather, the wetness prevented the powder in the pan from igniting.

If the musket-bearing redcoats were mainly from the lower strata of society, the officers who commanded them came from the elite. Hardly professionals in the modern sense, they had no Sandhurst, St. Cyr, or West Point to prepare them for their military roles. Most of them progressed through the officer corps because of wealth and family rather than performance. Commissions were bought and sold, and the prices were staggering; the lowest commission in the regular service, ensign in a foot regiment, cost £400. A lieutenant colonel paid £3,500 in the infantry, £5,200 in the cavalry, and £6,700 in the foot guards. Cornwallis, with all the right credentials, was a lieutenant colonel at twenty-three, a lieutenant general at thirty-eight. Not unexpectedly, the system threw up officers like George Osborne in Thackeray's *Vanity Fair*, like George Wickham in Jane Austen's *Pride and Prejudice*. But there were other young aristocrats and gentlemen who took their duties seriously, who were brave and competent. Lord Rawdon, Charles Stuart, Frederick Mackenzie, and various others gave good accounts of themselves in the War of Independence.

The head of the army was the king, who carried the military title of captain general. In the eighteenth century the office of commander in chief was seldom filled, although in 1778 (after France entered the war) that post went to Lord Amherst. All the Hanoverians took their military duties seriously, displaying a special pride in the army, which had known George II affectionately as the "Little Captain." General officers in particular had to be acceptable to the monarch in a century when loyalty to the king was a necessary prerequisite for military command, when the army was a force on which the social order might depend in the absence of a national police system. Thus Gage, Howe, Burgoyne, Cornwallis, and Clinton were from the top of the social structure. They were, except for Gage, prima donnas. Independent of mind, they were jealous and suspicious of each other, a partial reflection of their political and social rivalries back home, for the upper echelons themselves were splintered by factionalism. During the war twenty-three or more generals sat in the House of Commons, joined in the various coalitions of family and special interest that formed majorities in the House of Commons or, in other cases, constituted the

This British officer of the 26th Regiment probably was given his commission because of wealth and social position, and received little or no formal military training.

so-called opposition. Since Howe, Burgoyne, Clinton, and Cornwallis were all members of that body, the ministry was often fearful of censuring or relieving them, for to do so might drive them into the arms of Pitt (now Lord Chatham), Lord Rockingham, and other leaders of the "outs."

By the standards of the day, Britain's American commanders were not outstanding; they were competent at best. They were better trained to fight in Flanders or Germany than in America, to employ orthodox linear formations rather than to improvise in a war that called for rapid movements, innovative tactics, winter campaigning, and—most importantly—contending with a people in arms, a massive rebellion unknown in the memory of Europeans.

The British navy, relatively speaking, had always been considered stronger than the army, had been thought of as the island kingdom's first line of defense. The navy, however, was not in 1775 up to its traditional standard of being the numerical equal of its two Bourbon rivals, and the quality of a substantial portion of the fleet had for the first time fallen below that of its "antient foes." Historians have been quick to point an accusing finger at the Earl of Sandwich, first lord of the admiralty, who today is best remembered for the form of food named for him, or, perversely, for his celebrated affair with the actress Martha Ray, who bore his bastards. Present-day investigators maintain that Sandwich has been maligned, that he endeavored after 1770 to revive the navy and failed because of North's tight hold on the purse strings and because of a shortage of seasoned British oak. During the Revolution, the navy would feel the loss of thousands of American seamen who customarily manned its vessels in time of war, the loss of the colonial merchant marine (in 1775 one-third of all the tonnage of British register), and the loss of colonial naval stores and the New England white pine that were turned into lower masts of ships of the line.

The lot of the common seaman in the navy was worse than the life of the enlisted man in the army. Since bounties provided only a small fraction of the necessary naval enlistments, the service continued to resort to the age-old method of impressments. Beaten within an inch of his life, a country lad—or a sailor taken from an incoming merchantman—might come to after his unsuccessful effort to escape "the press," to find a life as bad as he had imagined. Subjected to the lash for minor infractions, he might see typhus and typhoid rampant on shipboard; he might many times see and feel the effects of scurvy, the most malignant of all sea diseases. His ship's biscuit might contain weevils, his meat maggots. The later mutiny on the *Bounty* arose from intolerable conditions not altogether unlike those a Jack-tar experienced in the American war.

For all its deficiencies, Britain's naval arm was formidable. Its greatest strength lay in its officers, who carried on the traditions of such sea giants as Vernon, Anson, and Hawke. In the Revolution, Lord Richard Howe, Rodney, Hood, Parker, Jervis, and Kempenfelt were the equal, some the superior, of Howe, Burgoyne, and company, although Graves, Arbuthnot, and Byron were lesser men. Though family counted for much, it never dominated appointment and advancement in the navy to the extent it did in the army. Captain James Cook was the son of a laborer. Aspiring naval officers, unlike their counterparts in the army, did not receive a commission before they studied seamanship and navigation, either at the Royal Naval Academy or as captains' servants. Vigorous competition produced a sense of responsibility and a genuine knowledge of maritime affairs.

In November 1775, Parliament passed the Prohibitory Act, which authorized a naval blockade of American ports and the forcible enlistment of American seamen into the Royal Navy. This act was to many colonists the final proof that Parliament wanted no reconciliation with the colonies.

One artist's version of the July 4,
1776, meeting of the
Continental Congress has
the delegates neatly lined up.
This same artist also depicted the
welcome of British troops in Boston.

One artist's version of the July 4,
1776, meeting of the
Continental Congress has
the delegates neatly lined up.
This same artist also depicted the
welcome of British troops in Boston.

The Americans could obviously not contest the sea lanes with this powerful navy, whose fast frigates and formidable ships of the line could blockade their coasts, raid their cities, and interrupt their commerce in weapons and military paraphernalia. Yet for the navy, as well as for its companion service, the Revolution was a different kind of war. The American coastline was too long to be blockaded at all points. There were too many rivers, bays, and inlets where stores could be landed. Fleets found it hard to stay afloat, whether in blockading or patrolling strategic sea routes, for more than six consecutive weeks without real suffering. Thus reasons of health combined with the absence of adequate facilities for repairs in the New World placed severe strains on the effectiveness of a navy that would find itself with even more demanding responsibilities after France entered the war in 1778.

If British weaknesses were more subtle, less apparent at the outset in view of certain obvious strengths, the Americans appeared to be afflicted with overwhelming disadvantages, which created in London an air of assurance that the colonial uprising would be of short duration. Britain had one chief magistrate, one cabinet, one Parliament, and—despite its creaky and overlapping machinery—a long-established central government that did not share authority with regional political entities, to say nothing of a well-stocked treasury. In contrast, America had fourteen congresses or legislatures and thirteen separate executives. In America, there was no national chief executive; and no separate or independent departments of government, such as war, treasury, and foreign affairs, existed until near the end of the conflict. In fact, the Continental Congress was an extralegal body, existing at the pleasure of the states prior to the ratification of the Articles of Confederation in 1781.

Congress, beset with myriad responsibilities, began its legislative day with prayers led by one of its chaplains, followed by a reading of the previous day's minutes from the journal, and then by the reading of letters from Washington, other officers, American diplomats in Europe, state governments, and private citizens. Many of these epistles were referred to appropriate committees. Finally came committee reports, which might be adopted, amended, recommitted, or rejected. At times, the legislators read newspapers, wandered about the white-paneled council chamber that served as their main meeting room, interrupted speakers on the floor, and addressed the chair without recognition. These faults—one can still see them in visiting our state legislatures today—are relatively minor, as are charges that Congress was too slow to act and that it catered to the whims and special interests of the states. When we consider its lack of a legal base and its dearth of military resources, then it may be that the men in Philadelphia performed as much or even more than might rightly have been expected of them. It should not be forgotten that the Continental Congress adopted an army, appointed Washington to the supreme command, declared independence, concluded an alliance with France, wrote the Articles of Confederation, organized a postal service, issued currency, and brought the war to a successful termination.

Congress, as the civil government, closely supervised the Continental army, although giving Washington substantial latitude in the conduct of operations. Solely in control of policy, it only occasionally tried its hand at strategy, when it ordered Schuyler's invasion of Canada in 1775 and when it instructed Washington to defend New York City the following year. A well-defined command system in the American army had to await the

Civil War. Although Congress created from time to time military departments with responsibilities for specific geographic areas—the northern, eastern (or New England), middle, southern, and western—each commander usually reported directly to Congress rather than to Washington, whose own field army operated in the middle department. Washington, to

Thomas John of Maryland nominated George Washington for the post of commander in chief of the new army on June 15, 1775, with John Adams seconding. Washington took formal command of his 14,500 troops at Cambridge on July 3. The button is from the uniform worn by Washington when he was a colonel in a Virginia regiment.

be sure, kept in touch with commanders elsewhere as best he could, and Congress was known to request the Virginian's advice about appointments and procedures in departments outside his own.

Since Americans were aware of the historic evil of "standing armies," which could turn upon the peaceful citizens to establish despotisms, Congress sought to anchor safeguards into its own military system. One, of course, was the choice of a commander in chief dedicated to civil control. A second was Congress's adoption of a military code, sixty-nine articles of war designed to keep its citizen-soldiers committed to virtue and the ideals of the Revolution and to keep them from becoming easy-prey robots for would-be caesars. Highly moralistic in tone, the articles were considerably less severe in their prescribed punishments for wrongdoing than similar codes in foreign armies. Congress, John Adams assured a friend, would never "new model your Army", that is, subject America to military rule as Oliver Cromwell's New Model army had done after its triumph over Charles I of England. Even so, the British influence was felt in the Continental army, especially in its battalion, division, and artillery organization.

Probably the biggest single advantage of the Continental army was that it had a vast reservoir of manpower to draw upon. In this unique war one nation could ask service of its entire male population, even productive citizens. But in Europe the productive citizen was normally spared a military obligation, since political and economic theory maintained that it was dangerous to arm people who might consequently wish to use force to reform society, and who, besides, should stay at their jobs in order not to disturb commerce and industry. Too much has been made of the fact that

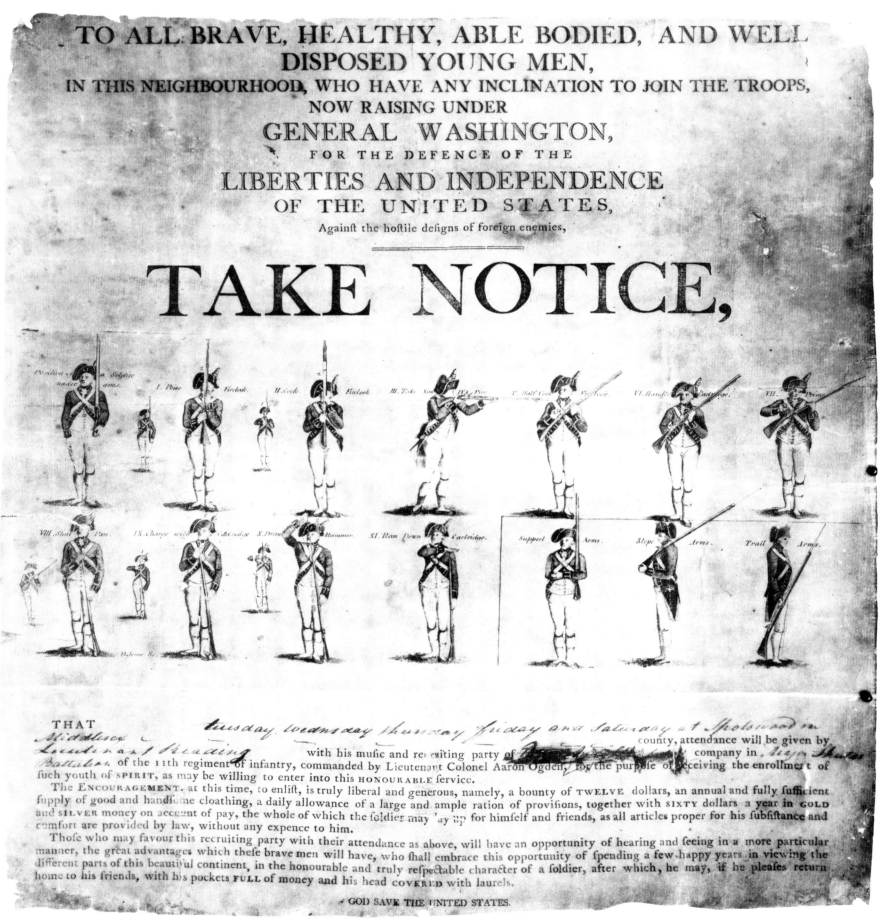

TO ALL BRAVE, HEALTHY, ABLE BODIED, AND WELL
DISPOSED YOUNG MEN,

IN THIS NEIGHBOURHOOD, WHO HAVE ANY INCLINATION TO JOIN THE TROOPS,
NOW RAISING UNDER
GENERAL WASHINGTON,
FOR THE DEFENCE OF THE
LIBERTIES AND INDEPENDENCE
OF THE UNITED STATES,
Against the hoftile defigns of foreign enemies,

TAKE NOTICE,

THAT tuesday, wednsday, thursday, friday and Saturday at Spotswood in Middlesex county, attendance will be given by Lieutenant Reading with his mufic and recruiting party of company in ... Battalion of the 11th regiment of infantry, commanded by Lieutenant Colonel Aaron Ogden, for the purpose of receiving the enrollment of such youth of SPIRIT, as may be willing to enter into this HONOURABLE service.

The ENCOURAGEMENT, at this time, to enlift, is truly liberal and generous, namely, a bounty of TWELVE dollars, an annual and fully fufficient fupply of good and handfome cloathing, a daily allowance of a large and ample ration of provifions, together with SIXTY dollars a year in GOLD and SILVER money on account of pay, the whole of which the foldier may lay up for himfelf and friends, as all articles proper for his fubfiftance and comfort are provided by law, without any expence to him.

Thofe who may favour this recruiting party with their attendance as above, will have an opportunity of hearing and feeing in a more particular manner, the great advantages which thefe brave men will have, who fhall embrace this opportunity of fpending a few happy years in viewing the different parts of this beautiful continent, in the honourable and truly refpectable character of a foldier, after which, he may, if he pleafes return home to his friends, with his pockets FULL of money and his head COVERED with laurels.

GOD SAVE THE UNITED STATES.

This recruiting poster proclaimed that Lieutenant Reading would be at Spotswood with his music and his party, to receive the enrollment "of such youth of spirit" as would be willing to join the 11th regiment of infantry. The promised salary was sixty dollars a year plus "a daily allowance of a large and ample ration of provisions."

troops were always in short supply in the Continental army. The point is that men were always coming and going. Long enlistments, notwithstanding offers of bounties in money or land, were not numerous. The citizen often felt an obligation, but it was one to be shared with others. Why should he serve longer than a one-to-three-year term when there were countless additional farmers and tradesmen to be called? Though the ranks always thinned out as the year waned, spring saw the arrival of new enlistees and draftees, the latter being resorted to at crucial times by some states and individual communities.

It is not simple to generalize about the composition of the American army. Recruiting officers sometimes paid little attention to instructions that every soldier should be healthy, at least sixteen years old, and five feet two inches tall or better. Two Pennsylvania Continentals were David Hamilton Morris, age eleven, and Jeremiah Levering, age twelve. A study of Massachusetts troops—admittedly a small sample—may be suggestive. The shortest man was four feet seven inches tall. The youngest was fourteen, the oldest fifty-eight, approximately two-thirds of the total under twenty-six. An extant Maryland muster role, unusually detailed, likewise provides data that may be reflective of trends, particularly late in the struggle. Approximately a third of the men were in the age bracket fourteen-to-nineteen, but only about 10 percent were in their forties or older. Much of the army must have been on the youthful side, and recruiting teams at times had to scrape the bottom of the barrel to come up with their quotas. Obviously then, not every soldier owned his own land or his own shop, although this does not mean that the yeoman's son, tenant farmer, farm laborer, ironworker, cordwainer, blacksmith, cooper, carpenter, and so on were nonproductive citizens, were not capable of advancing their station in life in subsequent years. It is claimed that enlistment in the army was one of the few opportunities for advancement available to recently freed indentured servants, who usually lacked capital or land. Yet we cannot necessarily assume that bounty inducements offered much of a financial gain when balanced against rampant inflation, modest army pay, and perennial shortages of basic necessities during the winter months.

British deserters and prisoners of war were eventually recruited, contrary to Washington's warning that dangers lurked in the enrolling of men "who are bound to us by no motives of attachment," lacking the "ties of Country, kindred, and sometimes property" that influenced American citizens. Recruited, too, were white servants, whose masters were usually rewarded for their loss. Some recruits were substitutes for wealthier men who were willing to pay another instead of going to war themselves, a practice permitted by the government as late as the Civil War. Blacks in bondage likewise found their way into Continental regiments, although at the outset there was a marked reluctance throughout America to deprive a master of his slave or to permit a Negro to shoulder a musket. Beginning in 1777, the New England states, feeling the pinch for human resources, filled out their battalions with Blacks, as did in time all the states north of Virginia, a state which did permit free men of color to join the standard.

Women, those "fair daughters of liberty," were never officially placed on the muster rolls, but females did their bit to collect goods and money for the benefit of the troops. In several states women set up organizations, with a treasurer in every county, who was to send her proceeds to the wife of the state's governor, who in turn would pass them on to Martha Washington, the general's lady, for distribution at camp. Other distaff patriots lived and traveled with the army, so-called camp followers, and they defy easy description. They were a mixed bag of prostitutes, wives, sweethearts, and rootless persons. Every army of that age had its share of them, and they were not without their considerable value to the army of Washington, as they cooked, sewed, washed, performed as nurses, and in a multiplicity of ways added their feminine touch to the lives of men away from home.

All the same, the war witnessed substantial restlessness in the ranks. After all, the American was a free man, not a professional but a citizen-

The American militiaman was not a professional soldier; he served out his enlistment, then went home to tend his farm. Washington constantly reminded his men that theirs was a conflict for individual liberties and national independence.

soldier not at all reticent about speaking his piece. "To attempt to introduce discipline and subordination into a new army," declared Washington's secretary Joseph Reed, "must always be a work of great difficulty, but where the principles of democracy so universally prevail, where so great an equality and so thorough a leveling spirit predominates, either no discipline can be established, or he who attempts it must become odious and detestable, a position which no one will choose." But if the state was asking more of its citizens than was true in Europe—rather than turning to a longtime professional army composed of flotsam and jetsam thrown up by economic tides—the citizens would likely be inclined to be assertive, to complain of late pay, of soaring prices, and sinking currency. Clothing supplies were inadequate much of the time. Probably a small percentage of the army had at any one time uniforms, which, contrary to popular thinking, were officially designated to be brown—until 1779 when Congress changed the basic color of army clothing to blue, and so it remained throughout the nineteenth century. But growling stomachs were as much of a concern as partially naked bodies, both problems resulting more from the malfunctioning of the supply departments than an absence of cloth or food in the country.

Military drum carried by a Revolutionary soldier from North Carolina.

The suffering at Valley Forge, which, incidentally, was not the hardest winter of the war for the army, sprang chiefly from an absence of wagons and teamsters to carry stores to the soldiers. In fairness to army administrators in the quartermaster, commissary, and other departments, however, it should be stressed that inflation and a shortage of funds severely hampered their endeavors. Occasionally Washington did have words of praise for the much-criticized administrators, as when, for example, he complimented Commissary General Joseph Trumbull in 1776, Commissary General Jeremiah Wadsworth in 1778, and Quartermaster General

Making soldiers out of raw recruits was the problem of every officer, including General Anthony Wayne at Fort Washington. Baron von Steuben, ex-Prussian captain, drilled the undisciplined troops at Valley Forge into an army. Photo courtesy of the Chicago Historical Society.

Nathanael Greene in 1778 and again on his stepping down from his station in 1780.

Faced with a variety of complaints from the troops, Washington labored long and hard to improve conditions, to maintain order, and to persuade the men that theirs was a cause worth suffering for, no matter what the hardship. He repeatedly called to the attention of Congress the material needs of the army, and he encouraged legislative committees to make on-the-scene investigations. Desertion posed an enormous problem. A recent investigator believes that perhaps as many as 25 percent of all the Continentals departed illegally sooner or later, an astounding statistic until one is reminded that desertion rates were actually much higher in European armies of the time. In the French and Indian War desertions reduced the Austrian army by 62,000 men, the French by 70,000, the Prussian by 80,000. Desertion had been a persistent problem for the British army in America since before the Revolution, but after 1775 it increased in magnitude, particularly among the German mercenaries. Only about 58 percent of them—17,313 of 30,000—returned to their native land in 1783; thousands of others survived the struggle and remained behind to add their ore to the great American melting pot. The motives of American deserters were complex, but no more than a small fraction went over to the enemy. Some skipped out to enlist under an assumed name in another regiment and collect new bounty money. Most did not depart because of their disenchantment with the cause; spring planting, fall harvesting, and pathetic letters from families back home were all primary reasons for unauthorized departures.

When Washington dealt with desertions and occasional mutinies— the most serious in the latter category was among the Pennsylvania line in 1781—he responded with firmness combined with practicality and realism, although by our standards he appears exceedingly harsh. Brutality was a characteristic of his time. Life was cheap when in England the theft of a penknife led a boy of ten to the gallows, as did the stealing of a handkerchief for a girl of fourteen; when various infractions in the British army could bring as many as 1,000 lashes to the bare back. If Washington approved Congress's increasing the permitted number of lashes in the American army from 39 to 100 (and even personally favored jumping the maximum to 500), he himself issued many pardons and reduced other sentences. A mere handful of men sentenced to receive the death penalty had their executions carried out.

All things considered, the core of the army was devoted to the revolutionary movement. Charles Stuart, a British officer, praised the dedication of the Continentals; and Baron von Closen of the French army exclaimed, "I admire the American troops tremendously! It is incredible that soldiers composed of men of every age, even children of fifteen, of whites and blacks, almost naked, unpaid, and rather poorly fed, can march so well and withstand fire so steadfastly." Washington, in his general orders, continually reminded his troops that theirs was not one of the "usual contests of Empire and Ambition" in which "the conscience of the soldier has so little share"; it was rather a conflict for their individual liberties and the independence of their nation.

And the army did improve. If it won few pitched battles, it usually made the British know they had been in a good fight. Its errors of inexperience became fewer and fewer; it almost always exacted a heavy toll of the enemy, who could not easily obtain reinforcements. Admittedly, it had a minimum of outstanding general officers—only Washington and Greene stand out as commanders of large field armies. Horatio Gates, a good administrator, triumphed over Burgoyne's army in the North and then proceeded to lose an American army in the South. Daniel Morgan and Benedict Arnold were excellent combat officers (before Arnold exchanged coats!), though neither probably had the talents or temperament to manage a full-scale campaign. Anthony Wayne, John Sullivan, Philip Schuyler, Edward Hand, William Smallwood, Francis Nash, and Robert Howe were competent generals, although they at times were victims of bad luck and their own weaknesses. Benjamin Lincoln and Henry Knox,

A chart of the placement of ships and troops during the siege of Charleston, South Carolina, in 1780. The city fell to General Clinton and his British forces on May 12.

both of whom served as secretaries of war after Congress created a Department of War in 1781, were steady and reliable, and Knox in fact may have been quite superior.

Among the horde of foreign adventurers to descend upon Washington, a handful were of real quality: Friedrich Wilhelm von Steuben, Baron Johann de Kalb, Count Casimir Pulaski, Thaddeus Kosciuszko, and the very youthful Lafayette, whose eagerness helped to compensate for the inexperience that was his as a nineteen-year-old reserve captain in the French army. Perhaps Washington's regimental officers were the best single element in the army. The vicissitudes of war eliminated scores of incompetents, and the initial inexperience of the others was somewhat compensated for by their zeal. In 1776, William Howe lamented that the flower of young American manhood was joining Washington's officer corps. Among those officers of quality were Henry Dearborn and Moses Hazen of Massachusetts; Eleazer Oswald and several Trumbulls of Connecticut; Alexander Hamilton, Jacob Morris, and John Lamb of New York; Alexander Graydon and Richard Butler of Pennsylvania; Henry (Light Horse Harry) Lee, William Washington, and John Marshall of Virginia; William R. Davie of North Carolina; and John Laurens of South Carolina.

Finally, it was no small advantage to the Americans to be fighting on their own soil and to be more flexible in their military operations than their opponents. If they did not contemplate a massive guerrilla war, if they stood eyeball to eyeball with the redcoats in various "open" engagements from New York to South Carolina, they nonetheless resorted advantageously at times to winter campaigning and night attacks, and they effectively employed backwoods riflemen, light infantry, and irregular or civilian partisan fighters in harassing the flanks, interrupting communication and supply routes, and raiding isolated posts.

In contrast, the British pluses became steadily negated by the frustrations of waging war 3,000 miles from home against an armed population diffused over hundreds and hundreds of miles. The land was forested, ravined, swampy, and interlaced by countless streams and rivers. It seemingly took forever for word of campaign plans to pass from London to British commanders in America, for supplies to arrive, and for naval units to appear to operate in conjunction with land forces. It was discouraging to win battle after battle and see Britain's armies bled of men in the process, whereas the beaten rebels always bounded back; their reservoir of men—on a short-term basis in any case—seemed endless. It was exasperating to seize somewhere along the way every single American urban center, including the capital city of Philadelphia, and have nothing to show for it other than the possession of territory, for America had no vital strategic center. Today Americans know from bitter recent experience that to hold the cities in a war in a so-called backward area of the world is not to insure victory in the countryside. Was the Revolution indeed Britain's Vietnam?

The lack of food and clothing at Valley Forge was due chiefly to a shortage of wagons to haul supplies.

Life on High Street in Philadelphia went on in spite of the war, but tales came back from the battlefields of patriots bravely manning their cannons against the British forces.

The North
1776-1778

The minutemen who threw down their plows to fight at Lexington and Concord are memorialized in this famous statue at Concord. Retreating down the road from Concord, the defeated British had to fight off harassing attacks.

DURING THE TWO years following William Howe's evacuation of Boston in early 1776, Britain focused her strategy on throttling the insurrection in the northern tier of states. She did not totally ignore the region that lay below the Susquehanna River, however. Prior to launching major operations in the summer of 1776, there was a diversionary stab at the Carolina coast by a British army force, under Sir Henry Clinton, and a Royal Navy squadron under the command of Sir Peter Parker. London authorities believed support for the rebel cause to be less extensive in the South than in the North. They harbored the absurd notion that Parker's small squadron and Clinton's few thousand troops might restore the king's standard everywhere with the help of the allegedly ubiquitous Tories. That theory collapsed when Parker and Clinton reached the Cape Fear River in North Carolina, where they learned that a Loyalist uprising had been smashed by patriot militia at the Battle

of Moore's Creek Bridge (February 27, 1776), eighteen miles from Wilmington. (*See Map 7*)

Since their expressed objective was hopeless, Clinton and Parker resolved to salvage something from a disappointing campaign before they joined Howe in waters outside New York City. They decided to assault Sullivan's Island, guarding the harbor of Charleston, South Carolina. Landing his troops on Long Island, Clinton proposed for them to wade across to Sullivan's Island; but to his "unspeakable mortification," water said to be seventeen inches deep turned out to be seven feet! Actually, the Carolinians, commanded by General Charles Lee, were ready for the enemy. Their batteries on Sullivan's Island outdueled Parker's ships in a furious artillery exchange on June 28, and the British withdrew to the north. (*See Map 8*)

If Whitehall, despite contrary evidence from the Clinton-Parker expedition, continued to nurse illusory opinions of royalist sentiment in the South, officialdom in London was somewhat more realistic about the northern regions of America. They knew the rebels were numerous, especially in New England, although the thought never entered their heads at this stage that a majority of the population might support the Continental Congress. The campaign of 1776, in order to bring the war to an end, would call for a massive military effort. And that effort, it was generally agreed, should involve two British armies: a lesser one under General Guy Carleton, governor of Quebec, should push the Americans from their toeholds in Canada and follow them down the Lake Champlain-Hudson River trough, which pointed like a dagger at the heart of America, which might be the means of cutting the states in half; a greater force under William Howe should take New York City with its splendid harbor, a strategic base from which it could advance up the Hudson, unite with Carleton, and overwhelm New England. (*See Map 9*)

The plans for 1776 were largely the work of William Howe and Colonial Secretary George Germain, both of whom were also in agreement that nothing would knock the props from under the rebellion more quickly than a decisive battlefield victory; that would have a profound psychological impact upon all America. Whatever his shortcomings, Germain's performance was superb that year. The huge concentration that had gathered off New York by August 1776—Howe's troops from Halifax, Clinton's regiments from Charleston, thousands of redcoats and Germans directly from Europe—numbered 32,000 soldiers, 10,000 seamen, 400 transports, and 73 warships; and the colonial secretary, by galvanizing the various boards and agencies of government, deserved the lion's share of the credit for the accomplishment, this the most formidable assemblage in British history up to that time, one that would not be repeated or paralleled in the American conflict or in many wars to come. (*See Map 11*)

From a strictly military point of view, Washington should not have attempted to hold New York City and its environs. The islands, rivers, bays, and inlets led the Americans to spread their forces too thinly, afforded Howe opportunities to hit the patriots at weak points—to outflank them and possibly seal off escape routes.

But Howe does not seem to have been eager to rush the campaign, nor was his brother Richard Howe, "Black Dick," the admiral, who shared the American command with William. In fact, not only were the Howes commanders of their respective services, but they also had been designated by the ministry as peace commissioners. The government, favoring a hard line, had accepted the idea of a peace commission as a sop to advocates of moderation, and it only allowed the Howes to hint to the Americans of modest imperial reform *after* they laid down their arms. The admiral, in particular, appears to have been eager to try to secure an immediate cessation of hostilities, his enthusiasm undimmed neither by his restricted negotiating authority, nor by the recent Declaration of Independence.

When Washington refused to receive emissaries from the admiral, the Howes turned to the sword. But did they really seek the knockout blow that the general had advocated earlier? This is one of the unsolved mysteries of the Revolution, and it will probably remain that way. To be sure, the Howes, well known as moderates on the American question, had close ties with the colonists, who had hailed their brother George Augustus—killed at Ticonderoga in 1758—as one of the great British-American heroes of the French and Indian War. If there is more direct evidence for the admiral's reluctance to use the navy aggressively against the patriots, the actions of the general, to say the least, were scarcely

British and Hessian brigades attacked Fort Washington, New York, in November 1776, taking 2,818 prisoners. Two months earlier, a peace conference on Staten Island had aborted when the British demanded revocation of the Declaration of Independence.

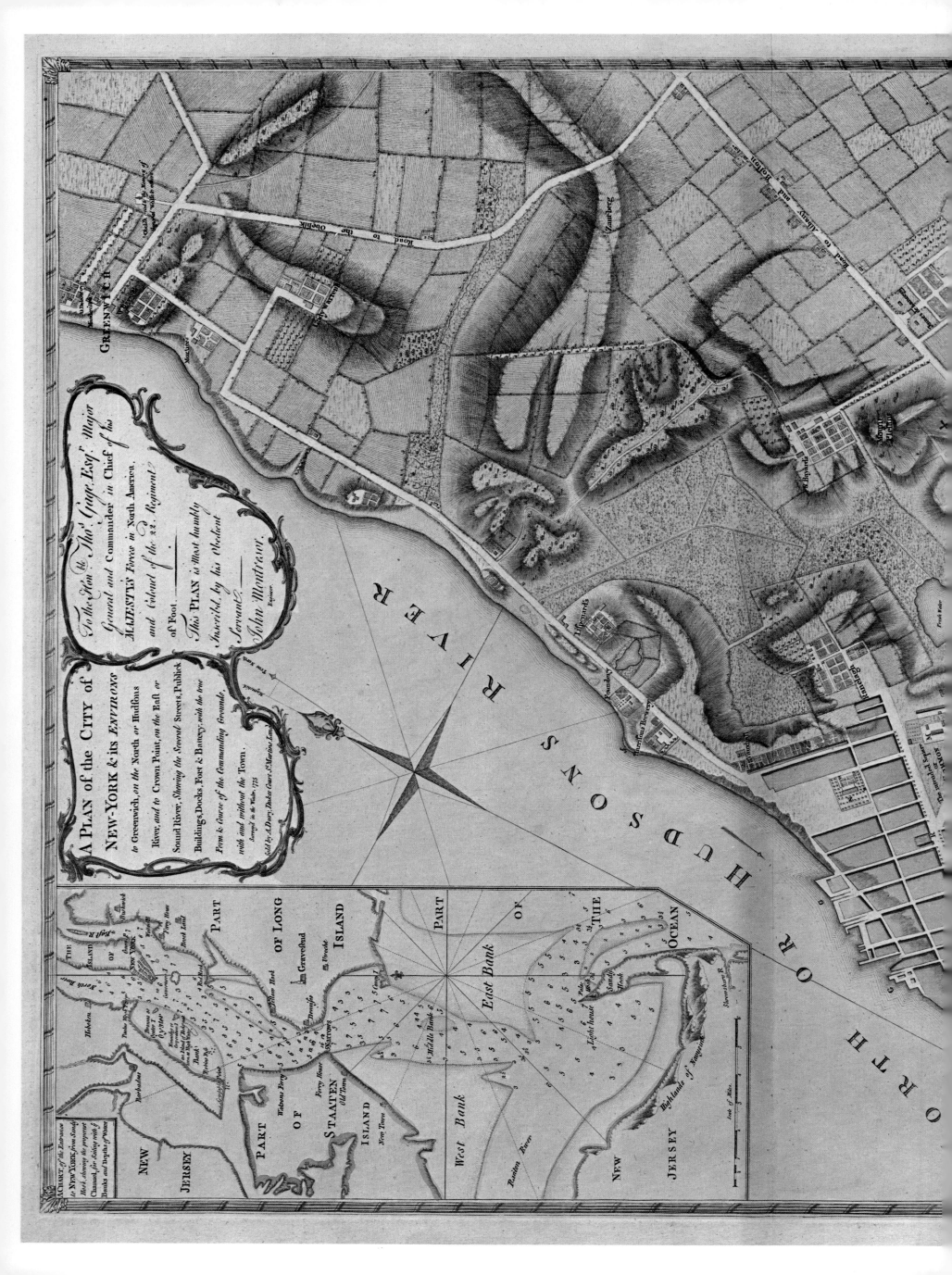

HUDSONS RIVER

NORTH or HUDSONS RIVER

Road to the Obelisk

Road to Greenwich and Boston

GREENWICH

PART OF LONG ISLAND

PART OF THE OCEAN

THE NARROWS

East Bank

West Bank

PART OF STAATEN ISLAND
Old Town
New Town

NEW JERSEY

NEW JERSEY

A CHART of the Entrance to New-York, from Sandy Hook, shewing the proper est Channel, for Sailing, with ye Banks and Depth of Water.

Scale of Miles.

New York in 1776

MAP 11. ¶ By reference to today's landmarks, New York's little grid of streets extended at the time of the Revolution northward along the Hudson to just beyond the World Trade Center and eastward to about the Brooklyn Bridge. In the center was the small suburb of the Bowery. The town of Harlem, although several miles away, had been annexed to the city in 1736. In between lay mostly farmland. At the top of the map is the peaceful village of Greenwich, where the Oliver De Lanceys (he was the senior Tory officer in America) lived with a few other families in their well-landscaped mansions. ¶ In spite of the disastrous and controversial fire of November 1776, following the British occupation in September of that year, New York emerged from the war to be the nation's first capital. After the British formally evacuated in November 1783, Washington led the American army through town to the Battery and a jubilant reception. Although he bade farewell to his officers at the celebrated dinner at Fraunces Tavern on December 4, 1783, he was to return to New York in April 1789 for his inauguration as first president of the United States at Federal Hall on Wall Street, shown on this map as "I," the City Hall. ¶ Captain John Montresor, the British military engineer who originally drew this accurate map in 1776, knew the area well. He had fought in America during the French and Indian War and Pontiac's War. Afterward he bought what is now called Randall's Island, which the Triborough Bridge spans today, and lived there with his wife and family. Montresor was present at Lexington, Bunker Hill, Long Island, the Delaware River forts (he designed the fortification of Mud Island), and Brandywine, but he returned to England in 1778, disappointed because his experience and professional ability were not appreciated by Sir Henry Clinton.

A Plan of the City of New-York & its Environs to Greenwich, on the North or Hudsons River, and to Crown Point, on the East or Sound River, Shewing the Several Streets, Publick Buildings, Docks, Fort & Battery, with the true Form & Course of the Commanding Grounds, with and without the Town. By John Montresor. Engraved by P. Andrews. London, A. Dury, 1776. (25" x 21")

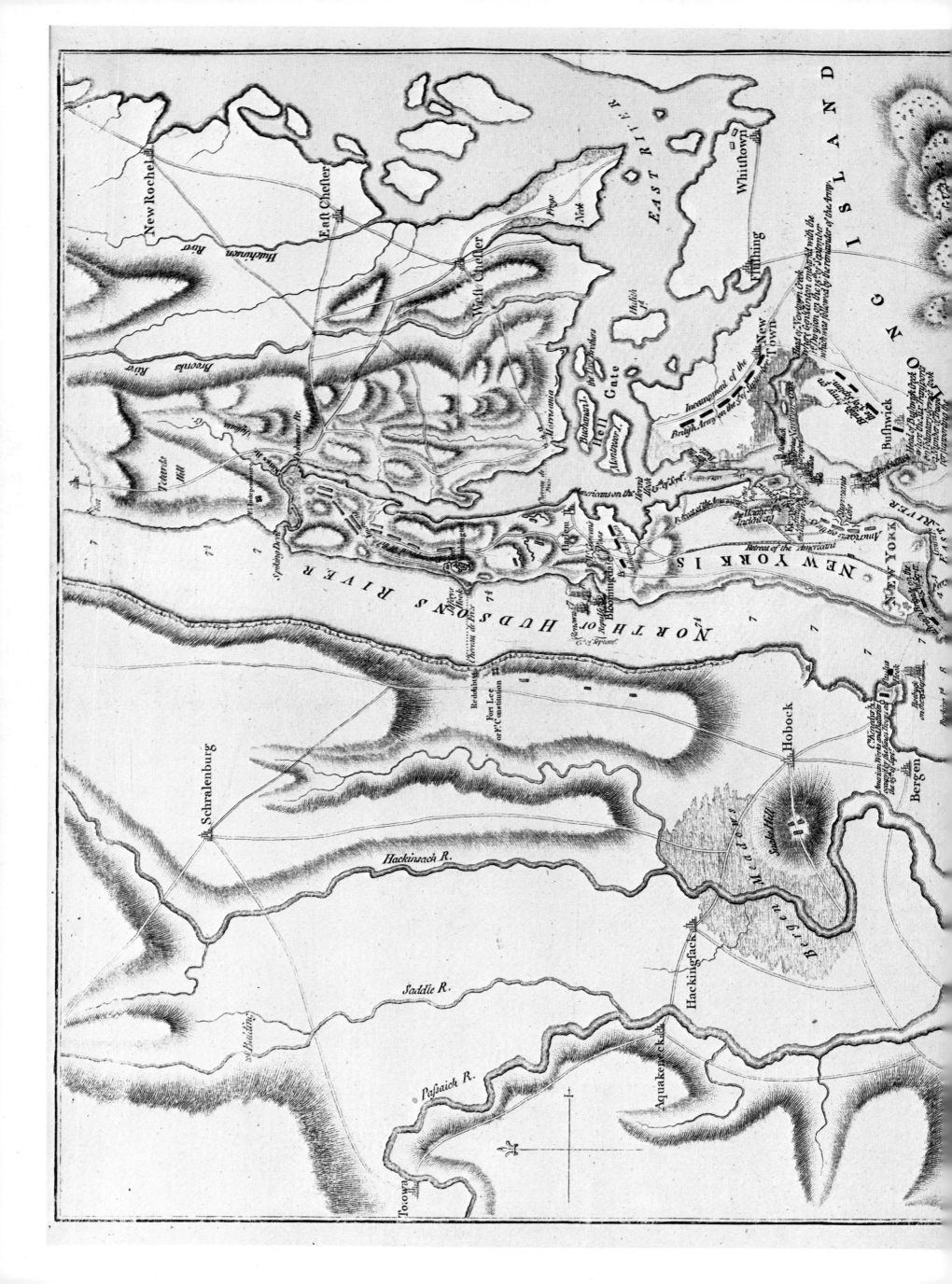

References to the Battle on Long Island.

A.A. *Landing of the British with Colonel Donop's Corps of Chasseurs & Hessian grenadiers, with 40 Pieces of Cannon on the 22.d of August.*
B.B. *Landing of 2.d Brigade of Hessians under Lieutenant-General de Heister, on the 25.th of August.*
C.C. *Lord Cornwallis with the Reserve, 2 Battalions of Light Infantry, Col. Donop's Corps & 6 Field Pieces on the 26.th*
D.D. *Lieutenant-General Heister, with his 2 Brigades on the 26.th*
E.E. *Lord Cornwallis with the British on the 26.th*
F. *Lieutenant-General Clinton with the Van, consisting of Light-Dragoons & Brigade of Light Infantry, the Reserve under Lord Cornwallis; excepting the 42.d Regiment which was posted on the Left of the Hessians,) the First Brigade & the 71.st Regt. with 14 Field Pieces.*
G. *The Main Body under Lord Percy, consisting of the Guards, 2.d 4.st & 6.th Brigade with 10 Field Pieces.*
H. *The 42.d Regiment.*
I. *The Baggage and its separate Guard.*
K. *A Battalion of Light Infantry, securing the Pass.*
L. *Keep: the House attacking the Front of the Enemy.*
M.M. *Maj.Gen. Grant with the 4.st & 5.th Brigade, the 10.th Regt. & 2 Companies of N. York Provincials with 10 Pieces of Cannon, attacking a large Corps on the Enemy's Right.*
N.N. *A Party of the Grenadiers, supported by the 71.st Regt.*
O.O.O. *Small Parties of the Enemy on the Coasts, who on the approach of the Boats, retired to the Woody Heights.*
P. *Lieutenant Colonel Dalrymple with 1 Brigade of Hessians, a Detachment of the 42.d Regt. from Virginia, now Convalescents*
Q. *Lines occupied by the Hessian Brigade after the Retreat of the Enemy to New-York.*

A PLAN of *NEW YORK ISLAND*, with part of *LONG ISLAND, STATEN ISLAND & EAST NEW JERSEY*, with a particular Description of the ENGAGEMENT on the Woody Heights of Long Island, between FLATBUSH and BROOKLYN, on the 27.th of August 1776.
between HIS MAJESTY'S FORCES Commanded by General HOWE and the AMERICANS under Major General PUTNAM. Shewing also the Landing of the BRITISH ARMY on New-York Island, and the Taking of the CITY of New-York &c. on the 15.th of September following, with the subsequent Disposition of Both the Armies.

Engraved & Published according to Act of Parliament Oct. 19.th 1776, by W.m Faden, (successor to the late T. Jefferys) Geographer to the King, Charing Cross, LONDON.

Washington's First Loss: First Victory

MAP 12. ¶ The siege of Boston had finally forced General Howe to move his army out of harm's way to Loyalist Halifax. It then became only a question of time until he would invade General Washington's domain and attempt to destroy the rebel army. Characteristically, Howe took his time building up the size of his army and his military stores, and it was not until five months after having left Boston that he was ready to launch his campaign. ¶ The British decision to attempt to take New York had been made early in the war, even before Howe had succeeded General Gage at Boston. The move was anticipated by the Americans, who had transferred troops to New York and begun erecting fortifications. ¶ The defense of New York against a full-scale invasion was considered impossible. Manhattan itself had fully navigable rivers running up both of its sides, and the general configuration of the entire area around New York made it accessible to whichever side had naval superiority. Since the Howe brothers put together what has been called the largest British armada in history, and the Americans scarcely had any navy at all, the occupation of New York was only a question of time and the price in men that could be extracted by the defenders. When the British landed on the western tip of Long Island, August 27, 1776, Washington could field only 60 percent of the number of combatants landed by Howe. He was further handicapped by those factors which were frequently to plague him: raw recruits facing regular army troops and an inadequate number of artillery. ¶ Actually, the British plan and execution was a great tactical success in the Battle of Long Island. Washington's inadvertent coup, however, was to extricate his army without crushing losses. Colonel Glover's Marblehead sailors, using muffled oars, managed to ferry the American army from Brooklyn to Manhattan, under the guns of the British warships. This left Howe with a somewhat empty victory. ¶ The map shows the movements of the opposing armies through the time of the disembarkation of the British army on September 15. Less than five weeks later this map was on sale in London to a public eager for details.

A Plan of New York Island, with part of Long Island, Staten Island & East New Jersey, with a particular Description of the Engagement on the Woody Heights of Long Island, between Flatbush and Brooklyn, on the 27th of August 1776, between His Majesty's Forces Commanded by General Howe and the Americans under Major General Putnam . . . with the Subsequent Disposition of Both the Armies. London, Wm. Faden, Oct. 19, 1776. (19" x 17")

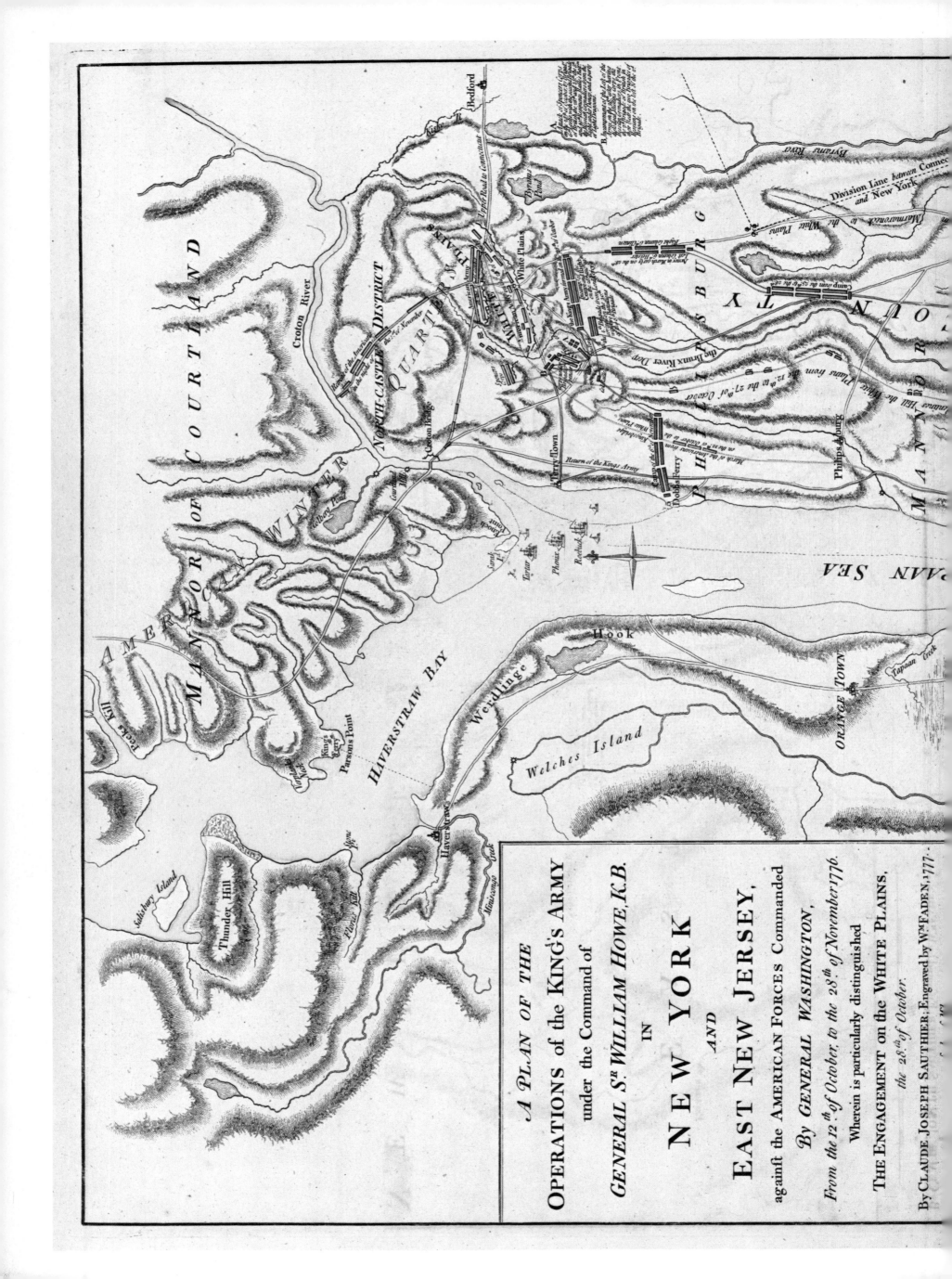

A PLAN OF THE

OPERATIONS of the KING'S ARMY

under the Command of

GENERAL Sr. WILLIAM HOWE, K.B.

IN

NEW YORK

AND

EAST NEW JERSEY,

againſt the AMERICAN FORCES Commanded

By GENERAL WASHINGTON,

From the 12th of October, to the 28th of November 1776.

Wherein is particularly diſtinguiſhed

THE ENGAGEMENT on the WHITE PLAINS,

the 28th of October.

By CLAUDE JOSEPH SAUTHIER; Engraved by Wm. FADEN, 1777.

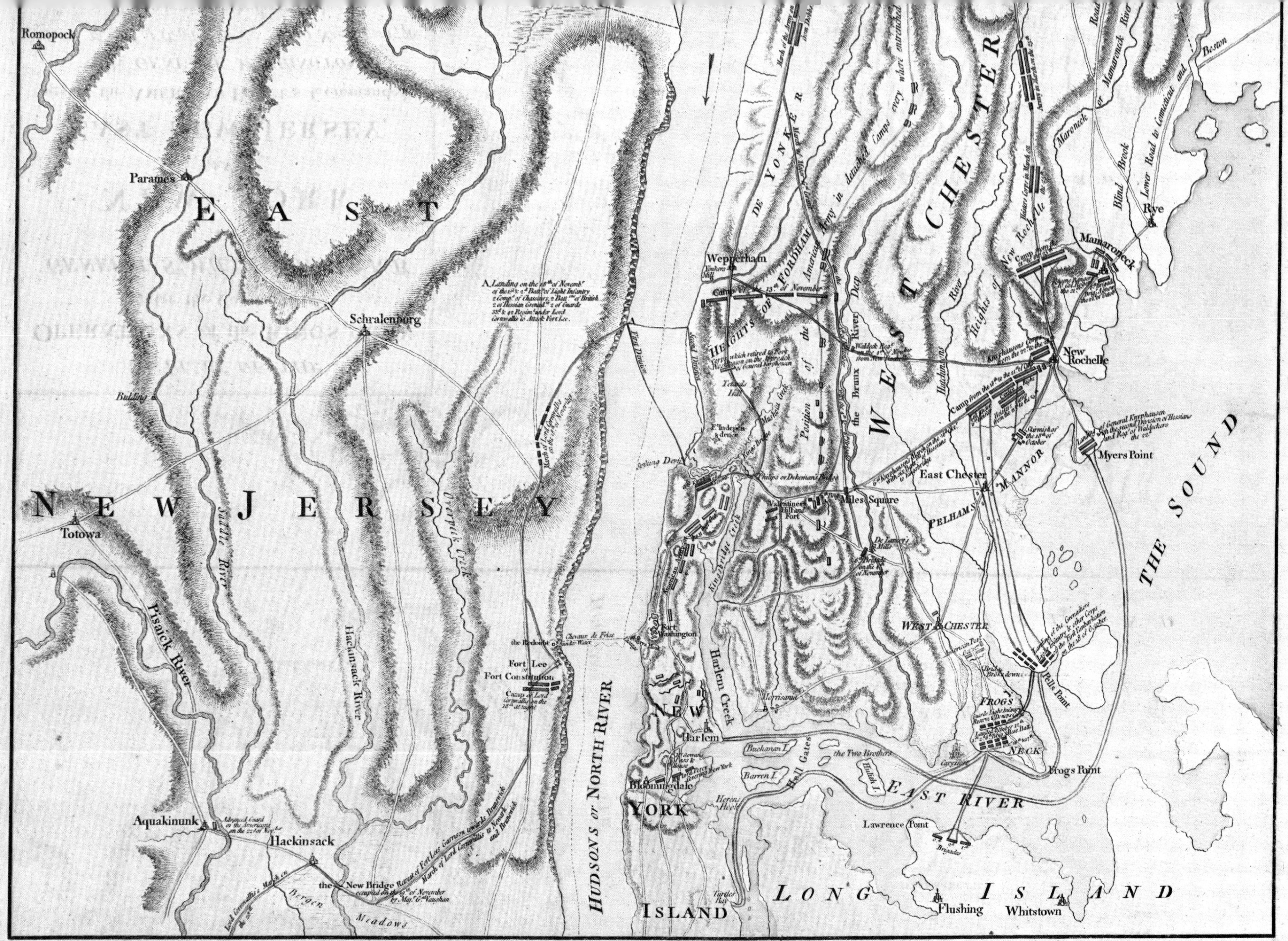

THE SOUND

LONG ISLAND

Flushing Whitstown

EAST RIVER

Lawrence Point

Hell Gates

Barren I.

Judith I.

the Two Brothers

Buchanan I.

Frogs Point

Pells Point

Myers Point

Mamaroneck

Rye

New Rochelle

Heights of New Rochelle

PELHAMS MANOR

East Chester

WEST CHESTER

FROGS NECK

YORK ISLAND

Harlem

Harlem Creek

Kingsbridge Creek

Miles Square

the Brunx River

Hutchinsons River

DE YONKER

WEST CHESTER

Heights of FORDHAM

Wepperham

Second Division

First Division

Position of the Heights of

NEW JERSEY

HUDSONS or NORTH RIVER

Fort Lee or Fort Constitution

Camp Lee

Overpeck Creek

Schralenburg

EAST JERSEY

Hackinsack River

Saddle River

Pisaick River

Hackinsack

Meadows

Aquakinunk

Totowa

Paramus

Romopock

the New Bridge

Blind Brook

War in Westchester

MAP 13. ¶ It has always been a challenge for the mapmaker to combine relief and cultural features. C. J. Sauthier, a cartographer who emigrated to the Carolinas from Strasbourg, drew this map, which is so filled with detail as to be at once among the most informative and the most difficult to study of all the battle plans. The persistent viewer will be rewarded with an excellent picture of the White Plains phase of the New York campaign. ¶ It is from Sauthier's manuscript that William Faden derived this military map of the area from the East River to the Croton and from the Hudson to Long Island Sound. It is the most accurate published delineation of the movements of the armies of Washington and Howe in Westchester, from the time of the British landing through November 28, particularly focusing on the Battle of White Plains. Other important features shown on the map are the British movement south toward Fort Washington, Cornwallis's landing in New Jersey, his taking of Fort Lee, and the British route toward Brunswick. It was published, in spite of the perils of a winter crossing, less than three months later in London.

SHOWN ON PRECEDING PAGE
A Plan of the Operations of the King's Army under the Command of General Sr. William Howe, K.B. in New York and east New Jersey, against the American Forces Commanded By General Washington, from the 12th of October, to the 28th of November 1776. Wherein is particularly distinguished The Engagement on the White Plains, the 28th of October. By Claude Joseph Sauthier; engraved by Wm. Faden. London, W. Faden, Feb. 25, 1777. (28¾" x 19¼")

German Victory at Washington Heights

MAP 14. ¶ The battle of Fort Washington is associated with several ironies. General Nathanael Greene, considered second only to Washington in judgment and leadership ability, advised the commander in chief well throughout the war. But it was Greene who convinced Washington to attempt the holding of Fort Washington against a vastly superior force. On the other hand, the German mercenaries certainly failed to distinguish themselves during most of the war — they are remembered principally for such disastrous defeats as Trenton and Bennington. And yet the Hessians did provide the brunt of this successful attack. ¶ The fortified hilltop post looked a great deal more impregnable than it turned out to be. While the site could have supported a very strong fort, General Washington as yet did not have a Kosciuszko to engineer one. A six-columned attack converged on the fort, causing the garrison to surrender. ¶ Washington experienced his most serious tactical defeat here. In all of the previous encounters with the British, he was able to get his army out intact, even when giving up ground. At Fort Washington he left over 2,800 men he could well have used in the New Jersey campaign to come. ¶ Faden's map was derived from the Sauthier manuscript prepared for Lord Percy. It was the most accurate delineation of Upper Manhattan to have been published up to this date.

SHOWN ON OPPOSITE PAGE
A Topographical Map of the Northn. Part of New York Island, Exhibiting the Plan of Fort Washington, now Fort Knyphausen, With the Rebels Lines to the Southward, which were forced by the Troops under the Command of the Rt. Honble. Earl Percy, on the 16th Novr. 1776. London, Wm. Faden, March 1, 1777. (18½" x 10¼")

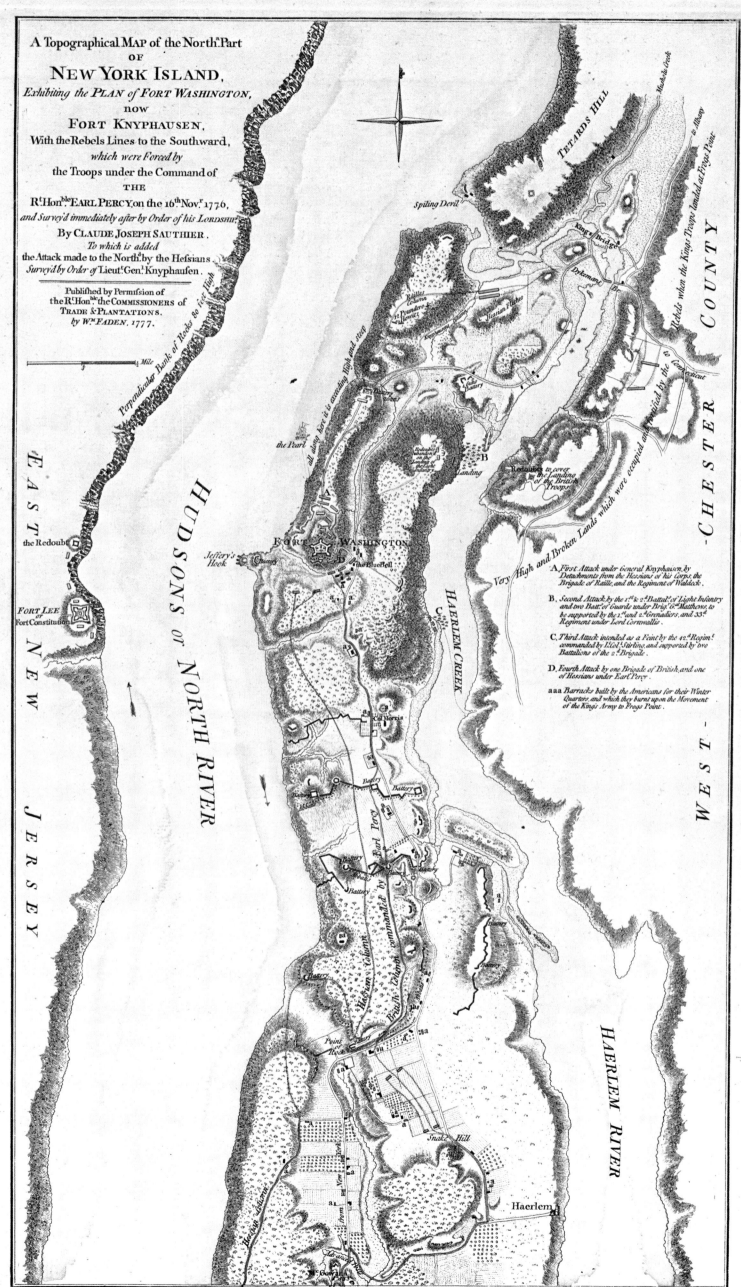

A Topographical MAP of the North.ᵗ Part
OF
NEW YORK ISLAND,
Exhibiting the PLAN of FORT WASHINGTON,
NOW
FORT KNYPHAUSEN,
With the Rebels Lines to the Southward,
which were Forced by
the Troops under the Command of
THE
Rᵗ Hon.ᵇˡᵉ EARL PERCY, on the 16.ᵗʰ Nov.ʳ 1776,
and Survey'd immediately after by Order of his Lordship.
By CLAUDE JOSEPH SAUTHIER.
To which is added
the Attack made to the North.ᵗ by the Hessians.
Survey'd by Order of Lieut.ᵗ Gen.ˡ Knyphausen.

Published by Permission of
the Rᵗ Hon.ᵇˡᵉ the COMMISSIONERS of
TRADE & PLANTATIONS.
by Wᵐ FADEN. 1777.

Perpendicular Bank of Rocks 80 feet High

EAST NEW JERSEY

HUDSONS or NORTH RIVER

CHESTER WEST COUNTY

HAERLEM RIVER

HAERLEM CREEK

FORT WASHINGTON

FORT LEE
or
Fort Constitution

the Redoubt

Jeffery's Hook

the BlueBell

Col Morris

Earl Percy

Point Rock

Snake Hill

Haerlem

TETARD'S HILL

Spiting Devil

King's Bridge

Dykeman's Br.

A. First Attack under General Knyphausen, by
Detachments from the Hessians of his Corps, the
Brigade of Raille, and the Regiment of Waldeck.

B. Second Attack by the 1.ˢᵗ & 2.ᵈ Battal.ⁿ of Light Infantry
and two Batt.ⁿ of Guards under Brig.ʳ G.ˡ Matthews, to
be supported by the 1.ˢᵗ and 2.ᵈ Grenadiers, and 33.ᵈ
Regiment under Lord Cornwallis.

C. Third Attack intended as a Feint by the 42.ᵈ Regim.ᵗ
commanded by Lt Col.ˡ Stirling, and supported by two
Battalions of the 2.ᵈ Brigade.

D. Fourth Attack by one Brigade of British, and one
of Hessians under Earl Percy.

aaa Barracks built by the Americans for their Winter
Quarters, and which they burnt upon the Movement
of the King's Army to Frogs Point.

London, Published as the Act directs, March 1ˢᵗ 1777. by Wᵐ Faden, Corner of St Martins Lane, Charing Cross.

91

those that would likely crush Washington in the New York area, were instead those that would occupy territory.

Rather than landing behind Washington's main army, concentrated at New York City on the lower end of Manhattan Island, Howe assembled his forces on Long Island, where Washington had erected fortifications on Brooklyn Heights. With his five-division army already widely dispersed, Washington took the dangerous gamble of reinforcing his division directly across from the city on the heights. Assuredly, his positions there were strong, and doubtless Washington hoped that Howe would hurl his scarlet ranks at the American entrenchments as he had done at Bunker Hill. But Howe was more subtle this time, his scheme of attack—suggested to him by Clinton—more in keeping with the eighteenth-century maxim of achieving one's ends by maneuver and economy of losses rather than by a draining head-on assault. It amounted to hitting the left flank of a 4,000-man American advance force guarding the roads and passes back to Brooklyn. As the contest opened on the early morning of August 27, British Major General James Grant and German General Philipp von Heister pushed against the American front. Meanwhile, Howe and Clinton marched silently during the predawn hours in a wide arc around the American left, held by General John Sullivan. Accompanying Clinton was Lord Charles Cornwallis, recently arrived from England with troop reinforcements. By dawn, the Continentals, though fighting stubbornly, were beginning to give ground in the center when the British right crashed down on Sullivan's unsuspecting rear. The panic that afflicted Sullivan's soldiers spread down the line. As the Americans streamed back into their Brooklyn entrenchments, Howe might well have capitalized on their confusion by carrying everything, had he pressed after them; but he chose not to do so. (*See Map 12*)

On the night of the 29th, under a heavy fog, Washington silently ferried the Brooklyn garrison over the East River to Manhattan. If Admiral Howe's vessels had made no effort to block Washington's escape route, and if General Howe had not quickly followed up on his victory, Washington was still in serious danger. And the Howes, albeit sluggishly, began a series of moves that threatened to block the American escape route that lay over Harlem Heights and across the Harlem River to the Bronx and the mainland. Reluctantly, and none too rapidly, Washington evacuated New York City and headed northward, his troops fending off British landing parties on his right flank until after he had left the island and taken up positions at White Plains, New York.

Howe's halfhearted doings of the past two months were repeated on October 28, in the Battle of White Plains, where the British general tested Washington's lines and, finding them strong, withdrew. Perhaps Howe was unwilling to pay the price in hard-to-come-by regulars. Perhaps he and his brother as peace commissioners sought another try at negotiations. Perhaps, too, they had relinquished any hope of terminating the war in 1776, an attitude that may explain their dispersing their forces by seizing (in December) Newport, Rhode Island, as a winter base for Admiral Howe's cruisers. Moreover, Carleton's Canadian-based army had been delayed in its drive southward by a small American fleet that Benedict Arnold put together on Lake Champlain. Consequently, Carleton, with winter coming on in the north country, closed his campaigning season and returned to Montreal. (*See Maps 10, 13, 16*)

Yet William Howe was not quite ready to ring down the curtain on

MAP 15. ¶ While George Washington can be credited with skillful generalship in extricating most of his army from New York, he desperately needed a victory to turn the strategic and psychological tides then running against him. Howe's army, deployed in New Jersey, was not the only menace. On December 31 the enlistments of three-fourths of his men would expire. Then the Delaware River, the only natural obstacle to the British army's advance, would freeze. ¶ The commander in chief's daring strikes against the Hessians at Trenton, and then against the British at Princeton, were to end the campaign of 1776 on a sufficiently optimistic note to sustain the rebel cause through the freezing winter at Morristown. ¶ This map, like the three which precede it, was on sale in London "immediately" after the action. It enables us to see the movements of the combatants just as a Londoner would have in April 1777. Beginning with the "Parade of the Troops on the evening of the 25th of Dec'r 1776," at McKenky's Ferry on the Delaware River, and continuing through "G'al Washington's March towards the Mountainous Parts," north of Princeton, the heroic maneuvers by the desperate Americans are traced for the British home audience.

SHOWN ON OPPOSITE PAGE
Plan of the Operations of General Washington against the King's Troops in New Jersey. from the 26th of December 1776, to the 3ᵈ· January 1777. By William Faden. London, Wm. Faden, April 15, 1777. (11½" x 17¼")

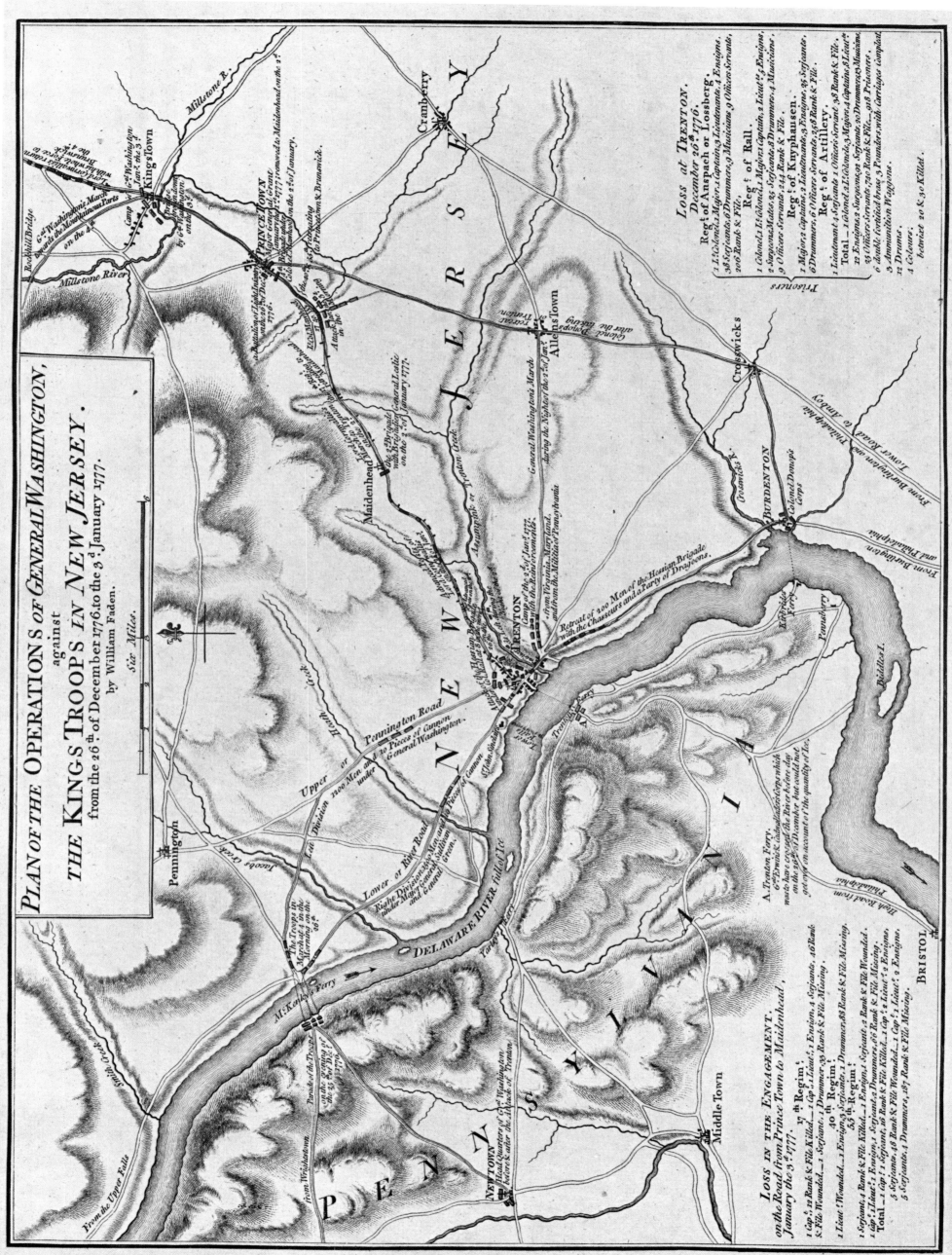

PLAN OF THE OPERATIONS OF GENERAL WASHINGTON, against THE KINGS TROOPS IN NEW JERSEY. from the 26th of December 1776, to the 3d January 1777. by William Faden.

London, Publish'd according to Act of Parliament, 15th April 1777, by Wm. Faden, corner of St Martins Lane, Charing Cross.

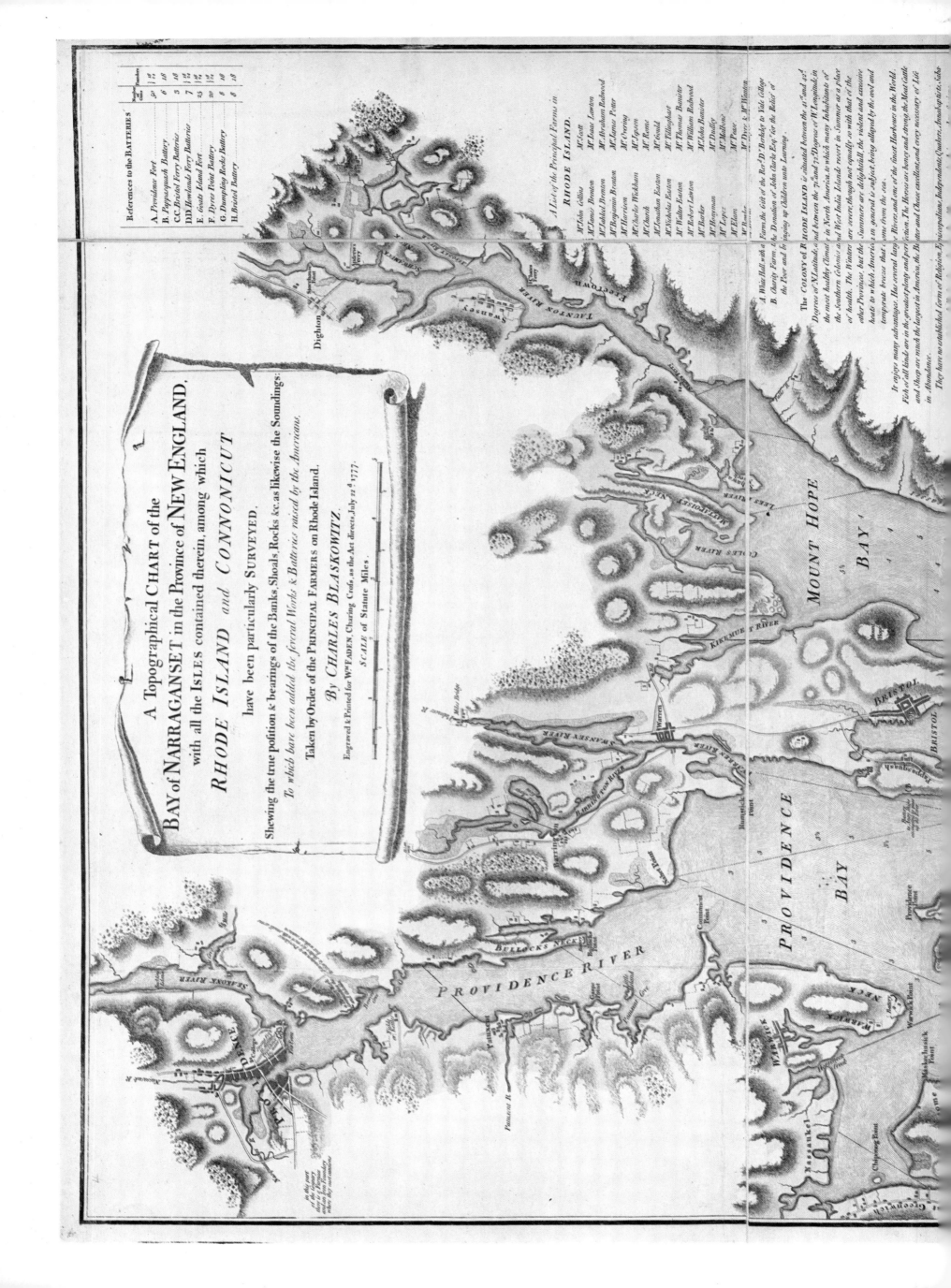

A Topographical CHART of the
BAY of NARRAGANSET in the Province of NEW ENGLAND,
with all the ISLES contained therein, among which
RHODE ISLAND and CONNONICUT
have been particularly SURVEYED.

Shewing the true position & bearings of the Banks, Shoals, Rocks &c. as likewise the Soundings:

To which have been added the several Works & Batteries raised by the Americans.

Taken by Order of the PRINCIPAL FARMERS on Rhode Island.

By CHARLES BLASKOWITZ.

Engraved & Printed for Wm. FADEN, Charing Cross, as the Act directs, July 22.d 1777.

SCALE of Statute Miles.

References to the BATTERIES

A. Providence Fort
B. Pappasquash Battery
C.C. Bristol Ferry Batteries
D.D. Howlands Ferry Batteries
E. Goats Island Fort
F. Dyres Point Fort
G. Dumpling Rocks Battery
H. Bristol Battery

A List of the Principal Farms in
RHODE ISLAND.

Mr. Scott
Mr. John Gibbs
Mr. James Brenton
Mr. Jahleel Brenton
Mr. Benjamin Brenton
Mr. Harrison
Mr. Charles Wickham
Mr. Church
Mr. Jonathan Easton
Mr. Nicholas Easton
Mr. Walter Easton
Mr. Robert Lawton
Mr. Barker
Mr. Hogman
Mr. Lopez
Mr. Elam
Mr. Pease
Mr. Dyre & Mr. Wanton

Mr. Isaac Lawton
Mr. Abraham Redwood
Mr. James Peter
Mr. Overing
Mr. Ogden
Mr. Rome
Mr. Gould
Mr. Tillinghast
Mr. Thomas Banister
Mr. William Redwood
Mr. John Banister
Mr. Dudley
Mr. Malbone
Mr. Bowler

The COLONY of RHODE ISLAND is situated between the 41.st and 42.d Degrees of N. Latitude, and between the 71.st and 72.d Degrees of W. Longitude, in the most healthy Climate in North America, to which many Inhabitants of the Southern Colonies and West India Islands resort in Summer as a place of health. The Winters are severe, though not equally so with that of the other Province, but the Summers are delightful, the violent and excessive heats to which America in general is subject, being allayed by the cool and temperate breezes that come from the sea.

A. White Hall, with a Farm, the Gift of the Rev.d Dr. Berkley to Yale college.
B. Charity Farm, the Donation of John Clarke Esq. for the Relief of the Poor and bringing up Children unto Learning.

It enjoys many advantages. Has several large Rivers, and one of the finest Harbours in the World. Fish of all kinds are in the greatest plenty and perfection. The Horses are hardy and strong, the Meat Cattle and sheep are much the largest in America, the Butter and Cheese excellent, and every necessary of Life in Abundance.

They have an established form of Religion, Episcopalians, Independents, Quakers, Anabaptists, (who ...

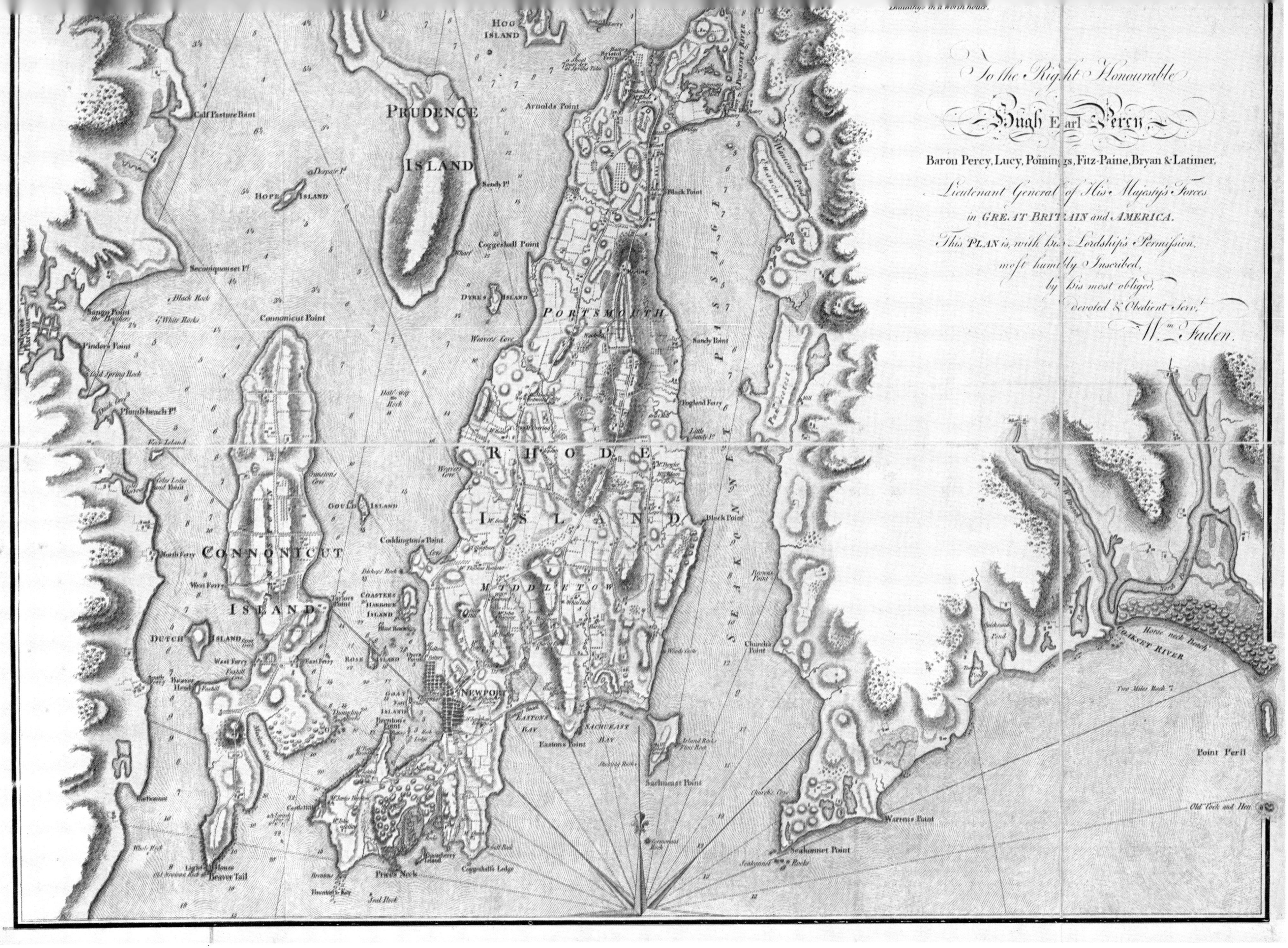

To the Right Honourable
Hugh Earl Percy

Baron Percy, Lucy, Poinings, Fitz-Paine, Bryan & Latimer,
Lieutenant General of His Majesty's Forces
in GREAT BRITAIN and AMERICA.
This PLAN is, with His Lordship's Permission,
most humbly Inserted,
by his most obliged,
Devoted & Obedient Serv.t
W.m Faden.

Lowlaridge in a North house.

HOG ISLAND

PRUDENCE ISLAND

CONNONICUT ISLAND

CONNONICUT ISLAND

RHODE ISLAND

PORTSMOUTH

MIDDLETOWN

NEWPORT

SEAKONNET PASSAGE

SEAKONNET

Point Feril

Point Feril

Warren Point

Seakonnet Point

Sakonnet Point

Eastons Point

Sachuest Point

Church's Point

SAKONNET RIVER

TAUNTON RIVER

Mantons Pond

Arnolds Point

Coggeshall Point

Dyers Island

Conanicut Point

Hope Island

Dutch Island

West Ferry

Gould Island

Coddington Point

Goat Island

Rose Island

Canonicut Point

Sandy Point

Black Point

Castle Hill

Brenton's Reef

Cull Pasture Point

Hunt Rock

White Rocks

Sandy Point

Prudence Island

Poor Start for the French Alliance

MAP 16. ¶ The original survey, followed by Faden to engrave this accurate chart, was done before the war by Charles Blaskowitz and Thomas Wheeler. These two mapmakers worked under Samuel Holland, surveyor general for the northern district of the British colonies. It is certain that the British, after occupying Newport at the end of 1776, used this map for their operations in this pivotal area. The detail shown is remarkable, including even the names of farmers on their land locations. ¶ It was in these waters during July of 1778 that the fleets of Admiral d'Estaing and Admiral Richard Howe faced each other. A major maritime engagement was about to begin when both fleets were dispersed by a devastating hurricane. ¶ The real dividends of the French Alliance were not felt until July 1780, when Comte de Rochambeau arrived with the French expeditionary force in Newport in time to help Washington end the war at Yorktown.

SHOWN ON PRECEDING PAGE
A Topographical Chart of the Bay of Narraganset in the Province of New England, with all the Isles contained therein, among which Rhode Island and Connonicut have been particularly surveyed. Shewing the true position & bearings of the Banks, Shoals, Rocks &c. as likewise the Soundings: To which have been added the several Works & Batteries raised by the Americans....by Charles Blaskowitz. London, Wm. Faden, July 22, 1777. (36½" x 25¼")

The Gibraltar of America?

MAP 17. ¶ The origin of this large-scale, detailed map of the key strategic area of Fort Ticonderoga and its environs is as interesting as the map itself. The map was prepared, along with the accompanying explanation, for Major General St. Clair's defense in his court-martial and published in the *Proceedings....* The account of the trial is considered the best contemporary documentation of the abandonment of the untenable outpost of Fort Ticonderoga after Burgoyne's army landed and laid siege in July 1777. This plan, which is the only contemporary graphic representation of the British attack at the south end of Lake Champlain, clearly outlines the insurmountable difficulties which St. Clair faced in defending the fort. ¶ The army and the public experienced a psychological reversal greater than merited by the loss of the fort. Fort Ticonderoga had undeservedly acquired the reputation as the Gibraltar of America. While it blocked the Lake Champlain-Hudson River invasion route from Canada, its fortifications were not adequate; nor was its garrison of 2,500 sufficient to stop Burgoyne's army of close to 10,000. ¶ Although St. Clair's decision to retreat was in fact wise, he was accused of everything from incompetence to disloyalty. Even though Burgoyne was crushed at Saratoga in October 1777, St. Clair was court-martialed the following year. In spite of his acquittal with honor, St. Clair's career as an important military leader was over. For the rest of the war his assignments were minor and mostly administrative. Washington's biographer has said of St. Clair, "His record was clean; the minds of some of his critics were not." ¶ Ticonderoga was Burgoyne's first encounter on the road to Saratoga. While Saratoga was a mere sixty miles to the south, the march there was to prove a long and bitter journey, which would end unexpectedly for him.

SHOWN ON OPPOSITE PAGE
Map of Ticonderoga, Mount Independence and the adjacent country. Philadelphia, 1778. (12¼" x 10¼")

In: *St. Clair, Major General Arthur. Proceedings of a General Court Martial . . . for the Trial of . . . Philadelphia, 1778.*

EXPLANATION of the DRAUGHT annexed.

A Old fort in very bad condition, wanting repair; could not be defended with lefs than 500 men.
B Stone redoubt, about 200 men would defend it, overlooketh the line Y, oppofite the Lake, in Fort Independence.
C Block houfe for 100 men.
D French redoubt upon the low ground for about 200 men, commanded by the oppofite fide.
E New breaft work for 200 men.
F New fleche for 100 men.
G New redoubt for 150 men.
H New redoubt for 100 men.
I Redoubt upon the low ground for 250 men, commanded by the oppofite fide.
K Jerfey redoubt upon the low ground for 300 men, commanded by the oppofite fide.
L Redoubt upon the low ground for 100 men.
M Redoubt upon the low ground for 100 men.
N French lines upon the high ground, overlooks all the works on Ticonderoga fide, for 2000 men, and not lefs, confidering the great length and importance of the place.
R P Q O New works, in addition to the French lines.
S High ground, occupied by the enemy, and overlooks the French lines.
T Mount Hope, overlooks ground S, occupied by the enemy.
U Block-houfe, burnt by the enemy.
V V High hill, overlooks Ticonderoga and Mount Independence.
X The bridge.

MOUNT INDEPENDENCE.

Y Line upon the low ground, commanded by the oppofite fide B, for 800 men.
Z Barbet battery.
2 Line only marked upon the ground.
3 Picket fort for 600 men.
4 Block-houfe for 100 men.
5 6 Line, with three new made batteries, for 1500 men, and not lefs.
7 Block-houfe for 100 men.
8 Battery made by the enemy.
9 Road made by the enemy to cut off the communication from Mount Independence to Skeenfborough.

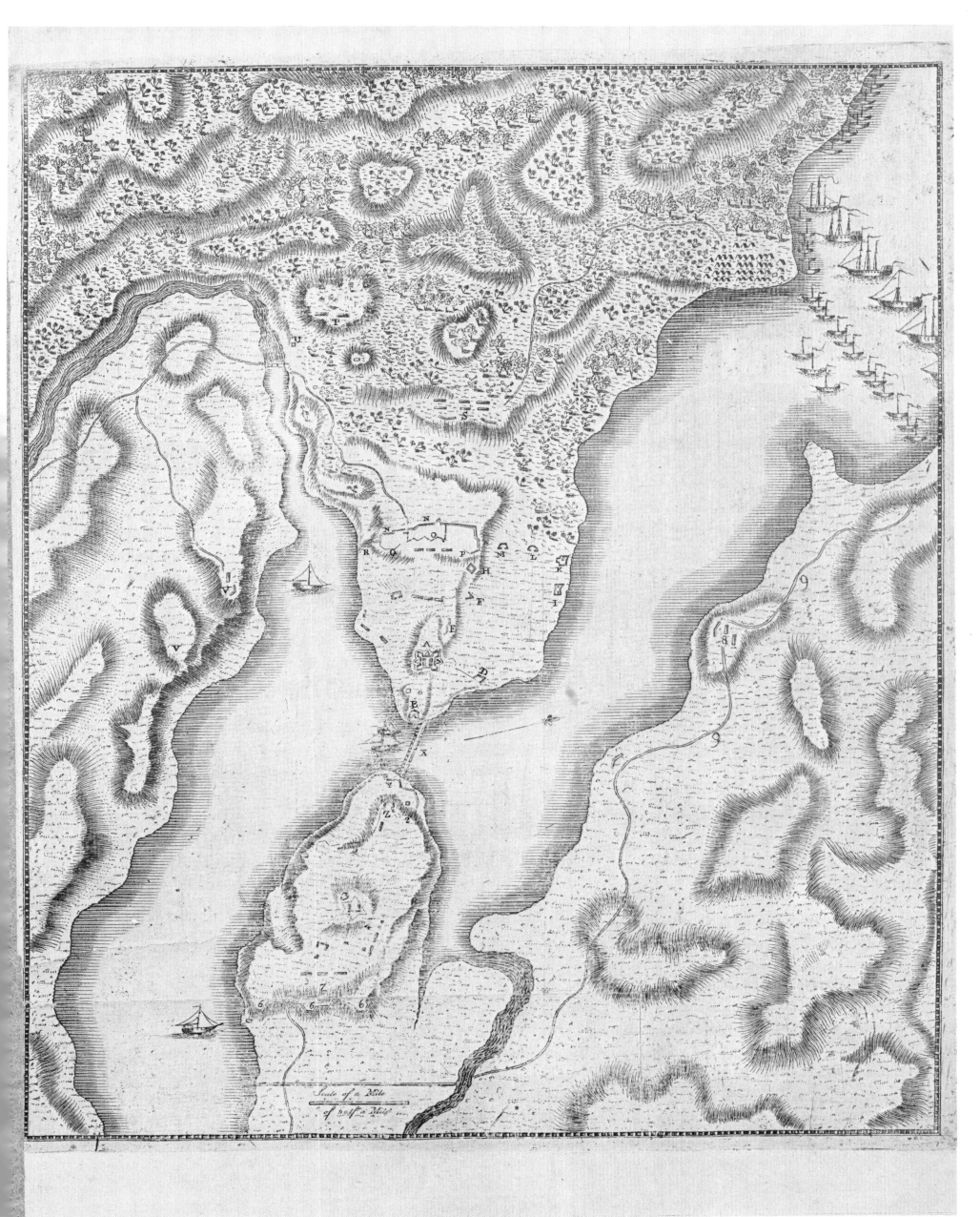

Scale of a Mile
of half a Mile

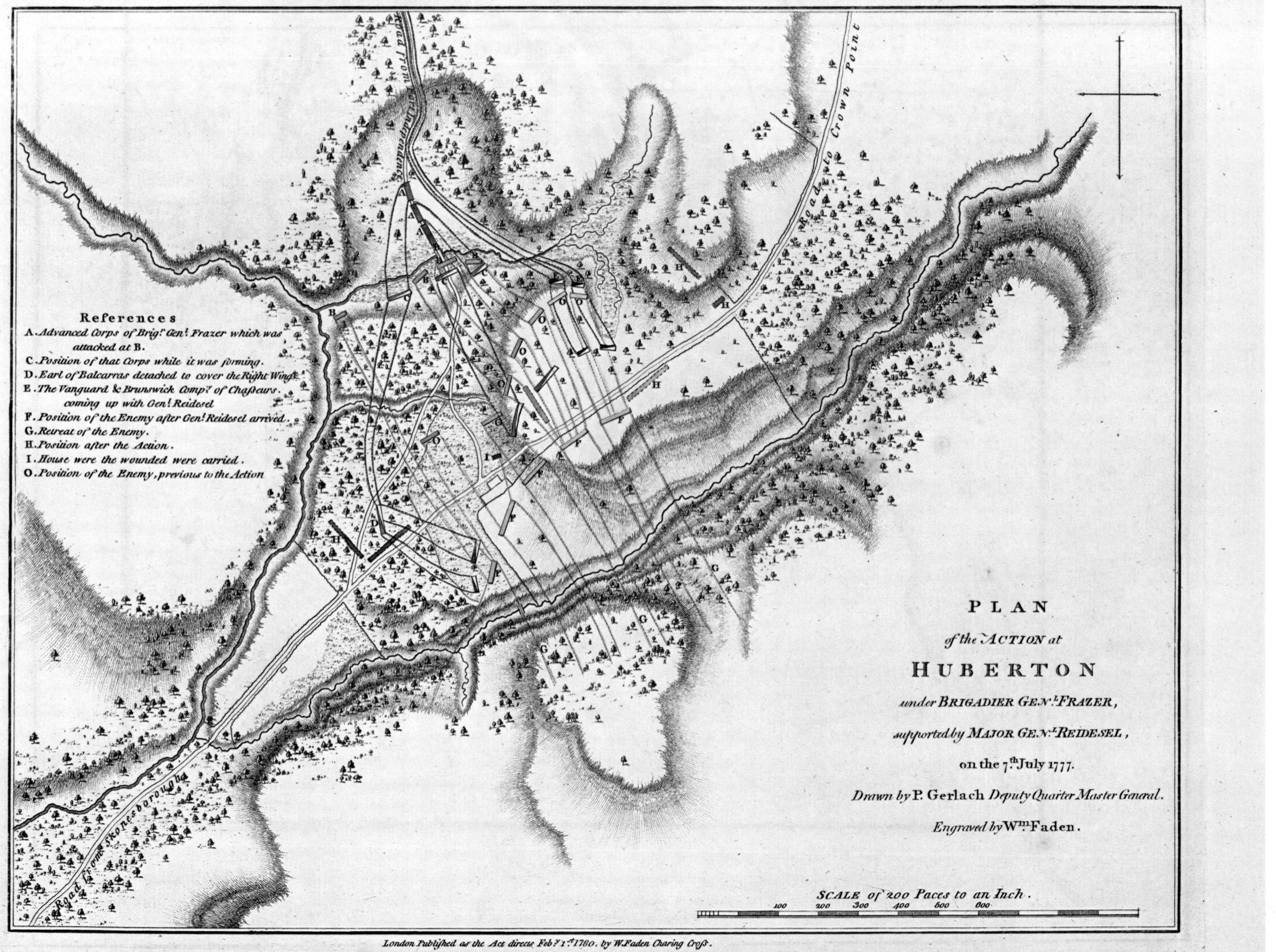

PLAN
of the ACTION at
HUBERTON
under BRIGADIER GEN.l FRAZER,
supported by MAJOR GEN.l REIDESEL,
on the 7.th July 1777.

Drawn by P. Gerlach Deputy Quarter Master General.

Engraved by Wm. Faden.

SCALE of 200 Paces to an Inch.

100   200   300   400   500   600
200   400   600   800

References

A. Advanced Corps of Brigr Genl Frazer which was
   attacked at B.
C. Position of that Corps while it was forming.
D. Earl of Balcarras detached to cover the Right Wing.
E. The Vanguard & Brunswick Compy of Chasseurs
   coming up with Genl Reidesel
F. Position of the Enemy after Genl Reidesel arrived.
G. Retreat of the Enemy.
H. Position after the Action.
I. House where the wounded were carried.
O. Position of the Enemy, previous to the Action

Road to Crown Point

Road from Fort Independence

London Published as the Act directs Feb.y 1.st 1780. by W.m Faden Charing Cross.

Disobeyed Orders at Hubbardton

MAP 18. ¶ After St. Clair's controversial evacuation of Fort Ticonderoga his army was still intact. Burgoyne had taken the legendary stronghold at minimal cost, but he had not destroyed the defending army. Seth Warner, the former hero of the Green Mountain Boys, headed the rear guard of St. Clair's Continental army. Had he followed his directions to consolidate the trailing regiments and bring them into the main camp at Castleton, a few miles farther south, the costly engagement at Hubbardton might have been avoided. ¶ General Simon Fraser's pursuing advance force, supported by a Hessian column under Baron von Riedesel, caught up with Warner's detachment, which in defiance of St. Clair's orders spent the night at Hubbardton. The action was intense, and most of Warner's men fought well. But a sweeping bayonet charge and the arrival of Riedesel's German troops, singing in chorus to their marching band, carried the day for the British. This was the only pitched battle fought in Vermont during the Revolution. ¶ Warner shortly redeemed himself in the important American victory at the Battle of Bennington. Vermont remembers him affectionately, and a highway named in his honor runs today from Manchester to Middlebury, right through the Hubbardton area. Simon Fraser later fought valorously at Saratoga, where he was mortally wounded; and Baron von Riedesel was to surrender with Burgoyne's army. ¶ This is a typical Faden battle plan. It presents clearly the positions and movements of the opposing units upon a topographical map, which enables the viewer to see where terrain features affected the action. Together with five of the six maps that follow, it was included in Burgoyne's apologia published after he returned to England.

SHOWN ON OPPOSITE PAGE
Plan of the Action at Huberton under Brigadier Genl. Frazer, supported by Major Genl. Reidesel, on the 7th July 1777. Drawn by P. Gerlach. Engraved by Wm. Faden. London, W. Faden, Feb. 1, 1780. (11" x 14½")

In: *Burgoyne, John. A State of the Expedition from Canada . . . London, 1780.*

the campaign of 1776. Seeking to close out the year on a positive note, he turned about and seized the remaining American post on Manhattan, Fort Washington, which Washington and Greene had thought able to withstand any assault. Howe sent Cornwallis over the Hudson to occupy Fort Lee on the Jersey shore, after which Cornwallis started after Washington, who had already traversed the Hudson and who now began his famous retreat through New Jersey toward the Delaware River. It was probably not so much Howe's intention to destroy Washington as it was his desire to remove him from New Jersey (where Howe intended to leave much of his army in winter garrisons) that prompted this undertaking. In any case, the Virginian was no match for Cornwallis, for he had left part of his own army in New York State to guard against a British stab up the Hudson or into New England. Neither the Americans nor the British proceeded at a very rapid pace; rains, muddy roads, and shortages of wagons slowed both armies. Collecting all the riverboats around Trenton, Washington fled across the Delaware to temporary safety in Pennsylvania on December 7. (*See Map 14*)

Had the Revolution reached its nadir? Conditions were definitely bleak, so depressing that Washington wrote his brother John Augustine on December 18 that if he did not receive new men, "I think the game is pretty near up." For the first time an entire American state, New Jersey, was in the hands of the enemy. All but 1,400 of his Continentals would serve out their enlistments on the last day of the year. But Washington, understandably given to unburdening his frustrations in private letters, did not mean what he had said. He already knew there were favorable straws in the wind. British efforts at pacification in New Jersey, feeble at best, had boomeranged in the face of confiscations and atrocities—particularly by German units—that royal officers later conceded candidly. And, as always was the case at the eleventh hour, new men *were* coming in, a few at a time, from here and there: a contingent from northern New Jersey minus their commander, Charles Lee, captured by a British patrol; a regiment from the Northern Department; and an assortment of militia and short-service volunteers.

If ever the cause needed a lift, it was now: to infuse fresh life into a people debilitated by the New York campaign and the loss of New Jersey; and to do so before the army unraveled from men returning home. Howe's widely scattered outposts in West Jersey were obvious targets. Trenton, held by Colonel Johann Gottlieb Rall's 1,400 Hessians, was the initial objective, after which Washington would play it by ear. While detached parties were to cross downstream to prevent the Bordentown garrison from hurrying to the relief of Rall, Washington's main force was to pass over the Delaware above Trenton and descend on the town from the north.

On Christmas night Colonel John Glover's regiment of ex-fishermen from Massachusetts manned forty-foot Durham boats normally used to transport grain and iron ore. By three o'clock in the morning they had safely carried the army through the churning, ice-filled stream to the Jersey side. Then the army set out on its nine-mile journey through wind, snow, and sleet. Many muskets became too wet to fire, but Washington had wisely brought along Colonel Henry Knox's artillery. While one wing of the army approached the town by a river road, another swung to the left and entered from almost the opposite direction, both columns overrunning unsuspecting outposts shortly after daybreak. Rall and his men had been drinking heavily and had retired for the night quite late.

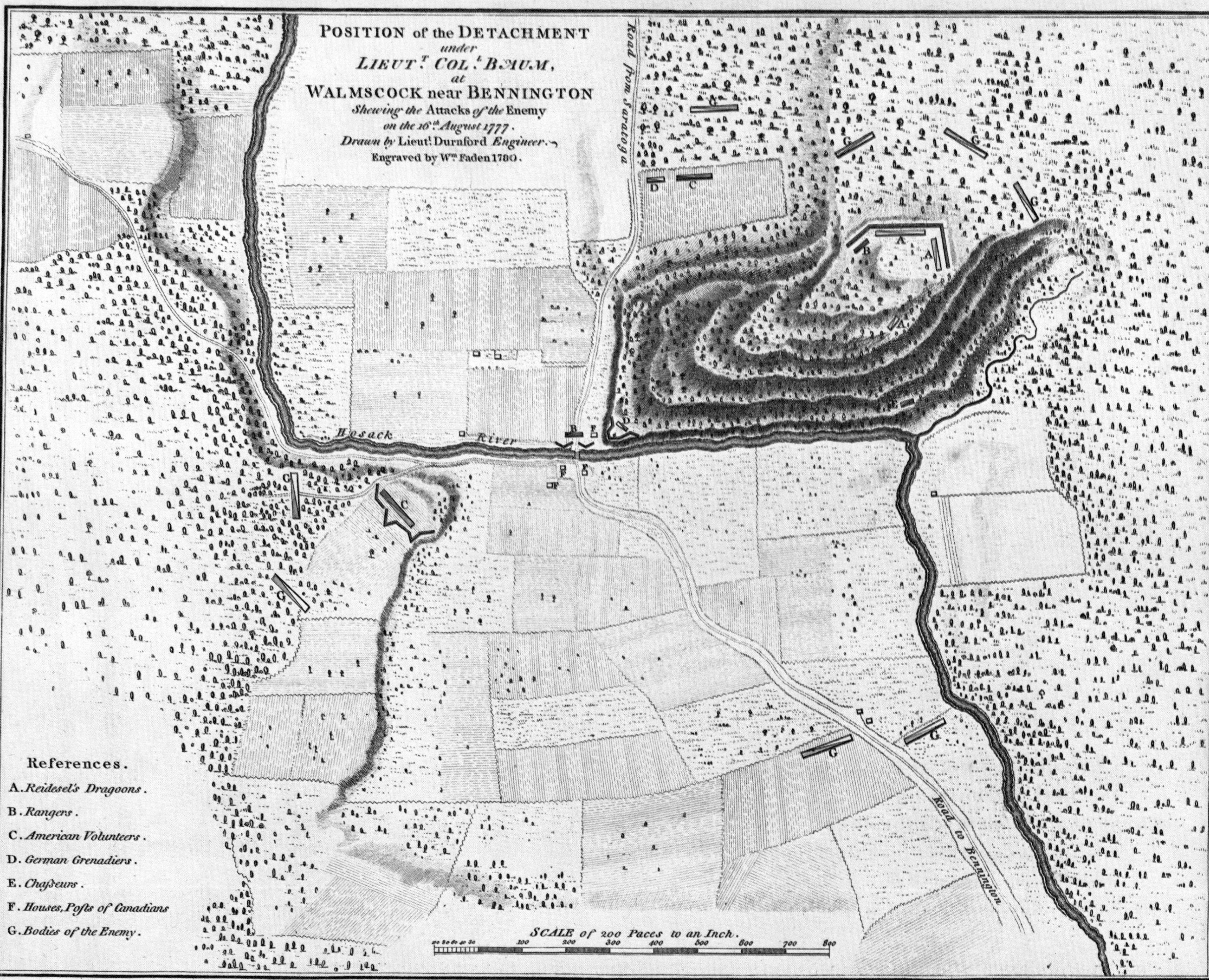

POSITION of the DETACHMENT
under
LIEUT. COL. BAUM,
at
WALMSCOCK near BENNINGTON
Shewing the Attacks of the Enemy
on the 16th August 1777.
Drawn by Lieut. Durnford Engineer.
Engraved by Wm. Faden 1780.

Road from Saratoga

Road to Bennington

Hosack River

References.

A. Reidesel's Dragoons.
B. Rangers.
C. American Volunteers.
D. German Grenadiers.
E. Chasseurs.
F. Houses, Poste of Canadians.
G. Bodies of the Enemy.

SCALE of 200 Paces to an Inch.
100 200 300 400 500 600 700 800

London Publish'd as the Act directs Feb.y 1.st 1780, by W. Faden, Charing Cross.

Fortune's Wheel
Takes A Turn

MAP 19. ¶ While not one of the largest battles of the war, Bennington was of great significance. It was born of Burgoyne's acute logistical problems that stemmed from the length of his line of communication from Canada. The raid was to have been a simple maneuver to enlist Tory support in the area and to procure the food, cattle, horses, and wagons that would enable the British expedition to promptly push through to Albany. ¶ Burgoyne sent a detachment of about 750 regular troops, half of them German, plus some 300 Tories, Canadians, and Indians. The brave but overconfident and stubborn commander of the Brunswick dragoons, Lieutenant Colonel Frederick Baum, led the operation. ¶ The affair was a monumental example of poor planning by Burgoyne. This, combined with the good fortune that favored the Americans, made Bennington a major British failure. Colonel John Stark happened to be nearby with 1,500 militia willing and able to fight. He was reinforced by the timely arrival of Seth Warner's regiment, which helped turn away Baum's tardy reinforcements of 650 Hessians led by Colonel von Breymann. Colonel Baum, who spoke no English, lost his life leading his dragoons in a great sword charge, attempting to break through Stark's encirclement. ¶ This engraving, somewhat schematic, shows the terrain where Stark annihilated Baum and denied Burgoyne his vital provisions. Of equal importance, Stark's victory raised the Americans' morale, which had reached a low point after the loss of Ticonderoga and the drubbing at Hubbardton. The word was soon afield that the feared Germans could be beaten.

SHOWN ON OPPOSITE PAGE
Position of the Detachment under Lieutt. Coll. Baum, at Walmscock near Bennington, Shewing the Attacks of the Enemy on the 16th August 1777. Drawn by Lieutt. Durnford. Engraved by Wm. Faden. London, W. Faden, Feb. 1, 1780. (10½″ x 13¾″)

In: *Burgoyne, John. A State of the Expedition from Canada . . . London, 1780.*

Washington crossed the Delaware River nine miles above Trenton in December 1776 to surprise and defeat Hessian troops in the city. This painting of the event is Thomas Sully's Passage of the Delaware.

Before Rall could arouse them and form an effective battle line, Knox's cannon were raking the town's principal thoroughfares. Rall's men never had a chance. Two hundred of them did escape on the Bordentown road, because Washington's detached parties were prevented by the elements from getting over the river. But thirty Germans were killed, including Rall, and over 900 were taken prisoner; Washington did not lose a man in action. (*See Map 15*)

It was a sparkling victory, and Washington returned to Pennsylvania to rest his weary men and to secure his prisoners. But not for long. Reports indicated that British garrisons in New Jersey were thrown into

a panic by Rall's debacle and that the militia of the state were taking heart and entering the field. Washington recrossed the Delaware and entered Trenton again on December 30. Addressing each regiment, he persuaded half the men whose enlistments were then expiring to give him another six weeks. He needed every one of them, for the commander in chief miscalculated the swiftness of the reaction of William Howe, who was spending the winter season comfortably in New York City, where his preference for the ladies, especially blonde, blue-eyed Mrs. Joshua Loring, wife of the British commissary of prisoners, was notorious. Would Sir William think it "proper to leave Mrs. Loring and face" his tormentors? asked a disgruntled English civilian in the city. No, but he wasted no time in sending Cornwallis. On January 2, His Lordship with 6,000 regulars rolled into Trenton to find Washington entrenched with his back to the Delaware. Cornwallis allegedly boasted of bagging "the fox" next morning, but daylight revealed that his animal was indeed a sly one.

Washington, slipping away in the night by a road leading south and then east, had swung around behind His Lordship and was rushing down the road to Princeton. There, after a brief but fierce contest, he sent three crimson regiments scattering in all directions. British losses in all categories were likely between 300 and 400, whereas Washington's were under 150.

At this point, the campaign of 1776—tardily according to the calendar—came to an end, not because Washington wished it, but because of forthcoming departures of Continentals and militia from his army. He

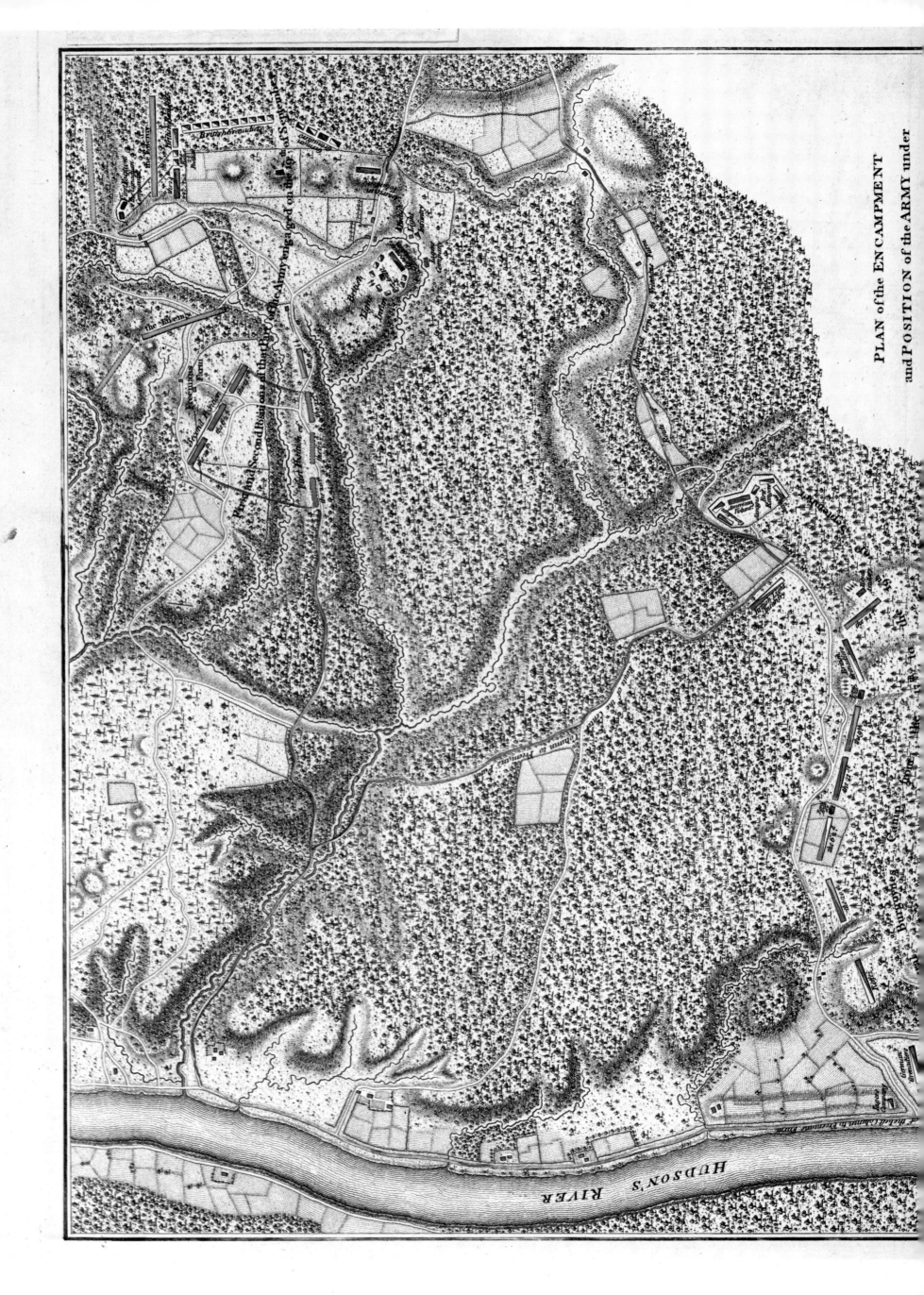

PLAN of the ENCAMPMENT
and POSITION of the ARMY under

HUDSON'S RIVER

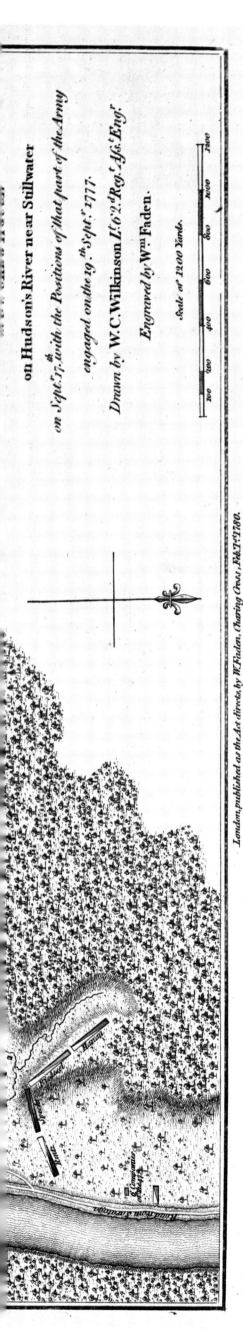

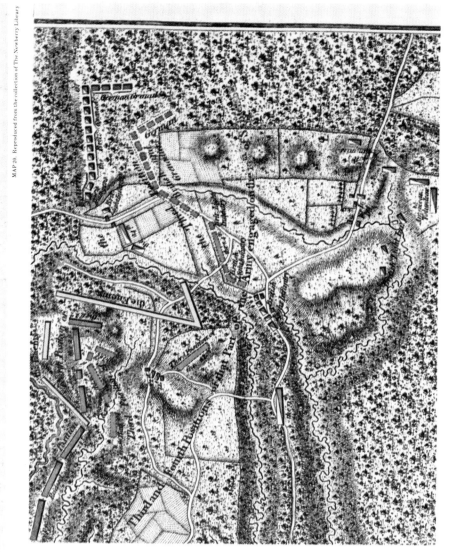

on Hudson's River near Stillwater

on Sept. 17, with the Positions of that part of the Army
engaged on the 19th Sept. 1777.

Drawn by W. C. Wilkinson Lt. 62d. Regt. As. Engr.

Engraved by Wm. Faden.

Scale of 1200 Yards.

London, published as the Act directs, by W. Faden, Charing Cross, Feb. 1st. 1780.

First Battle of Saratoga: The Gambler Sees His Odds Lengthening

MAP 20. ¶ Burgoyne's initially well-organized expedition had suffered two key reversals after a promising start at Ticonderoga. The western arm of the invasion, St. Leger's drive down the Mohawk, had been stopped by New York patriots and turned back by the ubiquitous Benedict Arnold. To the east there had been the disaster at Bennington, with significantly heavy losses. ¶ The British, having started confidently with 10,000 men in Burgoyne's army and 2,000 in St. Leger's, now numbered about 6,000. For the moment, Burgoyne could still field more troops than the Americans, but two factors were about to give the Americans the advantage. The British were straining precariously their line of communication with Canada, while at the same time, each British reversal drew enormous numbers of reinforcements into the American camp. Had Burgoyne retreated before Saratoga he might have returned to the St. Lawrence to fight another day. He eliminated this possibility when he moved his army across the Hudson. ¶ Variously referred to as the Battle of Sword's House, the first Battle of Freeman's Farm, Bemis Heights, Stillwater, or Saratoga, it was a violent encounter of some six hours' duration. Burgoyne's casualties were double those of General Gates's, but the British held the battlefield. ¶ This map, as well as Map 22, which depicts the second Battle of Saratoga, was taken by Faden directly from a very fine and large-scale survey, the manuscript of which is at the Library of Congress. (Note that north is at the bottom of these maps.) The cartographer was William Cumberland Wilkinson, a young engineer who was on the expedition. The map shows the positions before the battle, while the same area on the overlay gives the troop locations afterward.

Plan of the Encampment and Position of the Army under His Excelly. Lt. General Burgoyne at Swords House on Hudson's River near Stillwater on Septr. 17th, with the Positions of that part of the Army engaged on the 19th Septr. 1777. Drawn by W. C. Wilkinson. Engraved by Wm. Faden. London, W. Faden, Feb. 1, 1780. (12½" x 13¾")

In: *Burgoyne, John.* A State of the Expedition from Canada . . . *London, 1780.*

*The overlay appears at the end of the atlas for those who wish to hinge it to the main map as it was originally issued.

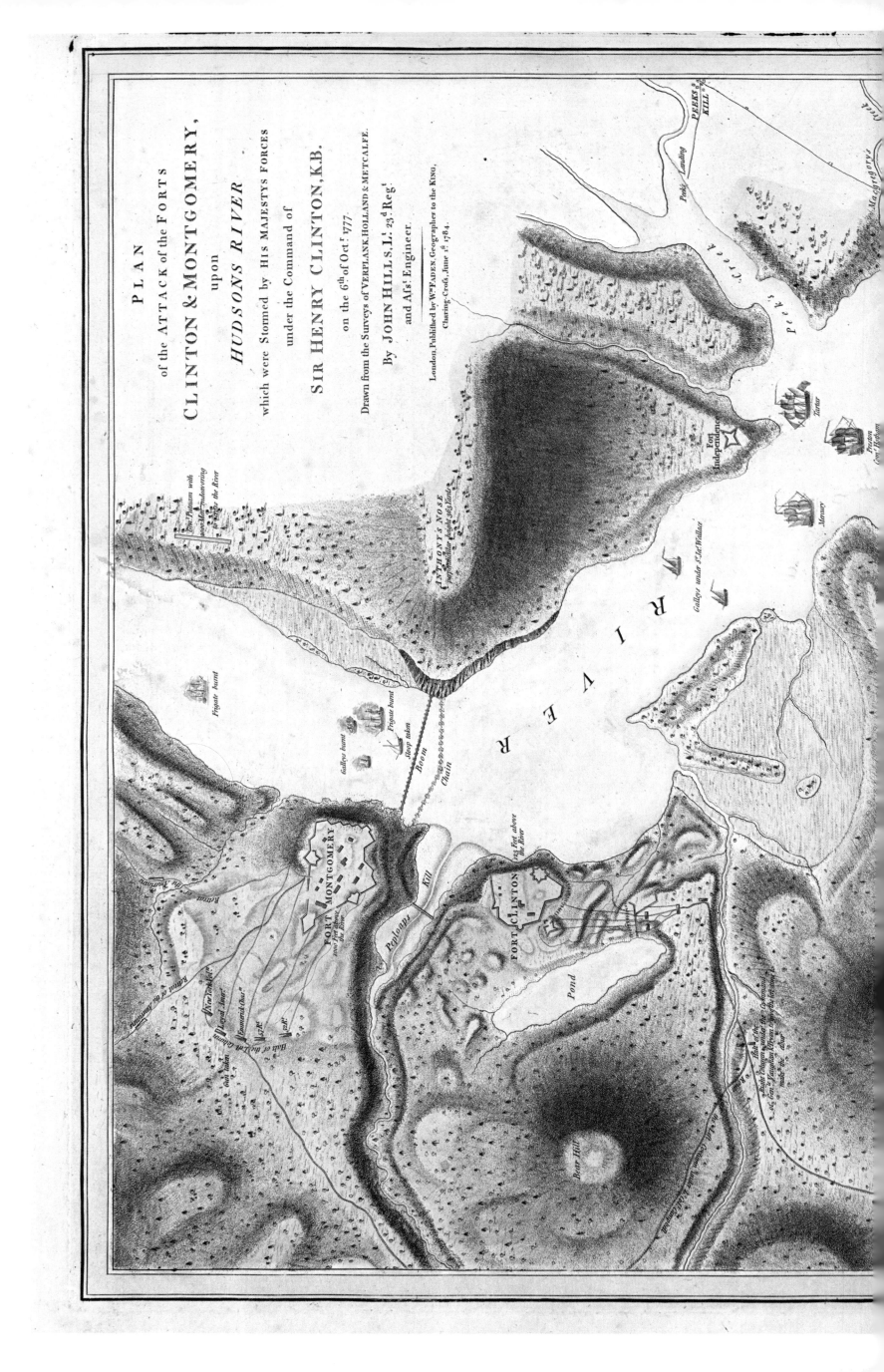

PLAN
of the ATTACK of the FORTS
CLINTON & MONTGOMERY,
upon
HUDSONS RIVER
which were Stormed by HIS MAJESTYS FORCES
under the Command of
SIR HENRY CLINTON, K.B.
on the 6th of Octr 1777.

Drawn from the Surveys of VERPLANK, HOLLAND & METCALFE.

By JOHN HILLS, Lt. 23d Regt.
and Asst. Engineer.

London, Published by Wm. Faden, Geographer to the King,
Charing-Cross, June 1st 1784.

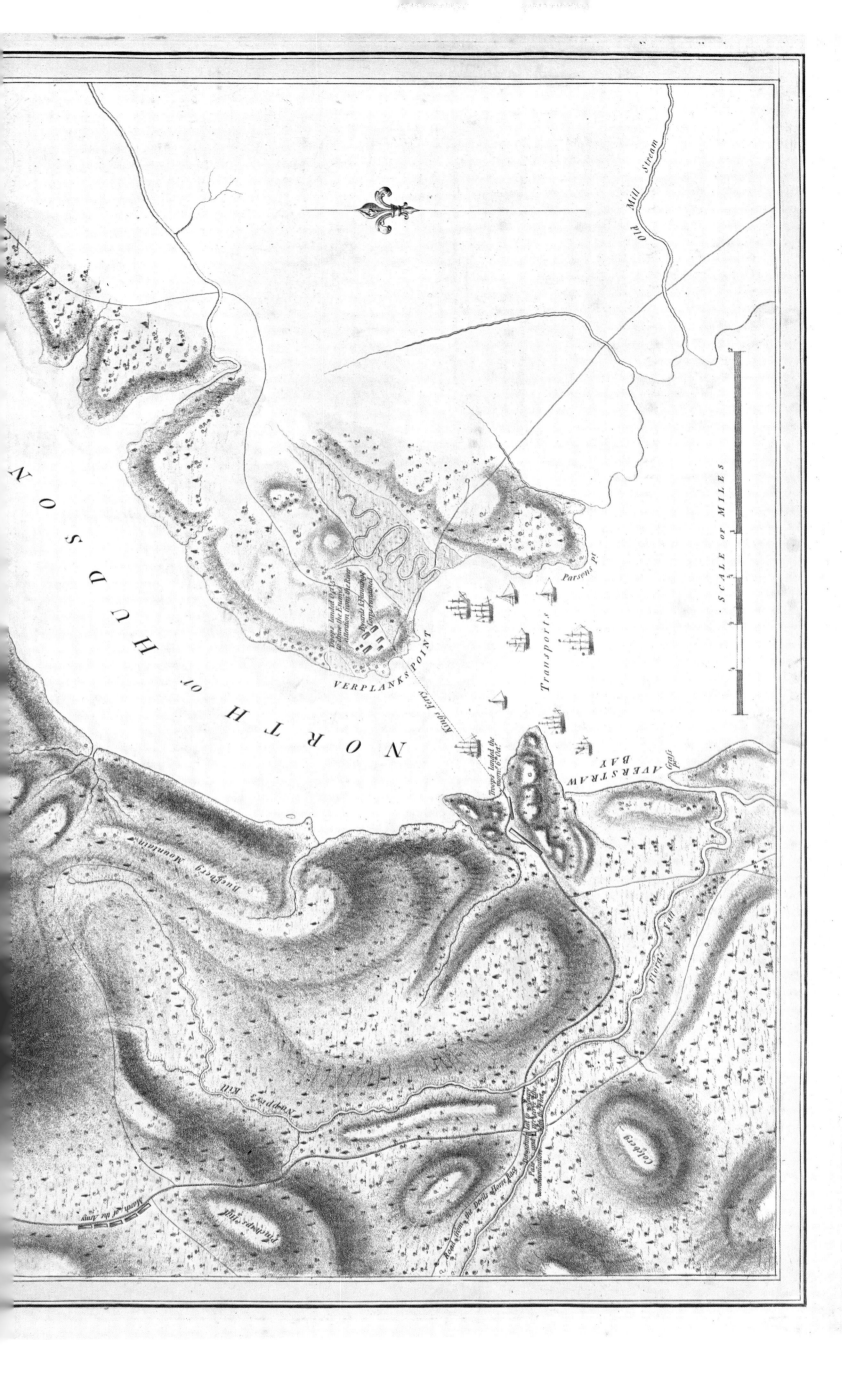

NORTH of HUDSON

Mill Stream

Old Stream

SCALE of MILES

Parsons pt.

Transports

VERPLANKS POINT

King's Ferry

AVERSTRAW BAY

Dunderberg Mountain

Kill

Timp Fall

Colsberg

March of the Army

Peekskill

A Very Limited Action in the Highlands

MAP 21. ¶ The complexities of Sir Henry Clinton's position at New York during the autumn of 1777 were considerable. General Howe had embarked for Philadelphia, leaving Clinton in charge with somewhat ambiguous orders, such as "act as occurrences direct." Burgoyne's early messages were so arrogant as to hardly inspire the assumption of great risk by Clinton. That tone changed after Bennington, St. Leger's retreat, the first Battle of Saratoga, and Brown's raid at Fort Ticonderoga. ¶ Before the American army was committed to Philadelphia, Clinton had feared an attack by General Washington on New York. Now reinforced by additional British and German troops from England, Clinton decided upon a limited action against the Hudson Highlands. This might have aided Burgoyne and worried General Gates at Saratoga, but would have committed Clinton neither too fully nor too far from New York City. ¶ It was a well-executed thrust, obviously conceived with accurate knowledge of the area and its defenses. Clinton began by landing at Verplank's Point, on the east end of King's Ferry (between today's towns of Peekskill and Croton), where he routed the garrison. He paused here long enough for Brigadier General Putnam to call for reinforcements from Forts Montgomery and Clinton, across the Hudson, before he crossed with 2,000 troops to attack those forts. ¶ The map shows the encircling actions made by the British through convoluted terrain to take the two forts from the rear, after landing at Stony Point. A frontal attack from the river would have been suicidal. Clinton sustained heavy losses, but was the victor. Howe's orders from Philadelphia for reinforcements forced the abandonment of the Highlands two weeks later. The thrust had done nothing real to relieve Burgoyne. However, it did strengthen the British position at the Saratoga Convention. John Hills, who prepared this map as well as several others in this atlas, was a lieutenant of engineers and one of the most talented of the topographical draftsmen in the British army. He served in America from 1778 until the end of the war, after which he remained in the United States as a commercial surveyor and draftsman.

SHOWN ON PRECEDING PAGE
Plan of the Attack of the Forts Clinton & Montgomery, upon Hudsons River which were Stormed by His Majestys Forces under the Command of Sir Henry Clinton, K.B. on the 6th of Octr. 1777. . . . By John Hills. London, Wm. Faqen, June 1, 1784. (26¼" x 20½")

withdrew to rugged positions in the hills about Morristown to spend the winter, while Cornwallis soon withdrew to New York, leaving outposts only at New Brunswick and Amboy. Britain's two-pronged strategy for 1776 had achieved mixed results. If Carleton had failed to penetrate the north country and connect with Howe, the latter officer had taken New York City. But that was a far cry from Germain's objective of bringing Washington to a decisive battle and ending the revolt. The Howe brothers' endeavors as peace commissioners had fared no better. The closest that they had come was to get Congress to send three of its members—Benjamin Franklin, John Adams, and Edward Rutledge—to talk unofficially with Admiral Howe to discover if he really had any significant powers to negotiate. The emissaries enjoyed the admiral's claret and mutton, but not his admission that he could do nothing until the colonies laid down their arms. As one British onlooker remarked, "They met, they talked, they parted. And now nothing remains but to fight it out."

For British strategists and policymakers in London and New York City, the winter months were spent not only in the customary revelries but also in planning the campaign of 1777. Once again, the focus would be on subduing the northern states, where Britain's land forces were already in a position to renew activities. There would be no southern sideshow this time similar to the Clinton-Parker expedition. In 1777, more would be expected of the Canadian-based army than before, because it would not first of all have to clear Quebec of rebels as in the previous year. Furthermore, it would be beefed up numerically, and it would have a new commander, supposedly more bold and enterprising than Carleton. He was Major General John Burgoyne, who had served under Carleton in 1776, and who, subsequently on leave in London, had missed no opportunity to knife his former chief.

Did Burgoyne and Howe agree that they should attempt to duplicate the plan of 1776, which contemplated a union of the two armies on the Hudson for a combined operation against New England? It seemed like such an apparent course of action that Americans assumed it would be the basis of the campaign, as did many in England. It was so obvious in fact that several generations of American historians were erroneously led to that conclusion, with the help—it may be added—of Burgoyne's testimony afterward somewhat to that effect in Parliament. But before the campaign opened and before Burgoyne lied to pull his chestnuts from the fire, he exuded confidence that his main army could plunge down the line of rivers and lakes from the Richelieu to the Hudson where, near Albany, it could link up with a smaller diversionary column he proposed to send southward by way of Oswego and the Mohawk River.

For his part, General Howe, now Sir William, seemed uncertain of what he wished to do, thereby reinforcing the web of theories about his motives and those of his brother. Perhaps they still hoped to resolve the conflict through their good offices as peace commissioners; and/or perhaps Sir William was becoming increasingly doubtful of the ability of Britain to achieve a military triumph in an exhausting land war. In any case, Howe bombarded Germain with four different plans in five months (November 1776–April 1777). In substance, they showed only marginal interest in the Canadian army, possibly because Howe, like other British generals, did not buy the idea of being yoked to the fortunes of another commander, in this instance an aggressive, glory-seeking kind of man who already had done his bit to tarnish the reputations of Gage and Carleton. Howe, though he kept shifting the details, had no desire to move any great distance from the coastline, to probe the interior as Burgoyne was about to do; and here he may have been influenced by his brother, the admiral, whose fleet would be of service. His objective became Philadelphia, and after dropping the notion of taking that city by a march through New Jersey, he notified Germain in his fourth plan that he would go by sea.

In the final analysis, neither Howe nor Burgoyne had corresponded with the other about the campaign—each would handle his own affairs! At best, Howe indicated that the garrison he would leave behind at New York under Clinton might be able to give Burgoyne limited assistance in opening the lower Hudson. As for Germain (who found that the exertions of 1776 could not be repeated, that only modest reinforcements were available for America), he eventually expressed his concern about the two armies operating in separate theaters with no coordination or cooperation; but the fault was more his than his generals, for he had sanctioned the campaign and had failed to give it a unifying concept.

To cope with Howe, Washington had assembled his annual new army of spring recruits sprinkled with returning veterans and militiamen. After Sir William advanced into New Jersey, possibly to determine Washington's intentions, he withdrew to New York and boarded his troops on transports. Both Clinton, who remained behind, and Colonel Charles Stuart thought the seaborne move to Philadelphia to be absurd since, among other things, it would deprive Howe of any intelligence of the Burgoyne campaign. On July 23, the armada cleared New York, put in

General Horatio Gates, having prepared an entrenched position on Bemis Heights near Albany, was joined by a flow of militiamen that swelled his force to over 6,000 men. General Burgoyne attempted to move against Gates but was held in check for three weeks. The British retreated to Saratoga.

briefly at Delaware Bay, and then, to the astonishment of many officers, returned to sea, not to unload its human cargo until it reached the head of Chesapeake Bay, even farther from Philadelphia, which was now fifty-seven miles away.

Washington, amazed at Howe's desertion of Burgoyne, had pressed southward with 11,000 men. After learning of the British landing and the direction of Howe's advance, he positioned his army astride Brandywine Creek, at Chad's Ford, to parry his opponent's obvious thrust at Philadelphia. The battle that opened on September 11 bore a striking resem-

Lord Howe's fleet sailed for Philadelphia in July 1777 with thirty-six battalions. In October 1777, General Burgoyne surrendered to Gates at Saratoga.

Second Battle of Saratoga: Burgoyne Walks Into Trouble

MAP 22. ¶ Gates had withdrawn his army to his well-chosen and strongly fortified position at Bemis Heights after the first Battle of Saratoga. He was content to make Burgoyne come to him as he sat athwart the way to Albany. ¶ Nineteen days later the British started somewhat tentatively to advance, and Gates counterattacked on both flanks. The second Battle of Saratoga had begun. The American commanders, Dan Morgan and Enoch Poor, took advantage of the irregular and heavily wooded terrain. The British were forced to retreat toward their defensive works. The battle might have ended at that, but again Benedict Arnold took to the field and led furious attacks on the two British redoubts, forcing the British off the battlefield and northward up the Hudson. ¶ William Faden engraved the maps of this campaign to accompany Burgoyne's published defense of his command, adding the overlays which interpret the secondary positions of the forces. These careful and detailed maps of the two battles of Saratoga have south at the top.

Plan of the Encampment and Position of the Army under His Excelly. Lt. General Burgoyne at Braemus Heights on Hudson's River near Stillwater, on the 20th Septr. with the Position of the Detachment &c. in the Action of the 7th of Octr. & the Position of the Army on the 8th Octr. 1777. Drawn by W. C. Wilkinson. Engraved by Wm. Faden. London, W. Faden, Feb. 1, 1780. (13½" x 14¼")

In: *Burgoyne, John.* A State of the Expedition from Canada... London, 1780

* The overlay appears at the end of the atlas for those who wish to hinge it to the main map as it was originally issued.

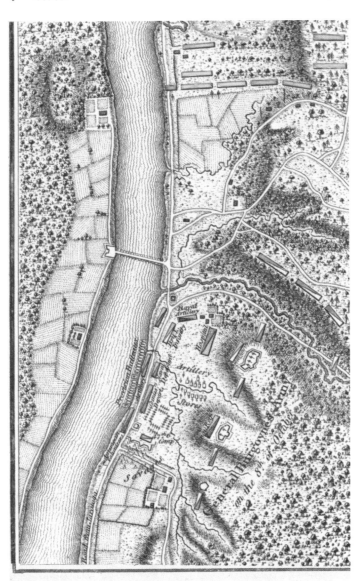

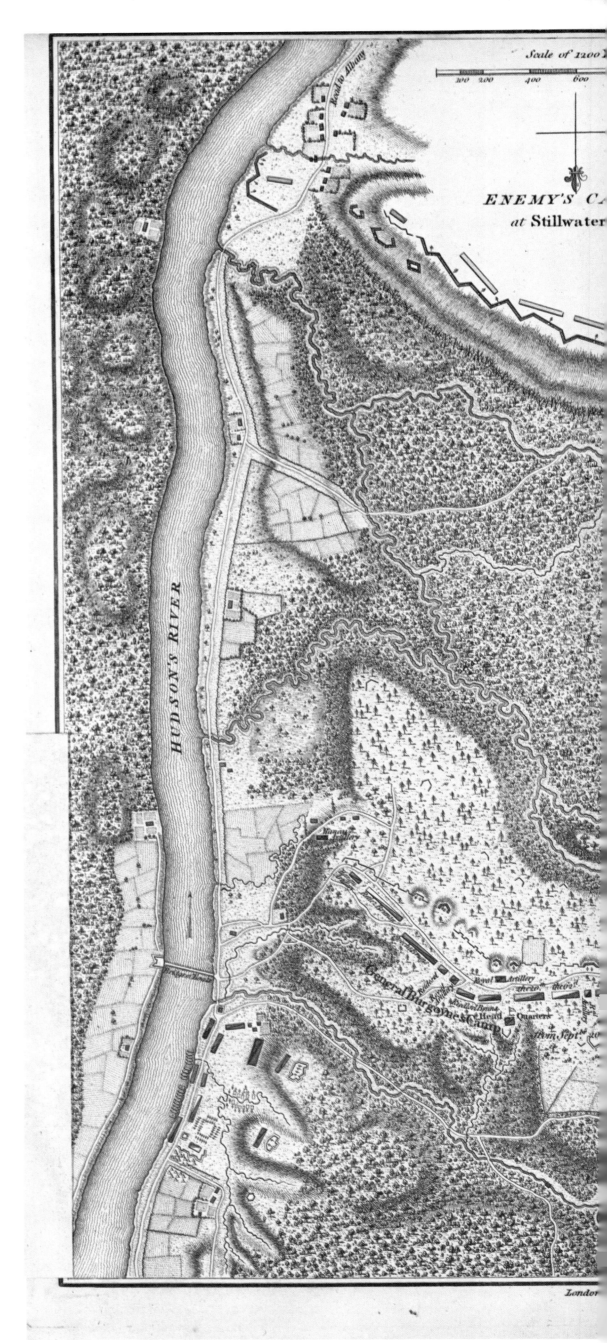

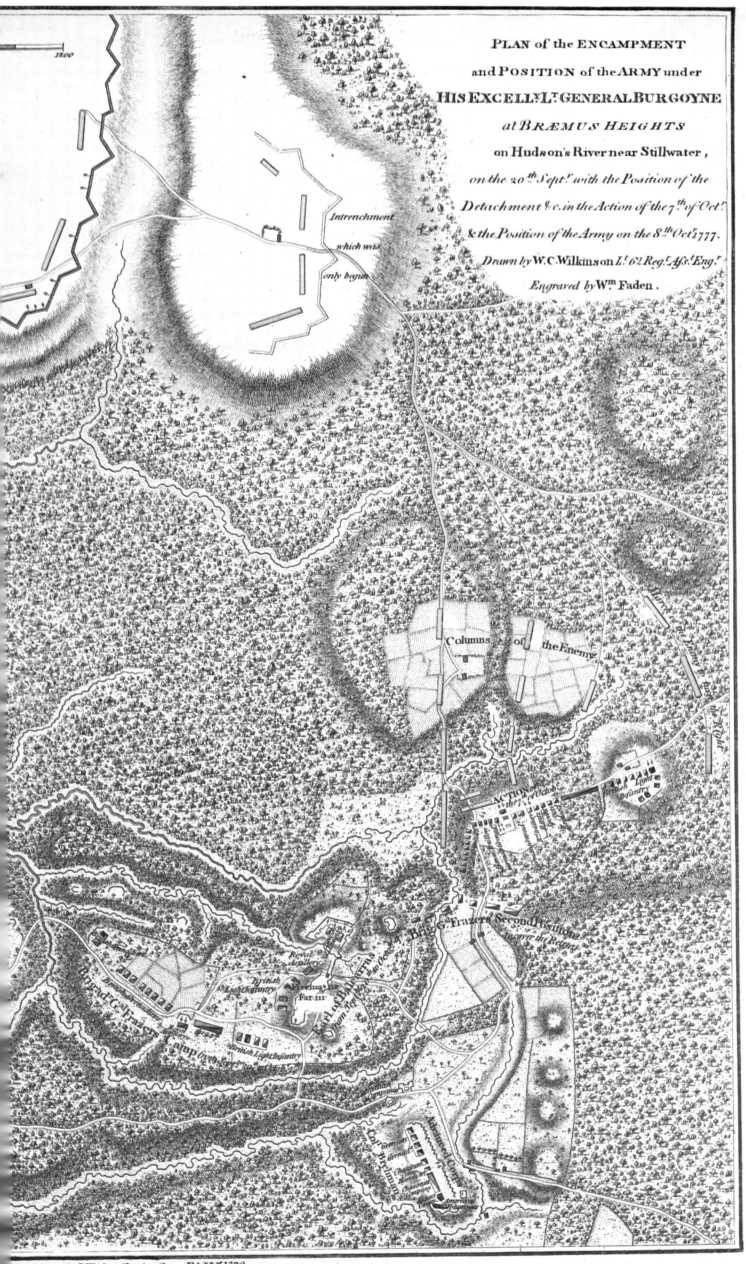

PLAN of the ENCAMPMENT
and POSITION of the ARMY under
HIS EXCELL.Y L.T GENERAL BURGOYNE
at BRÆMUS HEIGHTS
on Hudson's River near Stillwater,
on the 20.th Sept.r with the Position of the
Detachment &c. in the Action of the 7.th of Oct.r
& the Position of the Army on the 8.th Oct.r 1777.
Drawn by W. C. Wilkins on L.t 62 Reg.t Ass.t Eng.r
Engraved by W.m Faden.

Intrenchment
which was
only begun

Columns of the Enemy

Action of the Woods

Brig.r Gen.l Frazer's Second Position
during the Retreat

Royal
Artillery

British
Light Infantry

Germans

Freyman's
Farm

Plot of Balcarras

Gap from Fort

Dutch Light Infantry

Col. Breyman's

As the Act directs by W. Faden, Charing Cross, Feb.y 1.st 1780.

The Dramatist-General Gives Up One Profession

MAP 23. ¶ The second Battle of Saratoga spelled the end of Burgoyne's grand design. Thoroughly battered by the combination of Gates's cautious but sound strategy and the bold field leadership of Benedict Arnold, Dan Morgan, Enoch Poor, and Henry Dearborn, the British expedition was terminated at Saratoga on October 17, 1777. ¶ General Simon Fraser, Sir Francis Clarke, Colonel von Breymann, and Major Aclund were dead, and Burgoyne's dwindling army had suffered 600 more casualties in the second battle. Colonel John Brown's Ticonderoga raid in September had virtually severed the return route to Canada and Burgoyne's Bennington nemesis, John Stark, occupied the road north from Saratoga. This major turning point in the Revolution contributed strongly to France's entry into the war as America's first European ally, and in the long run assured the success of the rebel cause. ¶ Burgoyne bargained well with Gates for terms. Neither side knew what if anything would come of Clinton's Hudson River expedition and both were initially satisfied with the final terms of the Saratoga Convention. ¶ Burgoyne continued censuring his superior officers and colleagues; aside from that he was through as a general. He continued to write plays however; his drama "The Heiress" was published in 1786. ¶ The map, oriented with north at the right, shows the British units camped on high ground just to the north of Fish Kill. Farther north are the Hessian and Canadian troops. Gates's main army can be seen on the south bank of Fish Kill. Dan Morgan's riflemen appear to the north and west of the British camp.

Plan of the Position which the Army under Lt. Genl. Burgoine took at Saratoga on the 10th of September 1777, and in which it remained till the Convention was signed. Engraved by Wm. Faden. London, Wm. Faden, Feb. 1, 1780. (8¾" x 19")

In: Burgoyne, John. A State of the Expedition from Canada... London, 1780

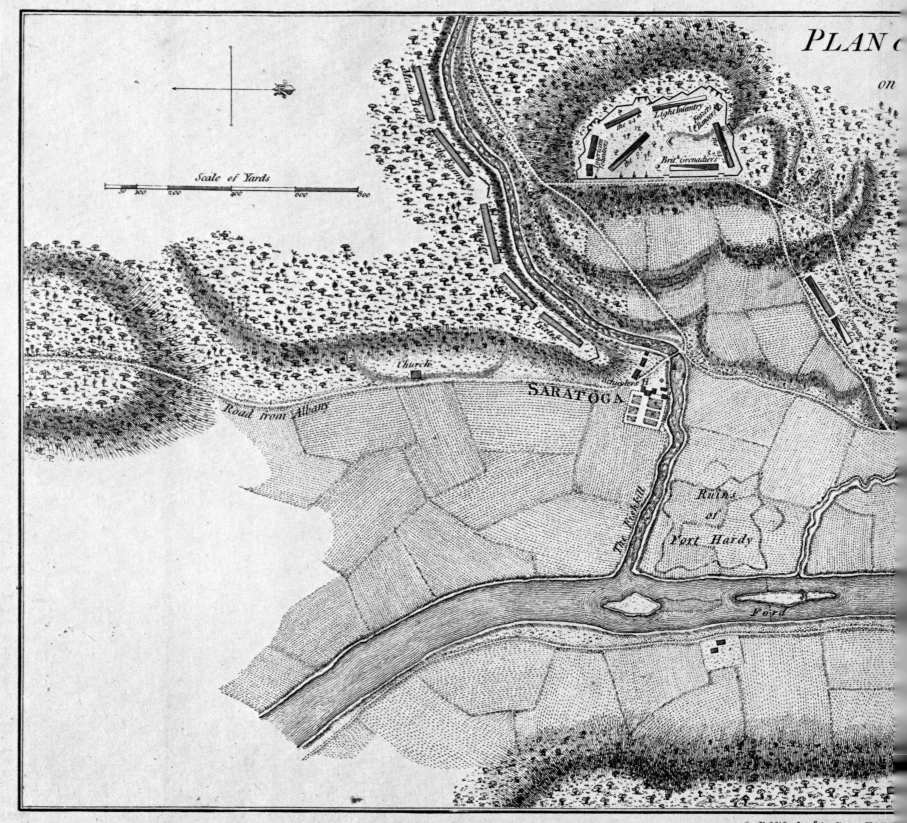

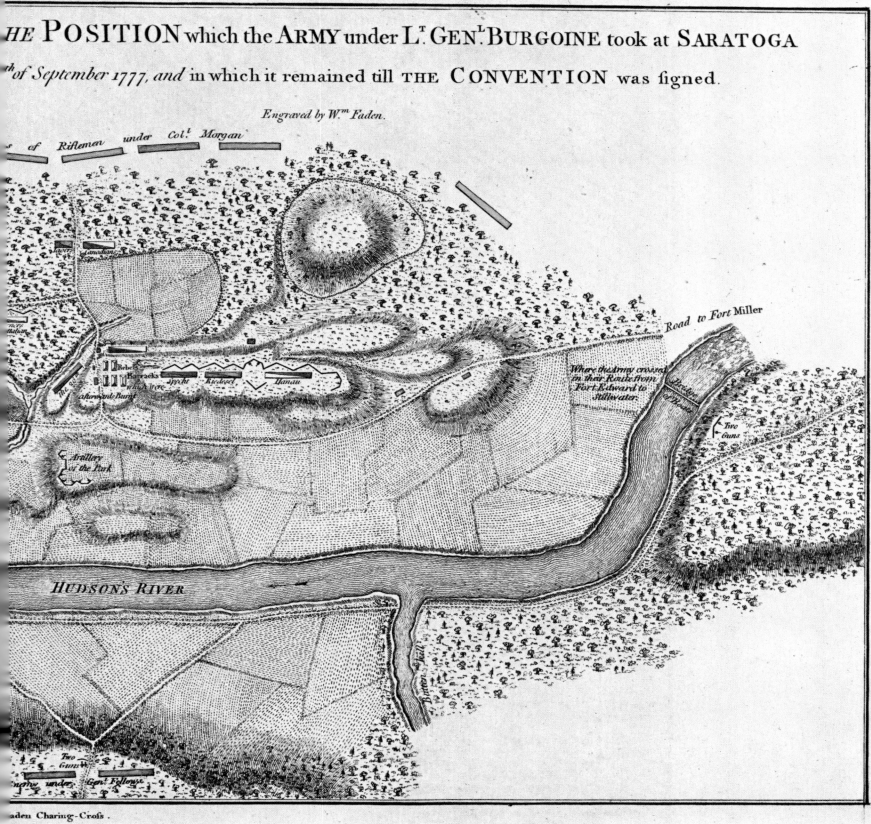

HE POSITION which the ARMY under Lr. Genl. BURGOINE took at SARATOGA

th of September 1777, and in which it remained till THE CONVENTION was signed.

Engraved by Wm. Faden.

s of Riflemen under Coll. Morgan

Road to Fort Miller

Where the Army crossed in their Route from Fort Edward to Stillwater

Two Guns

Artillery of the Park

HUDSON'S RIVER

Two Guns

aden Charing-Crofs.

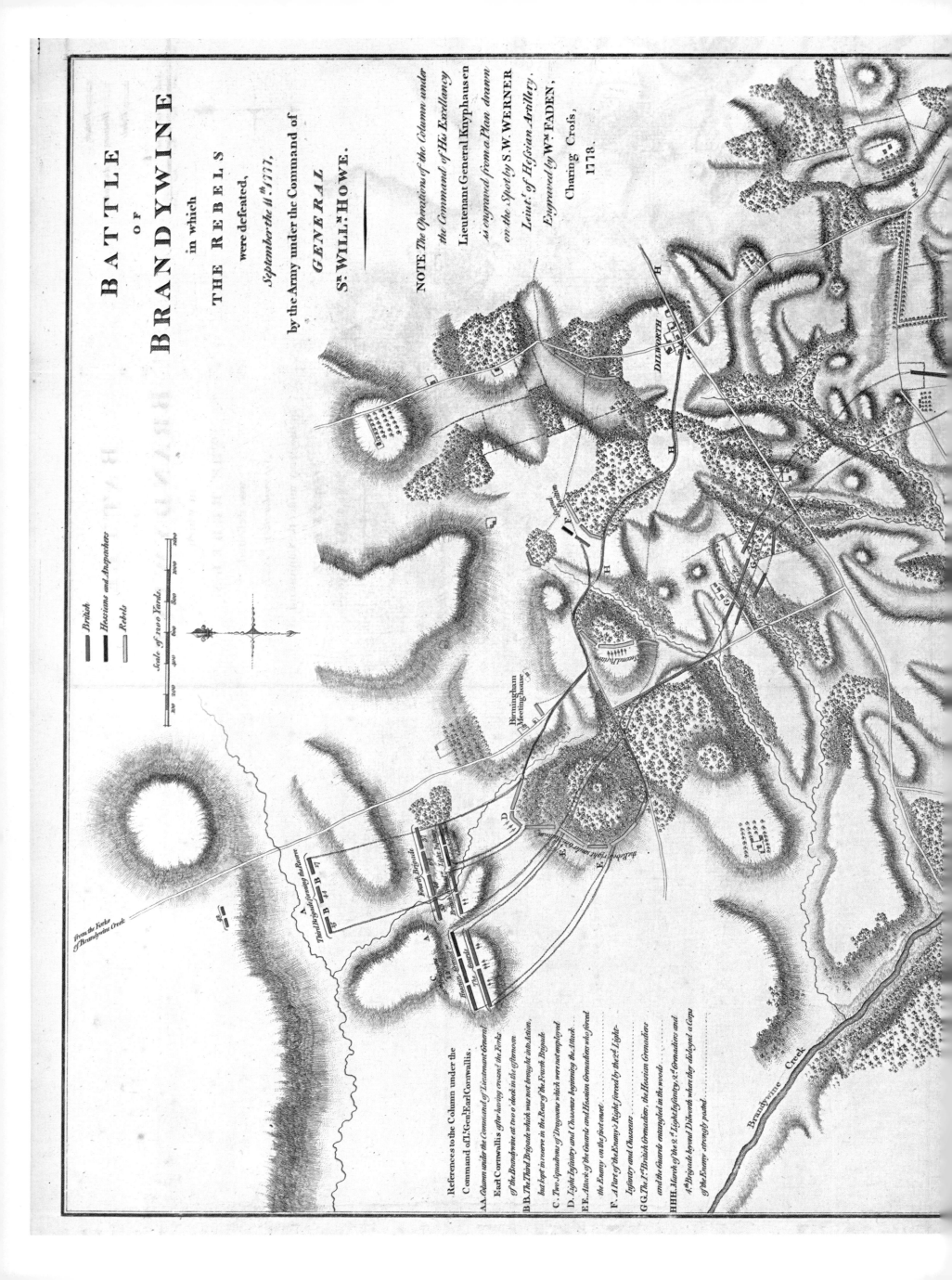

BATTLE
OF
BRANDYWINE

in which
THE REBELS
were defeated,

September the 11th 1777,

by the Army under the Command of

GENERAL
Sr WILLm HOWE.

NOTE. *The Operations of the Column under
the Command of His Excellancy
Lieutenant General Knyphausen
is engraved from a Plan drawn
on the Spot by S. W. WERNER,
Lieut.t of Hessian Artillery.
Engraved by Wm FADEN,
Charing Crofs,
1778.*

British
Hessians and Anspachers
Rebels

Scale of 1200 Yards.

from the Forks
of Brandywine Creek

Birmingham
Meeting house

DILWORTH

Second Brigade

the British right under the

The Guards

Fourth Brigade

Third Brigade forming the Reserve

Brandywine Creek

References to the Column under the
Command of Lt Genl Earl Cornwallis.

A A. *Column under the Command of Lieutenant General
Earl Cornwallis after having crossed the Forks
of the Brandywine at two o'clock in the afternoon.*

B B. *The Third Brigade which was not brought into Action,
but kept in reserve in the Rear of the Fourth Brigade.*

C. *Two Squadrons of Dragoons which were not employed.*

D. *Light Infantry and Chasseurs beginning the Attack.*

E E. *Attack of the Guards and Hessian Grenadiers who forced
the Enemy on the first onset.*

F. *A Part of the Enemy's Right forced by the 2d Light-
Infantry and Chasseurs.*

G G. *The 1st British Grenadiers, the Hessian Grenadiers
and the Guards entangled in the woods.*

H H H. *March of the 2d Light Infantry, 2d Grenadiers and
4th Brigade beyond Dilworth where they dislodged a Corps
of the Enemy strongly posted.*

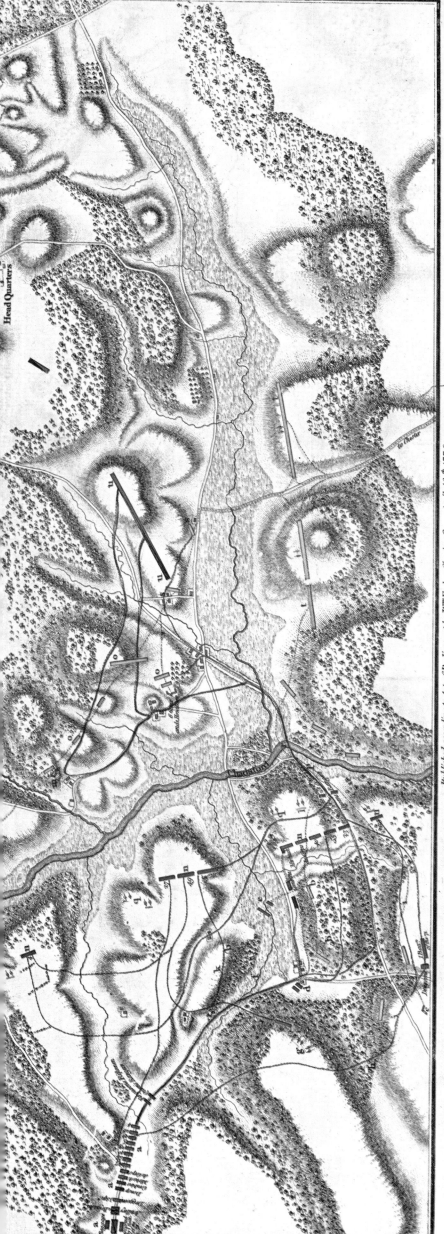

Published according to Act of Parliament by W.m Faden, Charing Cross, April 13.th 1778.

References to the Column under the Command of His Excellency Lieut.t Gen.l Knyphausen.

a . Column under the Command of His Excellency Lieutenant General Knyphausen, in march at 9 in the morning, he Van having drove back the Rebel Detachments which attempted to defend the Defile, from Welch Tavern to the Heights of Chadsford . . . .
b b . Heights and Woods occupied by the Rebels.   c . Small Works raised by D.o
d . The British Riflemen posted behind a House and supported by 100 men of Gen.l Stirn's Brigade. . . . .

e . The Queens Rangers pursuing the Enemy dislodged from the Wood x . . . . . .
g . Four Pieces of Cannon with the 40.th Reg.t to support the Attack of the Advanced Troops and the 28.th Reg.t who crossed the Valley 'h. to get to the Height i. which the Enemy abandon'd at their approach as well as the Fleche e . . . .
k . March of the Troops to take the Positions which was done under the Fire of Cannon in l and under that of the Enemy in m m . . . .

n n n . Position of the Column, from 4 after ten in the morning till four in the afternoon when Gen.l Howe made his Attack on the other side of the Brandywine Creek near Dilworth.. The Position of the Rebels was m . . that after some Resistance than in o o o o.
p . March of the Troops to the Ford under the Fire of the Cannon q. The Enemy fired from their Batteries m m . . . .
r . Ford where the Troops crossed the Creek and Charged the Enemy who at first opposed them with some resolution, but soon gave way. The Rifleman & Queens Rangers with the 71.st the 4.th and the 5.th followed by all the British Regiments and by Gen.l Starn's Brigade, forced the Enemy to abandon their Batteries m . . that after some Resistance near the House s s so to retreat t t, from which position they fired upon the Troops with four Pieces of Cannon. The Rebels afterwards retreated to Chester, the Right forming their escape and saved them from pursuit ... L.t Gen.l Knyphausens Column having joined General Howe remained in the position u u.

Long Island Repeated

MAP 24. ¶ It is just possible that Washington's serious defeat at Brandywine could have been avoided if he had had the aid of an accurate large-scale map, with additional copies for his field commanders, of the topographically complex area. There was confusion in the frantic field dispatches to and from the command post regarding place-names and terrain features. Even this detailed engraving, published the following spring, while helpful for tracing the troop positions and movements, does not master the course of the Brandywine and its tributaries and fords. ¶ Washington fielded an army in defense of Philadelphia that was not significantly inferior in size to the combined British-Hessian army. The Americans took up positions along the Brandywine. General Greene covered Chadds Ford; the militia were downstream to Greene's left; and John Sullivan guarded the fords upstream, with Stirling in reserve. ¶ Despite the lesson of the Battle of Long Island, Sullivan allowed Cornwallis to outmaneuver him by taking his column far to the northwest and crossing above the forks of the Brandywine. The British then were able to attack from the north and rout the Americans. Greene saved the army from annihilation by covering the retreat. General Howe was virtually in Philadelphia.

Battle of Brandywine in which the Rebels were defeated, September the 11th 1777, by the Army under the Command of General Sr. Willm. Howe. London, Wm. Faden, April 13, 1778. (19¼" x 17¼")

Mad Anthony's Nightmare

blance to Howe's victory on Long Island. For the British general again sent men forward as if to engage fully the American center, this time the Anglo-German push being directed by Lieutenant General Baron Wilhelm von Knyphausen; but, once again, it was primarily a feint, since Cornwallis had swung out in a wide half-circle so as to come in behind the American right. The parallel to Long Island was complete, because here, too, the victim was New Hampshire's John Sullivan, holding that end of the American line. When Cornwallis suddenly crashed down upon him, Sullivan saw his ranks crumble. Only an extraordinary effort by Nathanael Greene—cutting across four miles of broken country in fifty minutes with Virginia Continentals—averted a total disaster. While Greene held off Cornwallis and allowed Sullivan's remnants to filter through, Washington pulled back to Chester, his casualties in all categories reaching 1,000, twice the number of Howe's. (*See Map 24*)

If Washington and his lieutenants had been outgeneraled a second time, they scarcely allowed that fact to intimidate them, for soon after Howe moved on into Philadelphia, the Virginian struck him at night. (Did visions of Trenton and Princeton dance through his head?) This time, however, Washington did more than assault a garrison the size of Colonel Rall's at Trenton. On October 3, he went at the British advance post at Germantown, where Sir William had encamped about 9,000 men, the major part of his army. Though Washington's basic idea was militarily sound (there were few enemy outer defenses), his plan—four columns striking at different points in the darkness—was too complicated for the many inexperienced officers and men in the Continental army. Washington and Howe each suffered about the same losses they had sustained a few weeks earlier at Brandywine. Yet Howe was paying a price in men he could ill-afford, and Washington, after both Pennsylvania encounters, replenished his own depleted ranks. (*See Map 28*)

While Washington wanted still another round, Sir William, convinced the war would not be won in 1777, had no stomach for more indecisive bloodletting. He turned his attention to overrunning rebel fortifications along the Delaware River, finding as always in this war that victory exacted a heavy price; the capture of Fort Mercer cost him half his combined casualties at Brandywine and Germantown, along with one of Admiral Howe's ships of the line. General Howe now settled in for a winter at Philadelphia, with an endless round of social events—a weekly ball, suppers, music parties, and plays, the highlight being the celebration of the queen's birthday, which included salutes from the naval vessels, a dinner on board the *Eagle*, a supper and ball in town for two hundred ladies and gentlemen. It all contrasted sharply with the dreary scene twenty-five miles away in the desolate hills around Valley Forge, where the Continental army went through its annual agony of disintegration and rebirth. Under the facade of eighteenth-century formality, however, the Howes were unhappy men. They resigned their commissions as commanders in chief and peace delegates. They had failed, and they knew it, though they found it convenient to blame others, especially Germain in London for failing to provide more extensively for their military needs. (*See Maps 26, 27, 29*)

While William Howe won Pyrrhic victories in Pennsylvania and occupied a city whose strategic value was minimal, Burgoyne met with unmitigated disaster. Of course all began well, as was almost invariably true of British campaigning in the Revolution. The long procession of canoes and other craft glided down Lake Champlain in June 1777, carry-

MAP 25. ¶ After his victory at Brandywine, Howe started north to Philadelphia, while General Washington followed at a distance. ¶ Another American disappointment came when Anthony Wayne's division of 1,500 men and four cannon waited in ambush to attack Howe's flank or, failing that, to seize his baggage train. The British learned of Wayne's plan and his location. Cornwallis sent General Grey on a daring night raid against the Americans. With an advance guard of light infantry and two regiments, Grey moved silently and struck at midnight. Wayne lost 150 men in the bayonet attack at his bivouac, south of the Lancaster-Philadelphia road. ¶ The British camp at Trudruffrin is shown on the map, with the quarters of Lord Cornwallis and General Wilhelm von Knyphausen and their brigades. The line of march is indicated, as is the disorderly departure of Wayne's troops, who managed to rescue their cannon.

SHOWN ON OPPOSITE PAGE
British Camp at Trudruffrin from the 18th to the 21st of September 1777. with the Attack made by Major General Grey against the Rebels near White Horse Tavern. on the 20th of September. London, W. Faden, July 1, 1778. (10¼" x 16¼")

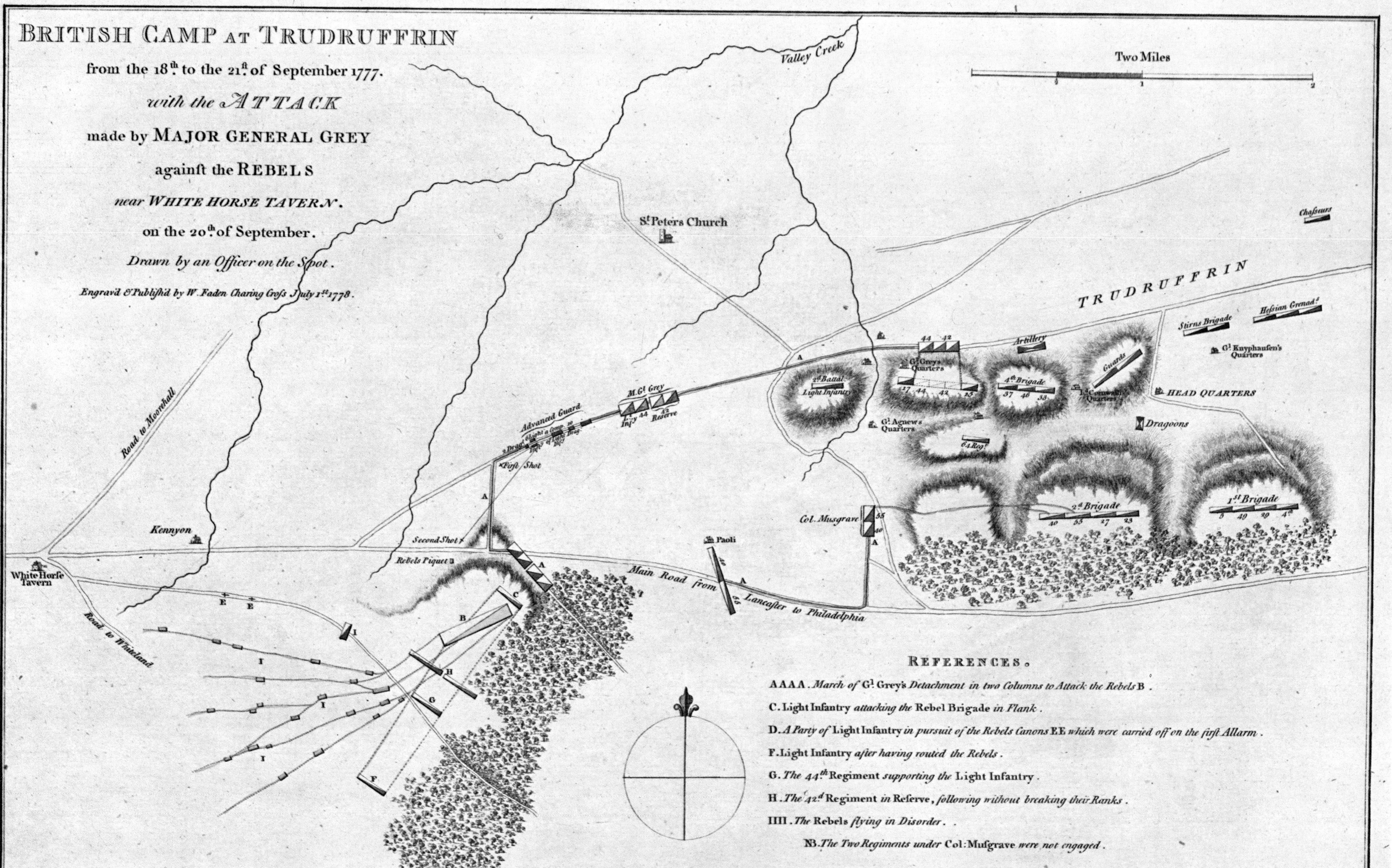

BRITISH CAMP AT TRUDRUFFRIN
from the 18th. to the 21st. of September 1777.
with the ATTACK
made by MAJOR GENERAL GREY
against the REBELS
near WHITE HORSE TAVERN.
on the 20th. of September.
Drawn by an Officer on the Spot.
Engrav'd & Publish'd by W. Faden Charing Cross July 1st. 1778.
Two Miles
0
1
2
Valley Creek
St. Peters Church
Chasseurs
TRUDRUFFRIN
Stirns Brigade
Hessian Grenad.
Gl. Knyphausen's Quarters
HEAD QUARTERS
Artillery
Guards
4th. Brigade
37 46 33
2d. Battal. Light Infantry
Gl. Greys Quarters
44 42
17 44 42 15
Gl. Agnews Quarters
64 Regt.
Dragoons
2d. Brigade
40 55 27 23
1st. Brigade
5 49 29 4th.
Col. Musgrave
55
40
A
M. Gl. Grey
Infy. 44
42 Reserve
Advanced Guard
First Shot
Second Shot
Rebels Piquet
Paoli
Main Road from Lancaster to Philadelphia
Road to Moorhall
Kennyon
White Horse Tavern
Road to Whiteland
E
B
C
F
G
H
I
REFERENCES.
AAAA. March of Gl. Grey's Detachment in two Columns to Attack the Rebels B.
C. Light Infantry attacking the Rebel Brigade in Flank.
D. A Party of Light Infantry in pursuit of the Rebels Canons EE which were carried off on the first Allarm.
F. Light Infantry after having routed the Rebels.
G. The 44th. Regiment supporting the Light Infantry.
H. The 42d. Regiment in Reserve, following without breaking their Ranks.
IIII. The Rebels flying in Disorder.
NB. The Two Regiments under Col: Musgrave were not engaged.

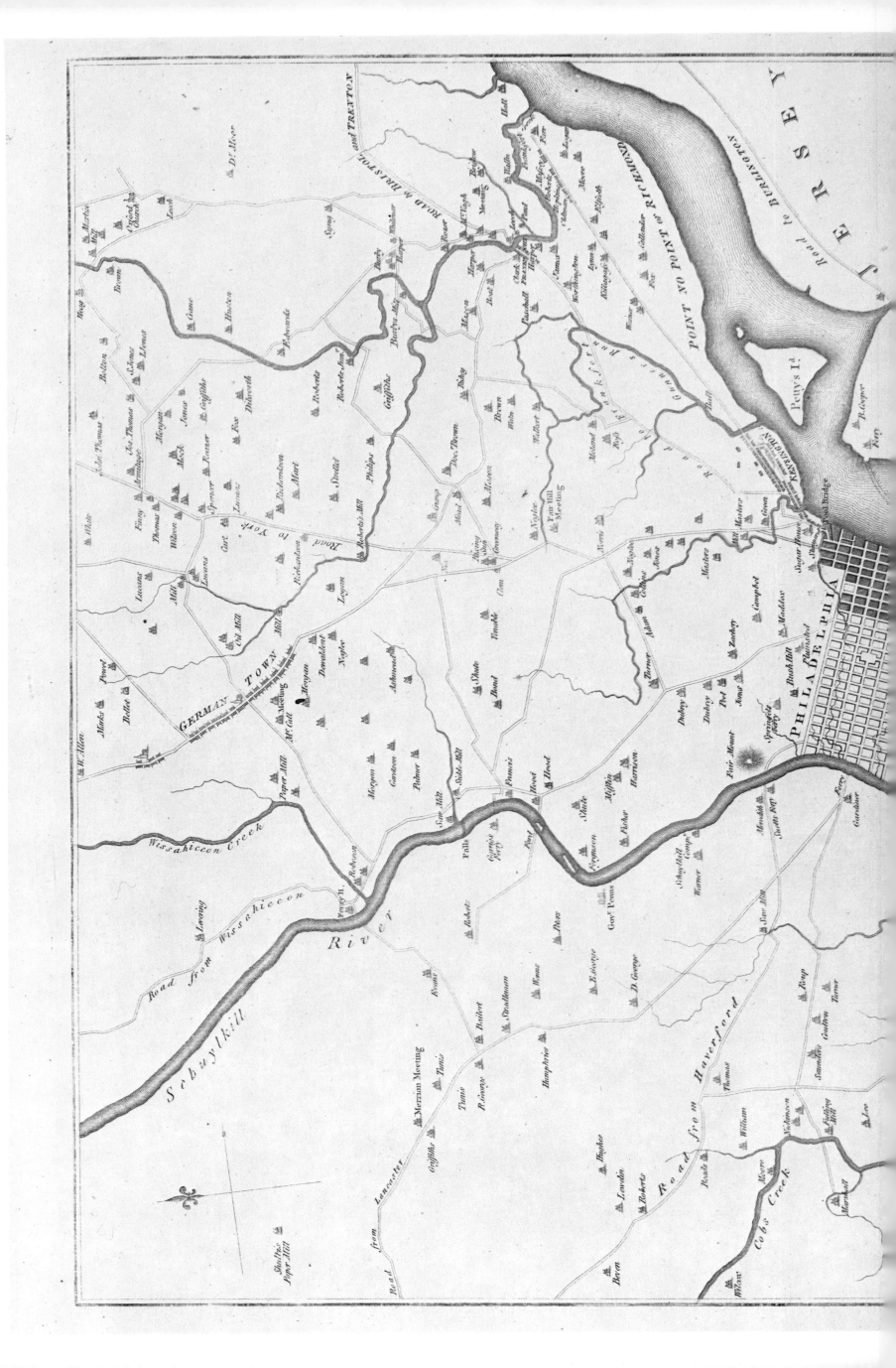

116

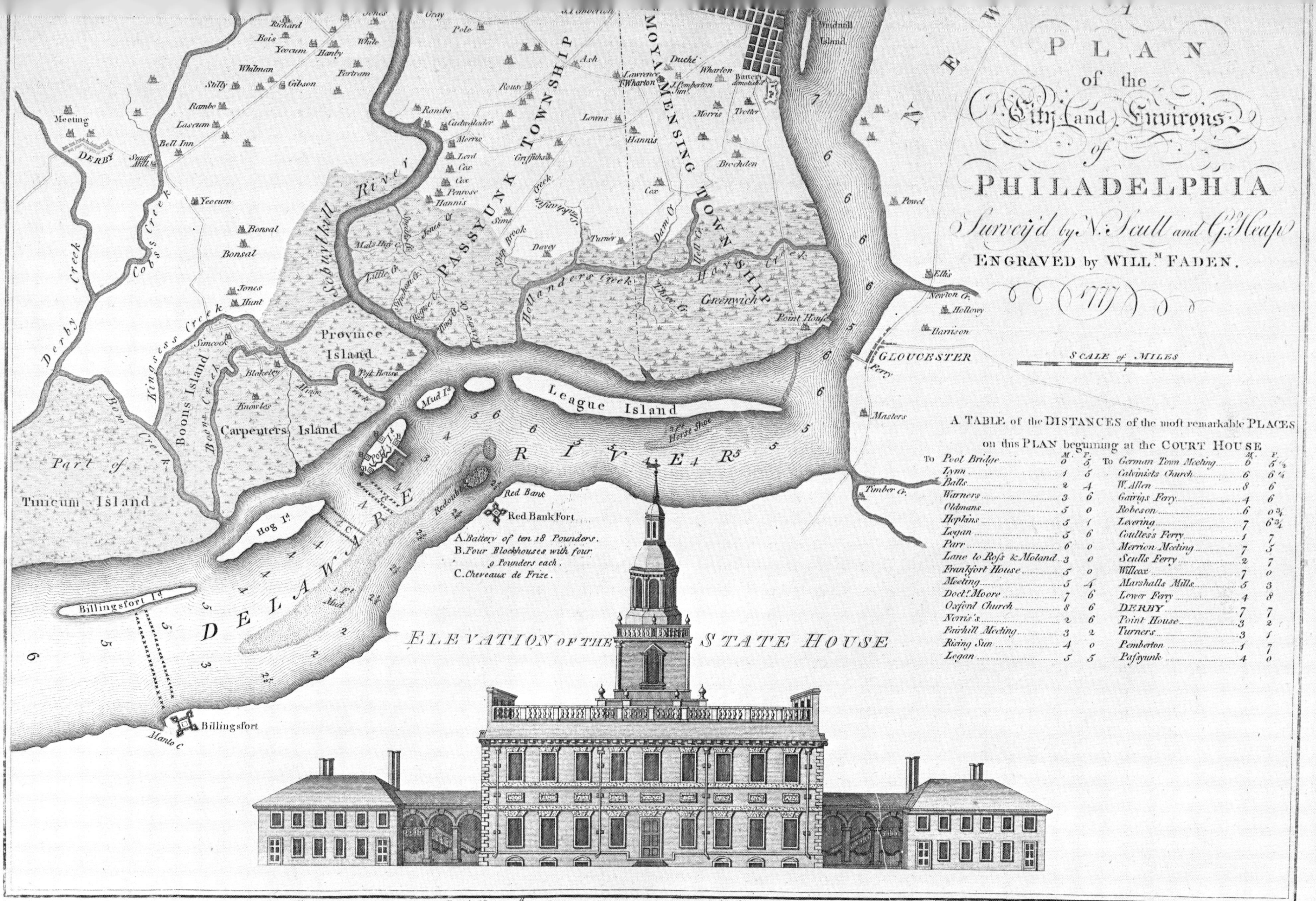

PLAN
of the
City and Environs

PHILADELPHIA
Surveyd by N. Scull and G. Heap

ENGRAVED by WILLᵐ FADEN.

1777

SCALE of MILES

A TABLE of the DISTANCES of the most remarkable PLACES
on this PLAN beginning at the COURT HOUSE.

	M. F.		M. F.
To Post Bridge	0 5	To German Town Meeting	6 0
Lynn	1 5	Cabinets Church	6 3
Balla	3 0	W. Allen	6 4
Warners	3 0	Gautips Ferry	4 0
Oldmans	3 5	Robeson	6 0
Hopkins	5 1	Levering	6 3
Logan	5 5	Goutleys Ferry	1 7
Parr	5 6	Merion Meeting	7 3
Lane to Rofs & Moland	3	Stalls Ferry	2 7
Frankfort House	3 0	Wilcax	7 0
Meeting	5 7	Marshalls Mills	3 8
Doct. Moor	5 7	Lower Ferry	4
Oxford Church	7 6	DERBY	7 7
Norris's	2 6	Point House	3 1
Bairhill Meeting	3 0	Turners	2 0
Rising Sun	4 0	Pemberton	1 0
Logan	5 5	Pafsyunk	4

ELEVATION OF THE STATE HOUSE

London Published according to Act of Parlᵗ March 12. 1777 by W. Faden Succefsor to the late Mr. Jefferys Geographer to the KING Charing Crofs

Map labels

MOYAMENSING TOWNSHIP

PASSYUNK TOWNSHIP

Schuylkill River

DELAWARE R.

League Island

Province Island

Carpenters Island

Boons Island

Tinicum Island

Hog Id.

Mud Id.

Red Bank

Red Bankfort

GLOUCESTER Ferry

Derby Creek

Bow Creek

Bottlers Creek

Kings Creek

Beans Creek

Cofs Creek

Windmill Island

Billingsfort

A. Battery of ten 18 Pounders.
B. Four Blockhouses with four
   9 Pounders each.
C. Chevaux de Frize.

Part of

Meeting

Derby

Heartland of the New Confederation

MAP 26. ¶ This most famous delineation of the Philadelphia area in the colonial period was first published in Philadelphia in 1752. Nicholas Scull, surveyor general of Pennsylvania, was no doubt responsible for the map, while George Heap, about whom little is known, is credited with the large perspective view of the State House. ¶ The engraving has always been rare; in fact, only one copy of the 1752 issue is known to have survived. When Philadelphia became the Revolutionary capital, demand for such a map caused it to be reprinted a number of times. The example shown here was published in London by William Faden in 1777, the year the British occupied the city. ¶ Faden enlarged the original plan and added information regarding fortification of the defensive posts along the Delaware River to the south of the city. Three distinct issues appeared, each adding more detail about the island forts and the obstructions placed in the river. This issue represents the final form, with the addition of Billingsport Island. Between this island and the Jersey shore was a double line almost a mile long of forts and obstructions called *chevaux de frise*—the first barrier the British had to clear to open the line of communication by water to the British army in Philadelphia. ¶ The map shows the location of the grid of the city between the two rivers, as well as the relationship of Germantown to the north and the river forts to the southwest. Because of its popularity, there were two editions published in Germany in 1777 and one in France the following year. ¶ The elevation of the State House, known today as Independence Hall, was the first published view of the building destined to become one of the nation's most historic shrines. It seems curious that the British, publishing this engraving early in 1777, did not delete the view of the seat of the second Continental Congress, which had adopted the Declaration of Independence there the previous July.

SHOWN ON PRECEDING PAGE
A Plan of the City and Environs of Philadelphia. Survey'd by N. Scull and G. Heap. Engraved by Willm. Faden. London, W. Faden, March 12, 1777. (24½″ x 18″)

ing Indian scouts, Loyalists, British regulars, and blue-coated Brunswickers. In all, Burgoyne had over 7,000 men, plus the proverbial assortment of women, children, dogs, and sutlers. Plus, too, Baroness Frederika von Riedesel of the German contingent, a delightful young woman, whose journal provides an intimate day-to-day account of the expedition, including the picnics, the all-night card games, the formal dinner parties. Which is to underscore the truism that war for the European aristocracy was romantic and glamorous, that notions of personal sacrifice and grim totality were lacking among officers who brought along their wives and mistresses, their resplendent wardrobes, their choicest wines to take up badly needed transport space in a campaign through a formidable wilderness. (*See Map 9*)

The American Northern Department, all but consumed by a bitter struggle for command between its two senior generals, Horatio Gates and Philip Schuyler, was scarcely ready to meet the invasion. Americans everywhere waited anxiously as word spread that Burgoyne's mighty expedition was approaching Fort Ticonderoga, which, it was commonly assumed, was the "key to a continent," another Louisbourg or Gibraltar in its strategic importance. A star-shaped fortress made of earth, timber, and stone, it sat upon high ground near the spot where Lake Champlain to the north and Lake George and Wood Creek to the south came together. To a degree, contemporary estimates were correct: its guns controlled all water traffic that passed beneath its ramparts; but the fort itself was in poor condition to withstand a siege. The British, after landing above the fort, sent detachments around behind its decaying walls and made preparations to plant cannon high atop Mount Defiance on the Lake George side. The American commander, sandy-haired General Arthur St. Clair, an ex-British officer, evacuated his post. Authorities at Fort Ticonderoga today (restored by the Pell family who had long owned the location) are not at all certain that Burgoyne's troops would have met with success in getting sufficient cannon up the rugged sides of Mount Defiance to enfilade "Old Ty." In any event, St. Clair was wise to preserve his small 3,000-man force, although Congress was outraged to the point of blaming Schuyler, then the supreme commander in that theater, and replacing him once and for all with Gates. (*See Map 17*)

The days before Schuyler departed were among the most crucial of the campaign. Burgoyne has been faulted for not proceeding down Lake George and then portaging his men and equipment the distance between that lake and the Hudson River. But one has only to examine that stretch of rocky mountains and ravines to see the inadvisability of that route. Burgoyne is exceedingly vulnerable, however, to criticism of a different sort: the way in which he did advance by land along the banks of Wood Creek in the direction of the Hudson. He halted at Skenesborough after a skirmish with St. Clair's rear guard, in no hurry to press on while the rebels were reeling. His decision gave Schuyler invaluable time to obstruct the already-arduous pathway from Skenesborough to Fort Edward with stones and fallen trees. Once Burgoyne did set out, it took twenty-four days to travel the twenty-three miles to Fort Edward. Burdened though Burgoyne was with excessive paraphernalia, he might have, by moving quickly earlier, accomplished his major objective of the campaign, which was to reach Albany, for there were several weeks in this period when the American Northern army would have been unable to make a defensive stand. (*See Map 18*)

Even so, it may be doubted that the arrival of the Anglo-German army in that old Dutch river settlement would have substantially altered the course of the war. Already Generals Thomas Gage and William Howe had found that the possession of particular cities and towns was of small advantage, no substitute for destroying rebel armies. Moreover, Howe had left Clinton in New York with scarcely enough men to cooperate meaningfully with Burgoyne. Both Washington and his perceptive young aide Alexander Hamilton doubted that Britain would ever have enough troops available to control the long Champlain-Hudson waterway, to cut off patriot supply routes, and to bludgeon the northern countryside into accepting passively a return to English rule.

As it was, neither Burgoyne's nor Washington's theories received a test. In mid-August, Burgoyne learned that his diversionary party swinging through the Mohawk Valley had been halted by patriot irregulars and compelled to pull back. More bad news came from Bennington, Vermont, where two of Burgoyne's German units in search of packhorses and provisions had been routed by a militia general named John Stark. By the time "Gentleman Johnny" Burgoyne finally crossed to the west bank of the Hudson and came within forty miles of Albany, he encountered Horatio Gates, now in command of a revitalized American Northern army, growing rapidly and solidly dug in on towering Bemis Heights, overlooking the river and blocking his southward progress. One gains immeasurably in perception of the impending clash if he climbs over Bemis Heights today with its deep ravines and towering bluffs unchanged by two centuries. For Gates could not have chosen better ground, and Burgoyne's advance parties had no idea of the exact location of the Northern army. Twice—on September 19 and October 7—Burgoyne sent substantial columns forward to probe blindly through the dense thickets for Gates's lines. Both times Gates sent out regiments to claw at his opponent from advantageous wooded locations. Burgoyne's casualties in the first and second battles of Bemis Heights exceeded those of Gates by roughly 1,200 to 470. When Burgoyne fell back to the northward, Gates dispatched units to surround him. Short of provisions and aware that militiamen by the thousands were swarming behind him, he decided against trying to fight his way back to Ticonderoga. Nor could he count on being saved by Clinton, who did undertake a stab up the river from New York, only to return with the realization that he could do little for the Canadian army. Burgoyne laid down his weapons on October 17 at the village of Saratoga. A European army was scarcely equipped for wilderness warfare, to say nothing of fighting a countryside in arms. Schuyler had provided the delaying tactics, and Gates had followed with the knockout blow, ably assisted by such excellent combat officers as Benedict Arnold and Daniel Morgan. (*See Maps 19, 20, 22, 23*)

While the year 1777 marked the end of full-scale warfare in the northern states, the year 1778 was a transitional period in the revolutionary conflict, largely because of British failures in New York and Pennsylvania and because of the expanded role of France. Already France during 1776–78 had made available to the patriots secret aid: chiefly in the form of invaluable quantities of arms, munitions, and clothing which the government of Louis XVI had turned over to the playwright Caron de Beaumarchais and his fake "Hortalez and Company," which in turn sent them across the Atlantic. Now in early 1778, thanks more to the efforts of Franklin than his fellow diplomatic commissioners, Arthur Lee

Philadelphia: Second Only to London in the English-Speaking World

MAP 27. ¶ The political and religious climate of Penn's town on the Delaware River rather quickly made it one of the leading cities of America, although New York and Boston each had a half-century head start. By the outbreak of the American Revolution, the Quaker city was first in population and cultural life and was the seat of the Continental Congress. While her population in 1776 was only 34,000, Philadelphia had become the second-largest city of the British Empire—more populous than Bristol and Dublin, and well ahead of New York City's 22,000, Boston's 15,000, and Charleston's 12,000. ¶ This fine large-scale town plan was published in London four months after the signing of the Declaration of Independence. While it was the best picture of the city available on the eve of the British occupation, it is surprisingly anachronistic. Publisher Dury credits the map to Benjamin Easburn, who was surveyor general of Pennsylvania from 1733 to 1741. The delineation of the streets and buildings, however, is almost identical to that of the plan prepared by Nicholas Scull, published in 1762, which contained information that was up to date at that time. The plan by Scull, who held the surveyor general's post after Easburn, was issued with copyright protection. Dury, perhaps attempting to avoid paying royalties, attributed the map to a man who had been dead for thirty-five years. ¶ The Loyalists and neutrals who remained in Philadelphia during the British occupation from September 1777 to June 1778, together with General William Howe and his staff, carried on a sparkling social life in the city. The brilliant scene of society at play was crowned by the famous *Mischianza* of May 18, 1777. This fantastic imitation of a great medieval festival was staged at vast expense in honor of William Howe's departure for England, after his replacement by Clinton as commander in chief in America. After sailing down the river in a Venetian-style water parade of ornately decorated barges and galleys, the participants went ashore at Walnut Grove, the country estate of the Whartons. The music rang out "God Save the King" as the procession passed between rows of redcoats at attention. They then beheld an elaborate triumphal arch erected in honor of Lord Howe. Nearby a jousting tournament was staged for the ladies. All these festivities were organized under the direction of the British officers John Andre and Oliver De Lancey.

SHOWN ON FOLLOWING PAGE
A Plan of the City of Philadelphia, the Capital of Pennsylvania, from an Actual Survey by Benjamin Easburn. London, Andrew Dury, Nov. 4, 1776. (19½" x 26½")

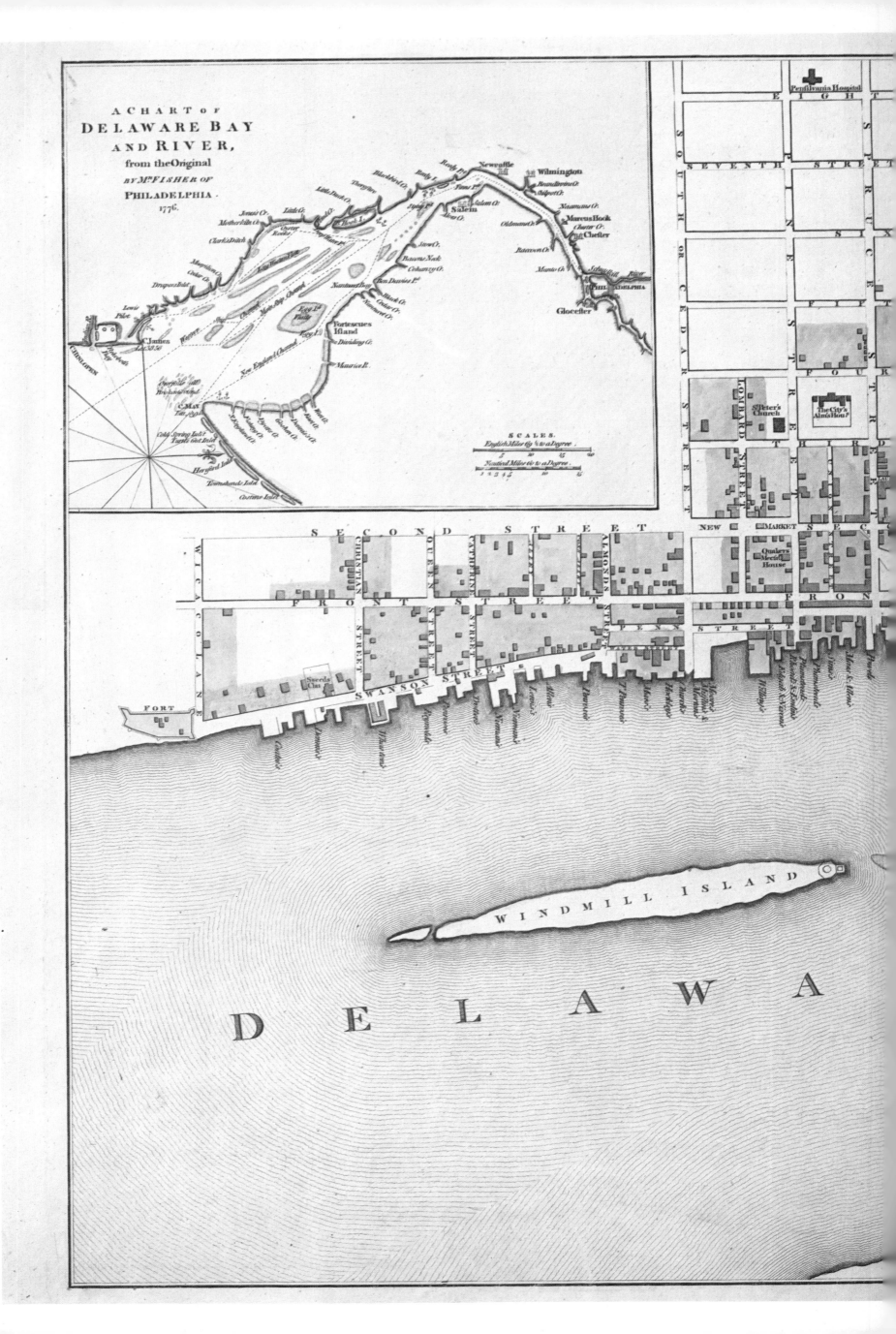

A CHART OF
DELAWARE BAY
AND **RIVER**,
from the Original
BY Mr FISHER OF
PHILADELPHIA.
1776.

SCALES.
English Miles 69 ½ to a Degree
Nautical Miles 60 to a Degree

SECOND STREET

FRONT STREET

SWANSON STREET

WICACO LANE

CHRISTIAN STREET

QUEEN STREET

CATHERINE STREET

ALMONDS STREET

NEW MARKET

FORT

Sweeds Chu.

PENN STREET

FRONT STREET

SEVENTH STREET

SOUTH or CEDAR STREET

EIGHTH STREET

SPRUCE STREET

SIXTH STREET

FIFTH STREET

FOURTH STREET

THIRD STREET

SECOND STREET

LOMBARD STREET

Pensylvania Hospital

St Peter's Church

The City's Alms Hou.f

Quakers Meeting House

WINDMILL ISLAND

D E L A W A

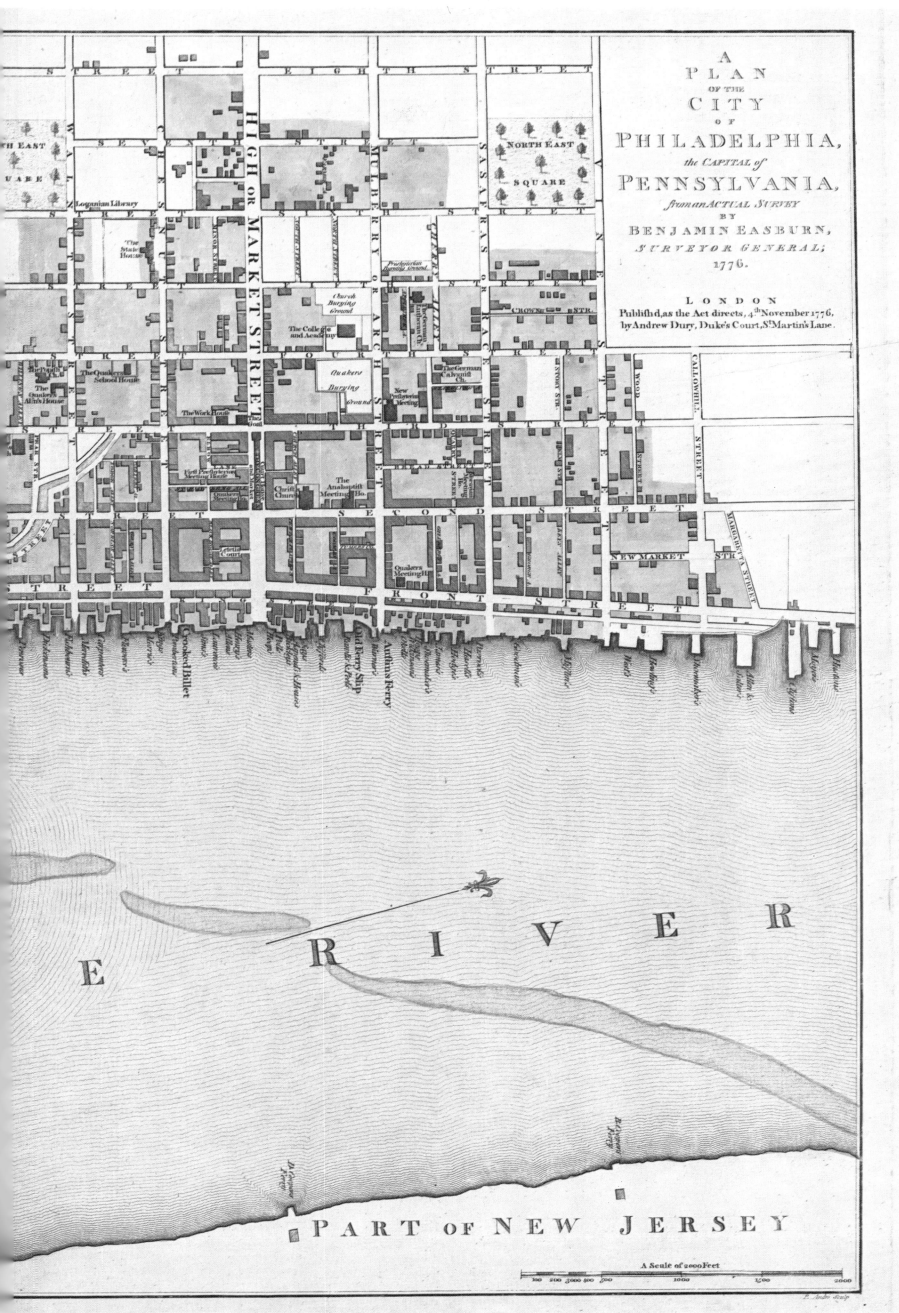

A
PLAN
OF THE
CITY
OF
PHILADELPHIA,
the CAPITAL of
PENNSYLVANIA,
from an ACTUAL SURVEY
BY
BENJAMIN EASBURN,
SURVEYOR GENERAL;
1776.

LONDON
Publish'd, as the Act directs, 4th November 1776,
by Andrew Dury, Duke's Court, St Martin's Lane.

NORTH EAST SQUARE

NORTH EAST SQUARE

HIGH OR MARKET STREET

E RIVER

PART OF NEW JERSEY

A Scale of 2000 Feet

121

Where the Tide Was Almost Turned

MAP 28. ¶ At Germantown, after his successes at Brandywine and Paoli, General Howe appears to have become overconfident and careless with the deployment of his troops. By October 4, 1777, when George Washington decided to attempt a four-column night attack from the north with his reinforced army, no fortifications yet had been erected by the British-Hessian army at Germantown. ¶ Although Washington undoubtedly erred by putting his militia troops in the outside columns and his stronger Continentals in the center, the rebels came within a whisker of a great victory. John Sullivan's center column had just forced its way through to the streets of Germantown when a dense fog descended upon the area. This, combined with the poor execution of the complex four-column advance and the drunken behavior of General Adam Stephen, turned potential triumph into tragedy. After the American disappointment at Germantown, little of significance occurred during the rest of the campaign of 1777. Washington went into winter quarters at Valley Forge two months later. ¶ The Germantown plan is one of a number of fine maps by Lieutenant John Hills, several of which are included in this atlas. It enables the viewer to see the hilly, bluff-strewn ground where the encounter took place. One can almost envision the chaos produced by the thick fog that moved into the ravines during the battle. The references in the legend explain the action from the British point of view.

Sketch of the Surprise of German Town. by the American Forces commanded by General Washington. October 4th 1777. by J. Hills. London, Wm. Faden, March 12, 1784. (18" x 21")

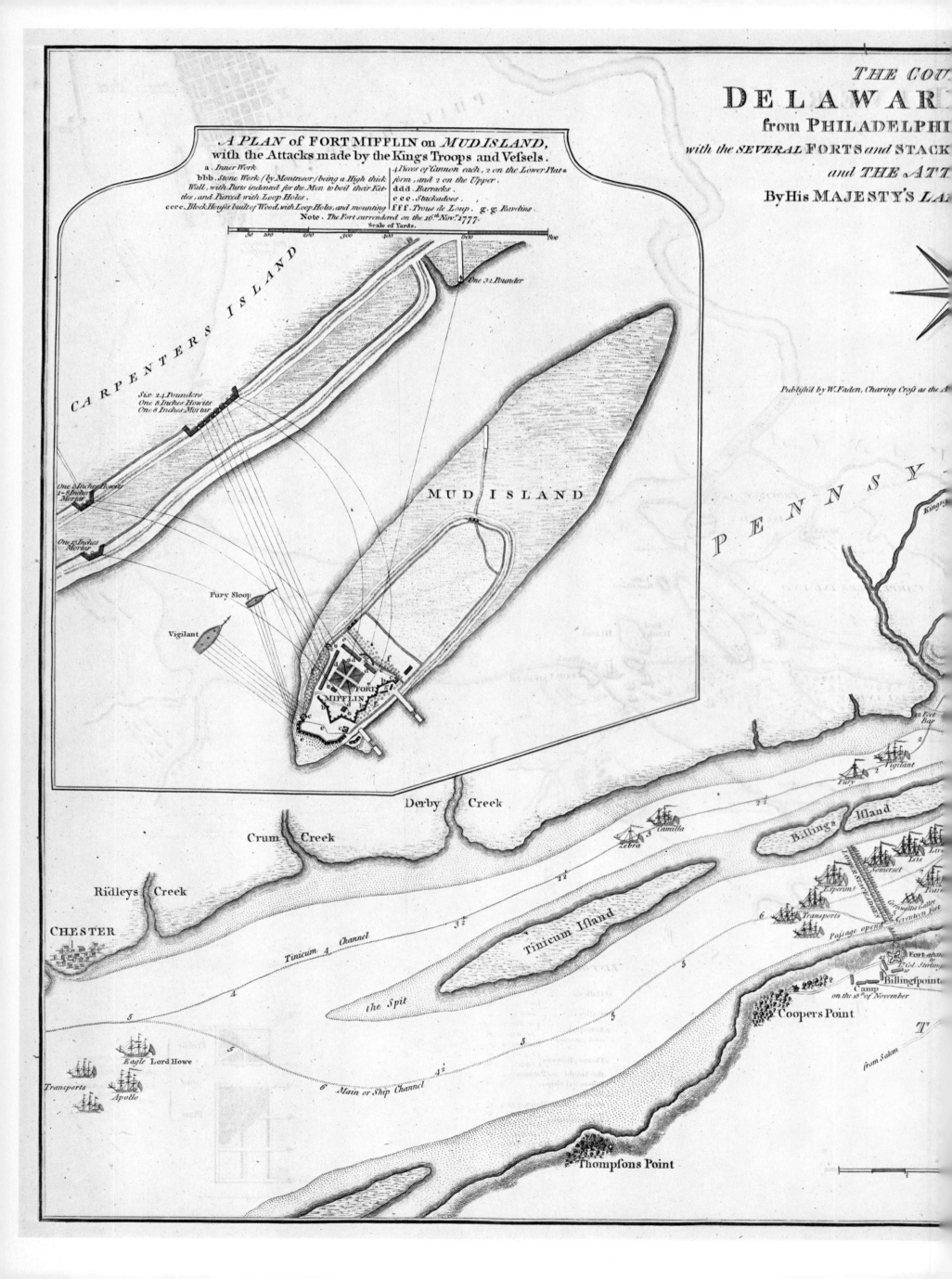

A PLAN of FORT MIFFLIN on *MUD ISLAND*,
with the Attacks made by the King's Troops and Vessels.

a . Inner Work
bbb . Stone Work (by Montresor) being a High thick
Wall, with Parts indented for the Men to boil their Ket=
tles, and Pierced with Loop Holes
cccc . Block Houses built of Wood, with Loop Holes, and mounting

4 Pieces of Cannon each, 2 on the Lower Plat=
form, and 2 on the Upper.
ddd . Barracks.
eee . Stackadoes.
fff . Trous de Loup. g.g. Ravelins.

Note . The Fort surrendered on the 16th Nov.r 1777.

Scale of Yards.

THE COU
DELAWARE
from PHILADELPHI
with the SEVERAL FORTS and STACK
and THE ATT
By His MAJESTY'S LA

Published by W. Faden, Charing Cross as the A

CARPENTERS ISLAND

One 32 Pounder

Six 24 Pounders
One 8 Inches Howits
One 8 Inches Mortar

One 8 Inches Howits
1=8 Inches Mortar

One 8 Inches Mortar

MUD ISLAND

PENNSY

Fury Sloop

Vigilant

FORT
MIFFLIN

Derby Creek

Crum Creek

Ridleys Creek

CHESTER

Tinicum 4 Channel

the Spit

Tinicum Island

Billings Island

Zebra

Camilla

Isis

Experiment

Somerset

Granvilla Gallies

Transports

Passage opend

Fort aban=
to
Lt. Col. Stirling

Billingspoint

Camp
on the 18th of November

Coopers Point

Main or Ship Channel

Eagle Lord Howe

Transports

Apollo

Thompsons Point

from Salem

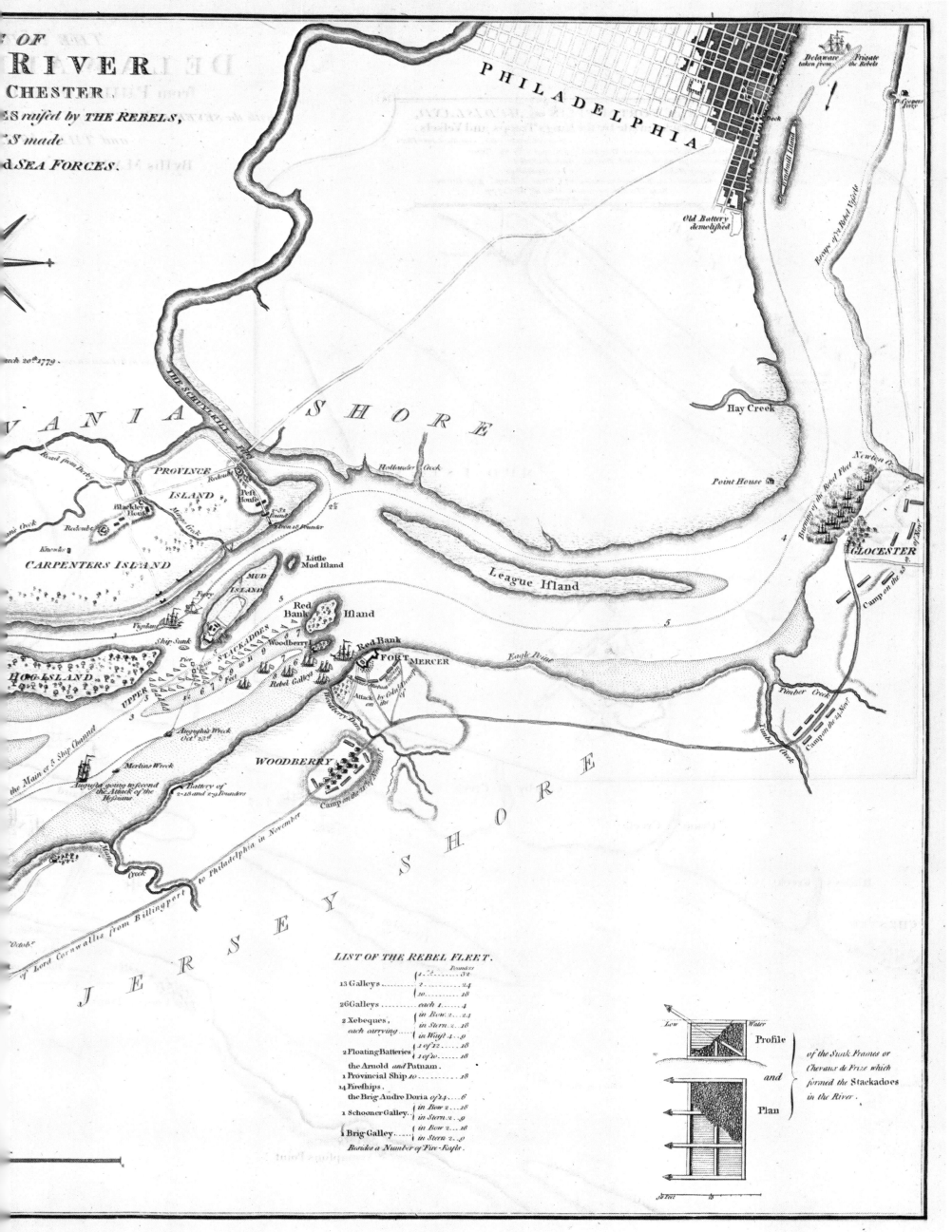

RIVER DELAWARE

OF THE CHESTER

ES raised by THE REBELS,

S made

d SEA FORCES.

ch 20th 1779.

VANIA SHORE

PHILADELPHIA

Delaware taken from the Rebels

Frigate

Escape of the Rebel Vessels

Province Island

Old Battery demolished

Hay Creek

Pest House

Hollander Creek

Point House

Newton Cr.

Burning of the Rebel Fleet

GLOCESTER

Camp on the 25 of Nov.

CARPENTERS ISLAND

Little Mud Island

League Island

Camp on the 24 Nov.

Timber Creek

MUD ISLAND

Red Bank Island

Ship Sunk

STACKADOES

Woodberry

Red Bank

FORT MERCER

Eagle Point

HOG ISLAND

UPPER

Rebel Galleys

Attack by Colo. Donop on the

Augusta Wreck Oct. 23d

Merlins Wreck

WOODBERRY

Woodbury

Battery of 2 18 and 2 9 Pounders

Augusta going to second the Attack of the Hessians

Camp on the 15 of Nov.

Camp on the 15th

the Main or S Ship Channel

Creek

of Lord Cornwallis from Billingsport to Philadelphia in November

JERSEY SHORE

JERSEY

October

LIST OF THE REBEL FLEET.

		Pounders
13 Galleys	{ 1	32
	{ 2	24
	{ 10	18
26 Galleys	each 1	4
2 Xebeques, each carrying	{ in Bow 2	24
	{ in Stern 2	18
	{ in Waist 4	9
2 Floating Batteries	{ 1 of 12	18
the Arnold and Putnam	{ 1 of 10	18
1 Provincial Ship 10		18
14 Fireships		
the Brig Andre Doria of 14		6
1 Schooner Galley	{ in Bow 2	18
	{ in Stern 2	9
1 Brig Galley	{ in Bow 2	18
	{ in Stern 2	9
Besides a Number of Fire-Rafts.		

Low   Water

Profile

and

Plan

of the Sunk Frames or Chevaux de Frize which formed the Stackadoes in the River.

The Delaware River Forts

MAP 29. ¶ This chart of the Delaware River below Philadelphia gives an indication of the network of protective strongholds erected for the defense of Philadelphia. Word of these and of the feared *chevaux de frise* had undoubtedly influenced the circuitous course taken by the British fleet, when they embarked from New York on the Philadelphia campaign. Instead of heading up the Delaware, the fleet sailed south around Cape Charles, Virginia, then northward up the entire Chesapeake Bay to a point near Elkton, Maryland, where Admiral Richard Howe landed the army of his brother, General William Howe. ¶ Even after their victories at Brandywine and Germantown, the British occupation of Philadelphia was not secure until they could gain control of the river. In a bitterly contested and costly series of engagements they eventually drove the Americans out of their positions at Billingsport, Fort Mifflin on Mud Island, and Fort Mercer at Red Bank. ¶ A second edition of this map, published after the war, in 1785, from the original copperplate, shows later positions of the British ships just east of the lower "stockadoe," or *chevaux de frise*. Most interestingly, Faden, the publisher, carefully reworked the plate to change the word "Rebels" to "Americans" in each place it appeared on the second edition. This was a characteristic of the post-1783 British maps published by positive-thinking map sellers.

SHOWN ON PRECEDING PAGE

The Course of Delaware River from Philadelphia to Chester with the several Forts and Stackadoes raised by the Rebels, and the Attacks made By His Majesty's Land & Sea Forces. London, W. Faden, Mar. 20, 1779. (17¾" x 26¾")

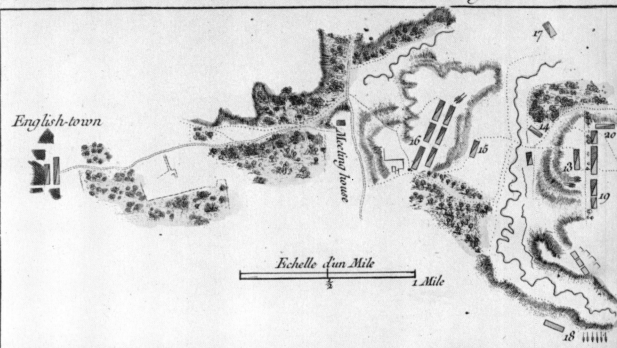

PLAN de la Bataille de Montmouth où le G.ˡ Washington Command..

Echelle d'un Mile ½ 1 Mile

Explicati...

a. *Position que les Anglais occupaient la veille de l'affaire.*
1. *Colonne Anglaise se déployant par sa gauche et d'où il a été detaché des dragons pour se porter sur la droite des colonnes Américaines qui débouchaient du bois.*
2. *Premiere batterie des Anglais qui faisait feu pendant qu'ils se déployaient.*
3. *Débouchement de la 1ʳᵉ brigade du détachement du G.ˡ Lée qui s'est retirée dans le bois où le reste du détachement débouchait sur 4 Colonnes.*
4. *Débouchement des 4 Colonnes.*
5. *Seconde batterie des Anglais.*
6 et 7. *Premiere et Seconde batterie des Americains.*
8. *Troupes formées à la droite des batteries 6 et 7 qui ont eu ordre de se retirer sans avoir fait feu.*
9. *Village de Mont-mouth où est Court-house*
10. *Troupes formées en avant de Mont-mouth qui se sont retirées sans attendre l'ennemi.*
11. *Premiere position occupée par toutes les troupes aux ordres du G.ˡ Lée, où l'on na pas attendu l'attaque, et d'où l'on s'est jetté dans le bois sur la gauche.*
12. *Attaque très vive des Anglais sur les troupes jettées dans le bois, pendant la retraite de la position 11.*

MAP OF THE BATTLE OF MONMOUTH WHERE GEN. WASHINGTON COMMANDED THE AMERICAN ARMY AND GEN. CLINTON LED THE BRITISH ARMY. JUNE 28, 1778

A Translation of the Explanation of Reference Numbers

a. Position occupied by the British on the eve of the Affair.

1. British column deploying on its left, and from which dragoons were detached to move on to the right of the American troops which were emerging from the woods.

2. First battery of the British, firing while they were deploying.

3. Emerging of Gen. Lee's detachment first brigade, which had withdrawn into the woods, where the rest of the detachment was emerging in 4 columns.

4. Emerging of the 4 columns.

5. Second British battery.

6 and 7. First and second American batteries.

8. Troop formation at the right of batteries 6 and 7, which have been ordered to withdraw without having fired.

9. Monmouth Village, where Courthouse is located.

10. Troops formed in front of Monmouth, which withdrew without waiting for the enemy.

11. First position occupied by all of the troops under Gen. Lee's orders, from where, without waiting for the attack, the men have flung themselves into the woods at the left.

12. Very lively attack by the British on the troops that had withdrawn into the woods, during the retreat from position 11.

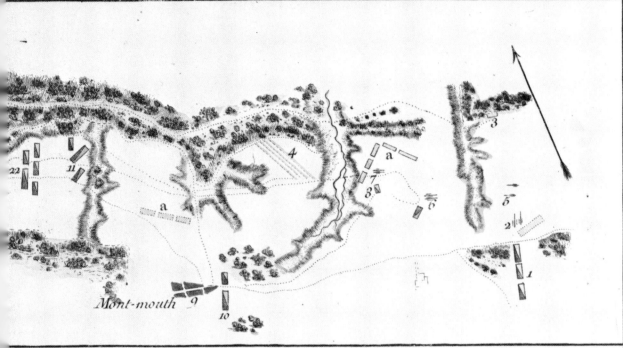

...mée Américaine Et le G.! Clinton l'Armée Anglaise, le 28 Juin 1778.

Mont-mouth

Chifres

13. Seconde position occupée par le reste des troupes et d'où elles se sont retirées étant chargées par les dragons Anglais, qui ont ensuite été dispersés par le Colonel Stuart.

14. Point où a débouché un corps d'Anglais qui a fait feu sur le reste des troupes qui occupaient encore la position 13.

15. Position que les troupes prirent en se retirant du point 13. et d'où le général Washington les fit passer en arrière de la ligne qu'il venait de former au point 16.

16. Position que le G.! Washington a fait occuper par les troupes qui arrivaient pour soutenir le détachement du Général Lée.

17. Colonne Anglaise qui s'avance pour attaquer la gauche et qui se retire après l'avoir reconnuë.

18. Batterie de 6 pieces commandée par le Chev.r du Plessis-Mauduit et soutenuë par 500 hommes.

19. Position occupée par les troupes Anglaises qui s'étaient retirées des point 14 et 17. et d'où elles ont été repoussées avec grande perte.

20. Terrein occupé par les Anglais après avoir été repoussés du point 19.

21. Nouvelle position prise par les Anglais lors que Washington les a fait attaquer et d'où ils ont été également repoussés.

22. Dernière position des Anglais et où ils ont passé la nuit.

13. Second position occupied by the rest of the troops and from where they retreated under charge by the British dragoons, who were later dispersed by Colonel Stuart.

14. Point of emergence of a British force which fired on the rest of the troops that were still occupying position 13.

15. Position seized by the troops as they were retreating from position 13, and from where Gen. Washington made them move to the rear of the line that they had just formed at point 16.

16. Position that Gen. Washington had assigned to the troops arriving to support Gen. Lee's detachment.

17. British column advancing to attack the left, and which retires after having reconnoitered it.

18. Six-gun battery commanded by the Knight of Plessis-Mauduit, backed by 500 men.

19. Position occupied by the British troops which had retreated from points 14 and 17, and from where they had been thrown back with heavy losses.

20. Area occupied by the British after having been repulsed from point 19.

21. New position taken up by the British as Washington had them attacked and from which they were also thrown back.

22. Last position of the British, and where they spent the night.

Neither Army Victorious in the Blazing Heat at Monmouth

MAP 30. ¶ When Sir Henry Clinton replaced the demoralized Sir William Howe as commander in chief of the British army in America, his first move was to abandon Philadelphia and retreat with his army to New York. After sending some of his less reliable Hessians and thousands of terrified Tories to New York by sea, he set off with 10,000 troops to march across New Jersey to New York. ¶ The army Washington brought out of Valley Forge in June 1778 was stronger and better trained than the starving and exhausted band of men he had led there six months before. Learning of the British departure for New York, he was anxious to engage Clinton and to prove his ability, as well as his army's, to win a major victory. ¶ Monmouth, the longest battle of the war, was fought under conditions made almost unbearable by a temperature that reached 100 degrees. After a terrible start, the discipline and drill introduced by Von Steuben at Valley Forge began to show results. The outcome was generally considered to be a draw, but Washington's army proved it could face the redcoat regulars on even terms. Neither Clinton nor Washington was aware of it at the time, but this was to be the last major battle in the North. ¶ This fine French map, with its details of the ravine-crossed area, and explanation (translated) of the movements, gives a vivid picture of the battlefield. The original draft has been attributed to Michel du Chesnoy, an aide to Lafayette at the Battle of Monmouth.

Plan de la Bataille de Montmouth où le Gl. Washington Commandait l'Armée Américaine Et le Gl. Clinton l'Armée Anglaise, le 28 Juin 1778. Brussels, 1782. (8¾" x 15½")

In: *Hilliard, D'Auberteuil.* Essais Historiques et Politiques sur la Revolution de l'Amérique Septentrionale. *Brussels, 1782*

Rochambeau at Newport: Prelude to Yorktown

MAP 31. ¶ Newport, at the mouth of Narragansett Bay, was founded by Antinomians in 1639. Nine refugees from Massachusetts Bay bought the land for their town from the Indians. It was at the southern end of the island then called Aquidneck and known since 1644 as Rhode Island. ¶ From 1739 to 1760 enormous fortunes were amassed by the "Triangular Trade": Newport's rum went to Africa to be exchanged for slaves; the slaves were then brought to Barbados and traded for sugar and molasses; these were shipped to Newport to be bartered for more rum. Before the Revolution the foreign trade of this key port was greater than that of New York. But unlike New York and Boston, Newport did not recover vigorously from the trying years of the war. ¶ It was in Newport's harbor that one of the first violent incidents which led to the American Revolution occurred. John Hancock's sloop *Liberty* had been seized by the British in an incident during 1768 at Boston which came close to precipitating open fighting between Bostonians and port officials. In May of 1769, the *Liberty,* then in the king's service, was destroyed by the patriots at Newport as an open act of defiance. ¶ The British occupation of Rhode Island lasted from December 1776 to October 1779. In 1778 the Americans under John Sullivan, supposedly supported by the French fleet under Admiral d'Estaing, attempted to take Rhode Island, but the result was a notable failure. ¶ The heralded French Alliance of 1778, optimistically anticipated by the beleaguered Americans, produced a series of acute disappointments during its first two years. D'Estaing had missed the British fleet in Chesapeake Bay; he had lost an opportunity to attack Admiral Howe when the Royal Navy squadron was inside Sandy Hook; the French "cooperation" with Sullivan at the Battle of Rhode Island during the summer of 1778 had been a fiasco. The final disaster of d'Estaing's presence in America was the unsuccessful large-scale Franco-American attempt to retake Charleston during autumn of 1779. ¶ The arrival of Comte de Rochambeau with his expeditionary force at Newport on July 11, 1780, signaled the beginning of a new and decisive phase of military cooperation between France and the Americans. Rochambeau and his army remained at Newport until the spring of 1781, when they began their historic march to Yorktown. ¶ The fine French plan, prepared by engineers on Rochambeau's staff, shows how the port of Newport in Narragansett Bay, Rhode Island, was refortified by the French. The shore batteries, the deployment of battleships and their intended lines of fire to defend the harbor, and the encampment of the various units of the French army are all shown.

Plan de la position de l'Armée Française au tour de Newport dans Rhode Island, et du Mouillage de l'Escadre dans la Rade de cette ville. Paris, le Rouge, 1782. (17" x 19¼")

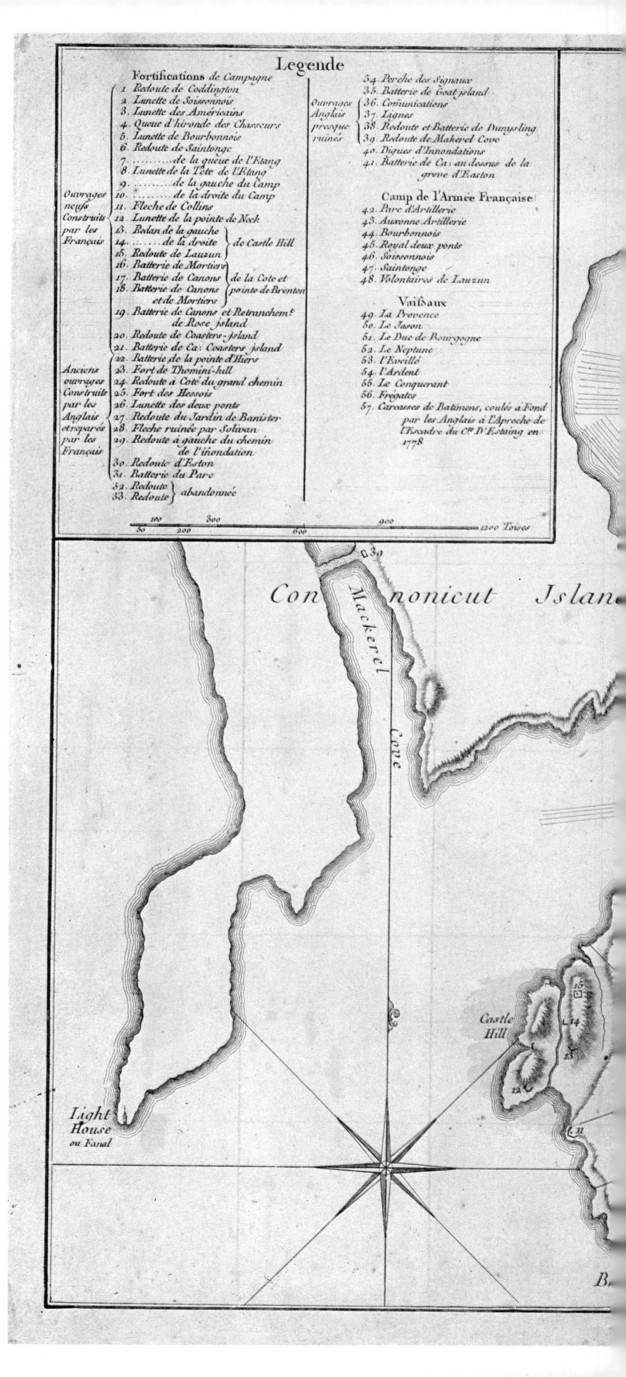

Legende

Fortifications de Campagne

1. Redoute de Coddington
2. Lunette de Soissonnois
3. Lunette des Américains
4. Queue d'hironde des Chasseurs
5. Lunette de Bourbonnois
6. Redoute de Saintonge

Ouvrages neufs Construits par les Français

7. .... de la queue de l'Etang
8. Lunette de la Tête de l'Etang
9. .... de la gauche du Camp
10. .... de la droite du Camp
11. Fleche de Collins
12. Lunette de la pointe de Noek
13. Redan de la gauche
14. .... de la droite } de Castle Hill
15. Redoute de Lauzun }
16. Batterie de Mortiers
17. Batterie de Canons } de la Cote et
18. Batterie de Canons } pointe de Brenton et de Mortiers
19. Batterie de Canons et Retranchem.t de Rose jsland
20. Redoute de Coasters-jsland
21. Batterie de Ca: Coasters jsland
22. Batterie de la pointe d'Hiers

Anciens ouvrages Construits par les Anglais et reparés par les Français

23. Fort de Thomini-hill
24. Redoute à Coté du grand chemin
25. Fort des Hessois
26. Lunette des deux ponts
27. Redoute du Jardin de Banister
28. Fleche ruinée par Solivan
29. Redoute à gauche du chemin de l'inondation
30. Redoute d'Eston
31. Batterie du Parc
32. Redoute } abandonneé
33. Redoute }

34. Perche des Signaux
35. Batterie de Goat jsland

Ouvrages Anglais presque ruinés

36. Comunications
37. Lignes
38. Redoute et Batterie de Dumpling
39. Redoute de Makerel Cove
40. Digues d'Innondations
41. Batterie de Ca: au dessus de la greve d'Easton

Camp de l'Armée Française

42. Parc d'Artillerie
43. Auxonne Artillerie
44. Bourbonnois
45. Royal deux ponts
46. Soissonnois
47. Saintonge
48. Volontaires de Lauzun

Vaisseaux

49. La Provence
50. Le Jason
51. Le Duc de Bourgogne
52. Le Neptune
53. l'Eveillé
54. l'Ardent
55. Le Conquerant
56. Fregates
57. Carcasses de Batimens, coulés à Fond par les Anglais à l'Aproche de l'Escadre du C.te D'Estaing en 1778

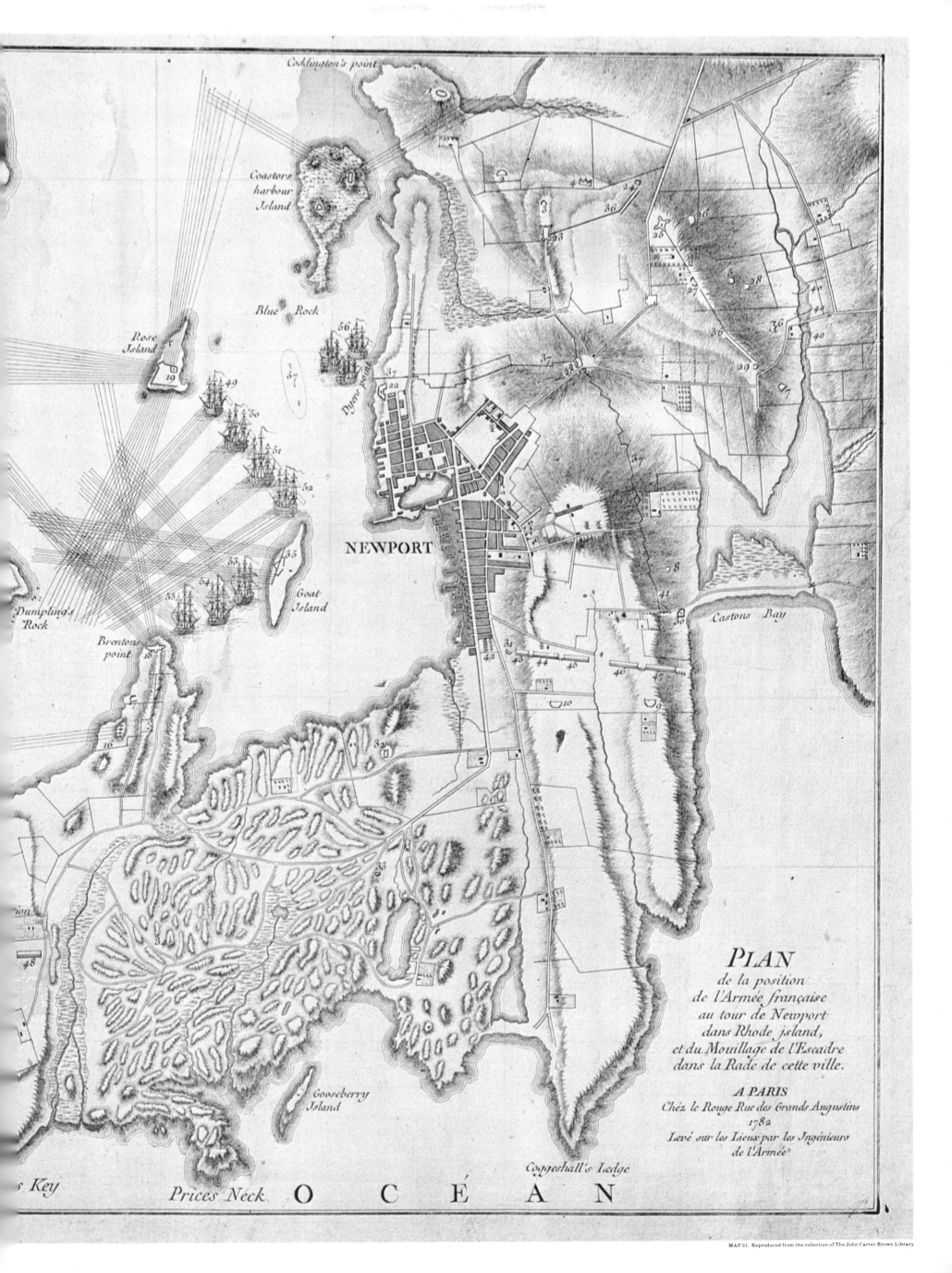

Coddington's point

Coastors harbour Island

Blue Rock

Rose Island

Dumpling's Rock

Brentons point

Goat Island

NEWPORT

Castons Bay

Gooseberry Island

Coggeshall's Ledge

Prices Neck   O C É A N

Key

PLAN
de la position
de l'Armée française
au tour de Newport
dans Rhode island,
et du Mouillage de l'Escadre
dans la Rade de cette ville.

A PARIS
Chéz le Rouge Rue des Grands Augustins
1782
Levé sur les Lieux par les Ingénieurs
de l'Armée

and Silas Deane, the French foreign minister, Comte de Vergennes, concluded, on February 6, treaties of commerce and alliance with the United States, an action that soon led to France's entering the war on the side of the patriots. France, ever ready to settle old scores with England, was now convinced the Americans were willing to see the contest through to independence. Consequently, British leaders were forced to spread their military and naval resources more thinly than ever in anticipation of Bourbon threats in Europe, the West Indies, India, and on the high seas. Sir Henry Clinton replaced William Howe as military commander in chief in North America. His orders were to constrict his operations by evacuating Philadelphia and concentrating his forces at New York City in order to free several thousand redcoats for duties in the West Indies.

Washington, meanwhile, found a new concern during the winter of 1777–78. There were reports, in and out of the army, of dissatisfaction with the performance of Washington in the Pennsylvania campaign, where his setbacks contrasted sharply with Gates's triumph over Burgoyne. Soon Washington's friends were convinced that a plot existed to remove Washington in favor of Gates, an episode known as the Conway Cabal, named for General Thomas Conway who was thought to favor such a change. If Valley Forge were alive with such talk, it was mostly groundless. Washington and his subordinates were overly sensitive owing to their battlefield reversals, their dismal winter at Valley Forge, and their un-

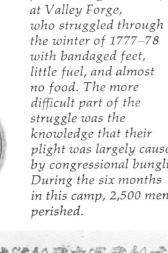

This silver medal was struck by Dupre to commemorate American liberty. But medals and money had little meaning for Washington's troops at Valley Forge, who struggled through the winter of 1777–78 with bandaged feet, little fuel, and almost no food. The more difficult part of the struggle was the knowledge that their plight was largely caused by congressional bungling. During the six months in this camp, 2,500 men perished.

Hard money was scarce and the colonies resorted to the expediency of printing paper money.

happiness with Congress over officers' pay and other benefits. Spring brought green foliage, new recruits, a healthier frame of mind at Valley Forge, and an end to the Conway Cabal, which was really a myth.

Finally, it led Washington to break camp and pursue Clinton across New Jersey following Sir Henry's evacuation of the City of Brotherly Love. Certainly Clinton's 10,000 men and long wagon train extending over a dozen miles were tempting to the general, who had been dogged by reversals in 1777. On June 28, American advance regiments under Charles Lee (who had been captured by a British patrol in December 1776, but later exchanged) caught up with Clinton's rear guard at Monmouth Courthouse. Lee's troops, after initial disorganized probes, fell back in confusion in time to meet Washington who arrived with the main army. Clinton, hurrying back reinforcements to Monmouth, now engaged Washington. With Washington now in command, the Continentals stood firm, exchanging volley for volley with the finest soldiers in Europe. The outcome was indecisive in military terms, but for American soldiers it was a moral victory. They were steadily improving, and some of the credit belonged to the balding Steuben, the Prussian drillmaster who had simplified and standardized the army's battlefield evolutions during the previous months. Lee's performance on the field and his subsequent angry attempts to justify himself eventually led to his censure and removal from the service. (*See Map 30*)

After the Monmouth Court engagement, Clinton continued to New York City, and Washington, too, moved northward, encamping at White Plains, New York. As Washington commented, the two armies were back in almost the same locations they had occupied two years earlier. The *London Evening Post* scarcely found pleasure in the unproductive meanderings of the Howe-Clinton army.

> Here we go up, up, up
> And here we go down, down, downy
> There we go *backwards* and *forwards*
> And here we go round, round, roundy.

At dawn on January 3, 1777, Americans under General Hugh Mercer surprised the British near Princeton. Mercer was killed, and the outlook was bad for the colonials until Washington rode up with the main forces.
Mercer's son William painted this picture.

Wayne Strikes Back

MAP 32. ¶ Stony Point provided the colorful, impetuous Anthony Wayne both revenge for his humiliating defeat at Paoli and the basis for his reputation as a fearsome fighting general. The bold three-pronged attack at midnight was carried out in silence. The two flanking columns had the flints in their muskets removed. This assured quiet and forced the men to rely on their bayonets, as had the British at Paoli. ¶ The bravery of the attackers was matched by their discipline and restraint. After a furious hand-to-hand engagement inside the hilltop fortifications, they gave quarter to the defenders and took about 470 prisoners. While not of great strategic value, Wayne's dramatic strike at Stony Point raised patriot morale and gained new respect for the increasingly competent American army. ¶ Although issued after the war, this splendid engraving is the only battle plan of this engagement published. The detailed rendering of the relief provides one with a dramatic picture of the setting of Wayne's stunning victory.

SHOWN ON FOLLOWING PAGE
A Plan of the Surprise of Stoney Point, by a Detachment of the American Army, commanded by Brigr. Genl. Wayne, on the 15th July, 1779. Also of the Works erected on Verplanks Point, for the Defence of Kings Ferry, by the British Forces in July, 1779. After Wm. Simpson and D. Campbell by John Hills. London, Wm. Faden, March 1, 1784. (19¾" x 27½")

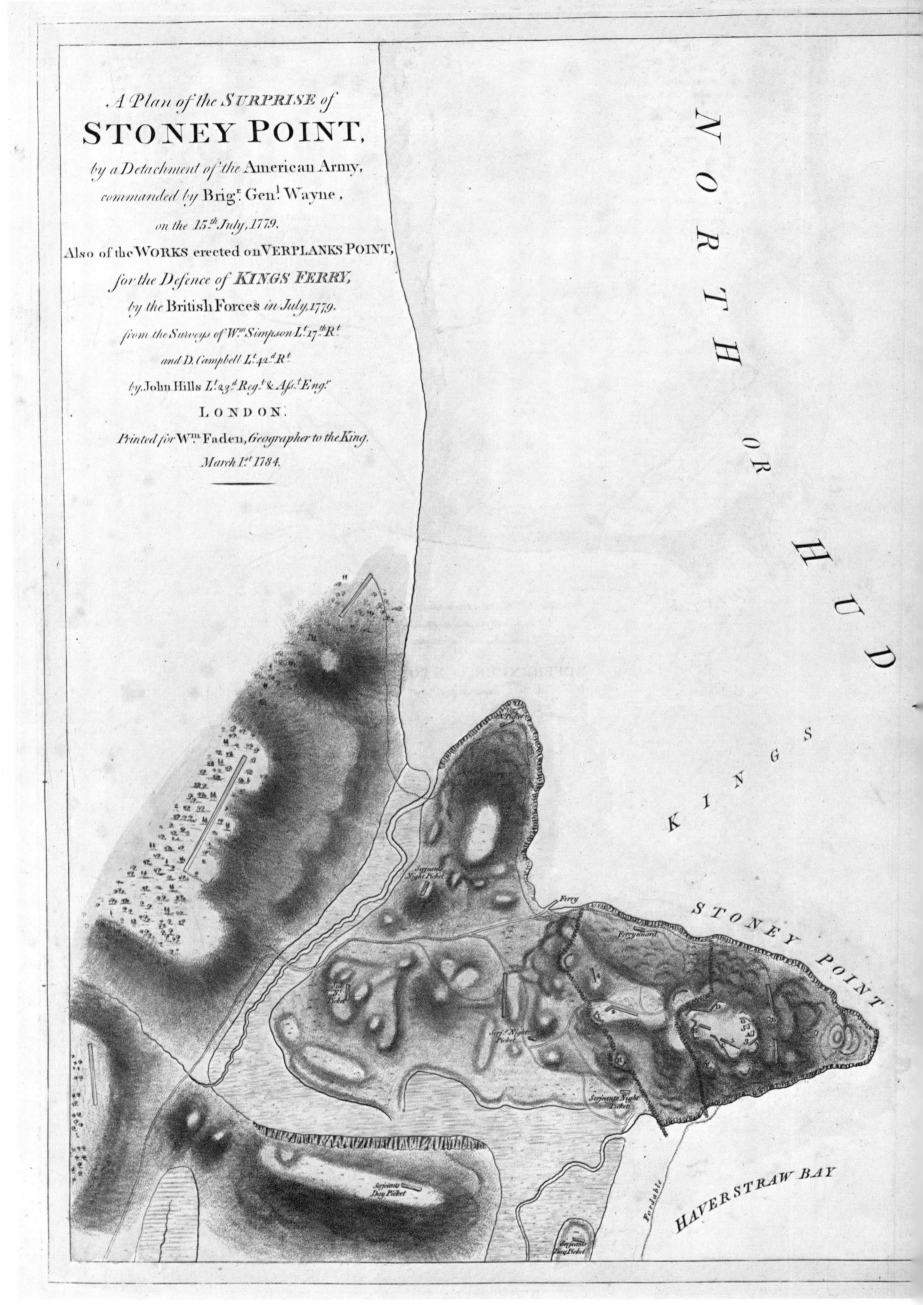

A *Plan of the* SURPRISE *of*
STONEY POINT,
by a Detachment of the American Army,
commanded by Brig.ʳ Gen.ˡ Wayne ,
on the 15.ᵗʰ July, 1779.
Also of the WORKS *erected on* VERPLANKS POINT,
for the Defence of KINGS FERRY,
by the British Forces in July, 1779.
from the Surveys of W.ᵐ Simpson L.ᵗ 17.ᵗʰ R.ᵗ
and D. Campbell L.ᵗ 42.ᵈ R.ᵗ
by John Hills L.ᵗ 23.ᵈ Reg.ᵗ & Aſ.ᵗ Eng.ʳ
LONDON.
Printed for W.ᵐ Faden, Geographer to the King,
March 1.ᵗ 1784.

NORTH OR HUD

KINGS

STONEY POINT

HAVERSTRAW BAY

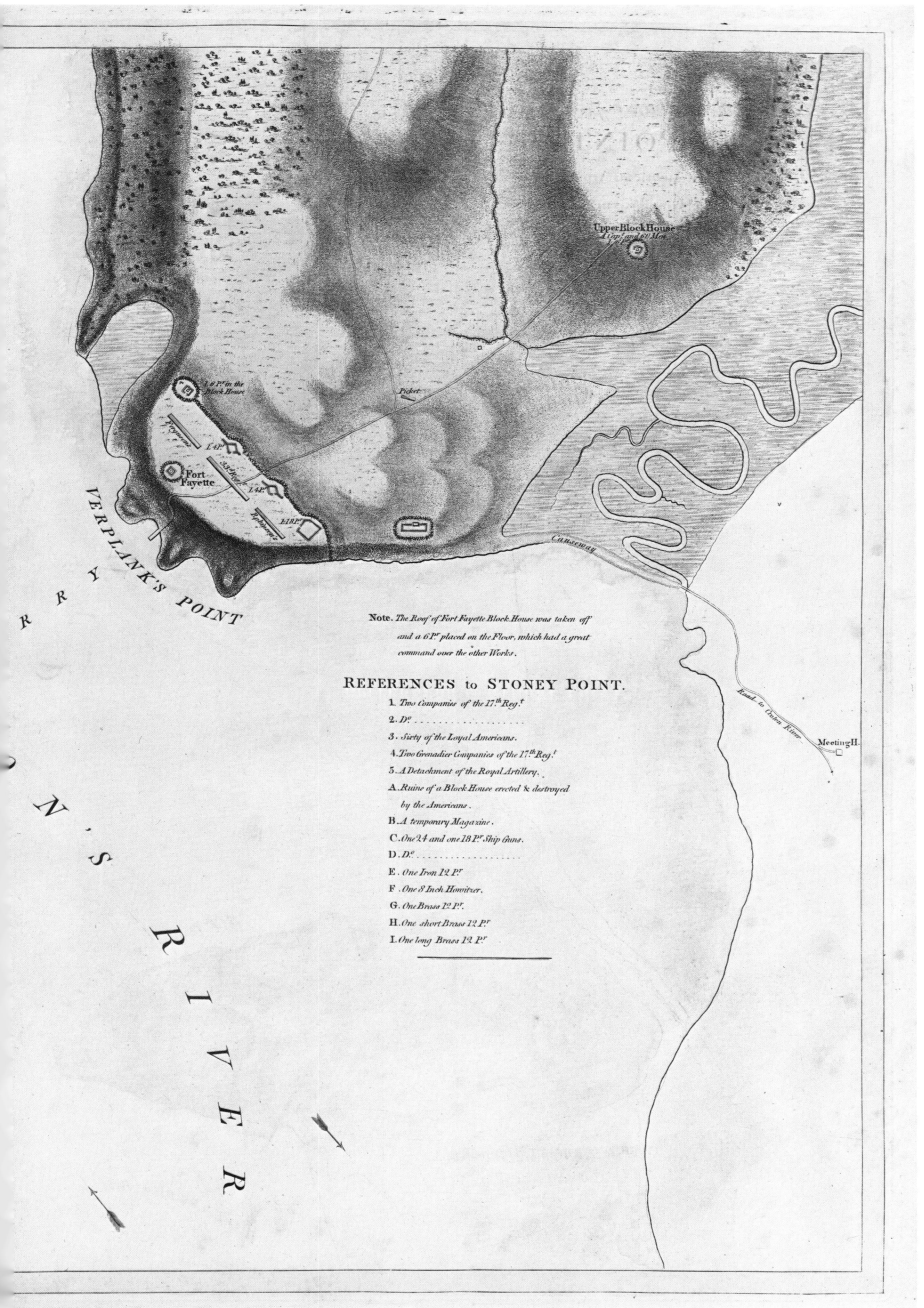

VERPLANK'S POINT

HUDSON'S RIVER

Upper Block House
1 Cap.t and 60 Men

1 6 Pr. in the
Block House

Fort Fayette

Picket

Causeway

Road to Onion River

Meeting H.

Note. The Roof of Fort Fayette Block House was taken off
and a 6 Pr. placed on the Floor, which had a great
command over the other Works.

REFERENCES to STONEY POINT.

1. Two Companies of the 17th Reg.t
2. Do. . . . .
3. Sixty of the Loyal Americans.
4. Two Grenadier Companies of the 17th Reg.t
5. A Detachment of the Royal Artillery.
A. Ruins of a Block House erected & destroyed
    by the Americans.
B. A temporary Magazine.
C. One 24 and one 18 Pr. Ship Guns.
D. Do. . . . .
E. One Iron 12 Pr.
F. One 8 Inch Howitzer.
G. One Brass 12 Pr.
H. One short Brass 12 Pr.
I. One long Brass 12 Pr.

133

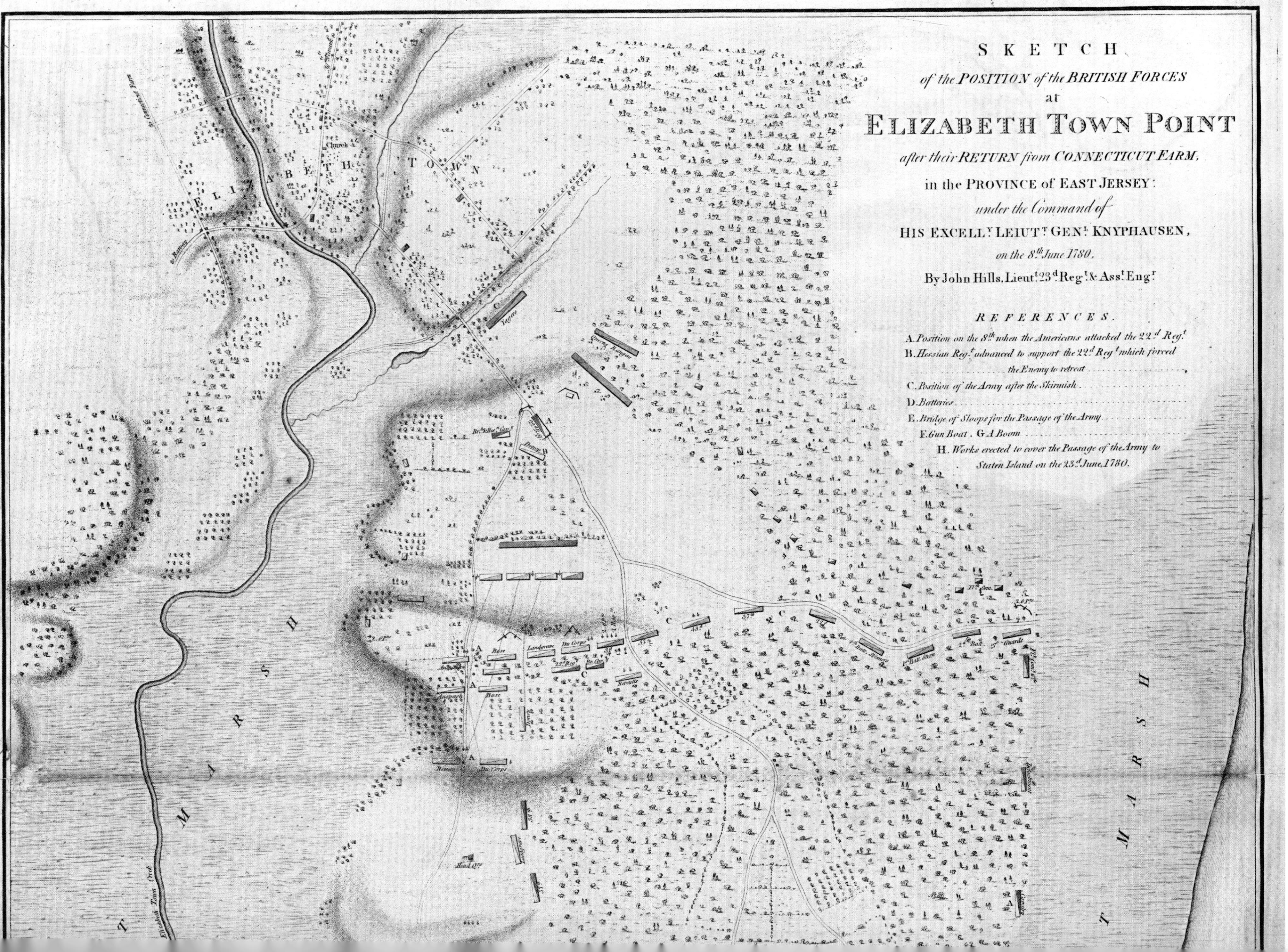

SKETCH
of the POSITION of the BRITISH FORCES
at
ELIZABETH TOWN POINT
after their RETURN from CONNECTICUT FARM,
in the PROVINCE of EAST JERSEY:
under the Command of
HIS EXCELL.Y LEIUT.T GEN.L KNYPHAUSEN,
on the 8th June 1780,
By John Hills, Lieut.t 23.d Reg.t & Ass.t Eng.r
REFERENCES.
A. Position on the 8th when the Americans attacked the 22.d Reg.t
B. Hessian Reg.t advanced to support the 22.d Reg.t which forced the Enemy to retreat
C. Position of the Army after the Skirmish
D. Batteries
E. Bridge of Sloops for the Passage of the Army
F. Gun Boat. G. A Boom
H. Works erected to cover the Passage of the Army to Staten Island on the 23.d June, 1780.
ELIZABETH TOWN
Church
MARSH
MARSH
Elizabeth Town Creek
Yagers
Queens Rangers
Landgrave
Du Corps
Bose
Anspach
Donop
Head Qr.s
Detachment
Cavalry
Guards

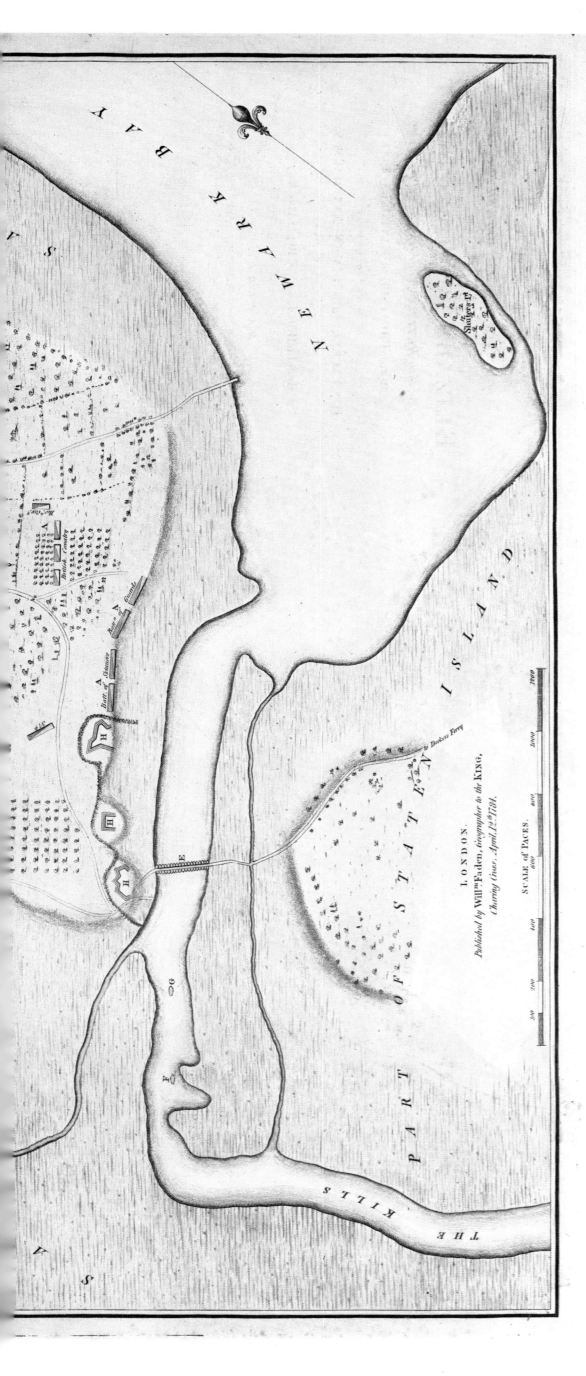

Invasion of New Jersey Repulsed

MAP 33. ¶ The colorless Prussian professional soldier, General Wilhelm von Knyphausen had been in command of all German mercenaries in America since the Hessian humiliation at Trenton. While Henry Clinton was at Charleston in 1780, Knyphausen was commandant of British forces at New York. ¶ Historians have either ignored or expressed bewilderment regarding Knyphausen's invasion of New Jersey with some 6,000 men in June 1780. The move apparently grew out of an earlier plan of Clinton's to attack the American forces at Morristown. Upon his return from the South, Clinton found the German column pulled back to the positions delineated on this map and fortified as if to resist a siege. They had been stopped at Springfield Bridge to the northwest by a much smaller force, and Knyphausen, acting almost as if offended by the hostile reception, retreated to the coast. Clinton reinforced the expedition, and they tried again two weeks later with the same results, whereupon Knyphausen picked up his army and went back the way he had come.

Sketch of the Position of the British Forces at Elizabeth Town Point after their Return from Connecticut Farm, in the Province of East Jersey: under the Command of His Excelly. Lieutt. Genl. Knyphausen, on the 8th June 1780. By John Hills. London, Willm. Faden, April 12, 1784. (24½″ x 20½″)

The Arch Street Ferry, Philadelphia, was one of the busiest of the many ferries crossing the Delaware River to New Jersey. Philadelphia, the center of manufacturing in the colonies, needed ships and boats to move manufactured commodities.

During the British occupation of the city in late 1777, many shops and factories closed and most of the men 18 to 55 years of age, a number of them Tories or Quakers, left the city.

Behind
the Lines

Though the recruiters promised ample clothing to those who joined and displayed pictures of soldiers in uniform, only a small percentage of the army was ever in uniform at any one time. Officers, however, supplied their own uniforms. The official uniform color was brown until 1779, when it was changed to blue.

THE REVOLUTION WAS more than a war for independence. While Washington waged battles and campaigns, civilians behind the lines were erecting new political institutions and taking a fresh look at society as a whole, besides laboring to sustain the Continentals in the field.

"Nothing has excited more admiration in the world than the manner in which free governments have been established in America," boasted James Madison, "for it was the first instance, from the creation of the world—that free inhabitants have been seen deliberating on a form of government, and selecting such of their citizens as possess their confidence, to determine upon and give effect to it." Madison might have added that the revolutionists were constructive statesmen, not negativists blinded by hatred of Britain, whose armies were then hammering at the gates of their cities and destroying their commerce. If they broke a relationship characterized by colonialism and monarchy, that was about the extent of their destructive activity. They maintained their respect for the British constitution, which they believed had been subverted by king and Parliament.

In writing their own state constitutions (except in Rhode Island and Connecticut where people revised their colonial charters), Americans made use of familiar British-American bricks and mortar. There were the usual executive, legislative, and judicial branches of government. But they had borrowed the best and eliminated the worst features. The executive was no longer a king or a royal governor, but an elective governor; the upper house of the legislature was no longer a royally appointed council, but an elective senate. In the colonial period, the lower house—like the British House of Commons—had always been the legislative branch closest to the people, and it continued to hold a preferred position in key areas of government. In several states, for example, the lower house elected both upper house and governor; and in Pennsylvania, which had only one legislative branch before the Revolution, the constitution makers decided to do without both an upper house and a governor.

The Americans in 1776 set out upon a political path they described as "republican." Tom Paine defined it as a system devoted to "the *public good*, or the good of the whole." The word, however, had been subject to various meanings, one being that it referred to a government run by the multitude and noted for its disorder and instability. Yet Americans' unfortunate experience with the British crown contributed to a fear of monarchy in general, as well as all hereditary titles and offices. The destruction of titles was a simple task; there were up until 1776 only two American baronets, Sir John Johnson and Sir William Pepperrell, both Loyalists. It is true that one of Washington's generals, hard-drinking and hard-fighting William Alexander of New Jersey, had put in a questionable claim to a lapsed Scottish earldom. But Lord Stirling, as he liked to be known, died before the termination of the war, and thus spared his state and himself any problem on that score. Several states forbade the passage of any office from one man to another by ties of blood. North Carolina's constitution echoed words found in other political parchments when it proclaimed that "no hereditary emoluments, privileges or honors ought to be granted or conferred in this state." Even the Society of the Cincinnati, founded at the close of the war, aroused a storm of opposition, for it was limited to Continental officers, whose memberships passed on to their eldest son, and so on in each generation.

Above all, however, political positions had to emanate from the people. If history demonstrated that republicanism had encountered travails in Greece, Rome, and elsewhere, it remained the most desirable form of government. Written constitutions, bills of rights, frequent elections, and (slightly later) judicial review, all would help reduce the danger of the legislative tyranny many thought to be a likelihood with republican forms. Certainly the revolutionary legislatures were far from perfect; for the first years there was an excess of power in the hands of the legislative branches, so that the executives and courts could not always function effectively. Before long a tightening up or slight restructuring of authority occurred, first of all in Massachusetts, where the constitution-making process was not completed until 1780. With the opportunity of gauging the positive and negative aspects of earlier political engineering from New Hampshire to Georgia, Massachusetts fashioned a document that made all branches of government viable, that provided meaningful separation of powers. Equally significant, Massachusetts, unlike other states, did not entrust writing and ratification to its legislature, or provincial congress. She elected to draft hers, a special convention which then offered its work to a direct vote of the people, a process that was afterward followed in the making of American constitutions everywhere.

It was primarily a political revolution that they were about when Americans cast off their imperial links and tailored independent governments. A revolution coupled with a foreign war, moreover, is hardly a time for thoughtful social experimentation, especially when—in the case of the Americans—men believed that they already lived in a remarkably free and enlightened society, where property was widely diffused, where suffrage belonged to many men and not just the few elite, and where legal privilege was nonexistent.

Yet Americans were imbued with the Enlightenment idea that institutions should be judged critically in terms of their usefulness to mankind, that the veil of dogma and tradition should not cover and perpetuate social and economic anachronisms in the Age of Reason. Besides, some of them stirred uneasily in the realization that there were contradictions between their revolutionary theories and their practices. Several of these eyesores were in fact already weakened or eroded by the degree of freedom and opportunity that existed in revolutionary America; but it was an appropriate time to strike them down in legal fashion. For example, inheritance laws were reformed. It was, in theory at least, mandatory hitherto in some states that the eldest son of a man who left no will would receive all his father's land, or that the owner of an estate could not break it up but must pass it on intact; these customs—known as primogeniture and entail—which tended to perpetuate concentrations of wealth were abolished in less than a generation.

If religious establishments had also been undermined in the twilight years of the colonial era, there was still work to do. Fortunately, the most influential trustees of the Revolution were committed to religious as well as political liberty. Christian in background, they had nonetheless become skeptical of claims by any one denomination or sect that it provided the one and only true path to personal salvation. Indeed, influenced by Newtonian physics and Enlightenment notions, some of the greatest names of the Revolution were deists, men who accepted the idea of a Creator but questioned or rejected the Doctrine of the Trinity—Washington, Jefferson, John Adams, Franklin, and Paine among them. Even religious conserva-

The Boston State House, from a drawing in the Massachusetts Magazine *of 1793, was reportedly built in 1713. It was replaced by a new structure in 1799, and this building still stands.*

*This is the first
published view of the
Philadelphia State
House. It was built
in 1734, with the
steeple added in 1751.
After 1776,
it was called
Independence Hall.*

tives ceased to defend the concept of allowing one denomination advantages to the exclusion of all others. But they fought a delaying action against the total separation of church and state by favoring government aid to all Protestant faiths. Although vestiges of favoritism to Congregationalism and some public support to other Protestant denominations continued for years in Connecticut, Massachusetts, and New Hampshire, Anglicanism was unable to maintain its privileges in the South owing to its association in the public mind with Britain and loyalism and owing to the numerical strength of dissenters there. Total separation of church and state prevailed, though there were illiberal provisions in the South as in all other parts of the country for some time denying public office to Catholics, agnostics, and atheists.

Obviously it was not enough for state bills of rights to acknowledge freedom of conscience and worship. Virginia, as she so often did in the Revolution, provided the leadership and the pattern for the future with her famous 1786 Statute of Religious Freedom, one of the outstanding documents of the age. The law proclaimed that "no man shall be compelled to frequent or support any religious worship, place, or ministry whatsoever, nor shall be enforced, restrained, molested, or burdened in his body or goods, nor shall otherwise suffer on account of his religious opinions or belief; but that all men shall be free to profess, and by argument to maintain, their opinion in matters of religion, and that the same shall in no wise diminish, enlarge, or affect their civil capacities." Could it have been more complete or explicit?

If Jefferson was so justly proud of his role in bringing the fullest kind of religious liberty to the Old Dominion that he wished it noted on his tombstone, it was yet another achievement that he also desired to be chiseled above his final resting place—the Declaration of Independence, which brought the severest internal agony to sensitive men of his time. When the sage of Monticello penned the phrase "all men are created equal," it was commonly read to mean that the mother country had not treated Americans as the equals of Englishmen. But the broader implications were obvious, and its relevance to chattel slavery inescapable, even to some Blacks. Individual slaves petitioned for manumission and in groups they memorialized their legislatures to end human bondage. One Negro, *Vox Africanorum*, summarized the feelings of many of his race: "Liberty is our claim. Reverence to our Great Creator, principles of humanity and the dictates of common sense, all convince us, that we have an indubitable right to liberty. . . . Though our bodies differ in colour from yours, yet our souls are similar in a desire for freedom. Disparity in colour, we conceive, can never constitute a disparity in rights."

From the standpoint of today, we are likely to see the eighteenth-century race problem as *the* great failure of the revolutionary generation, the fruits of which led inexorably to the disruption of the union in the 1860s and the persistence of "white over black" until after the current century had passed its midpoint. Yet it may be unnecessary, to say nothing of being unfair, to condemn the Founding Fathers as racists as some historians writing from a neoabolitionist corner have done.

First of all, it may be said that not even southerners of that era defended the peculiar institution as a positive good. Jefferson was joined by Washington, George Mason, Charles Carroll, William Pinkney, William Hooper, James Iredell, and Henry and John Laurens in considering slavery an abomination, destructive in its effects upon both races. But even in Virginia, possessed of more moderate and liberal thinking than any of her southern sisters, Jefferson discovered in 1779 there was no chance for a manumission bill he drafted in collaboration with George Wythe and Edmund Pendleton. Far from providing for instant and total abolition, it was a gradual measure, freeing only those blacks born after a particular date and requiring their subsequent departure from the state. The economic aspects of slavery were simply too deeply embedded, as were the social ramifications, not the least of which were a belief in the innate intellectual inferiority of Negroes and a fear of physical harm from exbondsmen.

Indeed, since slavery had always existed in some form, and since it was so inextricably woven into the fabric of the times, the significant fact may be that the revolutionists did accomplish some things that put it on the road to eventual extinction. Though idealistic in their hopes for mankind, they were also practical, reasonable men, who refused to allow a divisive internal issue to threaten the creation of a nation. They did destroy slavery in the North. While the war continued, Pennsylvania by statute provided for gradual emancipation, and the highest court in Massachusetts construed a phrase in the state constitution—"all men are born free and equal"—to mean that black servitude could not legally exist there. We may exaggerate the ease of these accomplishments above the Mason-Dixon line, for abolition was not total in New Jersey until the 1820s or in New York before the 1840s. Though Congress took another forthright step in prohibiting slavery above the Ohio River in the Northwest Territory, there was steady pressure in Illinois and Indiana into the 1820s to open those young states to slavery. The last positive step of the revolutionary generation occurred in 1808 when President Jefferson in unequivocal moral language persuaded Congress to end immediately the foreign slave trade in accordance with the twenty-year optional provision written into the Constitution. If slavery continued to exist at the time of Jefferson's death, it was not the institution it had been in 1776. Dying in the North, it was prohibited in the Northwest Territory and pressed deeper into the South. The tragedy of American Negro slavery lay not so much at the feet of Jefferson's generation, but rather it fell upon succeeding generations for failing to complete what had already been started, for not spelling out the remaining moral implications of the American Revolution.

Home-front activities involved more than building new political structures and improving the quality of American life; the war was an ever-present reality that at times took precedence over long-range goals and aspirations. Probably there was no greater concern in much of America than for the enemy within, the Loyalists, whose numbers were likely equal to between 20 and 30 percent of the white population. This admittedly imprecise estimate reflects recent studies which have scaled down sharply older interpretations that indicated possibly half the colonists retained their allegiance to the House of Hanover. The patriots were most numerous in states of purest English stock, while the proportion of Loyalists was highest among religious and cultural minorities who felt threatened by a ruling majority in church and state. Partly for these reasons, the Tories were ubiquitous in the heterogeneous middle states, but nowhere—not even in New York (contrary to long-accepted opinion)—did the king's friends balance the scale with the king's enemies. The South was heavily patriot, except for royal officeholders, backcountry pockets of royalists, and a scattering of others. There was never a problem of that nature for

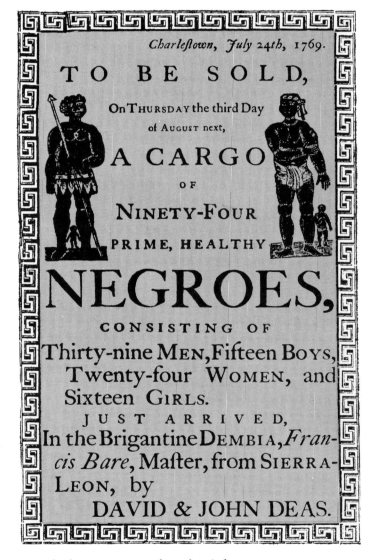

*Broadside announcing the sale of slaves
taken in Sierra-Leone.
Posters of this type were an
important advertising medium in the
eighteenth century for the sale of
all kinds of property, for recruiting,
and for public announcements.*

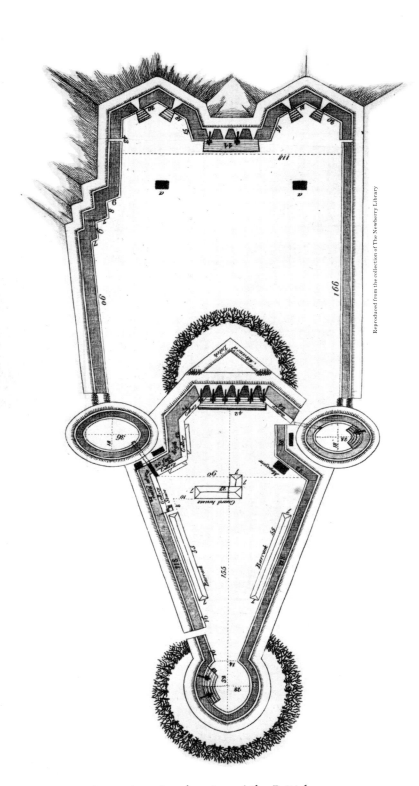

*An engineering drawing of the British
fortification on Bunker Hill, made at the
time the British evacuated Boston.
Figures on the drawing are paces of
three feet each and indicate that the
fort was approximately nine hundred feet long
and perhaps three hundred fifty feet wide.
The parapet was
from six to fifteen feet wide.*

the patriots in New England, where it is doubtful that 10 percent backed the crown.

Loyalists were a cross section of people, far from the standard image held by many modern Americans: of colonial high aristocrats—merchants, landowners, and placemen—who were ultraconservatives opposed to all change, or who for selfish or venal reasons were traitors to their fellow Americans. Most Loyalists were ordinary people—farmers, artisans, and laborers—whose behavior is understood by no monolithic explanation. Nor can we comprehend the responses of the Loyalist upper crust merely in terms of a wish to retain economic and political preferment. For they, like the patriots, came primarily from a background of reading the great English Whig writers, of glorifying 1688, and venerating the British constitution. Not a few of them agreed with "no taxation without representation" and other elements of the American creed.

But countless Loyalists, for all their Whiggery, drew back from still other American Whigs in their contention that a conspiracy to enslave them existed in the mother country. Why? It may be that the Loyalists were more imbued with traditional Whiggery, and the patriots more addicted to commonwealth, or radical, Whig writers who not only were shrill in their warnings to be ever alert for conspiracies, but who also espoused certain republican principles that were anathema to the king's friends. Or as William Smith of New York said, "If you want a New Government, it should have been in the British Model. I am a Whigg of the old Stamp."

If the Loyalists were also American Whigs, of sorts at least, they constituted a dangerous menace, a kind of potential fifth column in later terminology. The Continental Congress prodded the states into enacting treason statutes and laws detailing lesser crimes against the Revolution, such as praising the king, arousing disaffection in the militia, spreading rumors to undercut morale, and providing the British with intelligence. While Congress provided loyalty oaths for the army, the states did the same for their own civilians. These statements of fealty were not confined to those suspected of wavering sentiments or inimical acts. John Adams believed such declarations would stimulate the revolutionists to measure up to their sacred promise to battle for liberty and country. A welter of committees, commissions, courts, and individual officials enforced legislative edicts. The more drastic the danger the more severe the patriot response as when, for example, Tories were stirring in New York State with the Howe brothers threatening Manhattan Island in September 1776. A state public safety committee was set up to coordinate local committees and to gather information on disaffected persons. Formal legal action against Loyalists was usually the task of the state attorney general, who presented the government's charge before regular tribunals or specially convened judicial bodies. At the same time, the most serious disturbances brought out the state militias, and they were usually effective—maintaining order, seizing dangerous persons, and battling disaffection in all its forms. On the whole, prompt action early in the Revolution intimidated or coerced the Tories to the point that they were never a viable force to be seriously reckoned with except in small areas either occupied or menaced by British armies.

All told, approximately 60,000 Loyalists left America, either voluntarily or involuntarily. Nearly 1,000 departed from Boston in 1776, and there were mass exoduses at the end of the war when British troops evacuated Charleston and New York City. A substantial majority of the departing Tories settled in Canada, where their descendants today are members of the United Empire Loyalists, an active organization. Quebec, Ontario, Nova Scotia, New Brunswick, and Prince Edward Island received the exiles, as did other parts of the empire, particularly England and the

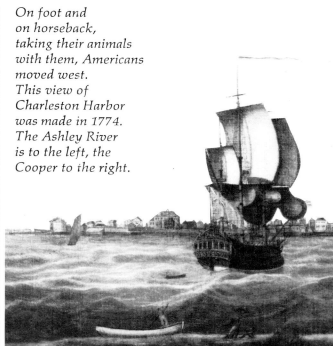

*On foot and
on horseback,
taking their animals
with them, Americans
moved west.
This view of
Charleston Harbor
was made in 1774.
The Ashley River
is to the left, the
Cooper to the right.*

West Indies. Many emigrants endured hardships in moving to pioneering areas of Canada, and there were difficult adjustments elsewhere as well, although Britain was reasonably generous to most of those who filed claims in London to document their loss of office and property. Over £ 3,000,000 were distributed among 4,118 American royalists.

There had been undeniable mistreatment of the Loyalists at the hands of the rebels, although it is well to remember that a revolution is never a placid affair; and to a large extent, American officials resorted to judicial processes in dealing with their internal opponents. A cluster of nonoffending Loyalists sat out the war unmolested. The mass slaughter and hangmen's harvests that have marked a multitude of later revolutions and civil wars simply did not occur. In his *Notes on Virginia*, Jefferson took satisfaction in stating that "not a single execution for treason" took place in the Old Dominion.

The patriots, too, did their share of suffering, and not only those who shouldered arms. There were massacres of civilians by Loyalists and Indians in western New York, and there were destructive raids in Kentucky and other frontier areas as well as along the coast. The fierce, partisan war in the southern backcountry took the lives of untold noncombatants on both sides. Banastre Tarleton's Tory Legion cut a swath of destruction across the South Carolina piedmont. After Tarleton leveled houses and burned fields, declared Francis Marion, it was not uncommon to find "Women & Children huddled . . . in the open Air round a fire without a blanket or any Cloathing but what they had on."

On the economic front, there were vicissitudes aplenty. The average Continental soldier had little leftover cash from his modest pay to send home to his family. It is doubtful that the lot of most officers was much better, since they were expected to purchase their own uniforms and meet their other needs from their salaries. Both soldiers and civilians experienced a multitude of hardships resulting from mounting inflation and skyrocketing prices. In a country lacking a stable national currency and possessing little in the way of manufacturers, such upward trends were almost inevitable. Congress and the states had no alternative to printing huge sums of paper money, which lacked specie backing and which consequently declined sharply in value.

The severest suffering occurred among people on fixed salaries: laborers, artisans, dockworkers, servicemen, clergymen, and public officials; for although wages went up, they rarely kept pace with the inflationary spiral. James Iredell, attorney general of North Carolina, found that a week of travel in May 1780 cost him $600. Between March and September of that same year Congressman James Madison spent $21,373 for room and board and other personal necessities in Philadelphia. Fortunately, only a small fraction of the population consisted of salaried persons.

At times planters and merchants accused each other of heightening inflation. On the whole, it was an argument that could scarcely point in a single direction. Yet merchants probably profited more than any other element in the country. Those who engaged in privateering and importing military stores often performed a vital public service in the course of making a private gain. To the merchant, the key was the volume of his business, which necessitated a constant turnover in goods and a constant turnover in ever-depreciating currency before it became valueless. Inflation, however, may have been a benefit to many a farmer whose obligations, mainly taxes and debts, did not increase at the rate of his produce; he and the larger planter as well might often sell only a part of their crops to meet obligations, then hold back the remainder in anticipation of still higher prices later.

A final economic question concerns the effects of the confiscation of land belonging to the Loyalists. Certainly the extension of social and economic democracy was not the objective of the American state governments in seizing Loyalist estates (which were sold to the highest bidders), but rather to raise money for prosecuting the war. The evidence currently available suggests that there was a fairly extensive subdivision of rural lands (hence, some acreage passed to common, landless people), while urban properties went from the affluent Tories to the affluent Whigs.

Since wartime hardships dampened morale among civilians as well as soldiers, newspapers performed a notable service in reviving patriotic sentiments. If printers themselves felt the adverse impact of war in soaring paper costs and having to move their presses to escape British troops, most of them remained in business, and they were not above personal humor about their own problems, as one can see from the March 22, 1780, issue of the *Pennsylvania Journal:*

> Says Thomas, our neighbours have wrote to the Printer,
> To stop sending news-papers during the winter;
> For living is hard, and provisions are dear,
> And there's seldom much news at this time of the year;
> But in summer the Papers more news will contain,
> And then or in spring we may take them again.
> Says John, neighbour Thomas, your scheme makes me smile;
> But how is the Printer to live the mean while?
> If times are so hard, as you do not deny,
> The Printer, unless he's supported must die.
> Till summer or spring, he can never survive,
> Unless thro' the winter you keep him alive.

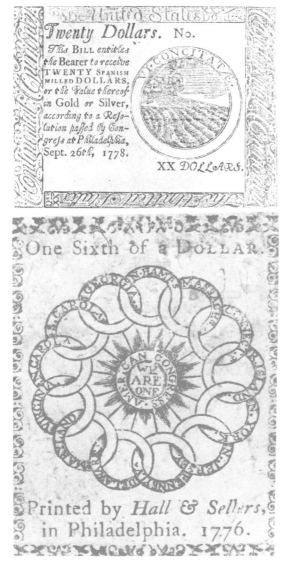

Money printed by the Continental Congress held its value during the first year and a half of the war and then dropped sharply in value, leading to the phrase, "Not worth a Continental."

And if you once starve him, it will be in vain
To expect that he ever will serve you again
Says Thomas, indeed we did none of us think
That Printers could feel, or could want meat or drink,
Or like other people would clothing require,
Or wood for the warming themselves with a fire.
And if none of these wants any trouble could pause,
They might live as the bears do, by sucking their paws.

Printers filled their columns with reports of battles, foreign news from London and Paris, proclamations of Congress, appeals for volunteers, and lists of deserters. British depravity, Loyalist treachery, and American virtue were themes designed to combat war weariness. It was the *Essex Journal* of Newburyport, Massachusetts, that started Washington's captured spy Nathan Hale on his path to immortality, although the prose of the hero as reported here is a bit less succinct than the much-quoted version that appeared years afterward. "If he had ten thousand lives," so he was quoted in the *Journal*, "he would lay them all down, if called to it, in defence of his injured, bleeding country." Myriad essays written under Latin pseudonyms—as was the custom then—sought to clarify the issues of the Revolution. "The consequences of this Struggle," predicted *Cato* in the *South-Carolina Gazette*, "will determine, whether Americans will be Freemen or Slaves." The "nature of the American Revolution," asserted another South Carolinian, was to secure for Americans greater freedom than men had ever known at any time in history. Still another essayist saw a "most just and holy war, in defence of our country, our wives, children, parents, sisters, and to secure to ourselves and our posterity the inestimable blessings of *Liberty*."

Occasionally, too, a song or ballad appeared in the *Boston Gazette*, the *Newport Mercury*, or the *Connecticut Courant*. Assuredly none compare with such songs of the Civil War as "Dixie" or "The Battle Hymn of the Republic." The closest thing to a ballad of that popularity was "Yankee Doodle," which seems to have predated the war in its original form. A number of the songs relate to events of the Revolution. So it is with the anonymously written "Ballad of Nathan Hale"; with Francis Hopkinson's "The Battle of the Kegs," about fighting near Philadelphia; and with Philip Freneau's "The British Prison Ship," about the sufferings of incarcerated Americans.

Americans, not yet a singing people as they would be by the Harrison presidential campaign of 1840, were more likely to be stirred by a rousing sermon, filled with what future generations, imbued with camp-meeting fervor, would describe as fire and brimstone. Steeped in a Calvinist tradition, most Americans were Protestants of the fundamentalist variety, whose clergymen found striking parallels between the Israelites and the Americans, each God's chosen people at a particular time in history. The Jews had known the yoke of oppressive rulers, just as Americans were feeling the sword of George III. The Almighty, as revealed in the Old Testament, had called for the tribes of Abraham and Jacob to throw off their oppressors, a message that rang with relevance from a host of American pulpits where, besides, the great warrior David was seen as only an early version of George Washington. The frequent recourse to Washington, by ministers and by printers, was also indicative of something else, the slow, at times almost imperceptible growth of American nationalism, of which Washington was the most powerful symbol and his army—drawn from all the states—the most tangible force.

A view of Philadelphia looking across the Schuylkill River made on November 28, 1777. The city had been occupied by the British two months earlier, and Congress had fled to York. Philadelphia was not to come back to American hands until after the surrender of the British.

The Fringes: Land and Sea

This primitive cart was used by the early settlers and was still in use at the time of the Revolution. The fort at Boonesboro, Kentucky, was built by Daniel Boone in 1775.

PICTURE A TOILING farmer, his muscles rippling under a summer sun as he guides a crude wooden plow through rich Ohio River bottomland. There are shots from trees along the edge of the clearing. The man falls across his plow. Soon there are war whoops, followed by screams from the nearby cabin. Before long neighbors a mile or so away see a thick column of smoke rolling up above the trees. Another family wiped out; another collection of drying scalps outside an Indian lodge.

That scene, repeated countless times, was also part of the Revolution, part of a conflict fought far from the long-settled areas. It is not so well remembered, this struggle for the West. To be sure, the West had yet to become romanticized in American poetry and prose. There were no legendary heroes—boatmen, trappers, gamblers, and other "bad men," and two-holstered marshals; no Mike Finks, Davy Crocketts, Jedediah Smiths, "Buffalo Bill" Codys, and "Wild Bill" Hickoks.

There was, of course, Daniel Boone, who in 1775 led the second division of settlers to Kentucky, founding Boonesborough in the month of Lexington and Concord. Soon after the Revolution, Boone did become a legend in his own time owing to John Filson's *Discovery, Settlement, and Present State of Kentucke* (1784), followed by treatment of the frontiersman in the eighth canto of Lord Byron's *Don Juan*, which gave him worldwide acclaim. Although hardly "the First White Man of the West" or a plethora of other things attributed to him, Boone—of only medium height, pleasant, and quiet-spoken, and free of traditional frontier vices—as a man had plenty of accomplishments. Possessed of real character, he imparted his mastery of woodcraft and expertness with the rifle to the pioneers of Kentucky, who were almost constantly menaced by Indians during the Revolutionary War.

Initially, however, neither the British nor the Americans seemed zealous to employ the aborigines, whose sympathetic neutrality was desired by both camps. Still, the idea of bringing down destructive raids upon one's opponents was too tempting for either side to eschew for long. Consequently, it is very likely impossible to say which one should bear the onus of first calling the hatchet and scalping knife into the fray. Of this we may be sure: nursing a host of age-old grievances against the colonists, the vast preponderance of tribesmen who set out along the war trails did so in the name of the king and not the Continental Congress. Many Indians, in fact, would have taken the field against the settlers without the consent or encouragement of British authorities. Among the British, General Thomas Gage and Lord George Germain seemed particularly anxious to secure redskinned allies.

Boone and his fellow Kentuckians, in the westernmost American outposts, felt especially vulnerable. Boonesborough, Harrodstown (named for the pioneer leader James Harrod), and St. Asaph (named for the Anglican bishop sympathetic to the patriot cause) were indeed designed for extermination by British officers at Detroit. The commander, Colonel Henry Hamilton, sent out a series of expeditions that made 1777—the year of the "Three 7's"—one of such horror that frontiersmen never forgot it. It was in the following year that a large raid resulted in the capture of Boone himself, who was taken as a prisoner to Detroit, from which he later escaped.

But the first Kentuckian whose fame reached the eastern seaboard was George Rogers Clark, not Daniel Boone. Clark, a twenty-five-year-old surveyor, planned a campaign of retaliation that would climax with the capture of Detroit. Without that base, the British could not send out small parties of Loyalists and redcoats to lead the painted warriors—the Miami, Wyandot, Ottawa, Wabash, and other tribes north of the Ohio—against the frontier hamlets stretching along that river from Fort Pitt (or Pittsburgh) southward. Nor would the Indians, dependent on Detroit for their arms, clothing, blankets, and liquor, act without succor from Hamilton. He was, according to the patriots, "the hair-buyer"—that is, he was believed to have paid the Indians for each scalp they brought in, an allegation he denied.

Traveling to Williamsburg, Clark received permission and financial support from Governor Patrick Henry, a necessary step since Virginia was Kentucky's parent state. Clark first proposed to seize Kaskaskia, Cahokia, and Vincennes in the Illinois country, which was inhabited by a few hundred Frenchmen, before proceeding against Detroit.

Clark, a tall, sinewy redhead, was made of the stuff of heroes. With only 175 men, he floated down the Ohio, then marched overland to occupy the French towns. So far, all had gone well; the townspeople welcomed him, and nearby Indians seemed impressed by his appearance. But Clark had to abandon temporarily notions of moving against Detroit, since many men left because their term of service was up. To compound his woes, word reached him at Kaskaskia that Henry Hamilton had responded to his invasion of the Illinois country by hastening southward from Detroit and had captured the garrison Clark had left at Vincennes. But if Hamilton intended to wait until spring to strike at Clark, Clark would not await seasonal changes to counter Hamilton. Surprise was the key to Clark, who wrote Patrick Henry that "Great things have been effected by a few men well conducted." Clark struggled westward through the most inclement weather imaginable, sloshing and fording the 180 miles to Vincennes, where the unsuspecting Hamilton put up only token resistance before surrendering.

Temporarily, at least, it seemed that British power might crumble in the interior, for to the south as well as to the north the patriots scored successes. The Cherokee and Creek nations dwelled along the southern frontier, and farther to the west were the villages of the Chickasaw and Choctaw. The Cherokee braves, despite warnings from some of their elders,

This view of the city of Detroit was made in July 1794. It was still occupied by the British at that time, not being turned over to America until 1796, and was little more than a military outpost. Philadelphia, by comparison, was a complex city.

needed no goading from British Southern Indian Superintendent John Stuart, who actually sought to restrain them until England could help them. Pouring from their "towns" in the mountain valleys of the lower

*General Nicholas Herkimer
led a force of
New York State farmers
against Burgoyne's troops
as they came south from
Canada in 1777. Though
he died in the attack at
Oriskany, he forced
Burgoyne to stop. In
February 1779, Lieutenant
Colonel George Rogers
Clark left Kaskaskia,
which he had captured the
previous summer, and
took Fort Vincennes from
the British, who were
under the command of
Colonel Henry Hamilton.*

Appalachians, they applied the torch and the hatchet to the outlying parts of Georgia and South Carolina. Settlers in the Watauga River communities of present-day eastern Tennessee repulsed similar onslaughts.

The militia, for all its inadequacies, could be exceedingly effective in border warfare. A sizable army of irregulars, drawn from Virginia, the Carolinas, and Georgia, invaded the heart of the Cherokee country, devastating fields and towns, compelling their adversaries to sign humiliating treaties of peace with various American states in 1777. Down but not out, Chief Dragging Canoe aroused some of the Cherokee, and intermittent fighting continued for several years, but the Indians were never the threat they had been, partly because they were deeply divided on their course of action. Repeatedly their forays were checked by James Robertson, Isaac Shelby, Arthur Campbell, and other frontier leaders.

From his headquarters at Pensacola, Stuart sought to mobilize the Creek, Choctaw, and Chickasaw; but not all their chiefs saw the danger of white settlements spreading upon their lands, and patriot emissaries pressed them to forgo their war chants. Only the Upper Creeks took up the hatchet, but they did so late and accomplished little.

The patriots recognized that the destruction of British power on the lower Mississippi would effectively curtail the Indians, who depended upon guns and supplies from the crown's agents there. It was Spain, not America, that overwhelmed the English in the Floridas. In May 1779 Spain entered the war, and under orders of her vigorous twenty-three-year-old governor at New Orleans, Bernardo de Gálvez, overran British stations at Baton Rouge and Natchez on the Mississippi in September 1779 before seizing Mobile on the Gulf coast in March 1780. With Gálvez's victorious siege of Pensacola in May of the following year, all of West Florida came under Spanish control.

In the northern borderlands, the story was not so favorable to England's enemies. George Rogers Clark, who never gained sufficient strength to move against Detroit, had checked his opponents only temporarily, though there remains the persistent historical myth that he "won the Northwest," assuring that the transmontane country would belong to the new republic in the 1783 peace treaty. The early 1780s once again saw the frontiers in flames and Clark and Boone—very real saviors of Kentucky—on the defensive.

On the upper Ohio, British-Indian raiding parties operated out of Fort Niagara, a strategic anchor point of royal power comparable to Detroit in the far northwest and Pensacola in the far southwest. Niagara was a provisioning base for the Iroquois, or Six Nations (Mohawk, Oneida, Cayuga, Onondaga, Seneca, and Tuscarora), of central New York and northern Pennsylvania. Culturally advanced compared to other Indians of the period, they formed a relatively stable confederation. They dwelled in log houses, sometimes with fireplaces and glass windows. Their noncombatants cultivated gardens and orchards. The Iroquois, for decades allies of the English, were somewhat slow to take the field, partly because Sir Guy Carleton, as governor of Quebec, had reservations about the savagery of Indian warfare. His successor in 1778, Swiss-born General Frederick Haldimand, was ready to use his forest satellites. With only a few troops to defend Canada, he feared an American invasion that would arouse the French Canadians as a consequence of the Franco-American alliance. He had able assistance in the Mohawk chieftain Joseph Brant, a devout Anglican, educated in England; in the Johnsons, John and Guy,

*Congress declared, on June 14, 1777, that
the new flag of the country should have
thirteen red and white stripes and
thirteen white stars on a blue field.
The Massachusetts expedition against the
British-held port of Penobscot Bay
failed in August 1779.
John Paul Jones, although only five feet
six inches tall, was a giant of the
Revolutionary navy.
Photo courtesy of the Chicago
Historical Soicety.*

relatives of British Northern Indian Superintendent Sir William Johnson; and in another family team, Major John Butler and his son Captain Walter Butler. Leading bands of Loyalists and Indians, they spread a dark hand of destruction over the Wyoming Valley of Pennsylvania and parts of western New York. Forty Fort (the "Wyoming massacre"), German Flats, Cherry Valley, and Minisink were place-names that conjured up visions of blood and gore. (*See Map 37*)

Although Congress had established a Western Department with headquarters at Pittsburgh, it always lacked sufficient forces to cope with Indian threats; the states, and usually the settlers themselves, more often than not had to devise defensive measures. Washington, however, felt that he could not allow the Indian depredations to continue unchecked. Consequently, he sent an expedition under General John Sullivan—Gates had first declined the command—into the Iroquois country of New York.

Here, as in the campaign against the Cherokee in 1776–77, Americans concluded that the best defense was a good offense, that carrying the war to the Indian villages was the way to bring the tribesmen to their knees. It was believed that the Indians, seeing a threat to their fields and homes, would finally be compelled to stand and fight in the fashion of the white man. (*See Map 37*)

Sullivan, dogged by bad luck previously, saw his fortunes change, and no doubt the explanation is that the campaign was well planned and therefore smoothly executed. Despite the opposition of the Butlers, Sir John Johnson, and Joseph Brant, their followers overruled them and insisted on offering battle. At Newtown, on August 29, 1779, 600 to 800 Tories and Indians fought a brief engagement with Sullivan's army of over 4,000 before the former scattered, leaving few casualties on either side. So ended the only real battle of the campaign, with the Butlers and Brant falling back to Niagara. In all, Sullivan destroyed an estimated 40 villages, 1,500 fruit trees, and acres of corn containing approximately 160,000 bushels. Both sides had committed cruelties and atrocities, as was usually true of border engagements. Lieutenant Erkuries Beatty told of entering Genessee Town and finding the bodies of a Lieutenant Thomas Boyd and an enlisted man. "They was both stripped naked, and their heads cut off, and the flesh of Lieutenant Boyd's was entirely taken off and his eyes punched out." On the other hand, Lieutenant William Barton encountered several dead Indians "and skinned two of them from their hips down for boot legs; one pair for the Major and the other for myself."

Major Jeremiah Fogg summed up the pluses and minuses of the Sullivan expedition when he declared, "The nests are destroyed, but the birds are still on the wing." The early 1780s saw renewed sweeps by Brant and his friends into the Schoharie and Mohawk valleys of New York. State forces retaliated under General Robert Van Rensselaer and Colonel Marinus Willett, and though they blunted several enemy thrusts, the Indian-Loyalist raiders usually escaped to the sanctuary of Niagara, so that permanent peace on the frontier had to await diplomatic events in Europe.

The war in the West rang down with neither side gaining a decided military advantage. And yet the Americans were not driven out. In fact, their numbers multiplied in spite of the dangers. According to some sources, 20,000 people poured into Kentucky in the last stages of the conflict, traveling through the Cumberland Gap and following what became known as the Wilderness Road. In the 1790s three frontier areas—Vermont, Kentucky, and Tennessee—would become the first additions to the original thirteen states. In the not too distant future, the tide of inland settlement would surge beyond the Mississippi River to French Louisiana, purchased in 1803 by President Thomas Jefferson, who hailed from Charlottesville, Virginia, the early home of that frontiersman who had helped pave the way, George Rogers Clark. Appropriately enough, it was Jefferson who sent William Clark, younger brother of George Rogers, as one of the leaders of an expedition to explore this "empire of liberty."

Along the Atlantic frontier the Americans also had their ups and downs as they endeavored to dispute the waves with mighty Britannia. In the early fall of 1775, even before Congress created a navy, the colonists were afloat.

Washington took the initiative in arming eight or more coastal vessels manned by Colonel John Glover's Marblehead regiment and other New England fishermen. That fall those vessels brought in twenty-three prizes, including the royal brig *Nancy*, which carried 2,000 muskets, 100,000 flints, and huge quantities of musket shot and round shot. By 1777, when Congress absorbed it into the regular sea service, the Yankee fleet—"George Washington's navy"—had seized fifty-five enemy ships.

The opening rounds of the war in 1775 had also seen private efforts to outfit sea raiders. "Privateering" was a tradition that extended back to the first intercolonial struggles, and it was Esek Hopkins, captain of a privateer in the French and Indian War, who was picked as the ranking officer in the American revolutionary navy. Privateers were owned by merchants and other investors, and they sailed under letters of marque (written authorization) from the colony-state governments or the Continental Congress, thus escaping the designation of pirates. Even so, there was the ever-present danger that Britain would treat captured privateersmen as pirates, particularly if a crew were composed of men of various nationalities, or if the captain were only recently English or Scottish. Since New England fishermen were now forbidden to cast their nets off the Grand Banks of Newfoundland, they eagerly signed on board privateers, where rewards were infinitely greater than in the Continental navy; all profits of privateering went directly to owners and crews, whereas the Continental government collected a percentage from the sale of captured maritime property.

It seems probable that well over 2,000 ships were commissioned as privateers, 600 by Massachusetts alone. Ranging from 100 to 500 tons,

This wood engraving published in 1838 shows five American prisoners escaping from a British prison ship during the Revolution. Battered battleship hulls, unfit for combat service, frequently served as prisons or floating barracks.

John Paul Jones,
commanding the Bon Homme Richard,
attacked the British Serapis,
which was convoying merchantmen.
The early fight
went against Jones, but
he refused to surrender, saying,
"I have not yet begun to fight."
Eventually, the Serapis struck
her colors. The Bon Homme Richard
sank, and Jones moved
his crew to the Serapis.

they carried as many as twenty guns and crews that averaged fifty men. And they caused Britain no end of trouble! In France, Benjamin Franklin personally supervised the activities of several privateers, whose chief aim was to provide the venerable Pennsylvanian with prisoners to exchange for American seamen in British prisons. The year 1777 found marine insurance rates in London jumping over 20 percent, solid proof of the impact of American privateering. During the war, these unofficial commerce raiders are estimated to have netted over 600 prizes compared to fewer than 200 by the small Continental navy.

Several state naval establishments also antedated the congressional naval arm. In time, eleven states (Delaware and New Jersey were exceptions) created some sort of armed maritime service, varying from New Hampshire with one ship to Massachusetts with a goodly number. They were chiefly small vessels—galleys, barges, and other makeshift craft— mainly concerned with the protection of rivers, harbors, and coastlines. A striking exception was the twenty-six-gun *Protector*, a Massachusetts frigate which in 1780 sank the thirty-two-gun *Admiral Duff* off the coast of Newfoundland, one of the severest actions of the war. Like the outfitters of privateers, state naval authorities rivaled Congress for seamen, and indeed the states competed with each other on occasion, one being when South Carolina attempted to enlist 500 seamen from the state of Massachusetts.

Rhode Island, a colony peculiarly vulnerable to the sea, took the initiative in the establishment of the United States Navy by instructing its congressional delegation to employ its "whole influence . . . for building, at the Continental expence, a fleet of sufficient force, for the protection of these colonies." Assuredly "defence" was a key word, for Americans recognized that they had neither the resources nor the know-how to assemble squadrons to match Britain's. In addition, however, an American

First
Major Battle
in the West Indies

navy would annoy and distract the enemy by disrupting Britain's sea communications and picking off individual vessels. To plunder Britain's commerce would cut into the supplies available to the army in America, supplies that Washington's own troops could put to good use.

Congress responded on October 30—the navy's birthday—by creating the first of several committees that directed naval affairs until 1779, when there was set up a Board of Admiralty, consisting of five commissioners, of whom three were not members of the national legislature. Two years later Congress theoretically launched a separate Department of Marine, which never really functioned, although Superintendent of Finance Robert Morris performed the functions that would have been exercised by a secretary of marine. Fortunately, many men who staffed the congressional committees and board were dedicated, hard-working individuals; they not infrequently sat from the close of Congress's legislative day, from six in the evening or so, until midnight, handling the thousand and one activities associated with creating and sustaining a navy. Among those who stood out were John Langdon and Josiah Bartlett of New Hampshire, Stephen Hopkins of Rhode Island, Richard Henry Lee of Virginia, Joseph Hewes of North Carolina, and Christopher Gadsden of South Carolina. Particularly valuable were such men as Hewes, who as merchants and shipowners brought real expertise to their work.

All told, 330 commissioned officers served in the navy and the marines. (Naval officers wore blue coats and red waistcoats, marine officers green coats and white waistcoats—when available.) Unlike the Continental army with its sprinkling of ex-British and foreign officers, the sea service had only one officer with real professional training, Captain Nicholas Biddle, who had entered the British navy as a midshipman in 1770. Later in the war Congress did bestow a commission on one Frenchman with a naval background, Captain Pierre Landais, who proved incompetent, if not half-crazy. Yet former merchant captains and mates—men highly knowledgeable of the sea—constituted a considerable percentage of those chosen to command American vessels. The ablest captains turned out to be Biddle, John Barry, Lambert Wickes, John Young and, of course, John Paul Jones. At the outset, though, politics played a part in the selections by Congress, so that Jones, a recent Scottish immigrant, was passed over in favor of master mariners with local backing.

So far, historians have told us relatively little about the common seamen of the period. They were called Jack-tar in both England and the colonies, as well as seamen, sailors, and mariners, although the last named might refer to a "master" or captain. Who was Jack-tar or whatever we may choose to call him? It was said that he walked with bowed legs, sometimes described as a "waddle." His uniform in the American navy, if he had one, might consist of a neckerchief, overly large jacket, red shirt, and loose-fitting trousers that were perhaps tarred for waterproofing. It was once assumed that most seamen were country lads who signed on for a voyage or more to get the wanderlust out of their system; but lately it has been demonstrated that many were a rather distinct element or class, men who had made their livelihood from the sea, and who—because of their long hatred of impressment by the British navy—were overwhelmingly patriot in their loyalties.

Certainly Jack-tar found conditions in the American navy less severe than in the royal fleet, and yet, as we have seen, the typical sailor preferred to sail on a privateer rather than on a Continental cruiser because of the

MAP 34. ¶ It is surprising how little has been written about the role of the West Indies during the Revolutionary War. The rich island colonies were of great significance to the British, French, Spanish, Dutch, and even the Danes. A number of notable battles between English and French naval and military forces took place in the Caribbean. ¶ After the French entered the war and were frustrated at Narragansett Bay, Admiral d'Estaing sailed from Boston for the West Indies. On the same day, November 4, 1778, Admiral Hotham left New York with a fleet carrying 5,800 men from Clinton's army, commanded by General James Grant. Admiral Barrington took command at Barbados and led the British attack on St. Lucia. Grant's troops were put ashore on December 12. They captured the French naval base minutes before d'Estaing arrived with a larger fleet convoying 9,000 troops from Martinique. ¶ The French fleet was unable to break Barrington's defense of Cul de Sac Bay. On December 16, d'Estaing put his army ashore at Anse du Choc and made two unsuccessful attacks against the British, sustaining heavy losses. The French eventually withdrew and returned to Martinique, a few miles to the north. Because of this hard-won victory over a superior French force, the British held St. Lucia throughout the war. ¶ A good indication of the terrain features and the locations and movements of the opposing armies can be seen on this informative plan. The successive alignments of both fleets are also clearly depicted. The inset shows the blockade of the French fleet established by Admiral Byron in Port Royal Harbor, Martinique, to the north.

SHOWN ON OPPOSITE PAGE
Attacks of St. Lucie with the Blockade of the French Fleet under Count D'Estaing in Martinico By Admiral Byrons Fleet. London, John Bowles, May 1, 1779. (9½" x 13½")

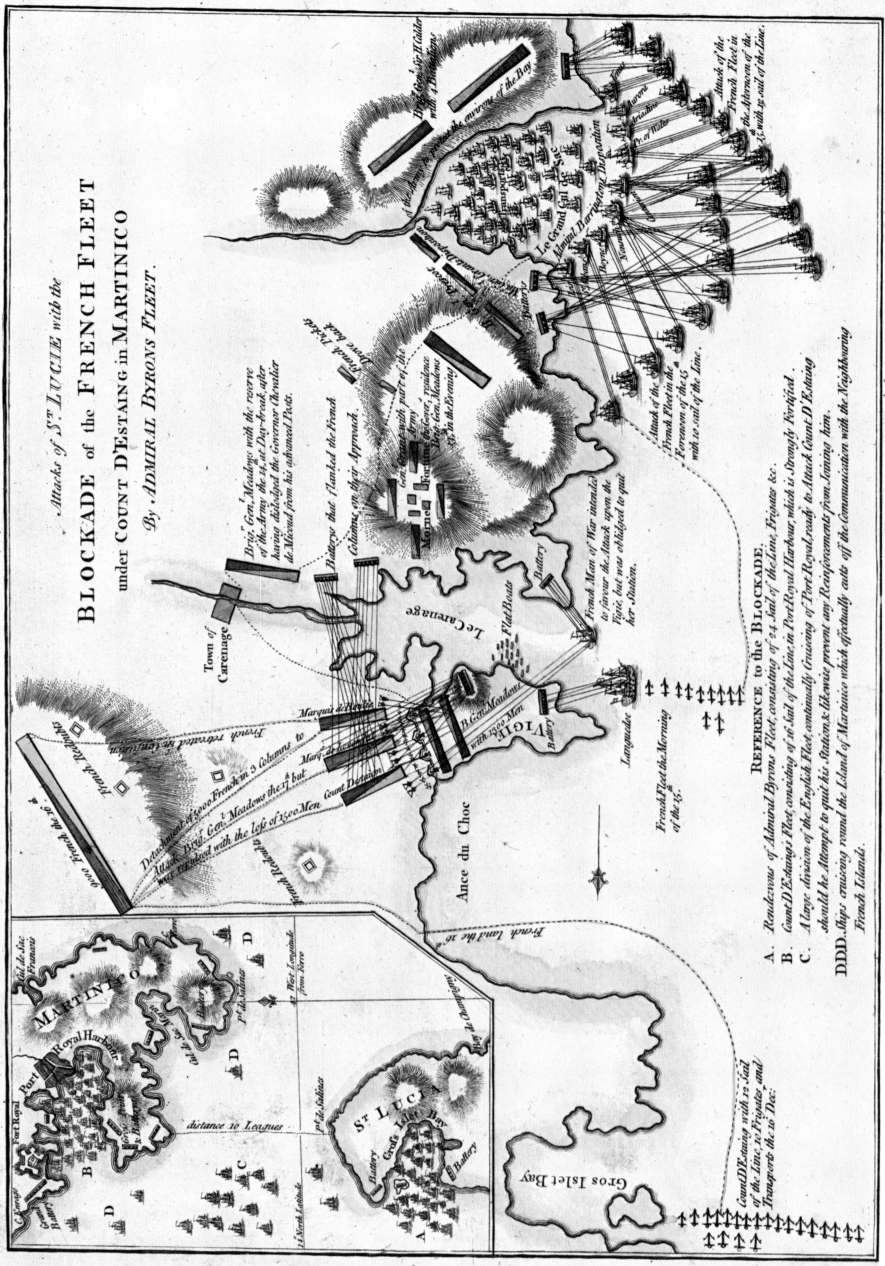

Attacks of St. LUCIE with the

BLOCKADE of the FRENCH FLEET
under COUNT D'ESTAING in MARTINICO
By ADMIRAL BYRONS FLEET.

REFERENCE to the BLOCKADE.

A. Rendezvous of Admiral Byrons Fleet, consisting of 24 Sail of the Line, Frigates &c.

B. Count D'Estaing's Fleet, consisting of 26 Sail of the Line, in Port Royal Harbour, which is strongly Fortified.

C. A large division of the English Fleet, continually Cruising of Port Royal ready to Attack Count D'Estaing should he Attempt to quit his Station, & likewise prevent any Reinforcements from Joining him.

DDD. Ships cruising round the Island of Martinico which effectually cuts off the Communication with the Neighbouring French Islands.

Publish'd as the Act directs 1st May 1779 by the Proprietor, & Sold by John Bowles No. 13 Cornhill. Price 1. 6d

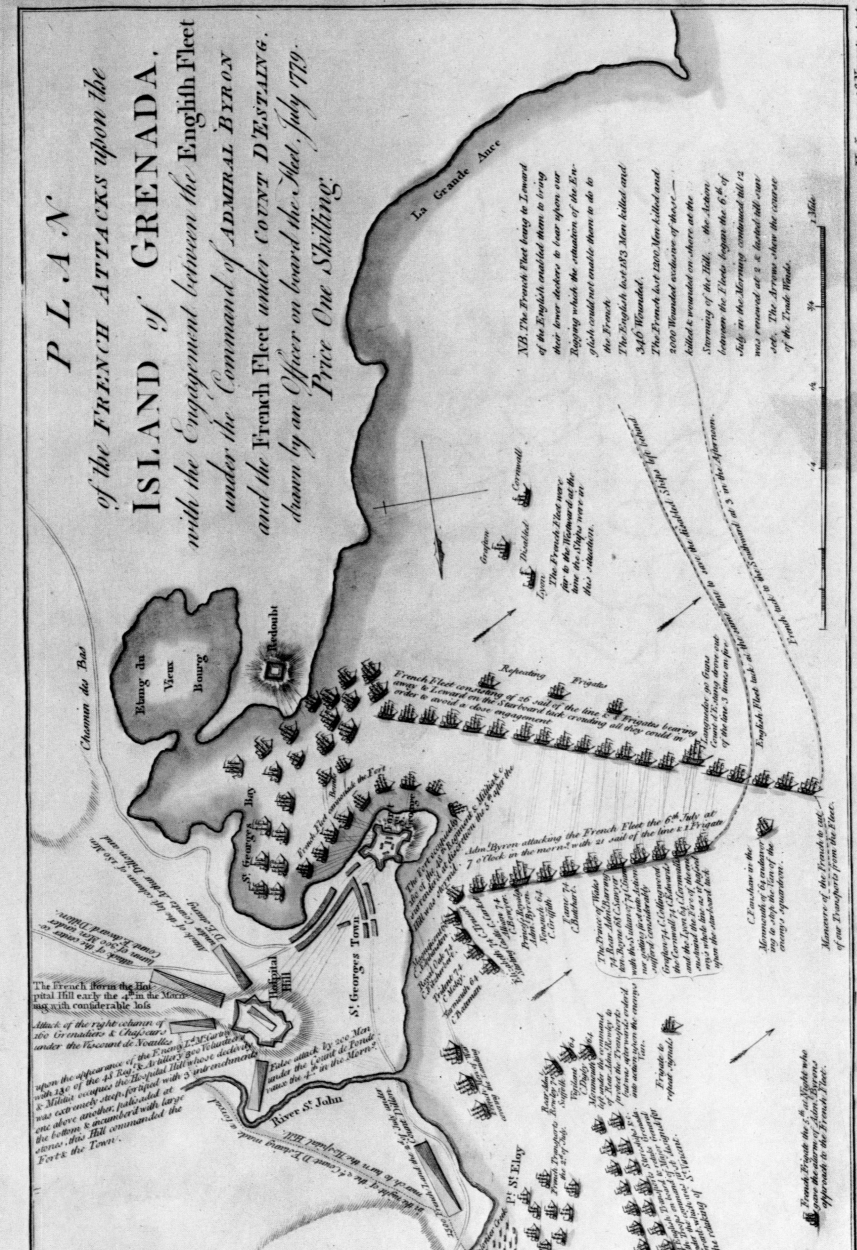

PLAN of the FRENCH ATTACKS upon the ISLAND of GRENADA. with the Engagement between the English Fleet under the Command of ADMIRAL BYRON and the French Fleet under COUNT D'ESTAING. drawn by an Officer on board the Fleet, July 1779. Price One Shilling.

Kauffman sc, 98 Newgate street.

London. Publish'd the 21.st Sept.r 1779. by J. Harris, Sweetings Alley, Cornhill.

D'Estaing Takes and Holds Grenada

MAP 35. ¶ When Byron's blockade lifted, de Grasse brought a French squadron into Martinique to reinforce d'Estaing. The French then took the islands of St. Vincent on June 16, 1779, and Grenada on July 4. On the following day Byron sailed with twenty-one ships-of-the-line and 1,000 troops under General Grant to retake St. Vincent. While under way, they changed their destination to Grenada. ¶ This plan shows the French army that d'Estaing led ashore to take Grenada. They assaulted fortified Hospital Hill above St. George's Town and took the island from the British. It also shows the major naval engagement of July 6, when the British fleet of twenty-one ships attacked d'Estaing's squadron of twenty-five ships. The action was fierce and the casualties heavy, but the results were indecisive, and Grenada remained in French hands. This southernmost of the Windward Islands was not restored to the British until the Treaty of Versailles in 1783.

SHOWN ON OPPOSITE PAGE

Plan of the French Attacks upon the Island of Grenada, with the Engagement between the English Fleet under the Command of Admiral Byron and the French Fleet under Count D'Estaing. Engraved by J. Luffman. London, J. Harris, Sept. 21, 1779. (9½″ x 14½″)

monetary advantages; he also doubtless found appealing the absence of regimentation and the opportunity to retire before serving a fixed number of years. Consequently, naval crews were often scraped together from the young and old, British deserters, and foreigners.

During the war, between fifty and sixty ships sailed under American emblems. Christopher Gadsden presented Esek Hopkins with what may have been considered only the fleet commander's personal standard, made of yellow silk, bearing a rattlesnake, and containing the motto Don't Tread on Me. The flag of the first fleet bore thirteen red and white stripes with British crosses in the upper canton next to the staff. Probably other insignias were in use here and there. In 1776 the *London Chronicle* reported the colors of the United Colonies to be a pine tree on a white field. Finally, on June 14, 1777, Congress resolved that "the flag of the United States be thirteen stripes, alternate red and white: that the union be thirteen stars, white in a blue field, representing a new constellation."

Congress, besides employing converted merchantmen and several ships purchased in France, began a modest program of naval construction. A small commerce-raiding navy did not need huge ships of the line, the counterpart of the modern battleship, which were stationed in a long battle line, with each fleet running by the other, firing round after round in the hope of hitting the enemy at the waterline or shredding his masts and sails. In fact, it seems somewhat ridiculous in retrospect that nations spent vast sums for such vessels, often 170 feet long and mounting 60 to 120 guns, with a crew of 450 to 1,000 men. For even observers in the eighteenth century acknowledged that naval battles between opponents of more or less equal strength were almost always indecisive. "Do you know what a naval battle is," asked an earlier French minister of marine, the Comte de Maurepas. "I will tell you: the fleets manoeuvre, come to grips, fire a few shots, and then each retreats . . . and the sea remains as salt as it was before."

In America, Congress quite appropriately turned to the building of frigates, which were noted for their speed and maneuverability vital to single-ship engagements. Similar to cruisers today, they were approximately 140 feet long, carried 200 to 300 men, and twenty-four to fifty guns. Some of the new vessels were extremely well constructed, a not surprising development since colonial shipyards had often repaired and refitted such British vessels in the past, and in fact had now and then produced ships for the Royal Navy as early as the 1690s.

Though the British blockade and the Americans own destruction of four frigates in the stocks to avoid their falling into enemy hands were serious setbacks to the infant navy, a number of the new commerce raiders escaped to sea. Captains Biddle, Barry, Wickes, Young, and Jones demonstrated their competence as naval officers as they roamed the Atlantic as far south as the West Indies, taking prizes, trading blows with British men-of-war, and convoying merchantmen. These single-ship actions were the key to the navy's modest accomplishments, although in the spring of 1776 Hopkins with a fleet of eight ships conducted a raid on Nassau in the Bahamas.

No account of the revolutionary navy can conclude without customary deference to that legendary figure John Paul, who had added the protective surname Jones after killing a mutinous sailor in self-defense prior to coming to the colonies. By the spring of 1777, Jones, operating along the Atlantic coast, had bagged an impressive collection of prizes. It was in

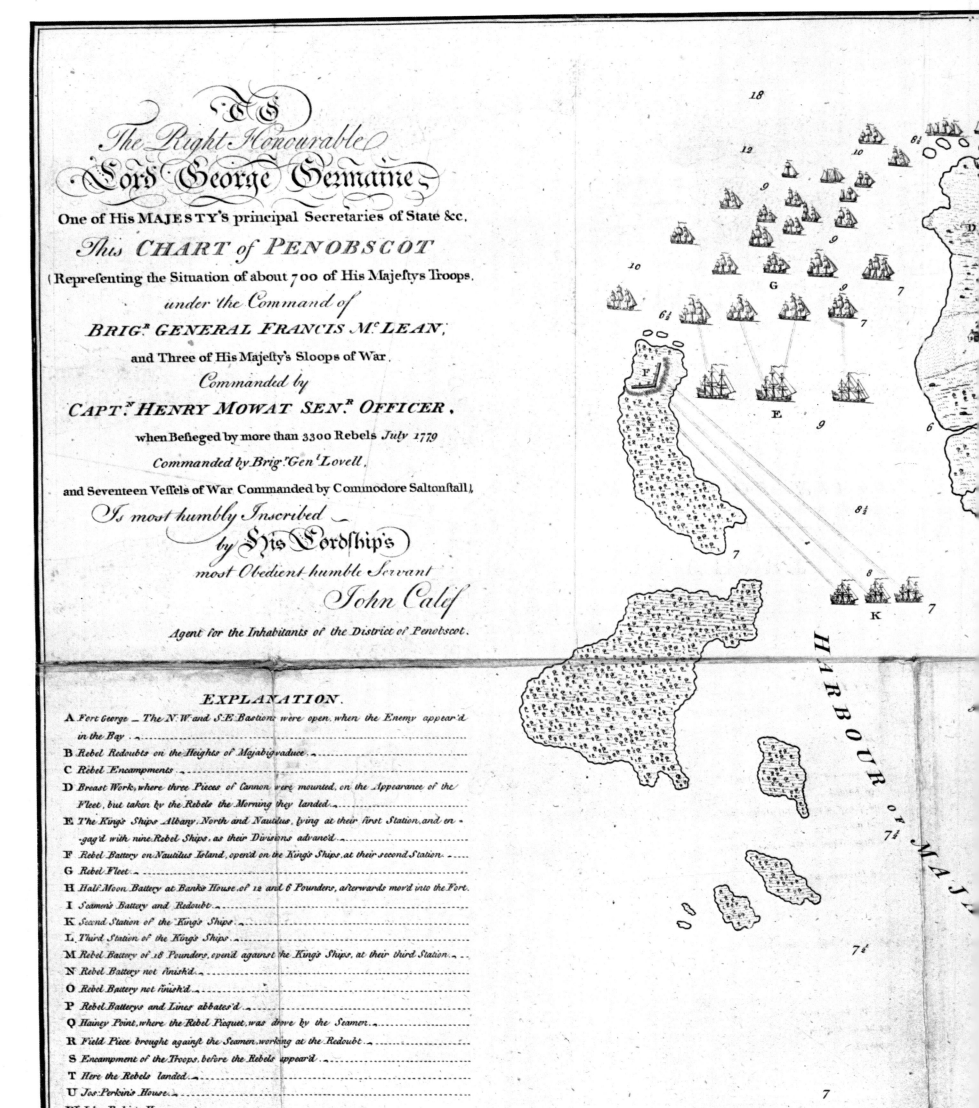

To
The Right Honourable
Lord George Germaine
One of His MAJESTY'S principal Secretaries of State &c.
This CHART of PENOBSCOT
Representing the Situation of about 700 of His Majestys Troops.
under the Command of
BRIG.ᴿ GENERAL FRANCIS Mᶜ LEAN,
and Three of His Majesty's Sloops of War.
Commanded by
CAPT.ᴺ HENRY MOWAT SEN.ᴿ OFFICER,
when Besieged by more than 3300 Rebels *July 1779*
Commanded by Brig.ᵣGen¹ Lovell.
and Seventeen Vessels of War Commanded by Commodore Saltonstall,
Is most humbly Inscribed
by His Lordship's
most Obedient humble Servant
John Calef
Agent for the Inhabitants of the District of Penobscot.

EXPLANATION.

A *Fort George* — The N.W and S.E Bastions were open, when the Enemy appear'd in the Bay ....
B *Rebel Redoubts on the Heights of Majabigwaduce* ....
C *Rebel Encampments* ....
D *Breast Work, where three Pieces of Cannon were mounted, on the Appearance of the Fleet, but taken by the Rebels the Morning they landed* ....
E *The King's Ships Albany, North and Nautilus, lying at their first Station, and engag'd with nine Rebel Ships, as their Divisions advanc'd* ....
F *Rebel Battery on Nautilus Island, open'd on the King's Ships, at their second Station* ....
G *Rebel Fleet.* ....
H *Half Moon Battery at Banks House, of 12 and 6 Pounders, afterwards mov'd into the Fort.*
I *Seamen's Battery and Redoubt* ....
K *Second Station of the King's Ships* ....
L *Third Station of the King's Ships* ....
M *Rebel Battery of 18 Pounders, open'd against the King's Ships, at their third Station* ....
N *Rebel Battery not finish'd.* ....
O *Rebel Battery not finish'd* ....
P *Rebel Batterys and Lines abbates'd* ....
Q *Hainey Point, where the Rebel Picquet, was drove by the Seamen.* ....
R *Field Piece brought against the Seamen, working at the Redoubt* ....
S *Encampment of the Troops, before the Rebels appear'd* ....
T *Here the Rebels landed* ....
U *Jos: Perkin's House* ....
W *John Perkins House* ....
X *Mark Hatch's House* ....
Y *A: Banks's House* ....
Z *Dyces House* ....
a *Soldiers Barracks* ....

Scale of 800 Yards.

100   200   400   800

Samuel Jn.º Neele sculp.ᵗ Russell Court

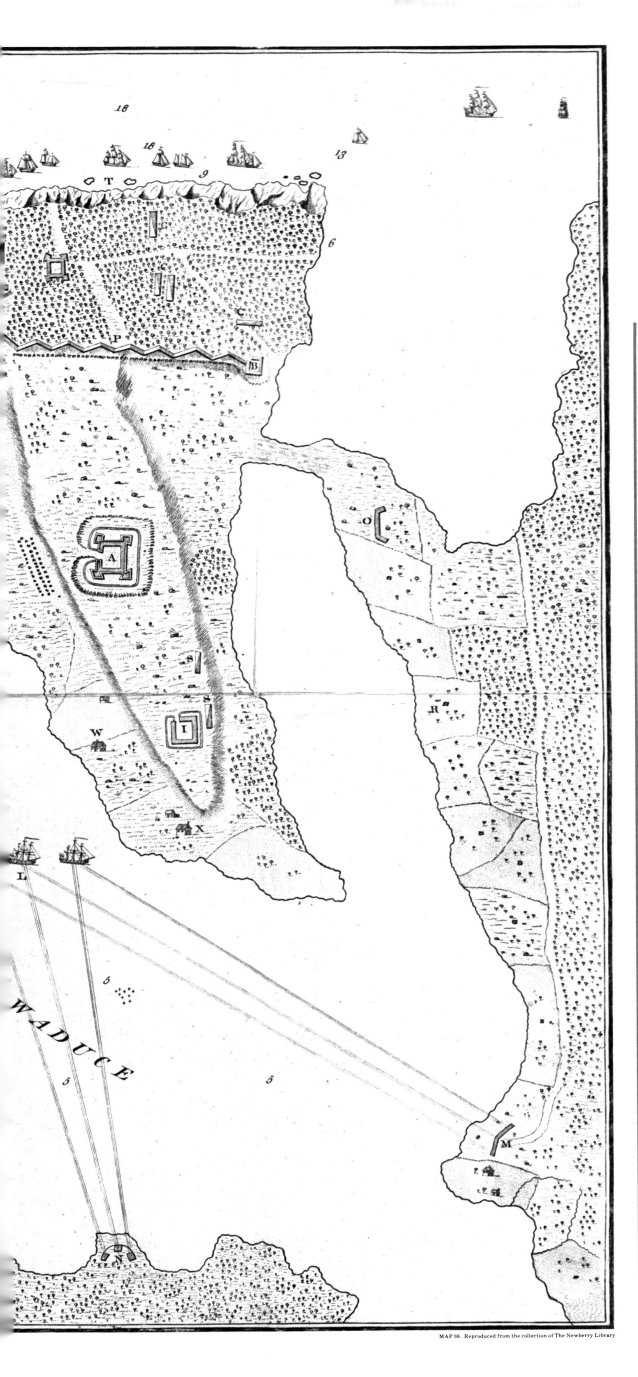

MAP 36. Reproduced from the collection of The Newberry Library

Fiasco on the Coast of Maine

MAP 36. ¶ In September 1779, John Paul Jones achieved his astonishing naval victory, which was one of the most brilliant patriot efforts of the war. The lesser known, disastrous defeat suffered at Penobscot a month earlier was, in contrast, one of the war's worst moments for the Americans. ¶ Apparently encouraged by recent successes of Continental navy raiders and of privateers, Massachusetts impetuously launched an expedition to capture the strong point that the British were establishing at the mouth of the Penobscot River, on the coast of Maine. The 750 troops from Halifax had not yet completed Fort George when the Massachusetts expeditionary force arrived in twenty-two transports convoyed by three Continental navy warships, three Massachusetts raiders, and thirteen privateers. ¶ Inadequate planning and poor execution doomed the project. Neither Congress nor General Washington were even aware of the arrangements. With Dudley Saltonstall commanding the fleet and its 2,000 men and General Solomon Lovell leading 900 militia, including Paul Revere as chief of artillery, a direct attack most likely would have succeeded. Instead, delay and excessive caution allowed time for a Royal Navy squadron, led by Sir George Collier, to arrive from Sandy Hook. Collier drove the American fleet up the Penobscot River, forcing the Yankees to burn every ship not taken by the British. All survivors, mariner and militia alike, had to make it back to the Boston area on foot. ¶ Subsequent recriminations after the fiasco brought an end to Saltonstall's career and even a court-martial for cowardice for Paul Revere—from which he was exonerated. ¶ This engraving, after the description of John Caleb, a Massachusetts Loyalist who became the agent in London for the Penobscot District, is rich in details of the land and naval activities, keyed by letter to the "Explanation" below the title. (North is to the right on this map.)

. . . Chart of Penobscot Representing the Situation of about 700 of His Majestys Troops, under the Command of Brigr. General Francis McLean, and Three of His Majesty's Sloops of War. Commanded by Captn. Henry Mowat Senr. Officer, when Besieged by more than 3300 Rebels July 1779 Commanded by Brigr. Genl. Lovell, and Seventeen Vessels of War, Commanded by Commodore Saltonstall. . . . By John Calef. Engraved by S. J. Neele. London, 1781. (14½" x 18½")

In: *Calef, John*. The Siege of Penobscot by the Rebels . . . *London, 1781*

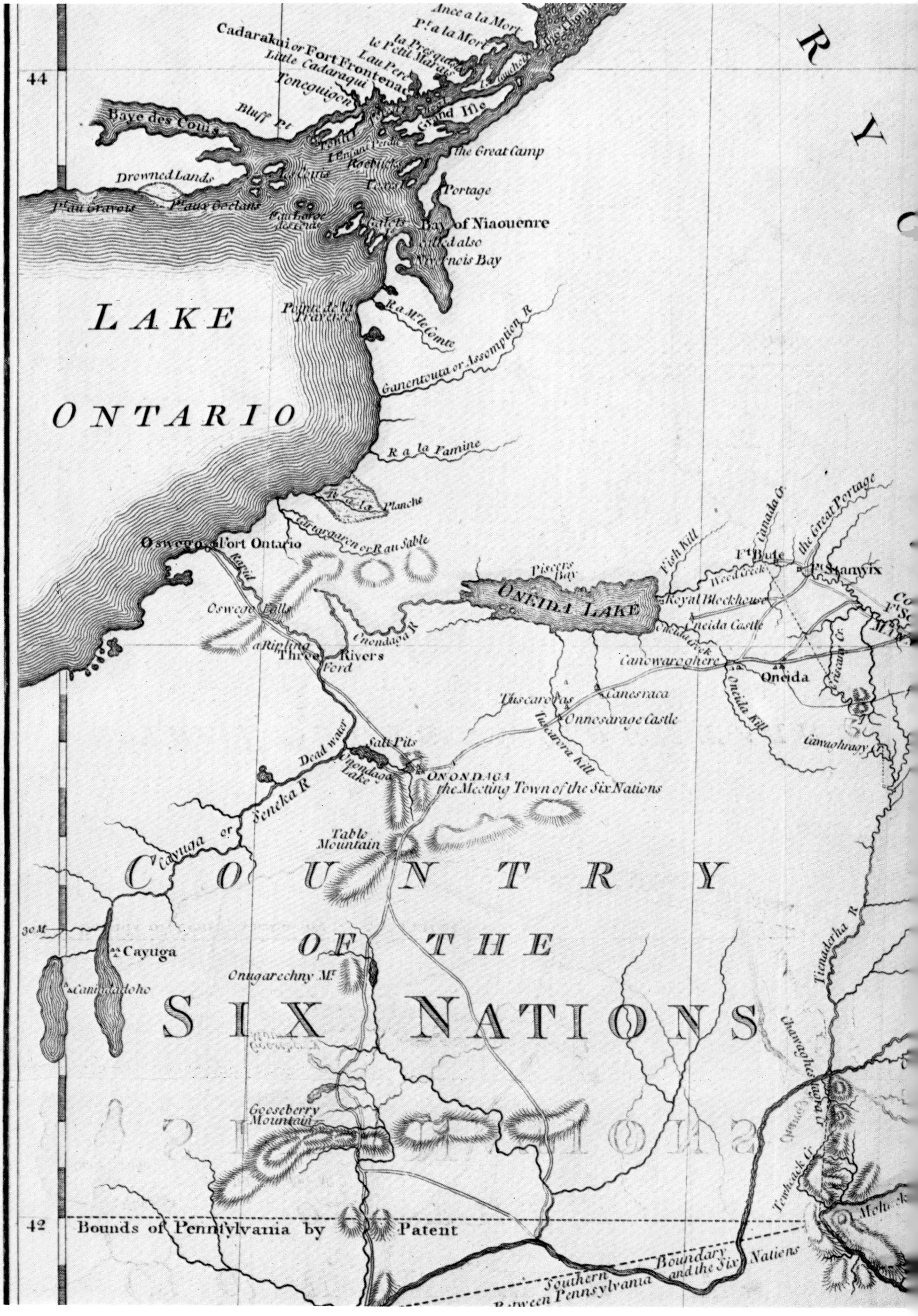

R Y O

LAKE

ONTARIO

Cadarakui or Fort Frontenac
Little Cadaraqui
Toneguigon
Bluff Pt
Baye des Cous
Drowned Lands
P.t au Gravois
P.t aux Goelans

Ance a la Mort
P.t a la Mort
la Presqu'ile
le Petit Marais
Lau Pere
Grand Isle
the Great Camp
I Enfant Perdu
Roebuc.
I. aux Louis
I. aux
Galets
Portage
Bay of Niaouenre
called also
Nivernois Bay

Pointe de la Traverse
R a M. le Comte
Ganentouta or Assomption R.

R a la Famine

Oswego or Fort Ontario
R a la Planche
Tartarraron or R au Sable
Rapid
Oswego Falls
a Rifling
Onondaga R.
Three Rivers Ford

ONEIDA LAKE
Piscer's Bay
Fish Kill
F.t Brute
F.t Stanwix
G.t Canada C.
the Great Portage
Weed Creek
Royal Blockhouse
Oneida Castle
Oneida Creek
CO.
P.t S.
MI.

Canowaroghere
Oneida
Oneida Kill
Tuscaroras
Canesraca
Onnosarage Castle
Tuscarora hill
Gawaghnagy

Dead water
Salt Pits
Onondaga Lake
Seneka R.
Cayuga or Seneka R.
Table Mountain
ONONDAGA
the Meeting Town of the Six Nations

COUNTRY

OF THE

SIX NATIONS

30 M.
Cayuga
Canindadeho
Onugarechny M.t

Tienaderha R.

Geeseberry Mountain

Tewhack Cr.
Tewhackhes
Niagra Cr.
Mohuck

Bounds of Pennsylvania by Patent

Boundary
and the Six Nations
Southern
Between Pennsylvania

Oswego to Albany— The Mohawk Valley Frontier

MAP 37. ¶ The road and river trails from Lake Ontario to Albany and the Hudson River connected numerous frontier settlements, towns, and forts. Supplied and encouraged by the British in Canada via the remote post at Niagara, 175 miles farther westward on the south shore of Lake Ontario, Tory-led Indian raiders kept this theater in turmoil for most of the six years of the war. ¶ There were two formal military expeditions into this area. In 1777, the British, with a large force under St. Leger, attempted to connect a column from the west with the Burgoyne army invading New York from Canada. Mohawk Valley militiamen stopped St. Leger's army at Ft. Stanwix, and the appearance of Benedict Arnold's column from the Hudson turned them back. In fact, Arnold's men chased St. Leger's army all the way to Lake Ontario, where the British hastily embarked for Canada. ¶ The second expedition in this area was sent by Washington under General John Sullivan in 1779 to punish the Tory and Mohawk forces that had kept the western New York border settlements in flames. Sullivan's army burned dozens of Indian villages and destroyed most of the year's harvest. ¶ To show this complex area as it was known at the time, where many events occurred during the war, a section was taken from a 1776 map of New York. (See key map below.) The scale bar from the legend was inserted in the margin and enlarged with the map section.

SHOWN ON PRECEDING PAGE
A section from . . . A Map of the Province of New-York, Reduc'd from the large Drawing of that Province, Compiled from Actual Surveys by . . . Claude Joseph Sauthier & B. Ratzer. Engraved by William Faden. London, 1776. (30" x 24")

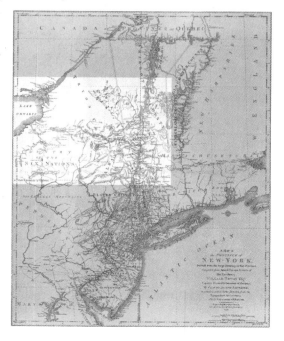

European waters, however, that the debonair little captain won his principal acclaim. His name became well known after he had the audacity to land a party at Whitehaven, Scotland, spiking guns and setting fire to ships in the harbor. Not in over one hundred years had a British seaport encountered such treatment. Soon afterward Jones was grounded for nearly a year for want of an adequate ship. He waited restlessly in France, making numerous conquests of the female variety and offering advice to everyone—to John Adams, he recommended a mistress as a most gratifying way to learn the French language!

Finally, America's ally France came up with a ship—of sorts—for Jones: an old, clumsy East Indiaman renamed *Bonhomme Richard*, in honor of Franklin, the "Poor Richard" of almanac renown. Setting sail with five vessels, Jones—after what appeared to be an unrewarding cruise—met fame head-on in the North Sea off the chalk cliffs of Flamborough Head on September 23, 1779. He matched up with Captain Richard Pearson's H.M.S. *Serapis* (fifty guns), a sturdy new copper-bottomed frigate. Everyone but Jones must have realized the decrepit *Richard* was out of her element. Luckily for Jones, when he was unable to get the tactical advantage of being able to rake the *Serapis* across her bow, a sudden burst of wind caused the two vessels to collide, whereupon the Americans lashed the vessels together. Then, as the guns of the two blazed away at each other, one of Jones's own ships—the *Alliance* under Captain Landais—mistakenly poured three broadsides into the *Richard*. Both the *Richard* and the *Serapis* were scenes of frightful carnage, but it was Jones who had the stronger will than Pearson, the latter's nerve giving way after his main mast began to tremble and an American boarding party lobbed a grenade down a hatch that blew a twenty-man gun crew to bits. After the British officer pulled down his standard, Jones abandoned the sinking *Richard*, took over the *Serapis*, and returned in triumph, bringing along the *Countess of Scarborough*, which had been taken by the *Pallas*, another of Jones's vessels.

The final years of Jones's service were anticlimactic. Picked to command the *America*, the only ship of the line constructed in the United States, as a reward for his fine achievements, he soon found that the ship would be transferred to France as a gesture of goodwill. Congress might have compensated Jones by promoting him to the rank of admiral, but several members of that body complained that this would bypass captains who outranked the enterprising officer on the seniority list. On the whole, Jones's declining fortunes were mirrored in the sorry condition of the navy as the war dragged to a close. Congress, perhaps unjustly, dismissed its ranking naval officer, Esek Hopkins, from the service on the grounds of incompetence. The very able Captain Biddle lost his life when the frigate *Randolph* blew up. By early 1782 frigates *Alliance* and *Deane* were the only ships of the United States Navy still afloat. The *Alliance*, taken from Landais, had at its quarterdeck John Barry, one of the few officers in any of the Continental services who can be positively identified as a Roman Catholic. The last accomplishments of the revolutionary navy belong to that fine mariner who, on a cruise in 1781, took several enemy privateers and two brigs. To Barry also goes the distinction of having fought the final naval action of the war when, on March 7, 1783, he severely damaged and put to rout a thirty-two gun enemy frigate off Havana.

A PLAN

of the several Villages in the

ILLINOIS COUNTRY,

with Part of the

River Mifsifsippi &c.

by

Thos. Hutchins.

Scale of Miles.

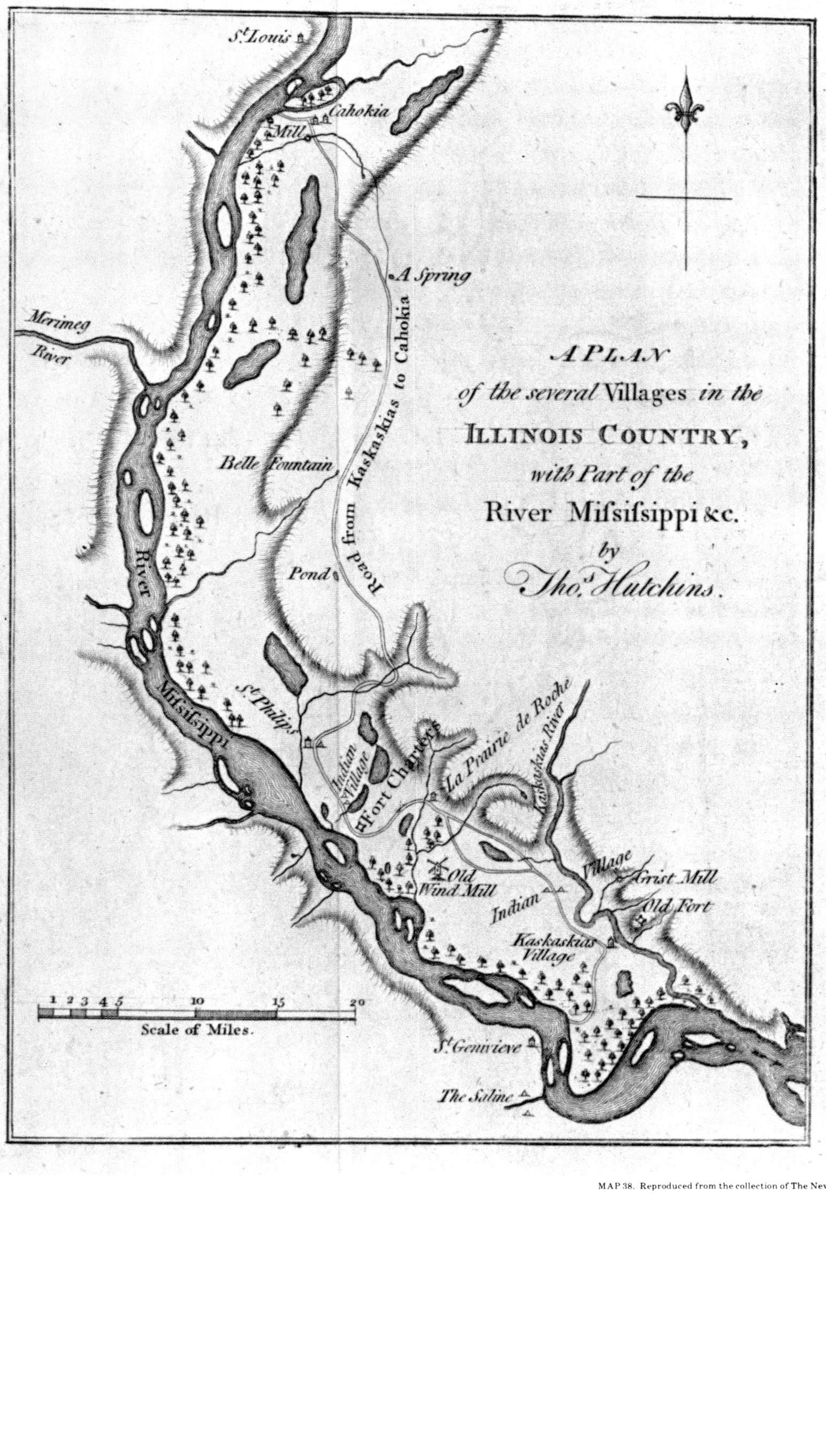

MAP 38. Reproduced from the collection of The Newberry Library

George Rogers Clark's Western Front

MAP 38. ¶ The old Illinois country towns along the Mississippi were not destined to become very populous, but they played a key role in determining the future of the vast Northwest Territory. It was George Rogers Clark's concept that offense was the best defense for Kentucky. This led him to propose taking the outposts of Kaskaskia, Fort Chartres, Cahokia, and Vincennes, on the Wabash River. With his little brigade of under 200, Clark took the towns without much resistance in 1778. ¶ The main problem of Clark's western campaign was that he was trying to conquer, with a tiny army, a region of thousands of square miles. After taking a post he was unable to leave a garrison to defend it. The British governor of the region, Lieutenant Colonel Henry Hamilton, set out to retake Vincennes with a force somewhat larger than Clark's. Using French Canadians, Indians, and a handful of regulars, he entered the town in December of 1778, five months after Clark's initial raid. ¶ Clark challenged Hamilton at Vincennes on February 24, 1779. His "long rifles" carried the day and captured Hamilton, who was taken to Williamsburg. Clark had also wanted to take Detroit and Michilimackinac, but troubles with British-sponsored Indian raids closer to home kept him from these expeditions. ¶ Thomas Hutchins, who published this map in England in 1778, had been stationed in Fort Chartres as a British officer before the war and lived in the area for a number of years. He was later to become the first "geographer to the United States." His accurate plan shows the struggling Spanish trading post at St. Louis and the small, chiefly French villages of Cahokia, Bellefontaine, Prairie du Rocher, and Kaskaskia on the Illinois side of the Mississippi.

A Plan of the several Villages in the Illinois Country, with Part of the River Mississippi &c. by Thos. Hutchins. London, 1778. (7¼" x 5")

In: *Hutchins, Thomas. A topographical Description of Virginia, Pennsylvania . . . The Rivers Ohio . . . Mississippi. . . . London, 1778*

High Street, Philadelphia, as it appeared from the Country Market-place. It was near here that Congress met during most of the war, moving to New York when the British entered Philadelphia for their nine-month occupation in September 1777.

The South
1778-1782

Because they were too weak to operate as a fleet, American ships in the Revolution worked effectively as single units. By 1778 they had taken 733 prizes. Land troops often moved at night, crossing rivers or moving about harbors in fishing boats.

THE WAR IN the North had been a stalemate at best for Britain. By mid-1778 she had little to show for three years of campaigning. Her troops occupied Newport, Rhode Island, and New York City; but they had voluntarily relinquished Boston and Philadelphia. Possessing only two enclaves in the upper states, she seemed unlikely to enlarge her areas of control, especially when France's entry into the struggle meant that British resources would be needed to defend the West Indies and perhaps other parts of the empire as well. (*See Maps 34, 35*)

Indeed, for a time Britain seemed threatened in the North by the Franco-American alliance, for French Vice-Admiral the Comte d'Estaing appeared in American waters in the summer of 1778. Yet bad luck dogged the initial Bourbon participation. The admiral just missed intercepting Admiral Howe's small fleet and bevy of Tory-laden transports heading from Philadelphia to New York. Subsequently, d'Estaing, hoping to bombard the latter city, found that his heavy ships drew too much water to cross the bar, and he made no effort to force his way into the harbor. Once again fortune smiled on Britain in the fall when a storm damaged d'Estaing's fleet and wrecked his favorable chances of defeating Admiral Howe off Narragansett Bay and trapping Major General Robert Pigot's redcoats in Rhode Island. Clinton later retrenched further by evacuating Rhode Island. Thus ended Franco-American campaigning in the North as both Washington and Clinton continued to eye each other over the next two and a half years. Both commanders conducted occasional raids—as, for example, when Washington sent Anthony Wayne to storm the enemy advance post at Stony Point and Henry (Light Horse Harry) Lee to raid Paulus Hook; when Sir Henry Clinton launched destructive coastal forays against New Bedford and New Haven in Connecticut, and when Sir Henry's subordinate General Wilhelm von Knyphausen swept in and out of eastern New Jersey. (*See Maps 16, 32, 33*)

All the while, the South was increasingly becoming the main theater of the war. If the North could not easily be brought back into the royal fold, London strategists felt that the South beckoned with fertile opportunities. It reputedly contained a high percentage of Loyalists in its population, and it was argued that Washington could not hasten reinforcements to the southern rebels as long as Clinton maintained a strong garrison in New York City. Furthermore, as Charles Jenkinson, treasury subminister, pointed out, the South produced goods of great value to England's mercantile scheme of things; consequently, if a choice must be made, it was better to save the realm of tobacco, rice, and indigo, better to let less valuable New England (with its "cursed puritanick spirit") go its own way. In short, vowed one Englishman, the war had "begun at the wrong end" of America.

Certain hard questions might have been asked at Whitehall prior to such a decided alteration of strategy. What evidence actually existed to support the idea—pressed by American exiles and royal officials from the South—that the king's friends were ubiquitous in the Carolinas and Georgia? And was there a danger in dispersing Britain's military resources from New York to the Floridas? If his majesty's Atlantic squadrons could not consistently dominate the waters off the American coast as d'Estaing's maraudings suggested, was there a likelihood that French naval detachments might cooperate with the rebels in picking off British bases?

But debating such theoretical points seemed hardly worthwhile in London, particularly in light of the first news from the South. Georgia, invaded by forces fron New York and Florida, was subdued during the period of December 1778 to January 1779. The "first stripe and star" had been taken from "the rebel flag of Congress," boasted Lieutenant Colonel Archibald Campbell. Yet the danger of the French navy presented itself again in September 1779, when the Comte d'Estaing made his second visit to America, this time to unite with Major General Benjamin Lincoln of the Southern Department in besieging the British forces at Savannah under Brigadier General Augustin Prevost. The Frenchman, having recently captured the islands of St. Vincent and Grenada in the West Indies and repulsed British naval units under Lord John Byron, was the momentary toast of America. But his repeat performance was more of a failure than his first venture to the United States. After a short time d'Estaing grew apprehensive about the approaching hurricane season and insisted on a direct assault on Prevost. In heavy fighting the allies were finally thrown back, their casualties reaching the staggering total of 837, Prevost's, 155. Count Casimir Pulaski, the Polish émigré who headed the American cavalry, received a mortal wound charging the enemy lines, while d'Estaing, twice wounded himself, soon set sail for France, a move that necessitated Lincoln's withdrawal. (*See Maps 35, 39*)

British planners—scarcely mindful of Prevost's narrow call at Savannah—were eager to expand the southern beachhead. With 8,700 additional troops, Sir Henry Clinton himself sailed from New York and on February 11, 1780, disembarked at North Edisto Inlet, near Charleston, South Carolina—the next state to be rolled up. While a naval squadron under Vice-Admiral Marriot Arbuthnot sealed off the harbor, Clinton inched his siege lines closer and closer to the beleaguered city situated at the tip of a peninsula between the Ashley and Cooper rivers. The portly, middle-aged Benjamin Lincoln, a sound if uninspiring officer, had bowed to the initial wishes of the South Carolinians, who begged him to defend their capital, but who now—as shot and shell rained upon them—clamored for the Massachusetts soldier to spare them further destruction by capitulating. His escape route to the north closed, Lincoln had no real choice but to surrender his over 8,500 men—which he did on May 12—the heaviest losses suffered by the Americans in the entire war.

Nor was Charleston the last bitter cup for the deep South patriots. A new, hastily assembled American Southern army, with a new commander, Horatio Gates—"the victor of Saratoga"—made its appearance in upper South Carolina in early August. It was a puny force compared to the first Southern army lost at Charleston; and for that reason, if no other, Gates should have jealously sheltered his 1,400 Maryland and Delaware Continentals, supported by artillery and cavalry companies and by Virginia and North Carolina militia. Historians remain at a loss to explain the rashness of the general who displayed prudence against Burgoyne, the general who immediately advanced—without adequate intelligence—into South Carolina, where, in the predaylight hours of August 16, he collided with a British column under Lord Cornwallis outside the village of Camden. Gates foolishly gave the militia the entire left side of his line instead of interspersing them with Continentals. Cornwallis, seeing that the American left was poorly formed, struck the militia a blow that scattered them in all directions, "a great majority" of whom "fled without firing a shot," reported Colonel Otho H. Williams of Maryland. On the American right, the Continentals fought heroically under Major General Johann de Kalb, who seemed to be everywhere at once, a splendid soldier, who fell at last, fatally wounded, hit in a half-dozen places. The American regulars were

A Franco-American Failure in the South

MAP 39. ¶ After the inept defense of Savannah in December 1778, by the American General Robert Howe under General Benjamin Lincoln, the British occupied the city until the end of the war. Before the fall of Charleston in 1780, Savannah served as British headquarters for the southern theater. ¶ In September and October of 1779, Lincoln with his small American army from Charleston joined forces with d'Estaing's seaborne French army to attempt the retaking of Savannah. D'Estaing demonstrated the same abrasive relationship with his American allies that prevailed at Narragansett Bay a year earlier; he even went so far as to declare to the defenders that he was taking Savannah for the king of France. The brave but unyielding Frenchman rejected Lincoln's plan to attack directly, although a *coup de main* had excellent possibilities. Instead he deployed for formal siege. This enabled Augustin Prevost, the British commander, to complete strong defensive works. When the Americans and French finally attacked, d'Estaing gallantly led his troops and was twice wounded. Count Casimir Pulaski was killed leading a cavalry charge. The well-designed British defenses held, and the attack failed. The success of Francis Marion's men at Spring Hill in the early stage could not be sustained. D'Estaing fought no more in North America. This had been his third defeat, following New York and Newport. Until Rochambeau's arrival, the Americans wondered just what the heralded French Alliance had accomplished. ¶ The action can be traced on this accurate map, although, in a rare oversight, we are not given a compass indicator. North is actually at the bottom. The French fleet downstream is off the map, but their line of fire is indicated. While destroying a few buildings in the town, the naval bombardment had little effect on the fortifications, which one can see were formidable.

SHOWN ON FOLLOWING PAGE
Plan of the Siege of Savannah, with the joint Attack of the French and Americans on the 9th October 1779. In which they were defeated by his Majesty's Forces Under the Command of Major Genl. Augustin Prevost. London, Wm. Faden, Feb. 2, 1784. (16½" x 23")

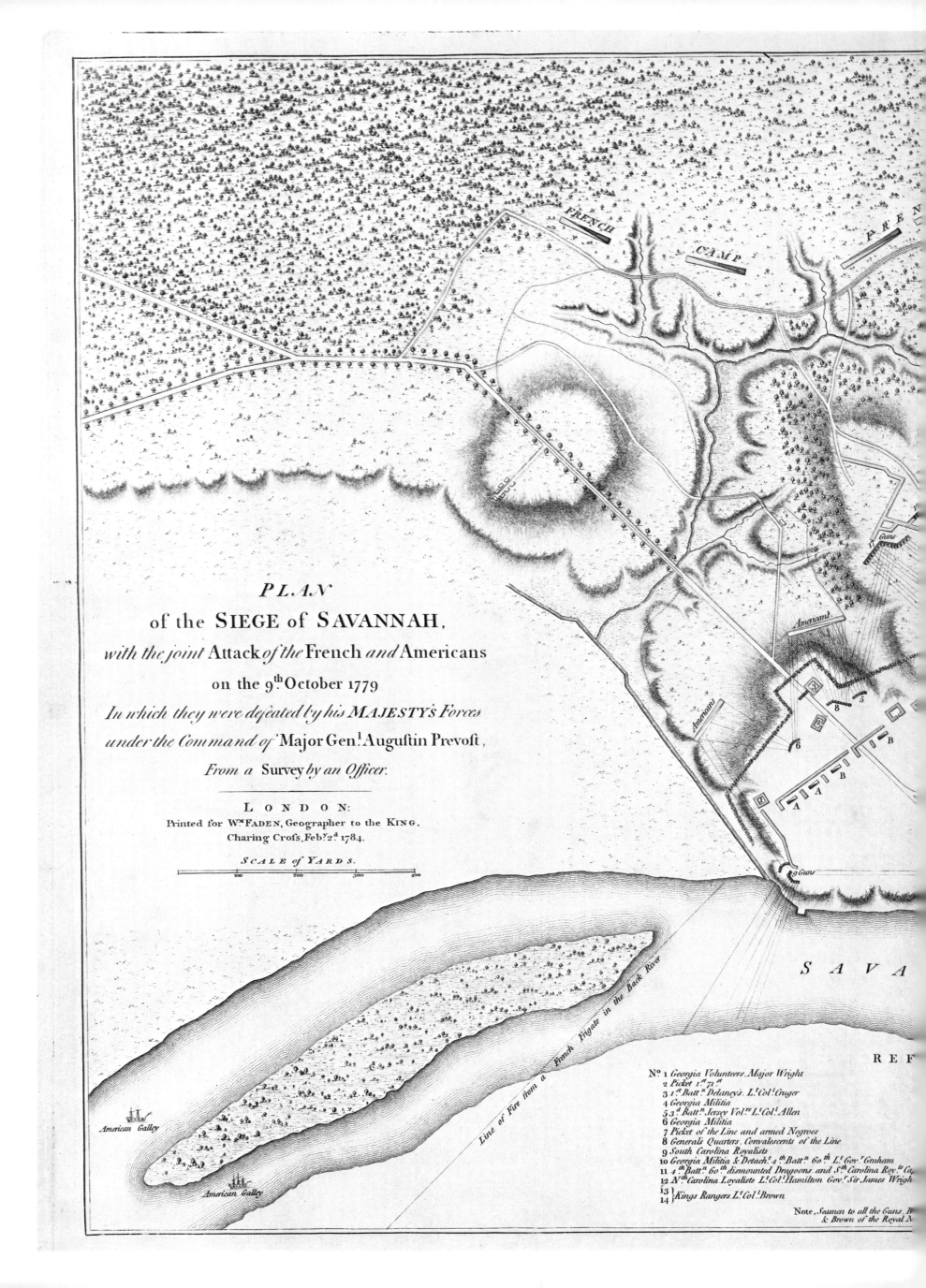

FRENCH CAMP

FREN...

French

Americans

Americans

Americans

Guns

6

7

8

5

3

A B

A A B

9 Guns

SAVA...

PLAN
of the SIEGE of SAVANNAH,

with the joint Attack of the French and Americans

on the 9.th October 1779

In which they were defeated by his MAJESTY's Forces

under the Command of Major Gen.l Augustin Prevost,

From a Survey by an Officer.

LONDON:
Printed for W.m FADEN, Geographer to the KING,
Charing Cross, Feb.ry 2.d 1784.

SCALE of YARDS.

100   200   300   400

American Galley

American Galley

Line of Fire from a French Frigate in the Back River

REF...

N.o 1 Georgia Volunteers. Major Wright
2 Picket 1.st 71.st
3 1.st Batt.n Delancey's. L.t Col.l Cruger
4 Georgia Militia
5 3.d Batt.n Jersey Vol.ts L.t Col.l Allen
6 Georgia Militia
7 Picket of the Line and armed Negroes
8 Generals Quarters. Convalescents of the Line
9 South Carolina Royalists
10 Georgia Militia & Detach.t 4.th Batt.n 60.th L.t Gov.r Graham
11 4.th Batt.n 60.th dismounted Dragoons. and S.th Carolina Roy.l Ca...
12 N.th Carolina Loyalists L.t Col.l Hamilton Gov.r Sir James Wrigh...
13 }
14 } Kings Rangers L.t Col.l Brown

Note., Seamen to all the Guns, B...
& Brown of the Royal N...

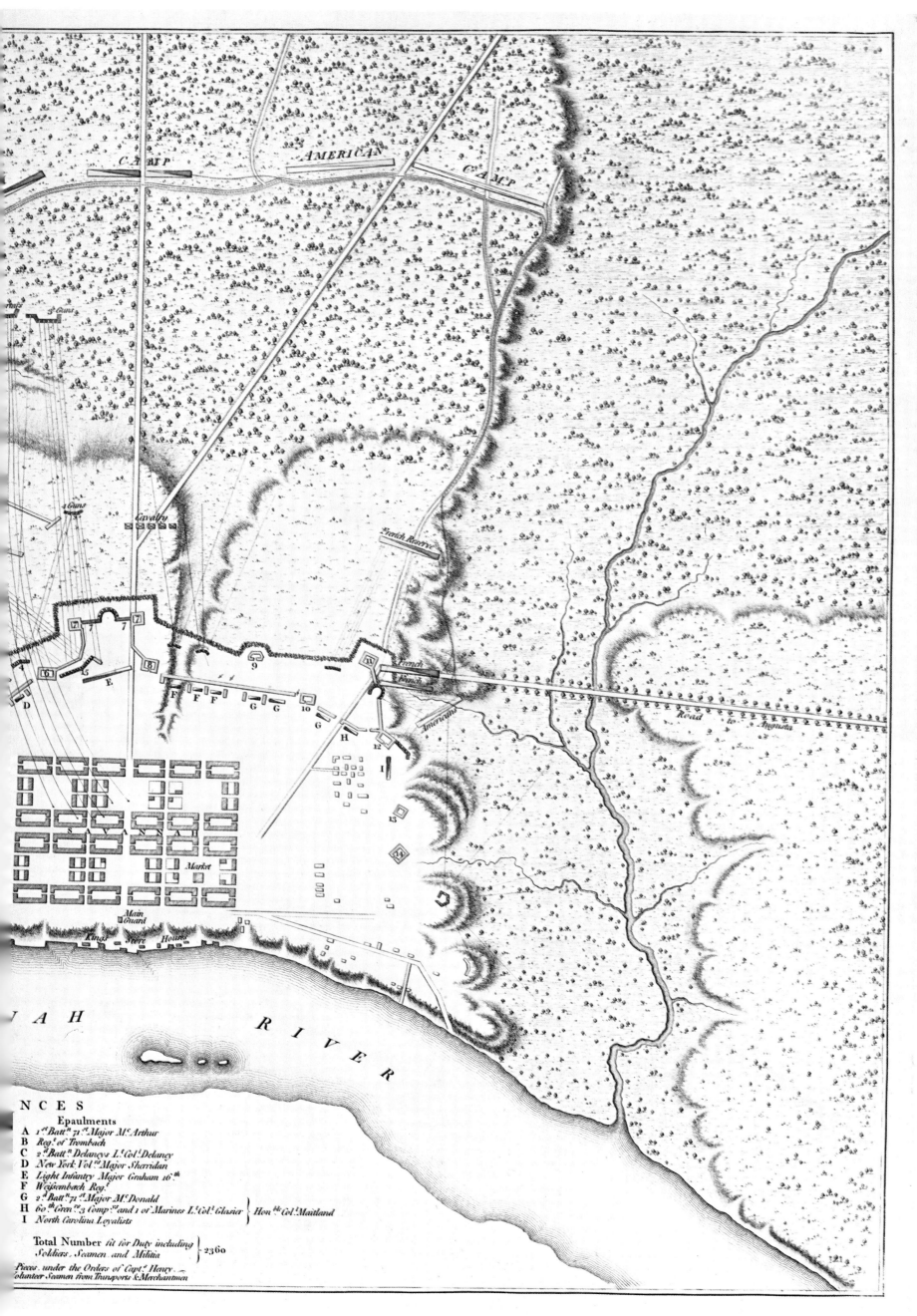

CAMP   AMERICAN   CAMP

3 Guns

4 Guns

Cavalry

French Reserve

17   7   7

4   6   5   8   9   10   French   IV
D   E   F   F   F   F   G   G   G   French
10   Americans
H   12
13

SAVANNAH

Market

Main
Guard

Kings Store Houses

Road   to   Augusta

JAH   RIVER

MAP 39. Reproduced from the collection of The Newberry Library

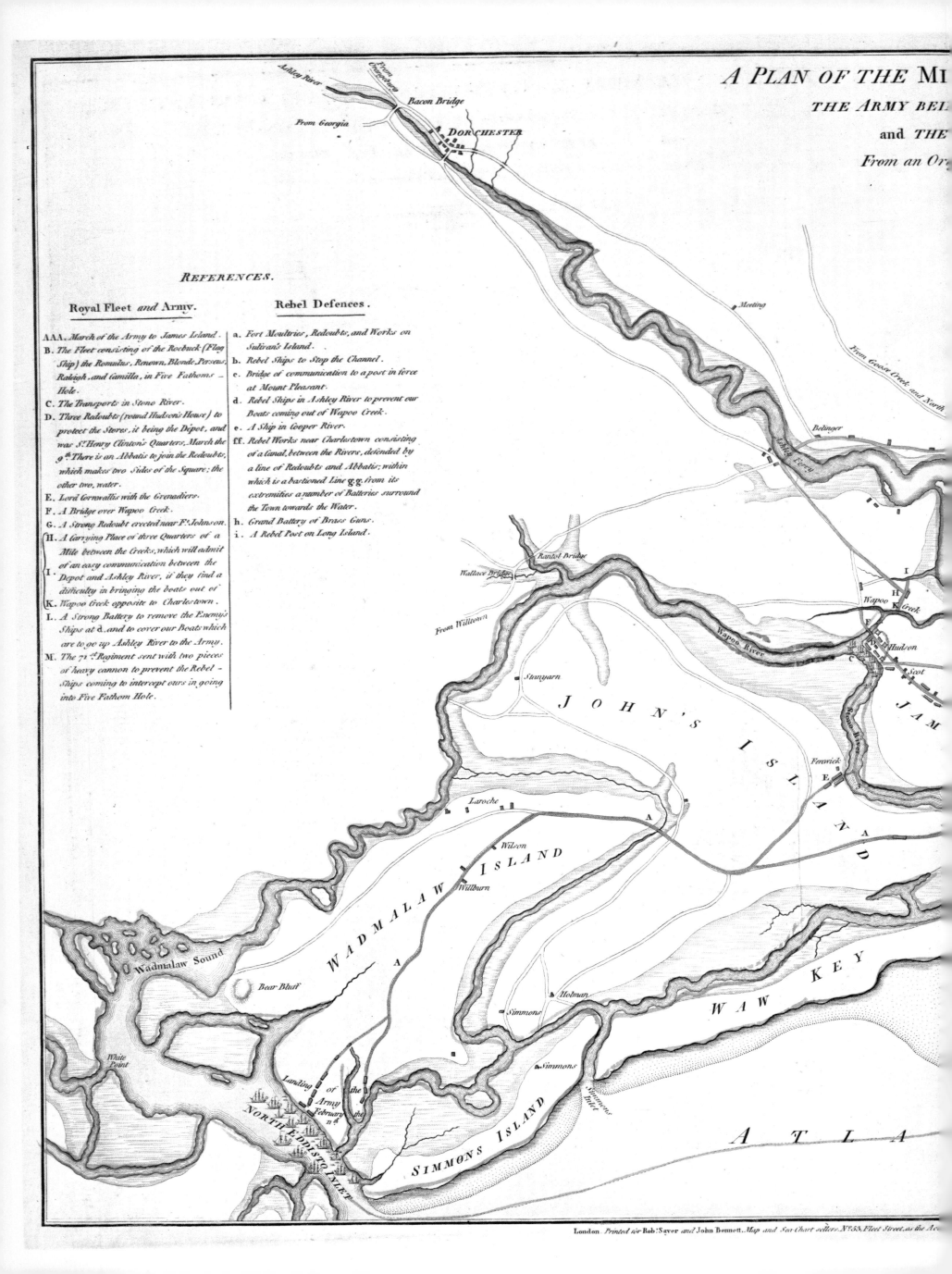

A PLAN OF THE MI[...]

THE ARMY BEL[...]

and THE [...]

From an Or[...]

REFERENCES.

Royal Fleet *and* Army.	Rebel Defences.

Royal Fleet and Army.

AAA. *March of the Army to James Island.*

B. *The Fleet consisting of the Roebuck (Flag Ship) the Romulus, Renown, Blonde, Perseus, Raleigh, and Camilla, in Five Fathoms Hole.*

C. *The Transports in Stono River.*

D. *Three Redoubts (round Hudson's House) to protect the Stores, it being the Dépôt, and was St. Henry Clinton's Quarters, March the 9th. There is an Abbatis to join the Redoubts, which makes two Sides of the Square; the other two, water.*

E. *Lord Cornwallis with the Grenadiers.*

F. *A Bridge over Wapoo Creek.*

G. *A Strong Redoubt erected near Ft. Johnson.*

H. *A Carrying Place of three Quarters of a Mile between the Creeks, which will admit of an easy communication between the*

I. *Depot and Ashley River, if they find a difficulty in bringing the boats out of*

K. *Wapoo Creek opposite to Charlestown.*

L. *A Strong Battery to remove the Enemy's Ships at d. and to cover our Boats which are to go up Ashley River to the Army.*

M. *The 71st Regiment sent with two pieces of heavy cannon to prevent the Rebel Ships coming to intercept ours in going into Five Fathom Hole.*

Rebel Defences.

a. *Fort Moultrie, Redoubts, and Works on Sulivan's Island.*

b. *Rebel Ships to Stop the Channel.*

c. *Bridge of communication to a post in force at Mount Pleasant.*

d. *Rebel Ships in Ashley River to prevent our Boats coming out of Wapoo Creek.*

e. *A Ship in Cooper River.*

ff. *Rebel Works near Charlestown consisting of a Canal, between the Rivers, defended by a line of Redoubts and Abbatis; within which is a bastioned Line g.g. from its extremities a number of Batteries surround the Town towards the Water.*

h. *Grand Battery of Brass Guns.*

i. *A Rebel Post on Long Island.*

Ashley River
From Orangeburg
Bacon Bridge
From Georgia
DORCHESTER
Meeting
From Goose Creek, and North
From Georgia
Belinger
Ashley Ferry
Rantol Bridge
Wallace Bridge
From Willtown
Wapoo Creek
Wapoo River
K Wapoo Creek
H
I
Hudson
Stono River
C
Scot
Stanyarn
JOHN'S ISLAND
JAM
Fenwick
E
Laroche
A
Wilson
WADMALAW ISLAND
Willburn
Wadmalaw Sound
Bear Bluff
A
WAW KEY
Holman
Simmons
White Point
SIMMONS ISLAND
Landing of the Army February the n d
NORTH EDISTO INLET
Simmons Inlet
ATLA

London. Printed for Robt. Sayer and John Bennett, Map and Sea Chart sellers, No. 53, Fleet Street, as the Ac[...]

Scale of Miles.

Cooper River

WANDO RIVER

COOPER RIVER

Town Marsh

Hobcaw Ferry

To North Carolina

LONG ISLAND

ARLESTOWN

NECK

Shutes Folly

Mount Pleasant

SULLIVAN'S ISLAND

North Channel

CHARLESTOWN

HARBOUR

L

Fort Johnson

Gummins P.t

the Swash

8 Feet

ISLAND

Ferry

Light House

8 Feet

COFFIN LAND

Ship Channel

Lawford's Channel

7½ Feet

ATLANTIC OCEAN

Charleston Falls, and So Does Benjamin Lincoln

MAP 40. ¶ The major catastrophe experienced by the Americans at Charleston during Clinton's 1780 expedition, coming after the loss of Savannah and the failure of the Franco-American attempt to retake the city, sank the American cause to one of its lowest points. ¶ Clinton's expeditionary force sailed from New York the day after Christmas, 1779. Admiral Arbuthnot's fleet of ten warships and ninety transports, with 5,000 sailors, brought Clinton's 8,700 troops from Sandy Hook to the South. The voyage took thirty-eight days, and the fleet encountered ferocious storms. Regardless of Clinton's original plan it became necessary to call first at Savannah for repairs. ¶ Shown on this remarkable and little-known map is the British landing at North Edisto Inlet, and their route toward Charleston. Also indicated are the American defenses of the city and the harbor. Published in London only fifteen days after the surrender of Charleston, it is a fascinating portrayal of the conditions immediately before the siege. ¶ It was from the positions indicated here that Clinton outgeneraled Benjamin Lincoln by silently moving his army several miles up the Ashly River, in order to make the crossing unimpeded. The civil leaders of Charleston coerced Lincoln into defending the city against the forthcoming siege, even though his army was vastly outnumbered. He had failed to learn from Washington's campaigns at New York and Philadelphia that the most important consideration in sustaining the Revolution was to keep his army intact—not to defend to the finish a specific place, no matter how important it might seem to be. ¶ The largest number of prisoners captured at any time during the war surrendered to the British on May 12, 1780. Shortly afterward Congress appointed Horatio Gates to succeed General Lincoln as commander in the South.

A Plan of the Military Operations against Charlestown, the Army being Commanded by L. G. Sir Henry Clinton, K.B. and the Fleet by Vice-Admiral Arbuthnot. . . . London, Robt. Sayer & John Bennett, May 27, 1780. (17" x 21¼")

Gates's Disaster

MAP 41. ¶ Camden was one of the worst defeats suffered by the Americans during the entire war. It has been called the most devastating reversal ever sustained by an American army. It was here that General Horatio Gates surrendered the laurels he had won at Saratoga. Not only was Gates's military reputation destroyed at Camden, but so was the Southern army, of which he had just assumed command. ¶ His strategy leading up to this engagement, his tactics when the armies made contact, as well as his apparent indecisiveness and lack of leadership during the action, all contributed to his crushing loss. All this, together with his controversial departure from the battlefield and headlong dash northward, made Gates's behavior difficult to defend even by his supporters. ¶ At the outset Gates's force occupied a superior position. As this map reveals, Cornwallis had his back to Saunders Creek and swampy areas protected the American flanks. The patriot force outnumbered the enemy, but two-thirds of the troops were inexperienced militiamen. They faced an army of seasoned veterans, led by three outstanding commanders. ¶ Lord Rawdon and "Bloody Ban" Tarleton were among those conspicuous for turning the battle into a rout. Gates's militia ran, many dropping loaded weapons, but his Continentals fought valorously, particularly the brigade under General de Kalb. That great Bavarian warrior was wounded a dozen times during the fight and died three days later.

Plan of the Battle Fought near Camden August 16th 1780. London, March 1, 1787. (8¾" x 7½")

In: *Tarleton, Banastre.* History of the Campaigns of 1780 and 1781. *London, 1787.*

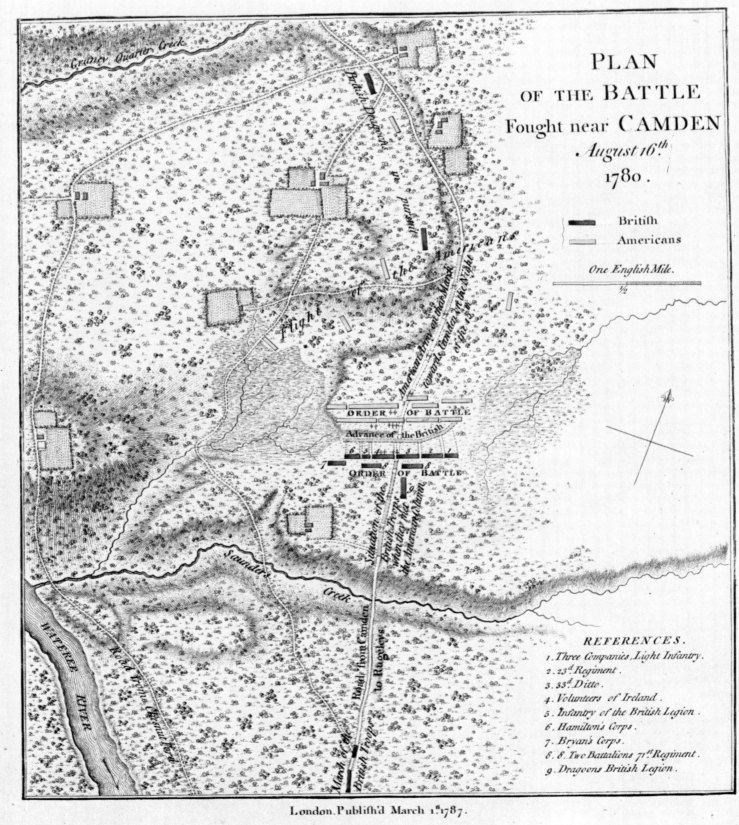

Cornwallis's Pyrrhic Victory

MAP 42. ¶ A major turning point in the war was the Battle of Guilford, near the site of modern Greensboro, North Carolina. It was here that General Nathanael Greene, the Rhode Islander who was to win back the South for the new nation, displayed his superb strategy. ¶ After winning his celebrated race with Cornwallis to the Dan River, following improved American fortunes at King's Mountain and Cowpens, Greene chose Guilford as the place for a showdown. He had passed through the area the previous month, while drawing Cornwallis far from the British supply bases. He now deployed his men somewhat the way General Daniel Morgan had at Cowpens. Both armies fought admirably. There was a moment during the hard-fought engagements at the three successive lines of battle indicated on the map when, if Greene could have had an aerial view of the battlefield, he might have committed his entire army and had a chance to destroy the British force. He was considered wise to have followed the alternative of an orderly, guarded retreat, keeping his army intact rather than gambling for all or nothing. ¶ The British at the time, and armchair tacticians since, considered Guilford to have been a victory for Cornwallis. He had driven the American army into retreat, as shown in this battle plan which accompanied Tarleton's account. The enormous number of British casualties suffered here, however, caused Cornwallis to withdraw to Wilmington, almost 200 miles away on the coast. At Wilmington, after being resupplied by sea, Cornwallis decided on his fateful march north into Virginia.

Battle of Guildford, Fought on the 15th of March 1781. London, March 1, 1871. (8¾" x 7½")

In: *Tarleton, Banastre.* History of the Campaigns of 1780 and 1781. *London, 1787.*

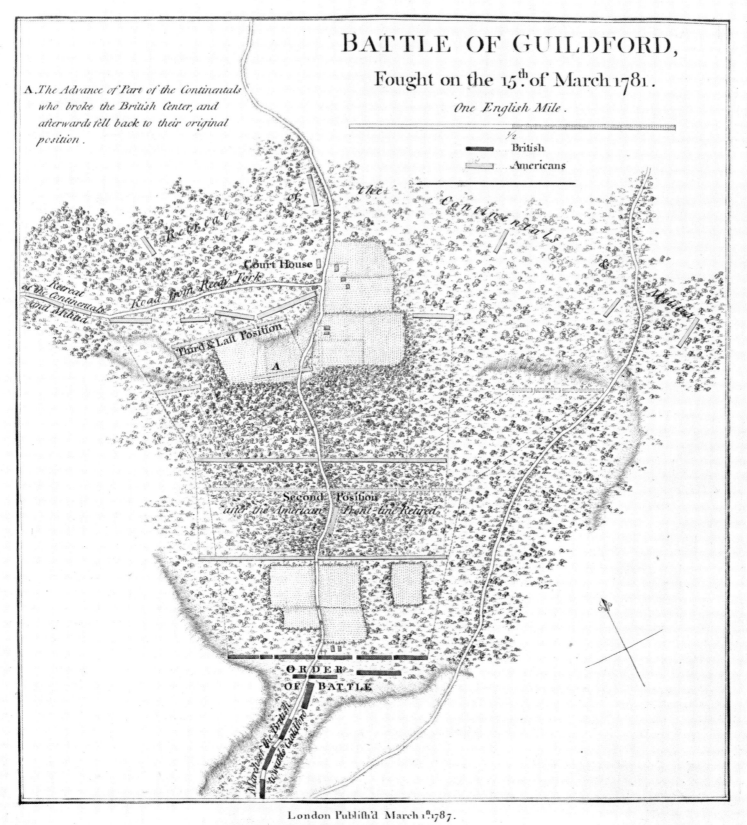

BATTLE OF GUILDFORD,
Fought on the 15th of March 1781.

One English Mile.

½

British
Americans

A. *The Advance of Part of the Continentals who broke the British Center, and afterwards fell back to their original position.*

Court House

Third & Last Position

Second Position
until the American Front line Retired

ORDER
OF BATTLE

London Publish'd March 1, 1787.

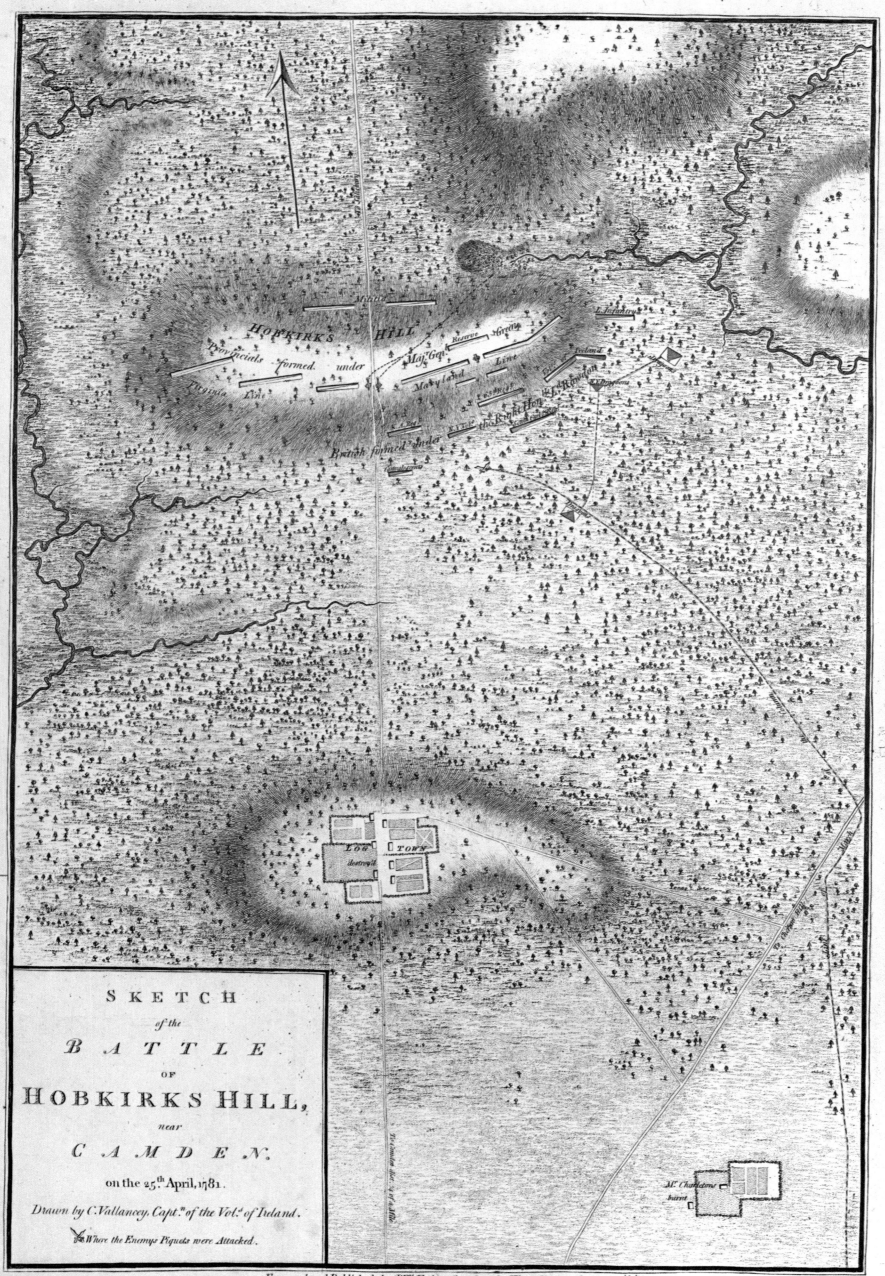

HOBKIRK'S HILL

Provincials formed under Maj. Gen.l Greene

Virginia Line

Reserve

Maryland Line

L. Infantry

British formed under the Right Hon.ble L.d Rawdon

SKETCH
of the
BATTLE
OF
HOBKIRKS HILL,
near
CAMDEN,
on the 25.th April, 1781.

Drawn by C. Vallancey, Capt.n of the Vol.rs of Ireland.

Where the Enemys Piquets were Attacked.

LOG TOWN
destroyed

Mr. Chisolms
burnt

Engraved and Published by Wm. Faden, Geog.r to the King, Charing Cross, Aug.t 1783.

Greene Versus Rawdon

MAP 43. ¶ The blistering action in the piney sandhills of South Carolina, north of Camden, was characteristic of General Nathanael Greene's pivotal campaign in the southern theater. He lost the battles, but won the war. Greene understood the type of strategy required to drive the British out of the South. With an army smaller than that of the British, he had worn the enemy down and made Cornwallis's long lines of communication indefensible. ¶ Cornwallis, marching to Virginia, had left the Carolinas in the hands of a dashing twenty-six-year-old Irish nobleman, Francis Rawdon-Hastings (usually known as Lord Rawdon), and 8,000 troops. This map reveals how the opponents lined up on April 25, 1781, just after the British extended the front line. Greene had stationed his units with care in expectation of Lord Rawdon's attack. In the hard fighting it first appeared as if Greene's men would hold the hill, but tactical errors and Rawdon's generalship allowed the British to carry the day. ¶ However, Rawdon's casualties were so great—over 30 percent—that he had no choice but to retreat toward Charleston. It was at this point that Greene penned his oft-repeated line, "We fight, get beat, rise and fight again." ¶ Little is known of Charles Vallancey, from whose drawing this map was engraved. He was an officer in a Tory regiment.

SHOWN ON OPPOSITE PAGE
Sketch of the Battle of Hobkirks Hill, near Camden. on the 25th April, 1781. Drawn by C. Vallancey. London, Wm. Faden, Aug. 1, 1783. (17¼" x 11¾")

finally overwhelmed, and the rout was complete, only 700 Continentals eventually making their way back to Hillsborough, North Carolina. (*See Map 41*)

Gates's debacle inspired this satirical piece in James Rivington's Loyalist *New York Royal Gazette:*

Millions!—Millions!—Millions!
REWARD

Strayed, deserted, or stolen, from the Subscriber on the 16th of August last, near Camden, in the State of South Carolina, a whole army, consisting of Horse, Foot, and Dragoons, to the amount of near ten thousand (as has been said) with all their baggage, artillery, wagons, and camp equipage. The subscriber has very strong suspicions, from information received from his Aid de Camp, that a certain Charles, Earl Cornwallis, was principally concerned in carrying off the said army with their baggage, & ....

As the stain of British conquest spread across the lower South, London talk from Whitehall to the coffeehouses had it that North Carolina and Virginia would also be under the royal standard in a matter of months. But had British victories in Georgia and South Carolina actually snuffed out the flames of rebellion there? And was the upper South such easy prey? It was true that state governments had ceased to function and that British posts stretched from the coast to the backcountry in both states. Yet we know from our experiences in Vietnam that pacification of the countryside is difficult, that guerrilla warfare often continues, and so it was in the Revolution.

Clinton, before returning to New York after the fall of Charleston, demanded that former rebels who had laid down their arms must take an oath of allegiance to pick them up again if called upon, this time to fight against their friends and relatives on the patriot side. These provisions in the oath led countless Georgians and Carolinians to rejoin the rebel forces, as did continued harassment by hard-core Tories who desired to retaliate for past harsh treatment, despite Cornwallis's pleas to stop the bloodletting. If Clinton's action had helped to create the rising tide of resentment, he had at least recognized that Cornwallis, now in command in the South, should not advance northward unless South Carolina was thoroughly subdued.

And the palmetto state was not. Even before the Battle of Camden, the legendary partisans of Thomas Sumter and Francis Marion were harassing British outposts and interrupting supply routes. Even so, Cornwallis, a restless, aggressive officer, launched an invasion of North Carolina, advancing as far as Charlotte when word of the destruction of the left wing of his army caused him to return to South Carolina. The blow had fallen at Kings Mountain, just below the Carolinas' border. There frontiersmen, mainly inhabitants of the Watauga settlements in present-day eastern Tennessee, caught up with 1,000 Loyalists under Major Patrick Ferguson, an able but arrogant and overconfident officer. Led by such backcountry stalwarts as Colonels Isaac Shelby and John Sevier, the patriots surged up the mountain; and in this all-American battle—patriots versus Tories—Ferguson's command was totally demolished: more than 300 dead or wounded and another 700 captured.

Particular truisms of the Revolutionary War seemed slow for Cornwallis to grasp. The defeat of Continental armies did not bring a termination of hostilities. Partisans and other irregulars—living off the land they knew so well, with all its forests, swamps, and other hideaways—did not have to be sustained by regulars in what was a people's war. In fact, Continental armies had a way of reappearing. Cornwallis learned in December that a third Southern army was forming at Charlotte under a third commander, a thirty-eight-year-old ex-Quaker from Rhode Island, Major General Nathanael Greene, Washington's most trusted subordinate and until only recently the quartermaster general of the Continental army.

Greene, a flexible, highly resourceful officer, resolved to play the guerrilla, or partisan, role himself, thus avoiding an all-out confrontation like Camden before he could turn his thin ranks into a respectable instrument of war. As Greene took up a position on South Carolina's Pee Dee River to rebuild his forces and observe Cornwallis, he boldly detached a part of his command under Brigadier General Daniel Morgan, whose orders were to advance southwestward from Charlotte and sit upon Cornwallis's left, support the South Carolina guerrilla bands, and keep the Tories in that neighborhood in check. Long before Mao Tse-tung and Vo-nguyen-Giap, the most influential theorists of guerrilla warfare, Greene recognized certain principles of irregular conflict that these two modern authorities have enunciated in the mid-twentieth century. As Giap of North Vietnam has expressed it, guerrilla campaigns can only evolve into full-scale warfare when the enemy is worn down by a thousand and one small strokes.

Cornwallis, stung repeatedly, was not about to be stung again. As Greene had predicted, his dispatching of Morgan into western South Carolina led the British general to divide his own army. Or, in the words of a recent British military analyst, Liddell Hart, "guerrilla war . . . inverts one of the main principles of orthodox war, the principle of concentration." Cornwallis sent after Morgan his own answer to the American partisans— Banastre Tarleton's Tory Legion of foot soldiers and dragoons. Morgan, aware that a partisan's chief value is in bedevilment rather than formal confrontation, fell back toward the Broad River. But with Tarleton closing in, he had no choice but to fight, even though half his men were militia and unfamiliar with orthodox warfare. On the morning of January 17, 1781, at a grazing area called the Cowpens, Morgan—blending his irregulars and Continentals superbly—nailed a decisive defeat on Tarleton, who rashly attacked upon making initial contact with the Americans. Tarleton lost 110 killed, 229 wounded, and 600 captured as compared to Morgan's 12 killed and 60 wounded.

The news of Morgan's victory sped throughout the backcountry. In Rutherford County, North Carolina, the Reverend John Miller offered up this prayer of thanks from his Presbyterian flock:

> Good Lord, our God that art in Heaven, we have great reason to thank thee for the many favors we have received at thine hands, the many battles we have won. There is the great and Glorious Battle of King's Mountain, where we kilt the great Gineral Ferguson, and took his whole army . . . and the ever-memorable and glorious Battle of the Coopens where we made the proud Gineral Tarleton run doon the road helter-skelter, and Good Lord, if ye had na suffered the Cruel Tories to burn Belly hell's [Billy Hill's] Iron Works, we would na have asked any mair favors at thy hands. Amen.

In his Scottish burr Miller might also have sought the Almighty's intervention against Cornwallis, who now pressed northward in an effort to smash the still-retreating Morgan. Greene, fearing the destruction of

Prelude to the Peninsula Campaign in Virginia

MAP 44. ¶ Published after the war, this fine detailed plan shows the minor action at Petersburg which preceded the crucial 1781 campaign in Virginia. It was General Peter Muhlenberg, not Von Steuben as the map states, who was defending this town on the Appomattox River when William Phillips struck with his 2,500 British regulars. Muhlenberg, a Lutheran-Episcopalian clergyman, American Revolutionary hero, and Philadelphia politician-to-be, is credited with putting up a stout defense of this supply depot south of Richmond before conducting an orderly retreat to the east (top of map). ¶ The map reveals that General Phillips staged a three-column attack to gain his objective of destroying the tobacco and supplies stored here. After this engagement, the British pressed on toward Richmond, only to find on April 30 that Lafayette had beaten them there by several hours with his 1,200 Continental troops. ¶ Cornwallis arrived at Petersburg less than a month after this action, having been driven out of North Carolina by Greene. He joined his Southern army with the British forces in Virginia under William Phillips and Benedict Arnold. ¶ This was the beginning of the peninsula campaign that was to end with Cornwallis's surrender at Yorktown. Phillips, Clinton's best artillery officer, was unfortunately not to be with Cornwallis on that campaign; he died in Petersburg of typhoid fever on May 13, 1781.

SHOWN ON OPPOSITE PAGE
Sketch of the Skirmish at Petersburg, between the Royal Army under the Command of Major Genl. Phillips, and the American Army commanded by Major Genl. Stewben, in which the latter were defeated, April 25, 1781. By John Hills. London, Wm. Faden, May 3, 1784. (10¾" x 14¼")

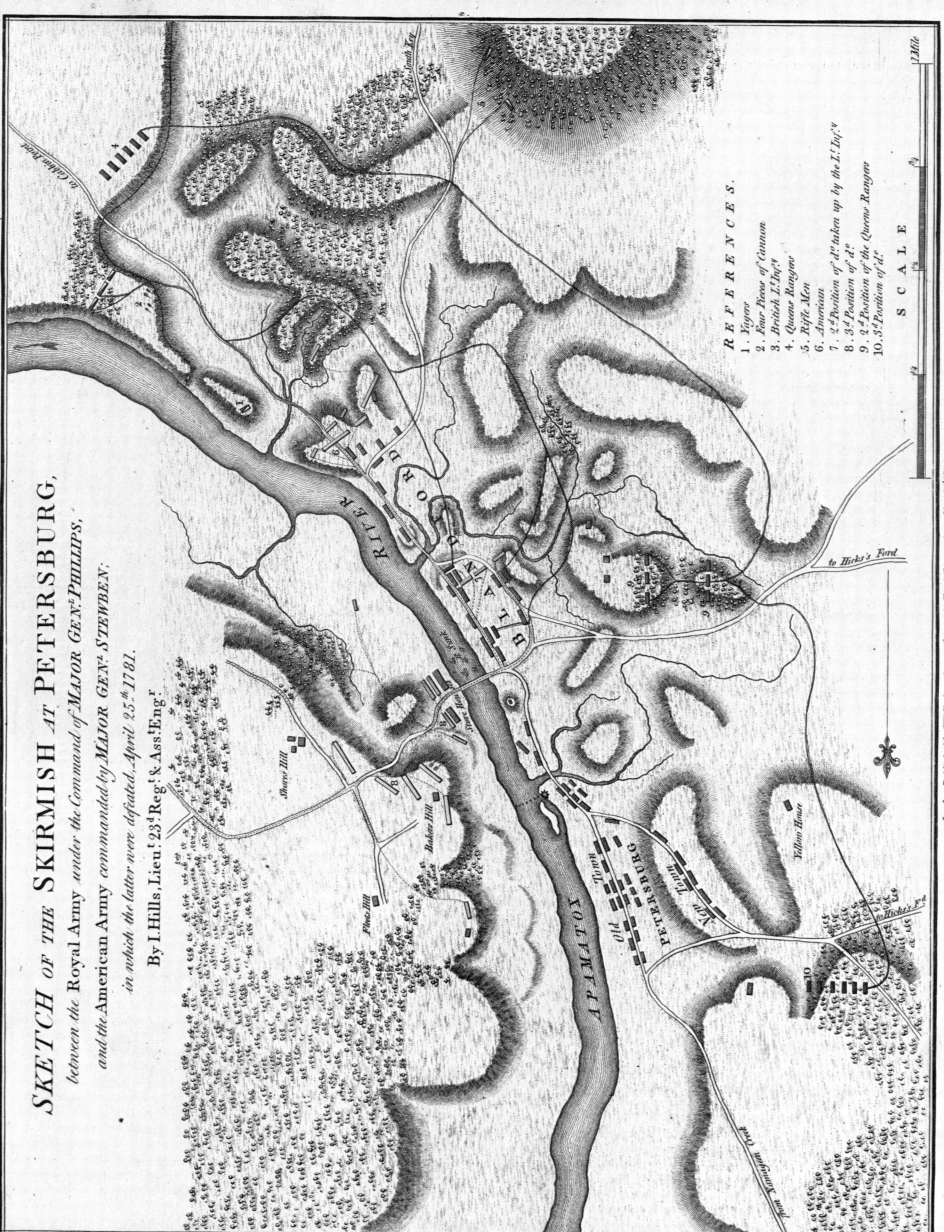

SKETCH of the SKIRMISH at PETERSBURG,

between the Royal Army under the Command of MAJOR GENᴸ PHILLIPS,

and the American Army commanded by MAJOR GENᴸ STEWBEN:

in which the latter were defeated, Aprilᵗ 25ᵗʰ 1781.

By I. Hills, Lieutᵗ 23ᵈ Regᵗ & Assᵗ Engᵣ.

REFERENCES.

1. Yagers
2. Four Pieces of Cannon
3. British Lᵗ Infᵗʸ
4. Queens Ranger
5. Rifle Men
6. American
7. 2ᵈ Position of dᵒ taken up by the Lᵗ Infᵗʸ
8. 3ᵈ Position of dᵒ.
9. 2ᵈ Position of the Queens Ranger
10. 3ᵈ Position of dᵒ.

SCALE

½   ¾   1 Mile

London. Published by Wᵐ Faden, Geographer to the King, Charing Cross, May 3ᵈ 1784.

RIVER APPOMATTOX

to Hicks's Ford

Sharp's Hill

Baker's Hill

Flint Hill

Old Town

PETERSBURG

New Town

Yellow House

to Hicks's Fᵈ

BLANDFORD

from Ronnagian Creek

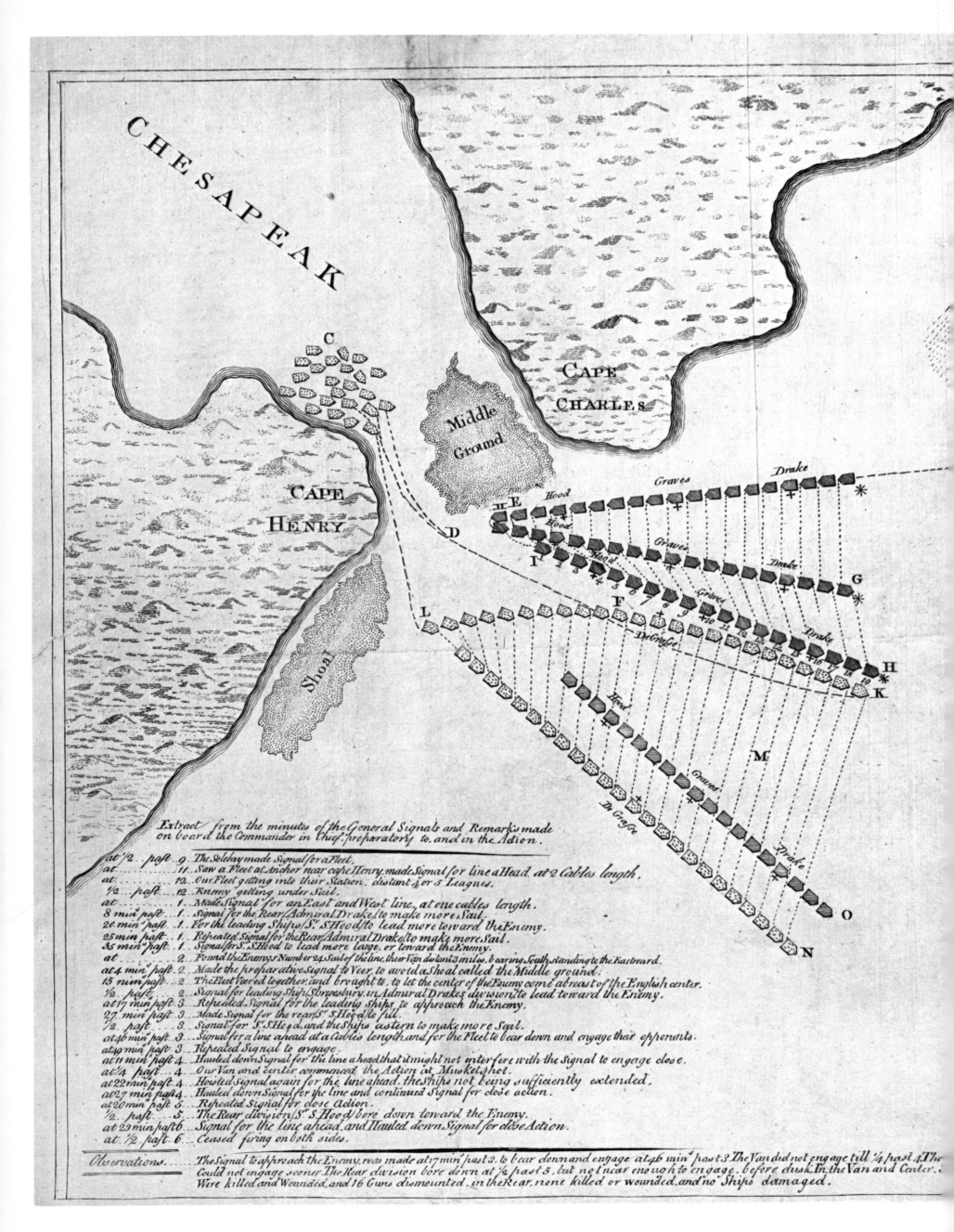

Extract from the minutes of the General Signals and Remarks made on board the Commander in Chief, preparatory to, and in the Action.

at 1/2 past 9 ... The Solebay made Signal for a Fleet.
at ...... 11 ... Saw a Fleet at Anchor near cape Henry, made Signal for line a Head, at 2 Cables length.
at ...... 12 ... Our Fleet getting into their Station, distant 4 or 5 Leagues.
1/2 past 12 ... Enemy getting under Sail.
at ...... 1 ... Made Signal for an East and West line, at one cables length.
8 min past 1 ... Signal for the Rear (Admiral Drake) to make more Sail.
20 min past 1 ... For the leading Ships (Sr S. Hood) to lead more toward the Enemy.
25 min past 1 ... Repeated Signal for the Rear, Admiral Drake to make more Sail.
35 min past 1 ... Signal for Sr S. Hood to lead more large, or toward the Enemy.
at ...... 2 ... Found the Enemy of Number 24 Sail of the line, their Van distant 3 miles, bearing South, standing to the Eastward.
at 4 min past 2 ... Made the preparative Signal to Veer, to avoid a Shoal called the Middle ground.
15 min past 2 ... The Fleet Veered together, and brought to, to let the center of the Enemy come abreast of the English center.
1/2 past 2 ... Signal for leading Ship (Shrewsbury) in Admiral Drakes division to lead toward the Enemy.
at 17 min past 3 ... Repeated Signal for the leading Ships, to approach the Enemy.
27 min past 3 ... Made Signal for the rear (Sr S. Hood) to fill.
1/2 past 3 ... Signal for Sr S. Hood, and the Ships astern to make more Sail.
at 46 min past 3 ... Signal for a line ahead at a Cables length, and for the Fleet to bear down and engage their opponents.
at 49 min past 3 ... Repeated Signal to engage.
at 11 min past 4 ... Hauled down Signal for the line a head that it might not interfere with the Signal to engage close.
at 1/4 past 4 ... Our Van and center commenced the Action at Musket shot.
at 22 min past 4 ... Hoisted Signal again for the line ahead, the Ships not being sufficiently extended.
at 27 min past 4 ... Hauled down Signal for the line and continued Signal for close action.
at 20 min past 5 ... Repeated Signal for close Action.
1/2 past 5 ... The Rear division (Sr S. Hood) bore down toward the Enemy.
at 29 min past 6 ... Signal for the line ahead, and Hauled down Signal for close Action.
at 1/2 past 6 ... Ceased firing on both sides.

Observations. The Signal to approach the Enemy, was made at 17 min past 3. to bear down and engage at 46 min past 3. The Van did not engage till 1/4 past 4. The ... could not engage sooner. The Rear division bore down at 1/2 past 5. but not near enough to engage. before dusk. In the Van and Center ... Were killed and Wounded, and 16 Guns dismounted, in the Rear, none killed or wounded, and no Ships damaged.

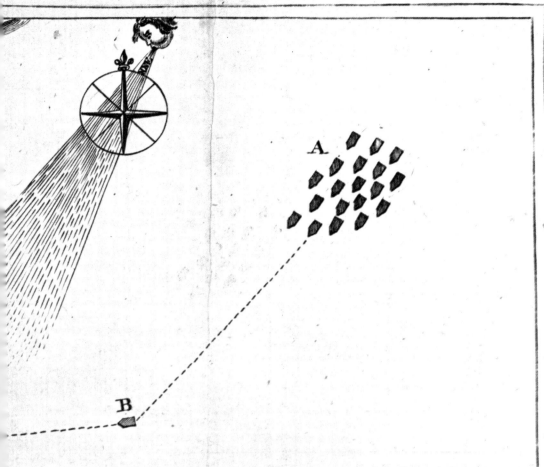

A·REPRE SENTATION,

Of the Sea Fight, on the 5th of Sepr 1781, between Rear Admiral GRAVES and the Count DE GRASSE.

- The English Fleet crowding toward Cape Henry. Wind NNE about 11 AM.
- English look out Ship.
- The French Fleet first seen at Anchor near Cape Henry, about 11 AM.
- Track of the French Van, Standing out at ½ past noon.
- The English Van Guard just before the Fleet wore to form upon the larboard, or same tack with the Enemy.
- The French Van Guard at the time the English Fleet veered and come to the larboard Tack.
- The English after having Veered on account of the Middle Ground, ½ past 2 & come to the larboard tack, which just Admiral Drake in the Van & Admiral Hood in the rear, who was at that time 2 miles nearer the Enemy than the center was
- The English partially engaged: the Van and center at Musket Shot, but the rear too distant to engage, being to Windward.
- The English rear when the Fleets engaged.
- The French Fleet when engaged.
- The French rear when the Fleets engaged K being their Van.
- The Track of the French declining from the English Van and center.
- The track of the French after Sun set.
- The English coming parallel to the Enemy after the firing had ceased on both sides.
- Admiral Drakes Division, or that part of the English Fleet, which form'd the Van in the Battle, in its three different positions, that is, just before the Fleet veer'd, after it had veered, and when it enterd into action, the French van being permitted to pass on with in cannon Shot from our center to our van, or nearly so, before the Signal was made to engage.

French	24 Ships	1822 Guns	18.200 Men	
English	19 Ships	1408 Guns	11.311 Men	

French Superior by 5 Ships   414 Guns   6889 Men

3. Neither Fleets had at this time any land Forces aboard or in Transports.

Alfred	Captn Bayne	8 Resolution	Capt L R Manners	15 Ajax	Captn Charrington	
Belliquex	Brine	9 Bedford	The Graves	16 Princessa	Knatchbull	
Invincible	Saxton	*10 London	Dd Graves	17 Alcide	Cha Thompson	
Barfleur	Hood	11 Royal Oak	Ardesoif	18 Intrepid	Molloy	
Monmouth	Reynolds	12 Montagu	Bowen	19 Shrewsbury	M Robinson	
Centaur	Inglefield	13 Europe	Child			
America	S Thompson	14 Terrible	Finch			

Had Britannia Ruled the Waves…

MAP 45. ¶ Admiral de Grasse's victory off the Chesapeake Capes on September 5, 1781, has been rightly regarded as one of the pivotal engagements of history. The defeat of the British fleet by the French in this engagement sealed the doom of Cornwallis at Yorktown, since it eliminated the possibility of either the reinforcement or evacuation of Cornwallis's troops. ¶ Before the French entered the war in 1778, Britain held almost unchallenged naval superiority in American waters. France's initial efforts, led by Admiral d'Estaing, were disastrous. It was the arrival of Rochambeau's army at Newport and of de Grasse at the Chesapeake Capes that yielded the benefits hoped for by Washington and the Continental Congress from the French Alliance. ¶ The Royal Navy had a reputation for superiority in seamanship, but they did not live up to it in this engagement. Captain Mahan, in his *The Influence of Sea Power on History* (1890), notes that the numerical superiority of de Grasse's twenty-four ships to Thomas Graves's nineteen did not deter the British fighting spirit. He suggests, rather, that on this day the French simply outsailed them. ¶ This English map gives details of the maneuvers of the two fleets and includes a list of the observations and orders signaled to the British fleet from their flagship, from 9:30 AM to 6:30 PM, when the firing ceased. The names and commanders of the nineteen British ships are included. Unlike many battle plans which were understandably partial in presenting what occurred, this British account is remarkably similar to French accounts of the battle.

A Representation, Of the Sea Fight, on the 5th of Sepr. 1781, between Rear Admiral Graves and the Count De Grasse. London, January 1784. (12½" x 15½")

In: Political Magazine VI (1784)

MAP 45. Reproduced from the collection of The Newberry Library

177

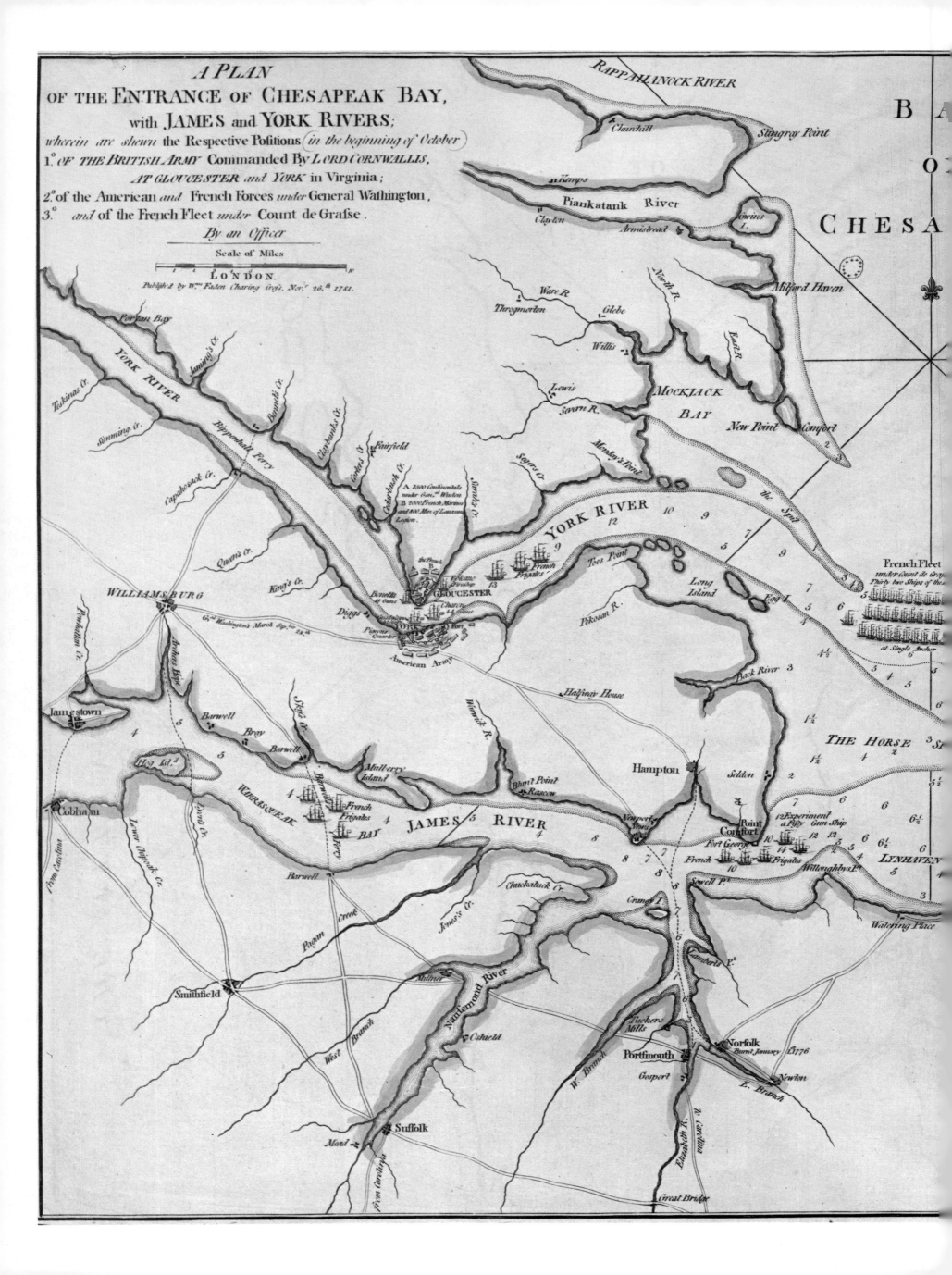

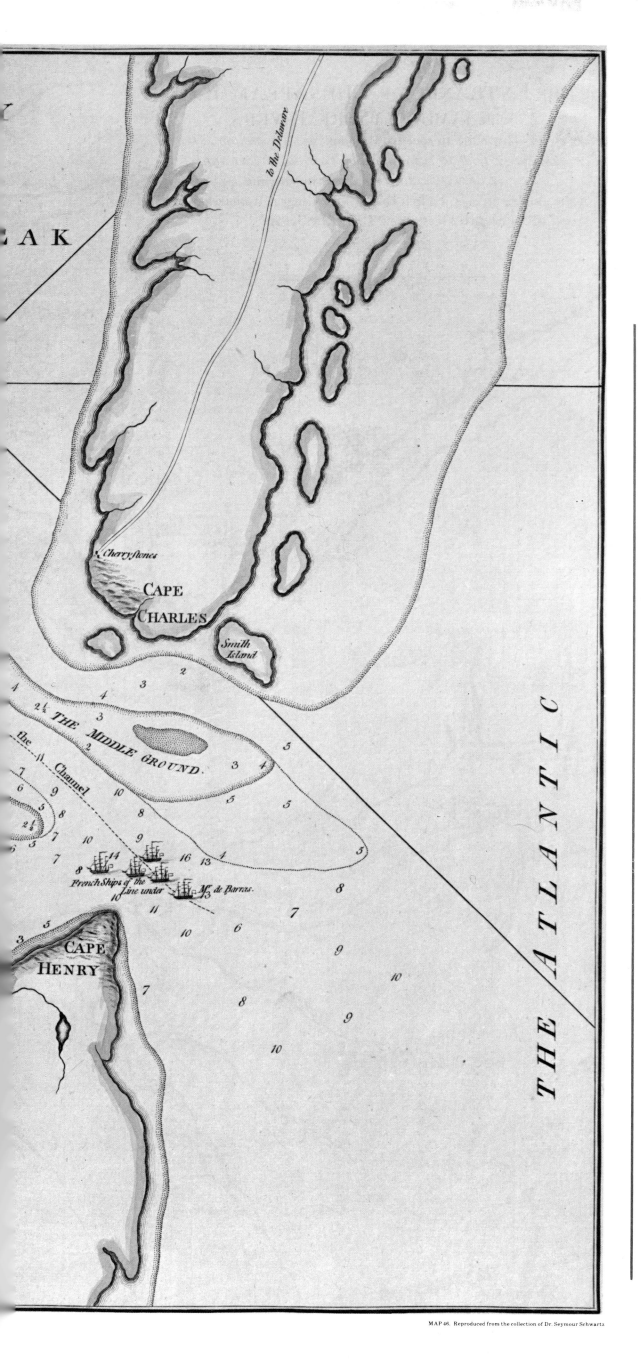

MAP 46. Reproduced from the collection of Dr. Seymour Schwartz

British View
of Unavoidable Disaster

MAP 46. ¶ When this map was issued in London, Cornwallis had already surrendered at Yorktown, but that fact could not have been known by then in Britain. The timeliness of this engraving, in addition to the clear picture it renders of the beginning of the end in Virginia, helps make it an exciting document. ¶ The road along which the allied French and American armies marched from Williamsburg to within less than a mile of Cornwallis's fortifications at Yorktown appears at the left of the map. The crucial presence of de Grasse's fleet and de Barras's squadron is depicted. The map shows French armed frigates on the James River just south of Yorktown, a number of ships off Fort Comfort at the mouth of the James, and frigates on the York River a short distance from the town. The American and French troops under Washington and Rochambeau are shown entrenched just outside Yorktown on the south shore and Gloucester on the north. ¶ There was one unsuccessful attempt by Cornwallis to break the siege. After this, he tried to gather boats, cross to the Gloucester side, and escape to the north. Even this was doomed to failure because a storm arose and swamped the small boats. ¶ Cornwallis asked for terms on October 17. These were worked out and the surrender executed on October 19. This terminated the last major action of the British army in North America in the eighteenth century. The end of the war and recognition of the independence of the United States were in sight.

A Plan of the Entrance of Chesapeak Bay, with James and York Rivers; wherein are shewn the Respective Positions (in the beginning of October) 1.° Of the British Army Commanded By Lord Cornwallis, at Gloucester and York in Virginia; 2.° of the American and French Forces under General Washington, 3.° and of the French Fleet under Count de Grasse. London, Wm. Faden, Nov. 26, 1781. (16¼" x 20½")

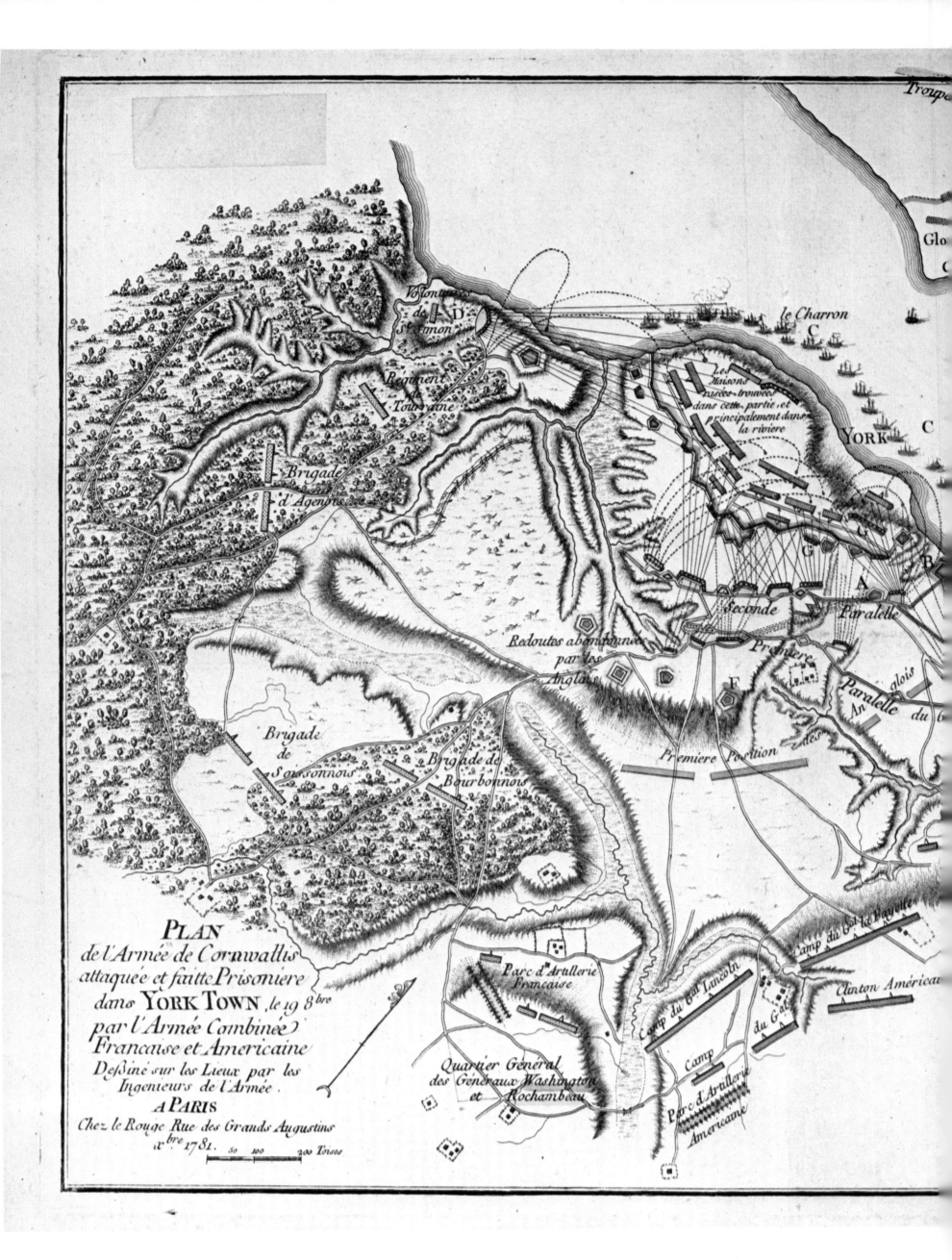

Troupe

Glo

le Charron
C

Volontaires
de St Simon
D

Regiment
Touraine

Les Maisons
rasées trouvées
dans cette partie et
principalement dans
la riviere

YORK
C

Brigade
d'Agenois

G

A

Seconde
Paralelle

Redoutes abandonnées
par les
Anglais

Premiere
Paralelle
Anglois

Paralelle du b

Brigade
de
Soissonnois

Brigade de
Bourbonnois

F

Premiere Position des

Camp du Gal le Fayette

Parc d'Artillerie
Française

Camp du Gal Lincoln

Clinton Américai

Camp
du Gal

PLAN
de l'Armée de Cornwallis
attaquée et faitte Prisoniere
dans YORK TOWN, le 19 8bre
par l'Armée Combinée
Française et Américaine
Dessiné sur les Lieux par les
Ingenieurs de l'Armée.
A PARIS
Chez le Rouge Rue des Grands Augustins
xbre 1781.   50 100   200 Toises

Quartier Général
des Generaux Washington
et Rochambeau

Camp

Parc d'Artillerie
Américaine

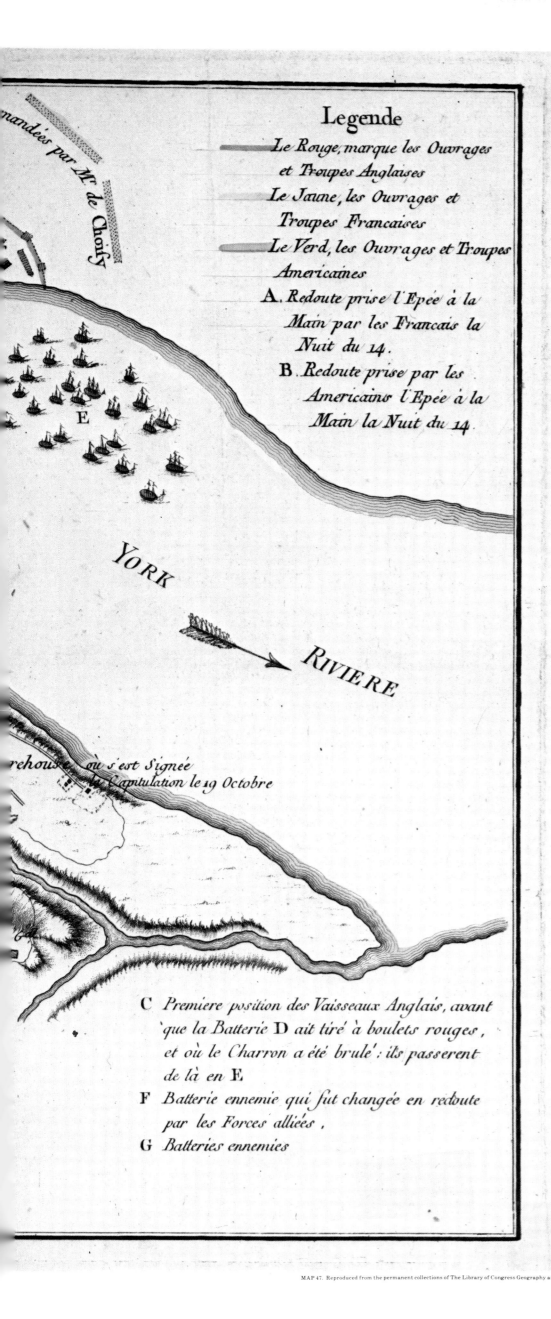

Legende

Le Rouge, marque les Ouvrages et Troupes Anglaises

Le Jaune, les Ouvrages et Troupes Francaises

Le Verd, les Ouvrages et Troupes Americaines

A. Redoute prise l'Epée à la Main par les Francais la Nuit du 14.

B. Redoute prise par les Americains l'Epée à la Main la Nuit du 14.

YORK RIVIERE

...mandées par Mr de Choisy

...rehouse ou s'est Signée ...la Capitulation le 19 Octobre

C Premiere position des Vaisseaux Anglais, avant que la Batterie D ait tiré à boulets rouges, et où le Charron a été brulé: ils passerent de là en E

F Batterie ennemie qui fut changée en redoute par les Forces alliées.

G Batteries ennemies

The End at Yorktown

MAP 47. ¶ Le Rouge's remarkable but little-known plan of the victory by the combined American-French armies over the British was among the first to have been published after Cornwallis surrendered. It was drawn on sufficient scale to permit considerable detail. The outer perimeter of defense posts, surprisingly abandoned by the British early and without contest, are shown, as are the two redoubts—one taken by an American charge and the other by a French charge on the night of October 14. The British warships are depicted in their first position on the Yorktown side from where they were driven by the French artillery ("D" on map), which set some of the ships afire with red-hot shot. The cluster of ships on the Gloucester side indicates the position of those which moved out of range. The first and second parallels of the siege entrenchments are delineated. Moore's house, where the articles of capitulation were signed, can be seen to the east. ¶ The activities at Gloucester leading up to the surrender are merely hinted at schematically on this plan.

Plan de l'Armée de Cornwallis attaquée et faitte Prisoniere dans York Town, le 19 8bre par l'Armée Combinée Francaise et Americaine....Paris, Le Rouge, Dec., 1781. (12½" x 15¾")

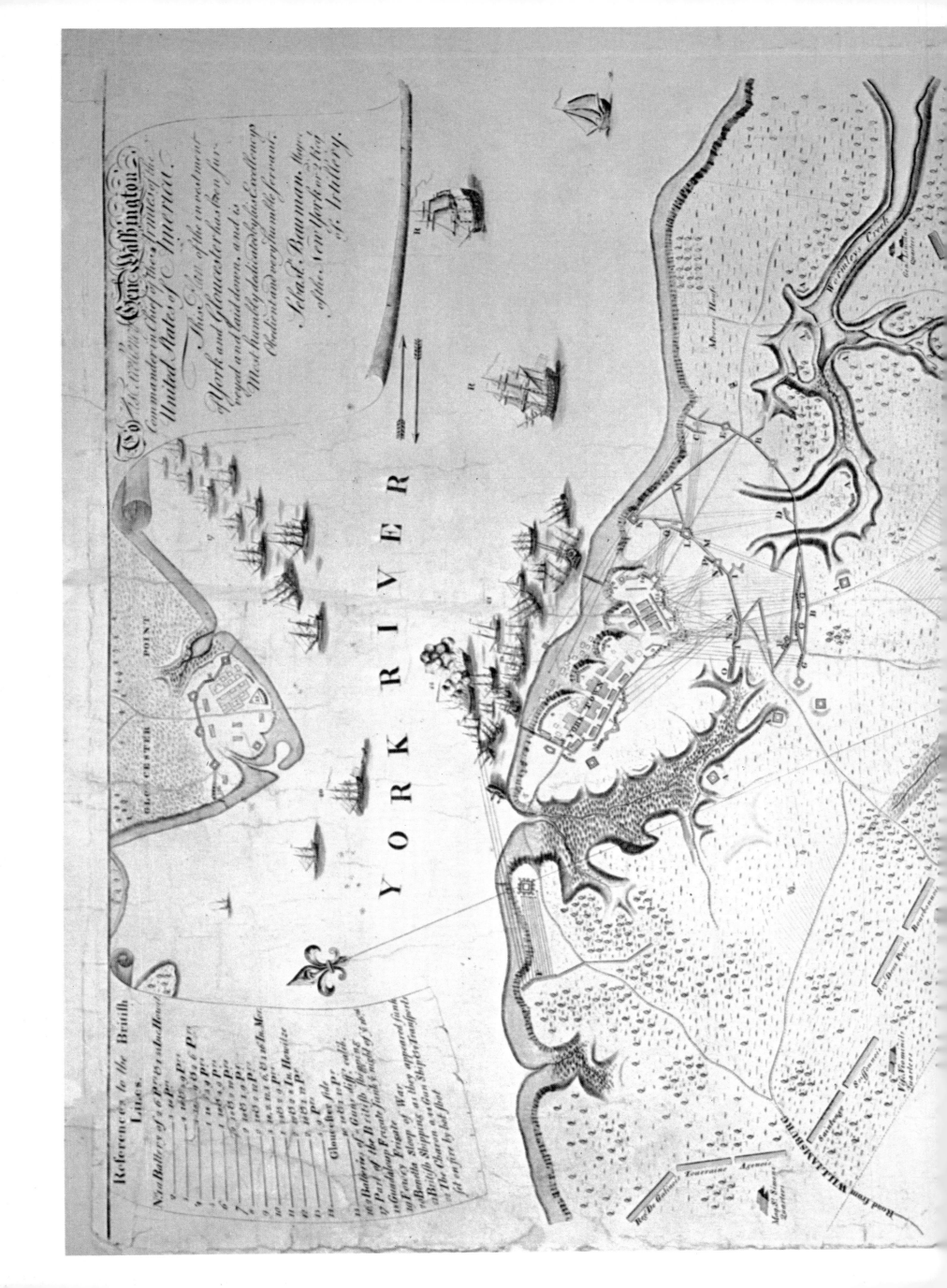

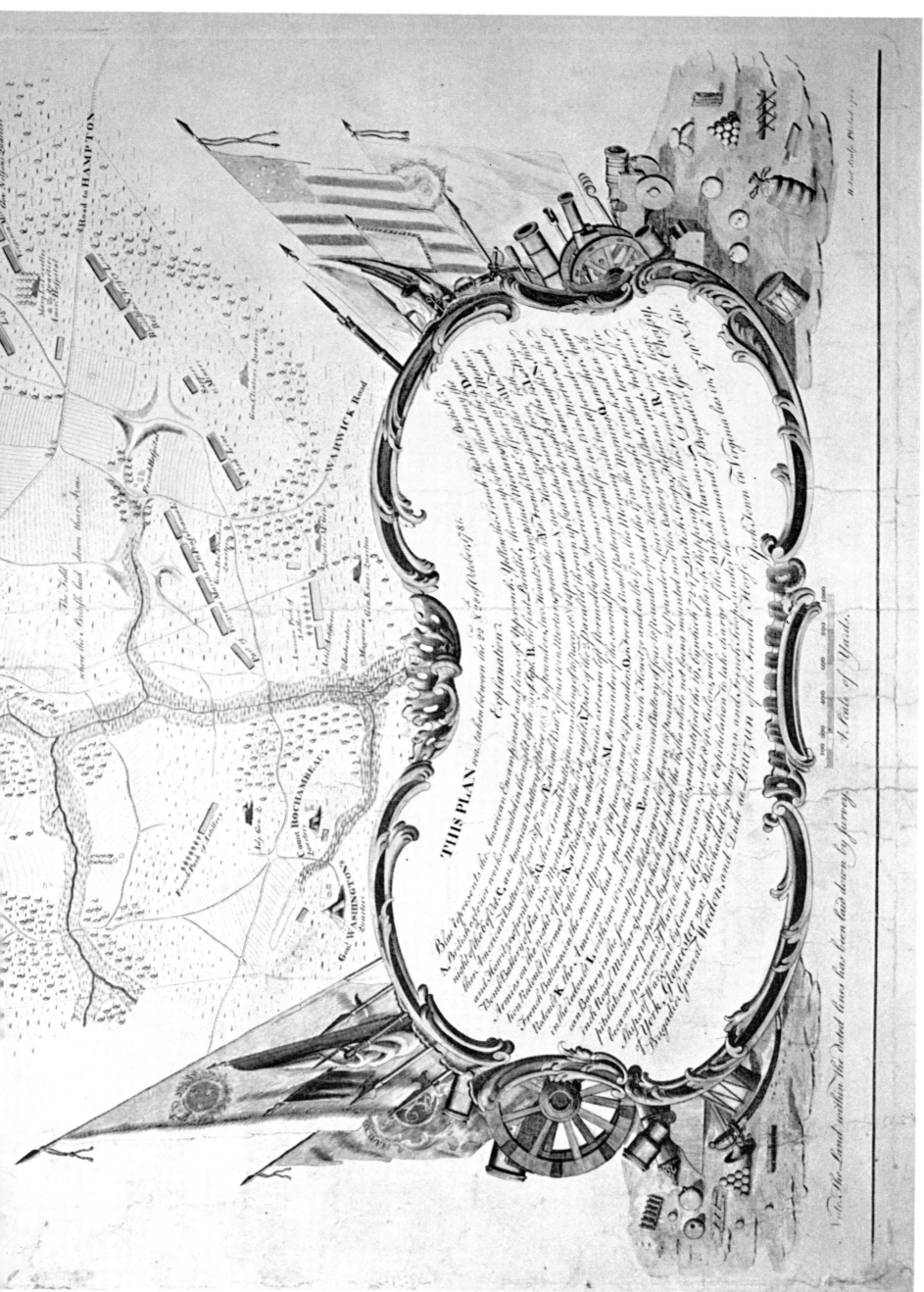

The First American Map of the War's Greatest Victory

MAP 48. ¶ Indefatigable men whose sense of history has brought them forward at moments of consequence have frequently provided the historian with his raw material. Such was the case when an American artillery officer took to the battlefield at Yorktown shortly after the guns became silent. ¶ Major Sebastian Bauman carefully surveyed the battle positions of both sides and the terrain on which this pivotal battle of world history was fought. He was well equipped for the task and had earned the honor of producing this important document of American history. A native of Germany, Bauman had emigrated to America as a young man after military training and service in the artillery of the Austrian army. He fought in the French and Indian War, and his regiment was cited by Washington. Bauman served loyally under Washington during the entire Revolutionary War. After action in the campaigns in New York, New Jersey, and Pennsylvania in 1776 and 1777, he was placed in command of artillery at West Point, before joining the besiegers at Yorktown. ¶ Bauman's splendid map, dedicated to General Washington, reflects his formal European training in topographical engineering. It is the only American survey of the culmination of the great struggle for independence and a cornerstone document of our national heritage.

SHOWN ON PRECEDING PAGE
Plan of the Investment of York and Gloucester by Sebastn. Bauman. Engraved by R. Scott. Philadelphia, 1782. (25½" x 18")

Morgan's command, withdrew himself into North Carolina and linked up with Morgan at Guilford Courthouse (near present-day Greensboro). With His Lordship nipping at his heels, Greene's reunited Southern army continued its flight, eventually passing over the Dan River to safety in Virginia. (*See Map 42*)

If, as Mao Tse-tung has said, "the ability to run away is the very characteristic of the guerrilla," then Greene had learned his role quite well. Yet another characteristic of guerrilla warfare—one that allows parallels to be drawn with Mao's war with the Chinese Nationalists and Giap's struggle against the French in Indochina—is this: sooner or later, after debilitating the enemy, the irregulars themselves may concentrate their forces and come out into the open in a more traditional manner of fighting.

And so it was with Greene, who fleshed out his army with new recruits and fresh militia units, and who knew that Cornwallis was bruised and battered by Kings Mountain, Cowpens, and his long, arduous chase through North Carolina. Returning to that state, Greene flung down the challenge of positional combat to Cornwallis, and Lord Charles accepted at Guilford Courthouse, where the Americans had a heavy numerical superiority, about 4,400 as opposed to 2,000. But Greene, with a tatterdemalion army, needed that advantage against Cornwallis's veterans. Had Greene counterattacked at a crucial stage in this contest of March 15, he might have won an impressive victory. As it was, after heavy British losses—over 500 in all categories as against Greene's 250 or so—the American general withdrew. Cornwallis, his army no longer an effective fighting machine, limped southeastward to Wilmington and then proceeded to Virginia, leaving his posts in South Carolina vulnerable to Greene.

"I am determined to carry the war immediately to South Carolina," the Rhode Islander informed Washington on April 5. Before Lord Rawdon, the British commander in that state, could call in his garrisons and concentrate against Greene, the American Southern army and the partisan bands of Thomas Sumter, Francis Marion, and Andrew Pickens were upon them. While the local irregulars struck elsewhere, Greene himself moved to contain the only sizable striking force at Rawdon's disposal: 1,500 men at Camden. Near that town, at Hobkirk's Hill, Greene fell short of victory when Colonel John Gunby's Maryland regiment became disorganized and gave up its place in the battle line, enabling Rawdon to counterattack, whereupon Greene—ever the daring strategist but cautious tactician—retired from the field. Since each side had suffered about the same number of casualties, Greene was able to maintain the pressure, leaving Rawdon and supporting the partisans, as one by one British stations fell. Rawdon soon abandoned Camden and rushed to the relief of his besieged post at Ninety-Six to the west. Although successful, Rawdon could not continue such a wide dispersal of his remaining troops, and he pulled back all his units to the coast.

Between April and July the Americans had eliminated the enemy from almost the entire lower South, except for a narrow strip from Charleston to Savannah. Greene's last important battle, like all his major encounters, ended indecisively: Eutaw Springs, where on September 8 he fought with Rawdon's successor, Lieutenant Colonel Alexander Stewart. Disorganization in the midst of battle, always a problem with Greene's mixture of regulars and militia, again kept him from carrying the day; but he netted 400 prisoners and inflicted nearly 500 casualties upon Stewart while suffering losses of 500 himself in various categories. The war wound down to occasional raids and skirmishes as Greene's army kept Charleston and Savannah under observation until the British evacuated those cities in 1782.

Greene in the South had been a masterful strategist. Consistently, he made the most of his resources, and he made the British play his game. Dividing his forces at key moments, he kept on the move, never letting up

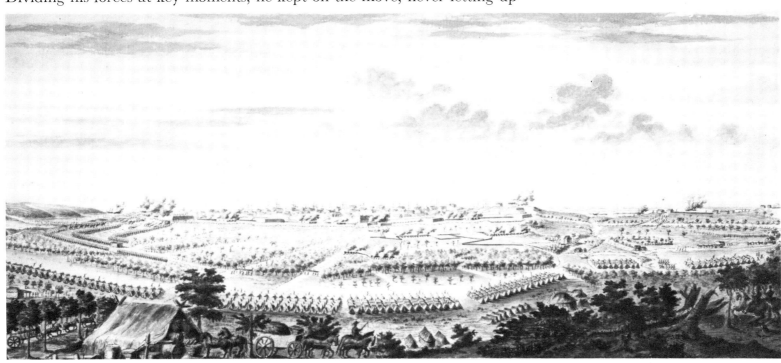

In late 1778, General Henry Clinton shifted British operations to the south, anticipating aid from southern Loyalists. On the 29th of December, the city of Savannah, Georgia, fell before an attack by 3,500 men under the command of Lieutenant Colonel Archibald Campbell.

to allow his opponents to collect themselves. He led Cornwallis on a chase that ultimately wore out His Lordship's army and prompted him to leave South Carolina to the mercy of the Continentals and partisans. Greene lived in a day when guerrilla warfare was little understood by professional soldiers. But in the lower South he used techniques that have been the stock-in-trade of revolutionists in our own time.

Meanwhile, in the upper South the Revolution was building toward a climax. On May 20, Cornwallis reached Petersburg, Virginia, and took command of British raiding parties that had been operating in the eastern part of that state since the past December. Those diversionary forces, led by the turncoat Benedict Arnold (who had gone over to the royal side in September 1780) and Major General William Phillips (who died a week before Cornwallis's arrival), had maneuvered up and down the peninsula skirmishing with Continentals and militia under Lafayette, assisted by Friedrich von Steuben and Peter Muhlenberg. Virginians were disheartened by the appearance of Cornwallis, plus two additional redcoat regiments that came by sea, raising the number of troops at His Lordship's disposal to 7,200. The Old Dominion was stirring, however, as fresh irregulars and supplies flowed in from the piedmont and Blue Ridge sections; and Continental reinforcements under Major General Anthony Wayne soon joined Lafayette. (*See Map 44*)

In July, after two months of indecisive campaigning in Virginia, Cornwallis retired to Yorktown near the coast and began erecting fortifications. Cornwallis seems to have given little serious thought to his objectives and his possibilities for achieving them. Cornwallis did assert that the possession of the Old Dominion was essential to holding securely the lower South. It was, to say the least, a doubtful assumption; in any case, it ignored the

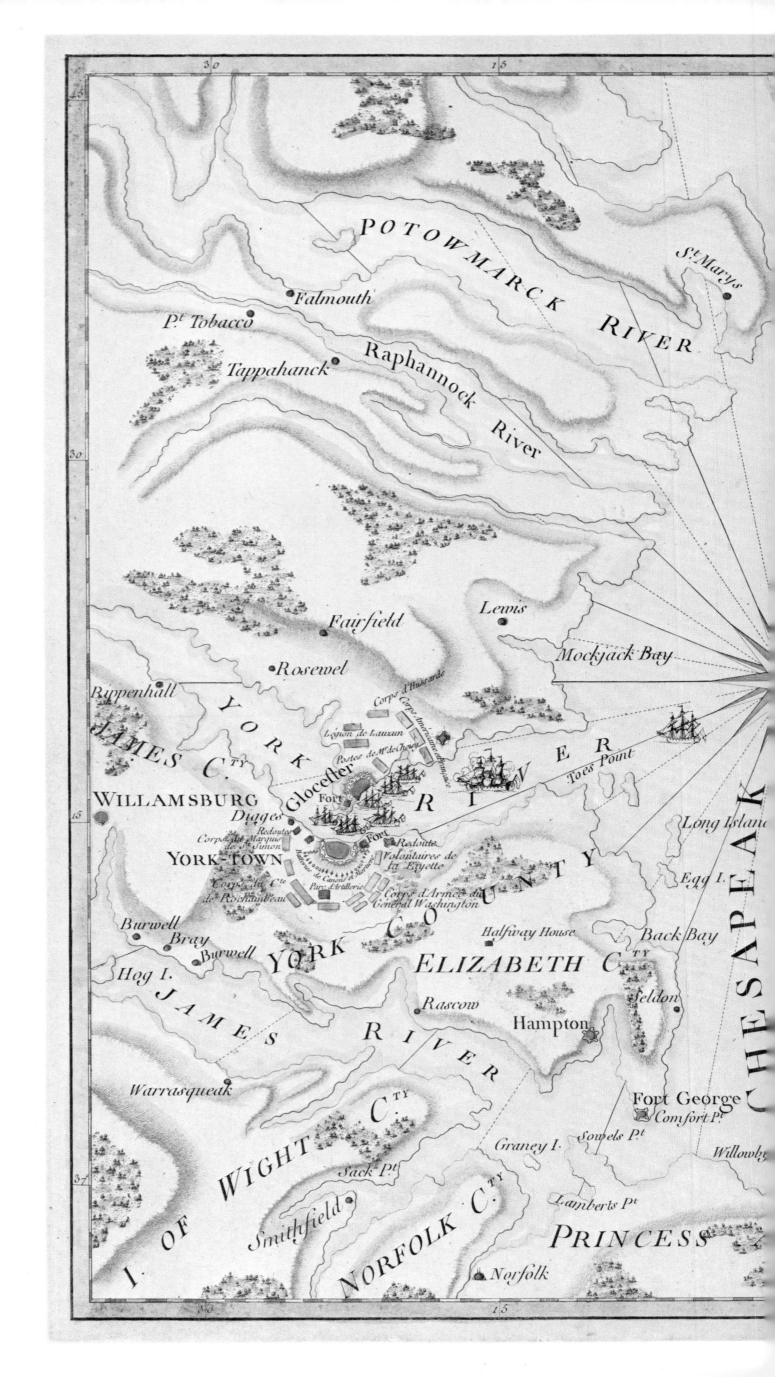

POTOWMARCK RIVER

S.t Mary's

Falmouth

P.t Tobacco

Tappahanck

Raphannock River

Fairfield

Lewis

Rosewel

Mockjack Bay

Rippenhall

YORK

JAMES C.TY

Corps d'Husards

Corps Invincil....ente

Légion de Lauzun

Postes de M.r de Choisy

WILLAMSBURG

Glocefter

Fort

RIVER

Toes Point

Digges

Redoute

Long Island

Corps du Marquis
de S.t Simon

YORK-TOWN

Redoute

Fort

Redoute
Volontaires de
la Fayette

Egg I.

Batterie de Canon et Mortiers

Corps du C.te
de Rochambeau

Parc d'Artillerie

Corps d'Armée du
General Washington

COUNTY

Burwell

Bray

Halfway House

Back Bay

Burwell

YORK

ELIZABETH C.TY

Seldon

Hog I.

Rascow

JAMES

RIVER

Hampton

Warrasqueak

Fort George

C.TY

Comfort P.t

OF

Sowels P.t

Graney I.

Willowby

WIGHT

Sack P.t

Lamberts P.t

Smithfield

NORFOLK C.TY

PRINCESS

Norfolk

CHESAPEAK

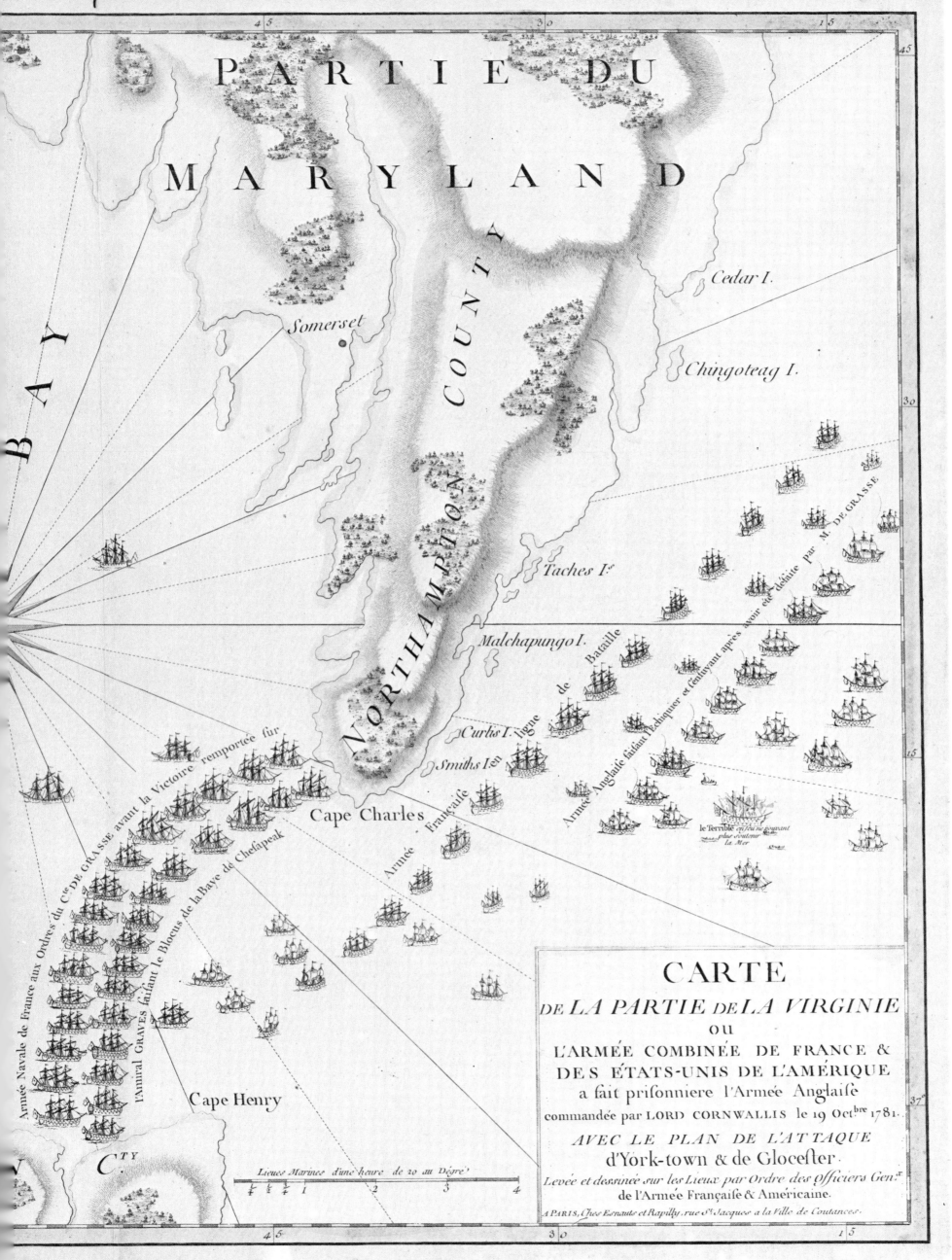

PARTIE DU

MARYLAND

B A Y

NORTHAMPTON COUNTY

Cedar I.

Somerset

Chingoteag I.

Taches Is.

Malchapungo I.

Bataille

Curlis I. ligne de

Smiths Ien

Armée Anglaise faisant l'échiquier après avoir été défaite par M. DE GRASSE

le Terrible en feu ne pouvant plus soutenir la Mer

Cape Charles

Armée Française

Armée Navale de France aux Ordres du Cte DE GRASSE avant la Victoire remportée sur

l'Amiral GRAVES faisant le Blocus de la Baye de Chesapeak

Cape Henry

C.TY

Lieues Marines d'une heure de 20 au Dégré
¼ ½ ¾ 1   2   3   4

CARTE
DE LA PARTIE DE LA VIRGINIE
ou
L'ARMÉE COMBINÉE DE FRANCE &
DES ÉTATS-UNIS DE L'AMÉRIQUE
a fait prisonniere l'Armée Angloise
commandée par LORD CORNWALLIS le 19 Oct.bre 1781.

AVEC LE PLAN DE L'ATTAQUE
d'York-town & de Glocester.

Levée et dessinée sur les Lieux par Ordre des Officiers Gen.x
de l'Armée Française & Américaine.

A PARIS, Chez Esnauts et Rapilly, rue St Jacques à la Ville de Coutances.

Homage to the French Fleet

MAP 49. ¶ Dramatically emphasized here is the effect of the presence of Admiral de Grasse's French fleet on the outcome of Yorktown. The French established control of the sea at the battle off the Chesapeake Capes two weeks after the British began to dig in at Yorktown and Gloucester. The French fleet helped to finish Cornwallis just as certainly as the allied armies of Washington and Rochambeau did by their siege. ¶ When de Grasse's fleet engaged the British, commanded by Admiral Thomas Graves with Admiral Samuel Hood's squadron included, the British losses were severe. During the encounter the two fleets drifted southward toward Cape Hatteras, which enabled the second French fleet, under the Comte de Barras, to arrive from Newport, bringing the heavy artillery for the siege of Yorktown. The British had to sail back to New York for repairs. De Grasse returned to the Chesapeake, and Cornwallis's army on the Virginia peninsula was surrounded by land and sea. ¶ This fascinating map also delineates the military positions at Yorktown and Gloucester and puts their locations in overall perspective. The British and French fleets are shown in their alignments before and during the battle.

SHOWN ON PRECEDING PAGE
Carte de La Partie de La Virginie ou l'Armée combinée de France & des Etats-Unis de l'Amérique a fait prisonniere l'Armée Anglaise commandée par Lord Cornwallis le 19 Octbre. 1781. Avec le plan de l'attaque d'York-town & de Glocester. . . . Paris, Esnauts and Rapilly, 1782. (18½" x 24")

question of whether Lord Charles could subdue Virginia, just as it avoided the fact that his superior Clinton had never intended to make that state the center of offensive operations in the South. Clinton realized that the Chesapeake area was vulnerable to French sea power, to say nothing of being fever-ridden and anything but an ideal location for warm-weather campaigning.

Whereas Clinton had seen Virginia only in terms of a diversion—to take pressure off his forces in the Carolinas and create a base as a refuge for Loyalists—Cornwallis now urged Clinton to make the Old Dominion the "Seat of war," even if that should necessitate the giving up of New York.

If Cornwallis's thinking was muddled, Clinton was at fault for not explicitly ordering Lord Charles to get out of Virginia and to consolidate British gains in the lower South before attempting anything else. Clinton, who had been an aggressive subordinate, invariably shrank from bold decision-making as commander in chief. The pattern of behavior is so clear that it was likely a part of his psychological makeup, a man who craved power until he possessed it and then found excuses to keep from using it. The summer of 1781 slowly passed as the two generals exchanged letter after letter, Clinton *suggesting* alternatives, Cornwallis—since matters were always left to his discretion—responding in the negative, his Yorktown base looming as an inviting target to the Franco-American allies.

The possibility of another attempt at cooperation between France and America had existed for some time, for in the spring of 1780 the Paris government dispatched its first contingent of troops to the United States. But the 5,500 troops under the Comte de Rochambeau had remained inactive in Rhode Island, as had a small French naval detachment at Newport. Washington for some months had turned over in his mind a direct assault on New York City, a scheme for which Rochambeau had little enthusiasm. The Virginian might have pressed the issue, since Louis XVI's ministers had instructed Rochambeau to take orders from Washington (but no other American general). Washington did not, however, partly because he wished to avoid offending the able, otherwise amiable foreigner, partly also because he doubted the success of an attack upon that city without French naval superiority. Prospects seemingly brightened in May 1781, when Washington learned that Rear Admiral Francois Joseph Paul, the Comte de Grasse, was sailing for New World waters. Would he join Washington and Rochambeau for a blow at New York? Washington now persuaded Rochambeau to participate in such an undertaking provided de Grasse could be a part of it. Then word arrived that de Grasse was in the West Indies and crowding sail for the Chesapeake with twenty ships of the line and 3,000 soldiers. Washington and Rochambeau on August 17 wrote the admiral that they would hasten southward to cooperate in snaring Cornwallis on the Virginia peninsula.

Clinton in New York was in the dark regarding the allied plans as Washington's garrison left behind made repeated feints at Sir Henry's outposts and constructed storehouses and bake ovens as if to put the city under immediate siege. Not until September 5—the day American and French armies paraded through Philadelphia—did Sir Henry realize that the allied thrust would be elsewhere, that Cornwallis might be the one under siege.

Given the absence of modern, instantaneous communications, the smooth synchronization of the massive operation is almost amazing in retrospect. As Lafayette's American forces in Virginia positioned themselves to hold Cornwallis on the peninsula, de Grasse arrived at the Virginia Capes in time to send transports to ferry the regiments of Washington and Rochambeau from Chesapeake Bay to the James River.

Only too late did Cornwallis comprehend what was happening, when there was no longer a reasonable chance of breaking out of the peninsula. If the allies needed the French fleet to seal His Lordship's fate, it was equally true that the one slim chance remaining to the British general was the Royal Navy. And whether it could have saved him is an unanswerable question, for the navy hardly rose to the occasion. The small Newport squadron under the Comte de Barras slipped out to sea with Rochambeau's artillery and hurried southward to pop in at the Chesapeake after De Grasse had cleared the ocean lanes. Subsequently, Rear Admiral Thomas Graves, acting British naval commander at New York, received a reinforcement under Rear Admiral Sir Samuel Hood from Admiral Sir George Rodney's West Indies fleet. Unfortunately for Cornwallis, Rodney had doubted that de Grasse would take his entire complement to the American coast, and therefore provided Hood with inadequate support. The fault lay also with the cabinet in London, which—after d'Estaing's earlier failures —had felt that any French naval activity in conjunction with the rebels could be easily dealt with.

On the night of August 29, 1776, Washington, after suffering severe losses in the battle of Long Island, secretly withdrew his forces to Manhattan Island. The next morning, the British were surprised to find the field before them deserted.

Although Graves was therefore outmanned when he headed southward from New York in a game effort to save Cornwallis, a better sailor might conceivably have turned the tide, notwithstanding the odds. For initially the French were caught napping when Graves hove into view, and consequently they were slow to put out to sea and form an effective line of battle. Graves, however, was not quick to align his own fleet. Once prepared, the fiery French Admiral de Grasse, who reputedly stood six feet two on ordinary days and six feet six on fighting days, expertly maneuvered his massive flagship, the *Ville de Paris*, and her companion ships. For two hours the two fleets exchanged a blistering fire. Then darkness descended, with the British having suffered heavy casualties and two vessels critically damaged. During the next four days the two commanders jockeyed for position, September 6–9, de Grasse luring Graves away from the capes to allow de Barras, with the vitally needed siege guns, to scoot into safety. The Battle of the Capes was over. Graves returned to New York, and Cornwallis's hour of reckoning was not far away. (*See Map 45*)

Rembrandt Peale, son of Charles Willson Peale, painted this portrait of Washington at Yorktown, where, on October 19, 1782, Cornwallis surrendered. General Benjamin Lincoln led the British soldiers between French troops and his fellow Americans.

At one time a thriving tobacco port, Yorktown was a sleepy village, not unlike it is today, where the old customhouse and the Moore House ("the surrender house") survive to give us a feeling of what life was like there 200 years ago. "This Yorktown, or Little-York," wrote a British soldier, "is . . . of approximately 300 houses . . . on the bank of the York River, somewhat high on a sandy but level ground. It has three churches, 2 reformed English and 1 German Lutheran, but without steeples, and 2 Quaker meeting houses, and a beautiful court or meeting house, which building, like the majority of the houses, is built of bricks."

Sometimes such hamlets—Gettysburg is another—are abruptly shoved forward into momentary prominence by the shifting sands of history. Yorktown occupied that role for about three weeks, beginning September 28 when the close to 17,000-man allied force, gathered at Williamsburg, advanced toward that town, where Cornwallis waited with approximately 8,000 troops.

As Cornwallis drew back to his entrenchments immediately before Yorktown, the allies began siege operations, constructing parallels at 600 yards and then 300 yards respectively from the enemy. The closer line was extended to the river after storming parties overran British redoubts numbers 9 and 10. Now it was up to the artillery, a military arm that had become increasingly significant in the eighteenth century. The French, in fact, were unexcelled at the time, though Henry Knox's American cannoneers had achieved considerable proficiency by 1781. Day after day the gun crews performed their work. Loading at the muzzle, the men poured in powder, ball, and wadding; then they elevated the barrel for the desired range and applied a length of burning match to the priming powder in the touchhole near the closed end of the weapon. To Dr. James Thatcher, a

Continental surgeon, the display of fireworks—particularly at night—was both magnificent and awesome to behold, "like fiery meteors with blazing tails, most beautifully brilliant, ascending majestically . . . to a certain altitude, and gradually descending to the spot where they are destined to execute their work of destruction." Nothing was spared as the artillerymen pinpointed gun batteries, ships in the harbor, troop encampments, and houses suspected of serving as command posts. (*See Map 47*)

On the morning of October 17, the anniversary of Burgoyne's surrender at Saratoga, a British drummer stepped forward and sounded the parley. He was followed by an officer waving a white handkerchief. Taken into the American lines, the officer handed Washington a letter from Cornwallis requesting a meeting of aides "at Mr. Moore's house, to settle terms for the surrender of the posts of York and Gloucester," the latter just across the York River and held by Banastre Tarleton. That night, wrote St. George Tucker of Virginia, "a solemn stillness prevailed" in anticipation of next day's conference at the handsome, two-story Moore House, which commanded a majestic view of the river. With Lieutenant Colonel John Laurens representing the Americans and the Viscomte de Noailles, Lafayette's brother-in-law, representing the French, the details were hammered out. The allies refused His Lordship only one article of importance to him: a guarantee that the Loyalists with his forces were "not to be punished on account of having joined the British army." That matter, explained Washington, would be determined by the state governments rather than by the Continental army.

At two o'clock on the afternoon of the nineteenth, the British, dressed in new scarlet uniforms, marched across the surrender field between long lines of white-coated French regulars and American Continentals, many of whom had finally received uniforms in what was the last campaign of the war in America. The British musicians appropriately played an old tune called "The World Turned Upside Down." Ironically, on the day of capitulation Graves and Clinton had set out for a final, desperate try to save Cornwallis. Five days later they encountered a schooner carrying refugees from Yorktown. At first disbelieving the news of Cornwallis's fall, they continued to cruise off the Virginia capes until they could confirm the results of Yorktown. As Lafayette noted, "the play . . . is over . . . the fifth act has just been closed."

Several days later an exhausted express rider clattered through the silent, predawn streets of Philadelphia. He clutched a letter for Thomas McKean, the president of Congress. Written across an outside fold were the words, "To be forwarded by night and by day with the utmost dispatch— Lord Cornwallis surrendered the garrison of York to General Washington. . . ." An old German, a member of the Philadelphia night watch, caught the glad tidings. Then, hastening on his rounds and swinging his lantern furiously, he exclaimed over and over, "Basht dree o'glock, und Cornwal-lis isht da-ken."

*The colonials stood firm,
manning the cannon,
as the redcoats,
some of Europe's finest
soldiers, advanced.*

Second Street, Philadelphia, looking North from Market Street with Christ Church (completed 1754) prominently depicted. There were many fine churches scattered throughout the city, several of them located on Second Street. Some were called meeting houses, such as the First Presbyterian Meeting House, and of course there were many Quaker meeting houses. Philadelphia was indeed a "City of Brotherly Love."

Culminating the Revolution

FOLLOWING YORKTOWN IT seemed obvious that America had, with the aid of France, won the war. There was scarcely a sign that Englishmen had any stomach for renewing the struggle after six trying years. It would have called for many thousands of additional redcoats and tons of supplies in order for the British to fan out from their isolated stations on the American coastline. Even so, Washington, who had returned to the North, and Greene, in the South, made no effort to drive the foe from those bases. Once again, with the victories in Virginia and South Carolina, and with the onset of winter months, American armies all but withered away. Of course, the Continental forces revived, as always; but there was hardly the incentive for men to come forward in generous numbers in response to recruiting officers' appeals when obviously no threat existed. The states also were less cooperative with Congress, and at times seemed irresponsible in meeting their obligations.

If the army was small and insignificant in size in 1782–83, it nevertheless frightened some Americans. The regiments were indeed in a most unhappy mood. The officers complained of their pay being in arrears, and they reminded Congress of its earlier promise in 1780 to award tham half pay for life as compensation for their extended services and sufferings. On this last point, however, the officers indicated a willingness to compromise and settle for something less, the commutation of such a pension into a lump cash settlement. Young Gouverneur Morris, assistant superintendent of finance, bluntly warned John Jay that "the army have swords in their hands." Rumors were rampant, including one that a part of the army had lost confidence in Washington for not pressing harder for the soldiers' demands. Discontent at Washington's camp at Newburgh, New York, reached its climax on March 10, 1783. That day there appeared the anonymous "Newburgh Addresses," which came from the pen of an intense young officer, twenty-four-year-old John Armstrong, whose father was a close friend of Washington. They called for a gathering of representatives from the officer corps and urged the officers not "to be tame and unprovoked when injuries press hard upon you." How extreme were the addresses? Their meaning, especially the possibility of taking violent action, is subject to differing interpretations, as is the question of whether the leaders wished to include or exclude Washington from their subsequent methods of seeking relief. The episode has been seen as "the only known instance of an attempted coup in American history." Whatever the movement, it appears to have been almost wholly confined to officers in their twenties and thirties. And it may well be that the whole affair was more an effort of disgruntled public creditors and advocates of a stronger central government to use the army than any undertaking initiated by the officers themselves.

In any case, Washington himself called a meeting of the officers and had no difficulty persuading them to work through him and other legitimate channels to secure their just rewards. No matter how oft-repeated, the Virginian's dramatic performance (was it planned?) bears retelling. Reading from a prepared statement, he faltered, reached for his eyeglasses, and said, "Gentlemen, you will permit me to put on my spectacles, for I have not only grown gray, but almost blind, in the service of my country." In time Congress responded by changing the half-pay proposal to a promise of full salaries for five years.

While the congressmen also sought to afford relief to enlisted men, that body faced a mutiny—the last of several—on the part of a few hundred troops in June. They surrounded the State House where Congress and the executive council of Pennsylvania were in session. The soldiers, soon boisterous from liquor, demanded an immediate redress of complaints. At length, the civilians inside steeled themselves and passed through the cordon of milling soldiers, who contented themselves with heaping verbal abuse upon the congressmen. Loyal regulars under Major General Robert Howe arrived on the scene, but word of their approach had already resulted in the mutineers' dispersing. Yet another crisis had been averted.

Behind Newburgh and the restlessness in the ranks lay something else: war-weariness on the part of a people engaged in an arduous struggle. Fortunately, the Revolution was not primarily a guerrilla war, which is

Philadelphia served during the Revolution as a seat of government, an enemy encampment, and a hub of travel and shipping from the north, south, and west.

usually destructive of society's most crucial institutions. Therefore, the War of Independence was not militarily a carbon copy of revolutionary upheavals in Indochina and elsewhere in Asia and in Africa, although we have noted earlier a few similarities, such as Greene's campaign in the Carolinas. Yet recent events do offer additional insights into our own struggle with Britain. If the motherland had problems that seem analogous to today's wars in the backward parts of the world—distances, terrain, and so on—the war itself was fought on American soil. Civilians were killed, property destroyed, and lives disrupted. The "triangularity of the struggle" —two armed forces in competition for the civilian population—meant that at the end of the conflict there would be hard questions about dealing with the civilians—the Loyalists—who had sided with the crown. Even though the internal chaos could have been much worse, and was in fact less than in recent more physically destructive revolutions, an eight-and-a-half-year war is a lengthy time. Prior to Vietnam, the Revolution was America's longest conflict.

America required an extended period of peace in which to recover and complete its unfinished domestic business, which meant getting the nation solidly on its feet. There was the need to disband the army, to make provision for determining and paying the public debt, to settle and or-

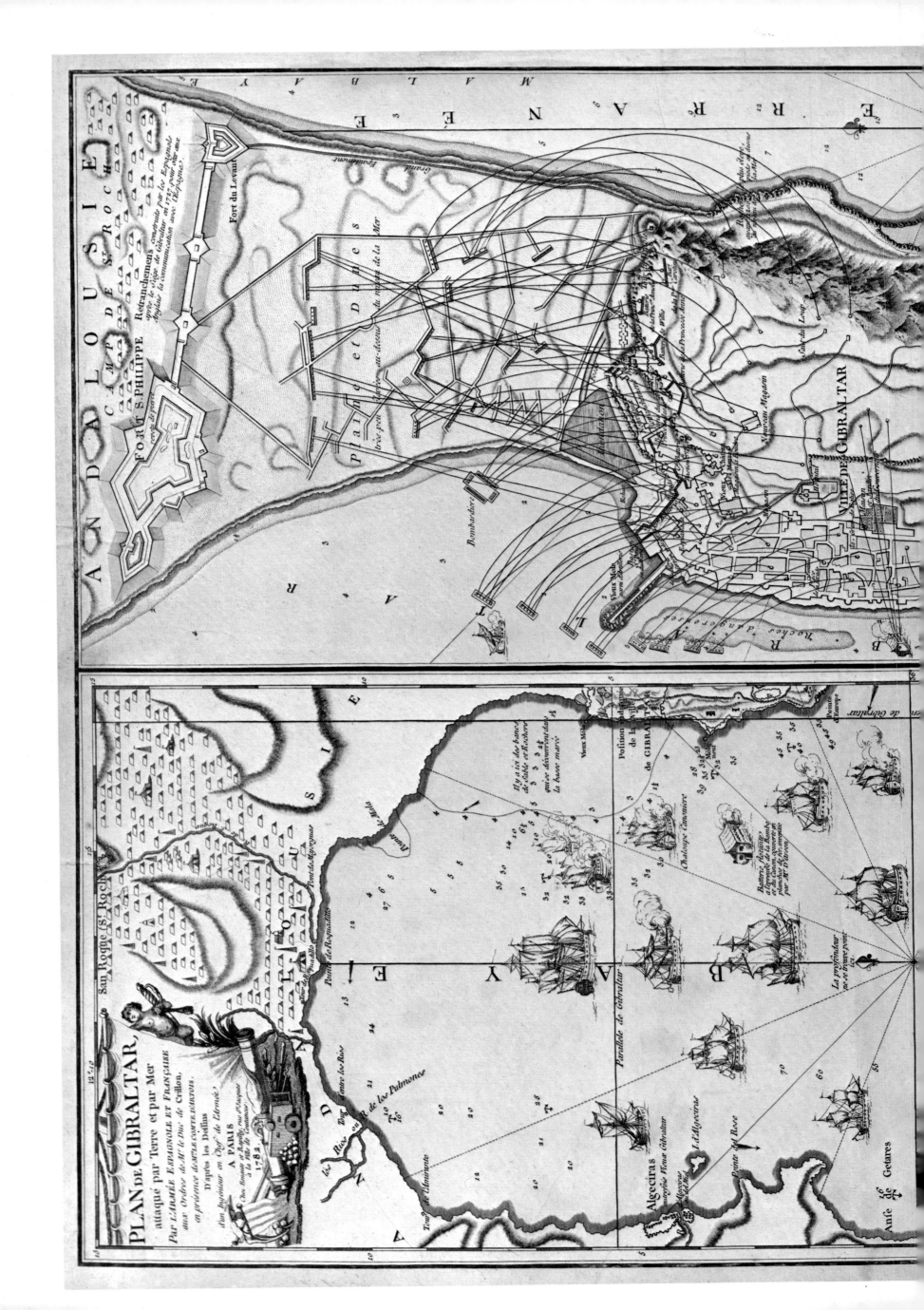

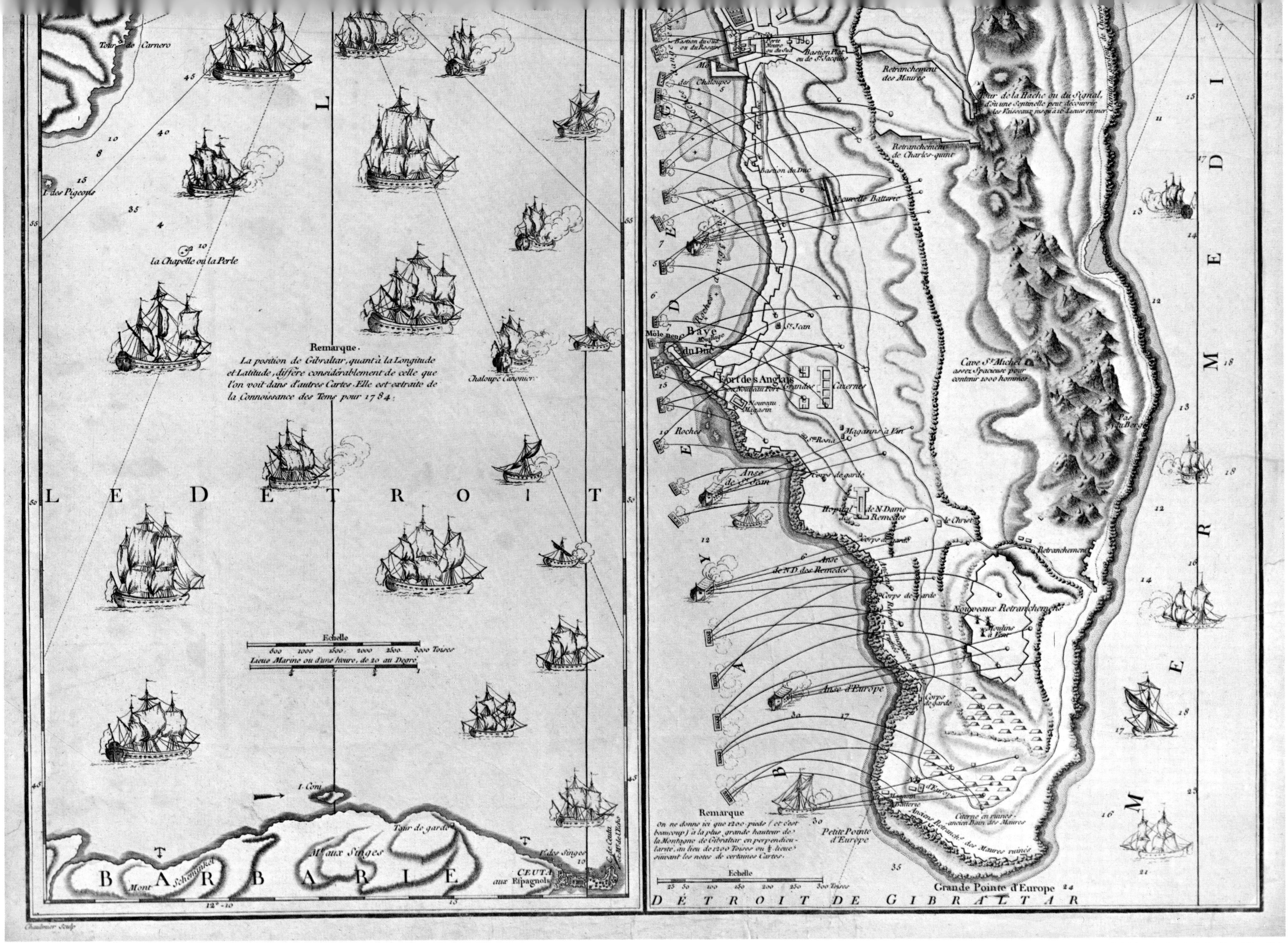

MER MEDITERRANÉE

DÉTROIT DE GIBRALTAR

Grande Pointe d'Europe

Petite Pointe d'Europe

Remarque

Echelle

LE DÉTROIT

Remarque.

La position de Gibraltar, quant à la Longitude
et Latitude, diffère considérablement de celle que
l'on voit dans d'autres Cartes. Elle est extraite de
la Connoissance des Tems pour 1784.

BARBARIE

Ceuta aux Espagnols

Isle Singes

Mont de Singes

Tour de garde

One of the Most Memorable Sieges in History

MAP 50. ¶ In 1704, during the War of Sutrian Succession, the British took the key stronghold of Gibraltar, and they have held it ever since. ¶ The greatest test of the defending garrison came in 1779. Spain, always watching for a chance to drive out the British, finally joined France as an ally of the Americans against Britain. The Spanish then wasted no time in turning their guns on Gibraltar. For over 1,300 days — three years and seven months — the British held out against artillery barrages from the north and naval bombardments from all around the peninsula. Many times during the siege British naval squadrons fought their way through the blockade to reprovision the defenders. ¶ Early in 1782, after Yorktown but before the end of the war, a "grand attack" was mounted against Gibraltar by a combined French-Spanish fleet commanded by the duc de Crillon. The left half of the plate shows the harbor and the attacking navies. Crillon's chief engineer, d'Arson, had devised covered, "unsinkable," gunships for the occasion. These armored artillery arks, clearly visible in the large-scale map on the right of the plate, withstood the accurate cannonading of hard-shot by the British, and it appeared as if the Union Jack's tenure at Gibraltar would end. Then the gallant General Sir George Augustus Elliot, later Lord Heathfield, who had commanded the post all during the war, played his trump card. Elliot, in anticipation of this assault, had ordered grates constructed for the heating of shot. When the British artillerymen, who were scoring 93 percent hits at 1,400 yards, switched to the red-hot shot, they blew up or burned to the waterline every one of the gunships. The attack of September 13 and 14, 1782, was over. The siege continued until the following February 6, when the duc de Crillon advised Elliot that the preliminaries of peace had been signed and that the war was over. Appropriately for the time, the duc then paid a state visit to the fortress, and he and Elliot drank a toast to one another. ¶ Spain, after doing comparatively little during the Revolution, walked away from the peace table with Florida. She failed, however, to win back "the Rock."

SHOWN ON PRECEDING PAGE

Plan de Gibraltar, attaqué par terre et par Mer par l'Armée Espagnole et Francaise aux ordres de Mr. le Duc de Crillon, en présence de Mgr. le Comte D'Artois. . . . Engraved by Chaulmier. Paris, Esnauts and Rapilly, 1782. (29½" x 20½")

ganize the western lands beyond the Appalachians. Then, too, many Americans felt that the Articles of Confederation were inadequate without amendments to strengthen the hand of Congress in order that it might cope with the internal and external responsibilities of a viable nation.

By all odds, the first priority was to bring the war to an official end, to conclude a peace that would recognize the independence of the United States and acknowledge American claims to the West. Despite Yorktown and Britain's unwillingness to try to conquer America, the prospects for a satisfactory peace treaty were cloudy in 1782. America seemed tied to the aspirations of Spain, a kingdom that had not recognized the independence of America, much less extended a helping hand. For America, according to the terms of the French alliance, could not conclude a separate peace; and France, in turn, had agreed to fight on until the objectives of *her ally* Spain were achieved.

Moreover, in 1782 Britain bounced back against her Bourbon enemies. In April, Admiral Rodney got his revenge on Admiral de Grasse, who had tricked him a year earlier: a decisive victory—the Battle of the Saints in the West Indies—that netted five French vessels and the capture of de Grasse himself. Almost simultaneously in India, the French under the Bailli de Suffren were repulsed by Admiral Sir William Hughes. Nor did the Bourbons fare better at Gibraltar, where Lord Howe's outnumbered fleet and General George Elliot's determined resistance saved that rocky eminence for Britain.

America's future, in a real sense, was in the hands of the congressionally appointed peace commission, of which one member, Thomas Jefferson, declined to serve owing to the loss of his wife; and a second member, Henry Laurens, captured by the enemy, was locked up in the infamous Tower of London. Of the three commissioners on the European continent, John Adams did not reach Paris until October, 1782, since he had been involved in negotiating a loan in Holland; another commissioner, John Jay, also unavailable for opening conversations, was in Madrid—unsuccessfully seeking substantial aid from Spain in the last stages of the war—prior to his joining Benjamin Franklin in Paris during the summer.

What were the chances for Franklin and, later, Jay? True enough, the North ministry had fallen in London, replaced by a coalition led by the Marquis of Rockingham and the Earl of Shelburne, both desirous of future American friendship. But while Rockingham, the first minister, favored recognizing American independence, George III wanted to hold the parts of the former colonies still in British hands, and Shelburne hoped to retain some sort of a loose union with America.

Then there was the problem with France, caught between the conflicting aspirations of her very separate allies, the United States and Spain. In Madrid, King Charles III continued to seek military conquests over Britain before a peace should come about; and, of equal or greater concern to American diplomats, Spanish Foreign Minister Floridablanca wished to confine the new nation east of the Appalachians, wished to head off the ambitions of an upstart rival in the New World, particularly a republican one that might infect Madrid's own colonies with notions of revolution and independence.

The American diplomats were further handicapped in their apparent lack of room to maneuver. In 1781, when creating the peace commission, Congress was disturbed by British gains in the South and was influenced by certain pressures from France. First, the commissioners were required to secure no more than the recognition of American independence, leaving the question of the trans-Appalachian region up in the air. And, second, they were "to undertake nothing" without the "knowledge and concurrence" of the French; "and ultimately to govern yourselves by their advice and opinion. . . ."

One might well ask how could the American diplomats have been in a worse position. How could they come home with their shirts? Or, to abandon the metaphor, could they even have achieved the admission of the independence of a confined and constricted United States, given their instructions, given Britain's evident unwillingness to sever wholly the American connection, and given Spain's insistence—now demonstrably hopeless after the success of Howe and Elliot—upon gaining Gibraltar?

Yet things are not always as they seem to be, especially if men are willing to be tough-minded and battle the odds, and so it was with the American commissioners. Franklin and Jay never followed literally Congress's prohibitions, and doubtless the lawmakers in Philadelphia would have accepted any such departure had they been demonstrated to be to the benefit of the United States; probably, too, these original instructions were in part designed to encourage additional French military assistance in 1781. Assuredly those tactics bore fruit that year, not only in the cooperation of Rochambeau and de Grasse at Yorktown, but also on the economic front: grants and loans amounting to approximately $1,000,000 more than all previous French allocations.

Actually, all the nations involved in the peacemaking proved more flexible than their official private and public utterances would indicate. In early 1782, Lord Shelburne proposed to fish in the troubled waters of the Franco-American alliance. He dispatched Richard Oswald, an old friend of Franklin, to Paris to confer with the Pennsylvanian in hopes of prying the Americans from their Gallic orbit. If French Foreign Minister Vergennes knew of this contact, he was unaware that Franklin (on July 12, 1782) advanced concrete proposals that later formed the core of negotiations. But Rockingham's death and the question of complete American independence temporarily stalled the talks. At this point, Jay arrived from Madrid, and since Franklin had fallen ill, the New Yorker took charge of the peacemaking.

Almost immediately two developments caused Jay to initiate quick, unilateral action. French and Spanish officials informed him that they favored a plan dividing the trans-Appalachian region between Britain and Spain. Then, when Jay learned that Vergennes's secretary had left secretly for London to get British support for their scheme, the commissioner notified Shelburne, now head of the ministry, that he was ready to conduct separate and confidential negotiations, a move Franklin subsequently concurred in. The rest was soon history. For the British, eager to split America from France, now dropped their illusory thoughts of holding America to some formal tie with the empire. On November 30, 1782, Oswald, Jay, and Franklin approved a preliminary treaty to take effect when Britain and France came to terms. The details need not concern us, except to say that America's all-important western boundary was to be the Mississippi River.

If the Americans had not complied with the details of their instructions or the literal terms of the French alliance, it could be argued that France, in showing favoritism to Spain, had scarcely shown her concern for the best interests of the United States. Since the preliminary treaty was contingent upon peace between Britain and France, then Vergennes might still have scotched the Anglo-American accord, although that step involved the risk

Benjamin Franklin, here in an engraving copied from a portrait painted in London in 1762 by Mason Chamberlain, was one of three agents who went to France in 1776 and successfully negotiated vital loans and a treaty of alliance with the French.

that Franklin, Jay, and now, Adams might go ahead and terminate the conflict without France. In fact, Vergennes had no desire to prolong the war for Spain's foolish schemes, and he wisely persuaded his Bourbon partner to accept the realities of the situation and to settle instead for recovering the Floridas, which she had lost to Britain in 1763.

As the moment for the final signing drew near, the British plenipotentiaries remembered that it was the custom to give presents to the diplomats of the various nations involved. The traditional practice often called for

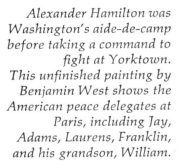

Alexander Hamilton was Washington's aide-de-camp before taking a command to fight at Yorktown. This unfinished painting by Benjamin West shows the American peace delegates at Paris, including Jay, Adams, Laurens, Franklin, and his grandson, William.

presenting diamond-encased portraits of the monarch, but the British delegation intelligently concluded that the Americans would prefer cash to a jeweled picture of a king whose rule they had foresworn. On the morning of September 3, 1783, the American commissioners repaired to the quarters of British representative David Hartley at the Hotel d'York, still standing in the Quartier Latin, and affixed their signatures to the definitive treaty, a scene recaptured (with certain errors) in Benjamin West's famous painting.

It is doubtful if Parisians saw the peace as any kind of turning point in world history, as the beginning of a revolutionary cycle of people seeking freedom and independence that would be repeated endlessly in the next two centuries. Nor did John Adams and the Conde de Aranda, the Spanish minister, fully recognize the long-term import of their light banter—when Aranda exclaimed, "*Tout, en ce monde, a été Révolution,*" and when Adams replied, "History is but a string of them." As for the Parisians, they were caught up in the successful balloon flights of the Montgolfier brothers, who achieved heights of six thousand feet.

In America, the final treaty brought great rejoicing, a realization that America's peace commissioners—"militia diplomats," as Adams phrased it —had won out over the low arts of European backstage dealings and power politics, had triumphed in spite of basic hostilities everywhere to what the American Revolution stood for. In Pennsylvania, the assembly appropriated a sum not to exceed £ 600 for building a victorious arch at the end of

Market Street, to be designed and constructed by the gifted artist Charles Willson Peale.

The most poignant reactions were seen in Washington's farewells to the officers of the army and to Congress. When definitive word of peace reached America, Sir Guy Carleton, who had replaced Clinton, evacuated New York City. Several days after Washington's small knot of remaining Continentals entered the city, the general met with his subordinates for a final time at Fraunces Tavern, which today had been restored and is once more offering culinary delights, to say nothing of its being the oldest surviving building on Manhattan Island. He wrote no message; but after the decanters of wine were passed around, he said simply, in words choked with emotion: "With a heart full of love and gratitude, I now take leave of you. I most devoutly wish that your later days may be as prosperous and happy as your former ones have been glorious and honorable." Then, after calling each man present to come forward—from major general to lowest lieutenant —and "take my hand," he was off to Annapolis, Maryland, where Congress was in session, where once again emotions surfaced. "Having now finished the work assigned me," he told the lawmakers in a short speech, "I retire from the great theatre of action; and bidding an Affectionate farewell to this August body under whose orders I have so long acted, I here offer my commission, and take my leave of all the employments of public life."

Yet Washington's generation had relatively little time to rest on its laurels. History—or so it has been said—is the story of one crisis after another; some periods of the past, at least, appear to sustain that contention, and so it was for the revolutionary generation. It had won on the military fronts, and it had triumphed at the peace conference, but it remained to be seen whether it could complete the task—started during the war—of setting its house in order. The lead everywhere was usually taken by men who had played an active role outside their own states during the war years, in the army, in Congress, and in administrative or diplomatic posts under the Confederation. Their experience with Continental affairs gave them a perspective on American problems often denied to individuals who had spent those same years at the local level. Alexander Hamilton said they were men who thought "continentally"; to Jefferson, they saw things "from a high ground." Indeed, "nationalists" is the best word to describe them.

The claim has been made that the nationalists from the end of the war or even before had schemed to abolish the Articles of Confederation in favor of a more conservative form of government that would favor mercantile groups and social elites. In short, that the nationalists were counter-revolutionary, intent on repudiating the principles of 1776. To be sure, the nationalists felt that the Articles did not give Congress sufficient control in areas of concern to the entire nation. It could not tax or regulate commerce. Nor did it have a way to enforce its authority in areas where the Articles gave it jurisdiction: making war and peace, conducting foreign affairs, dealing with Indian tribes, and handling postal matters—among others. In truth, the nationalists' aims were broad, not narrow; their concerns were for all Americans, not special interests. Practical, flexible men, they would likely have been willing enough to retain the Articles if that document could have been made workable. But repeated efforts between 1781 and 1786 to secure amendments to bolster Congress chiefly in financial and commercial areas had been defeated; and further attempts did not seem promising when unanimous approval of all the states was necessary. In the meantime, Congress struggled to survive. Or as James Madison said it, the task was like that

*Washington's estate
at Mount Vernon,
overlooking
the Potomac River,
served as his
retreat between
periods of service
to Virginia and to
the United States.
Both Washington and
his wife, Martha,
are buried
on the grounds
of the estate.*

of constantly manning the pumps to keep a ship afloat, a ship that now seemed beyond permanent repair. It was especially depressing to men who had become desectionalized by their revolutionary experience now to see the states violate the Articles by treating with the Indians, building state navies, and generally thumbing their noses at the Confederation government. Or to learn that American diplomats abroad—notably John Adams in England and Jefferson in France—had trouble persuading Europeans that they represented one nation and not thirteen.

The revolutionary years have quite properly been described as the "experimental period" of American history; and the years after the peace of 1783 were particularly "critical" ones in the sense that the poet Joel Barlow expressed it in 1786: "The revolution is but half completed. Independence and government were the two objects contended for; and but one is yet obtained."

So the nationalists scrapped the Articles, not to repudiate the Revolution, but to preserve and extend the fruits of the Revolution. The result was the Federal Constitution, written at Philadelphia in 1787 and adopted by the people in conventions by the following year. The architects of the new parchment and the strategists for its ratification were, in many cases, men who have repeatedly crossed the pages of this book: Washington, Madison, Hamilton, Schuyler, Jay, Knox, Lincoln, Morris, Wilson, Iredell. And let us not forget the eldest statesman, Franklin, now eighty-two. He had recently remarked of his countrymen, who seemingly would never allow him to retire from public service: "They have eaten my flesh, and seem resolved now to pick my bones."

The new political system insured the rights of the states at the same time that it gave the nation a central government capable of maintaining domestic tranquillity, preserving individual liberty, providing for the common defense, and raising the status of America in the family of nations. The fundamental political problem for America between 1763 and 1787 was how governmental power should be distributed; first, between Parliament and the colonial assemblies; later between Congress under the Articles of Confederation and the state legislatures. The solution to that problem, found in Philadelphia in 1787, brought the American Revolution to its culmination.

*Emerging from the terrible winter
at Valley Forge, Washington's forces
pursued Howe's army across New Jersey.
General Lee, with an advance corps,
attacked Howe at Monmouth Courthouse
on June 28, 1778, then retreated as British
reinforcements came up. Washington's
arrival checked the retreat.*

The Bank of the United
States was chartered
in Philadelphia in 1791.
Its charter expired in 1812,
and a second Bank of the
United States was chartered
from 1816 to 1836.
From then until 1863,
there were only state banks.
The Federal Reserve System
was established in 1914.

List of Participants

A

Adams, John.....*American patriot, second president*
Adams, Samuel.....*American patriot and statesman*
Alexander, William.....*American officer*
Allen, Ethan.....*American officer*
Amherst, Jeffery.....*British officer*
André, John.....*British officer and spy*
Arbuthnot, Marriott.....*British naval officer*
Arnold, Benedict.....*American officer and traitor*

B

Barras, Jacques-Melchior, Comte de.....*French naval officer*
Barry, John.....*American naval officer*
Biddle, Nicholas.....*American naval officer*
Boone, Daniel.....*American frontiersman*
Brant, Joseph.....*Mohawk chief, pro-British*
Burgoyne, John.....*British officer*
Butler, John.....*Loyalist*
Butler, Richard.....*American officer*
Butler, Walter.....*Tory leader*
Byron, John.....*British naval officer*

C

Carleton, Guy.....*British officer*
Carroll, Charles.....*American statesman*
Clark, George Rogers.....*American officer and explorer*
Clarke (Clerke), Sir Francis.....*British officer*
Clinton, Henry.....*British commander in chief in America (1778-1782)*
Collier, George.....*British naval officer*
Conway, Thomas.....*American officer*
Cornwallis, Charles.....*British officer*

D

Dartmouth, William Legge, Earl of.....*British statesman*
Davie, William Richardson.....*American patriot*
Dawes, William.....*American patriot*
Deane, Silas.....*Continental congressman*
Dearborn, Henry.....*American officer*
De Lancey, Oliver.....*British officer*

E

Estaing, Charles Hector Théodat, Comte d'.....*French naval officer*

F

Ferguson, Patrick.....*British officer*
Franklin, Benjamin.....*American statesman*
Fraser, Simon.....*British officer*

G

Gadsden, Christopher.....*American merchant, statesman, officer*
Gage, Thomas.....*British commander in chief in America (1763-1775)*
Gates, Horatio.....*American officer*
George III.....*King of Great Britain and Ireland*
Germain, George Sackville.....*British colonial secretary*
Glover, John.....*American officer*
Grant, James.....*British officer*
Grasse, Francois Joseph Paul, Comte de.....*French naval officer*
Graves, Thomas.....*British naval officer*
Greene, Nathanael.....*American officer*
Grey, Charles.....*British officer*
Gunby, John.....*American officer*

H

Haldimand, Sir Frederick.....*British officer*
Hale, Nathan.....*American officer*
Hamilton, Alexander.....*American officer and statesman*
Hamilton, Henry.....*British officer*
Hancock, John.....*American patriot*
Hand, Edward.....*American officer*
Hazen, Moses.....*American officer*
Heath, William.....*American officer*
Heister, Philip von.....*Hessian officer, British army*
Henry, Patrick.....*American patriot and statesman*
Herkimer, Nicholas.....*American officer*
Hood, Samuel, First Viscount.....*British naval officer*
Hopkins, Esek.....*First commander in chief of the Continental navy*
Hotham, William.....*British naval officer*
Howe, Richard.....*British naval officer*
Howe, Robert.....*American officer*
Howe, William.....*British commander in chief in America (1775-1778)*

J

Jay, John.....*American statesman and diplomat*
Jefferson, Thomas.....*American statesman*
Johnson, Sir John.....*Loyalist*
Johnson, Sir William.....*Loyalist*
Jones, John Paul.....*American naval officer*

K

Kalb, Johann de.....*American officer*
Knox, Henry.....*American officer*
Knyphausen, Wilhelm, Baron von.....*German officer, British army*
Kosciuszko, Thaddeus.....*American officer*

L

Lafayette, Marquis de.....*American officer*
Lamb, John.....*American officer*
Laurens, John.....*American officer*
Lee, Arthur.....*American diplomat*
Lee, Charles.....*American officer*
Lee, Henry ("Light-Horse Harry").....*American officer*
Lee, Richard Henry.....*American congressman*
Lincoln, Benjamin.....*American officer*

M

Madison, James.....*American patriot*
Marion, Francis.....*American officer*
Marshall, John.....*American officer*
Montgomery, Richard.....*American officer*
Montresor, John.....*British officer*
Morgan, Daniel.....*American officer*
Moultrie, William.....*American officer*
Muhlenberg, John Peter Gabriel.....*American officer and politician*

N

Nash, Francis.....*American officer*
North, Sir Frederick (Lord North).....*British prime minister*

O

Oswald, Eleazer.....*American officer*
Oswald, Richard.....*British diplomat*

P

Paine, Thomas.....*American patriot*
Parker, John.....*American officer*
Parker, Sir Peter.....*British naval officer*
Pepperrell, Sir William.....*Loyalist*
Percy, Hugh.....*British officer*
Phillips, William.....*British officer*
Pickens, Andrew.....*American officer*
Pigot, Robert.....*British officer*
Pitcairn, John.....*British officer*
Pomeroy, Seth.....*American officer*
Poor, Enoch.....*American officer*
Prescott, Samuel.....*American physician*
Prescott, William.....*American officer*
Preston, Charles.....*British officer*
Prevost, Augustine.....*British officer*
Pulaski, Casimir.....*American officer*
Putnam, Israel.....*American officer*

R

Rall, Johann Gottlieb.....*Hessian officer, British army*
Rawdon-Hastings, Francis (Lord Rawdon).....*British officer*
Revere, Paul.....*American patriot*
Riedesel, Baron Friedrich.....*German officer, British army*
Rochambeau, Jean Baptiste, Comte de.....*French officer, American army*
Rockingham, Charles, Marquess of.....*British prime minister*
Rodney, George.....*British naval officer*
Rutledge, Edward.....*American congressman*
Rutledge, John.....*American congressman*

S

St. Clair, Arthur.....*American officer*
St. Leger, Barry.....*British officer*
Saltonstall, Dudley.....*American naval officer*
Sandwich, John Montagu, Fourth Earl of.....*British politician*
Schuyler, Philip John.....*American officer*
Sevier, John.....*American officer*
Shelburne, William, Earl of.....*British statesman*
Shelby, Isaac.....*American officer*
Smallwood, William.....*American officer*
Smith, Francis.....*British officer*
Spencer, Joseph.....*American officer*
Stark, John.....*American officer*
Stephen, Adam.....*American officer*
Steuben, Friedrich Wilhelm von.....*American officer*
Stewart, Alexander.....*British officer*
Stuart, John.....*British Superintendent of Indian Affairs for the South*
Sullivan, John.....*American officer*
Sumter, Thomas.....*American officer*

T

Tarleton, Banastre.....*British officer*
Thomas, John.....*American officer*
Trumbull, Joseph.....*American officer*

V

Vergennes, Charles Gravier, Comte de.....*French foreign minister*

W

Wadsworth, Jeremiah.....*American officer*
Ward, Artemas.....*American officer*
Warner, Seth.....*American officer*
Warren, Joseph.....*American officer and doctor*
Washington, George.....*American commander in chief*
Washington, William.....*American officer*
Wayne, Anthony.....*American officer*
Wickes, Lambert.....*American naval officer*
Willett, Marinus.....*American officer*
Williams, Otho.....*American officer*
Wooster, David.....*American officer*
Wythe, George.....*American statesman*

A Compendious Account of the British Colonies in North-America.

These descriptions of the colonies were printed with *The Theatre of War in North America* map. London, R. Sayer & J. Bennett, March 20, 1776. (See front and back endsheets)

GOVERNMENT OF NEWFOUNDLAND.

By the Proclamation of the 7th of October, 1763, this government includes 1. The isle of Newfoundland, and all the islands adjacent to its coasts, except those of *Miquelon* and *St. Peter's*, which are left in the possession of the French; 2. The isles of Anticosti and Magdalen, in the Gulf of St. Laurence; 3. All the coast of Labrador, from St. John's River to Hudson's Straits. The soil of this government is barren, but the sea is an inexhaustible mine of treasure, and its coasts are full of harbours, very safe and commodious for the fishery. The chief town is *St. John*, on the south-east part of Newfoundland.

CANADA OR THE PROVINCE OF QUEBEC.

By the Royal Proclamation of the 7th of October, 1763, this province is bounded on the East by the river St. John, and from thence, by a Line drawn from the head of that river, through Lake St. John, to the south end of Lake Nipissing; from whence the said Line, crossing the river St. Lawrence and lake Champlain, in the 45th parallel of north latitude, passes along the high lands which divide the rivers that empty themselves into the said river St. Laurence, from those which fall into the sea; and also along the north coast of the Baye des Chaleurs, and the coast of the Gulf of St. Laurence, to Cape Rosiers, and from thence crossing the mouth of the river St. Laurence, by the west end of the island of Anticosti, terminates at the aforesaid river St. John. An Act of Parliament, passed in 1774, has removed the northern and western limits of the Province of Quebec, adding to its jurisdiction all the lands comprized between the northern bounds of New-York, the western line of Pennsylvania, the Ohio, the Missisippi, and the southern boundaries of Hudson's Bay Company.—The *Towns* of note are Quebec, Montreal, and Trois Rivieres. Quebec, which is a city, and the capital of the whole province, is a fortified place, situated at the confluence of the rivers St. Laurence and St. Charles, on the north side of the former: it consists of an Upper and Lower Town, well-built of stone, and contains 12 or 14,000 inhabitants.—Montreal is built on a fruitful island of the same name, in the river St. Laurence, 60 leagues south-west of Quebec; it is also divided into and Upper and Lower Town, well-built and populous. Near Montreal, on the river Richelieu, are two forts, Chambly and St. John, taken by the Provincials.—Trois Rivieres lies at the confluence of the three rivers so called, running into St. Laurence: it is much frequented by several nations of Indians, for the purpose of trading; and there is a very good foundry in its neighbourhood.—*Lakes:* The five principal, which communicate, are Lake Superior, 500 leagues in circuit; the Lakes Ontario, Erié or Oswego, Huron, and Michigan, all navigable by vessels of any size, as also their communications, except that between lakes Erié and Ontario, where is a stupendous cataract, called the Falls of Niagara. The stream is about a mile wide, divided by a rocky island in the form of a half-moon. The perpendicular height is 148 feet; and the noise may be heard upwards of fifteen miles.—The chief *River* is that of the St. Laurence, navigable from the sea to Montreal; it receives the rivers Outaouais, Richelieu or Sorel, Trois Rivieres, Saguenay, Bustard, and an innumerable quantity of lesser ones. Cape Roisers is the most remarkable Cape of the Province of Quebec, and of the Gulf of St. Laurence.

NOVA-SCOTIA,

Is bounded on the N. by Canada. E. Gulf of St. Laurence. S. Atlantic Ocean. W. New-England. The chief town in Nova-Scotia is Halifax, founded in 1749, by an embarkation of near 4000 families. It is situated on Chebucto-bay, where there is one of the finest harbours in the world, capable of containing 1000 ships in security, and very commodious for the fishery. Annapolis Royal was formerly called Port-Royal by the French, but received its present name in honour of Queen Anne; its harbour, which is as fine as that of Halifax, has the disadvantage of a very difficult entrance.—Lunenburg, a small town to the west of Halifax; Canso, another little town to the eastward.—*Capes:* Cape Sable, the most southern point of the province, Sambrô, Cansô.—*Bays*, the great bay of Fundy, with those of Chignicto, St. Mary's, Chebucto, Milford, Bayverte, Miramichy, and Chaleur-Bay.—*Rivers:* Ristigouche, Nipissiguit, Minaqua, St. John's, and river St. Croix, which divides the province from New-England. By the Royal Proclamation of 1763, the isles of *Cape Breton* and *St. John's*, in the Gulf of St. Laurence, are annexed to the government of Nova-Scotia. The former, where the French had the fortress of Louisbourg, now in ruins, has several good harbours, and plenty of coals; its inhabitants are very few. St. John's Island, which is settled by the English since the peace, has a fruitful soil, and several good harbours; its chief palace is Charlotte-town.

NEW ENGLAND,

Is bounded on the E. by Nova-Scotia. E. and S. by the Atlantic Ocean. W. New-York. N. Canada.—Boston, its metropolis, is situated upon a peninsula, joined to the continent by a neck of land, about half a mile long, 60 yeards broad, where General Gage erected fortifications. The town, which stands at the bottom of a capacious harbour, defended from the violence of the sea by numerous small islands, is nearly two miles in length, and half a mile in breadth; it contained about 3000 good houses, forming spacious streets, 10 churches, and near 18 or 20,000 inhabitants; and was divided in 12 wards, each of which kept a company of foot. At the bottom of the harbour is a noble pier, near 2000 feet in length, along which, on the north side, extends a row of warehouses. A light house was on one of the islands, called the Brewsters, at the entrance of the harbour; as also a castle on another island 1½ mile from the town.—Cambridge has no regular streets, but is remarkable for Harvard College, now turned into barracks for the Provincial soldiers. The Rev. Mr. John Harvard, minister of Charles-Town, left towards it a legacy of 800 l: An additional building was afterwards erected, called Stoughton-Hall; of these consists the university.—New England consists of the four following Provinces: New-Nampshire, Massachusets-Bay, Rhode-Island, Connecticut.—New Hampshire, though laid out in townships, is not formed into counties; nor are there but few towns; Portsmouth, Hampton, Lichfield, Dunstable, and Exeter, are the chief, Portsmouth being the seat of government.—Massachusets-Bay contains the following counties and towns; *York* (formerly the Province of Main): York, Kittery, Wells, Biddiford, Falmouth, Yarmouth, Brunswick: with several forts.—*Essex:* Salem, Marblehead, Lynn, Andover, Bradford, Haverill, Salisbury, Newbury, Ipswich, Wenham, Gloecster, Beverly, &c.—*Middlesex:* Cambridge (an university), Charles-Town (burnt by the King's troops, June 17, 1775), Concord, Lexington, Medford, Malden, Waltham, Woburn, Wilmington, Reading, Billerika, Groton, Chelsea, Weston, Stow, Marlborough, Sudbury, Sherburn, Natick, Holliston, &c.—*Hampshire:* Northampton, Hadley, Hatfield, Sunderland, Deerfield, Northfield, Narraganset, Petersham, Pentusok, Springfield, Springfield East and West, Sheffield, &c.—*Suffolk:* Boston, the metropolis of New-England, Roxbury, Dorchester, Milton, Brantree, Weymouth, Hingham, Konohasset, Stoughton, Wrentham, Walpole, Bellingham, Medway, Medfield, Deadham, &c.—*Worcester:* Oxford, Leicester, Sutton, Rutland, Old Rutland, Westborough, Mendon, Uxbridge, Douglas, &c.—*Ancient Colony of Plymouth:* Plymouth, Abingdon, Duxbury, Marshfield, &c.—*Bristol:* Attleborough, Easton, Raynham, Bridgewater, Taunton, Dighton, Swansey, Dartmouth, Rochester, Barrington, Rehoboth, &c.—*Barnstaple:* Barnstable, Sandwich, Falmouth, Yarmouth, Harwich, Eastham, Silver-spring, Belingsgate, Truro, Chatham, &c.—*Duke's County,* or *Island of Martha's Vineyard:* Edgar, Tisbury, Chilmark, &c.—*Nantuckket County* and *Island:* Sherburn, &c.—Besides the above, to the

Massachusets-Bay province also belongs the territory of *Sagadahok*, where, among other small settlements, are two forts, George's Truckhouse and Fort Frederic.—The counties, &c. of Rhode-Island and Providence Plantation, are, Providence, Warwick, Coventry, Scituate, Glocester, &c.—*Bristol:* Bristol.—*Newport:* Newport (capital of the province), and Portsmouth, in Rhode-Island;—*Tiverton,* Fagland and Little Compton.— *King's:* Richmond, Exeter, Kingston, Greenwich, &c.—The counties, &c. of Connecticut are, *Windham:* Windham, Mansfield, Ashford, Killingsley, Pomfret, Canterbury, Voluntown, Plainfield, &c.—*Lichfield:* Lichfield, Woodbury, New Milford, Kent, Cornwall, Sharon, Wiatiak, or Salisbury, &c.—*Hertford.* Hertford (the chief town of the colony), New Cambridge, Farmington, Hadham, Middletown, Glassenbury, Wethersfield, Willington, Somers, Windsor, Simsbury, &c.—*Newhaven:* Newhaven, Milford, Brentford, Guildford, Derby, Durham, &c.—*Fairfield:* Fairfield, Norwalk, Stamford, Stratford, Ridgfield, Newtown, Danbury, New Fairfield, &c.—*New London:* New London, Groton, Stonington, Norwich, Lime, Killingworth, Seabrook, &c—The principal *Capes,* headlands, and points of New-England, are, Pemaquid and Small Points, Cape Elizabeth, Black Point, Porpus and Nidduck, or Bald-head Capes, York Nubbles, Lock's Point, Great Boar's-head, Pigeon-hill, Cape Ann, Nahant, Pullein's, Alderton, Marshfield, Gurnet, Monument and Sandy Points, Murray's Cliffs, Sandy, Belinsgate, and Race Points, Cape Cod, Head of Pamet, Cape Malebar or Sandy Point, Gooseberry Neck, Ninigret, Quakoragox, Watch, Black, Pipe-staves, and Hemunasset Points, Sachem's Head, South, Long-Neck, and Elizabeth Points, and Lion's Tongue; also Cape Pope, and Gay Head, in Martha's Vineyard.—The chief *Bays* are, Penobscot, Kennebek, Casko, Sawko, Wells, the great bay of Massachusets, Cape-Cod bay (including Plymouth Bay), Buzzard's and Narraganset Bay; to which may be added the Devil's-Belt, or Long Island Sound, between that Island and Connecticut, and Winipissioket Pond, in New-Hampshire.—*Harbours:* Winter, Piscataqua, Cape Ann, Boston, Konohasset, Scituate, Yarmouth, Slokum's, New-haven, Ship, and Old Town (in Martha's Vineyard Island).—The principal *Rivers* are, Connecticut, Thames, Patuxet, Merrimack, Piscataqua, Sawko, Caskow, Kennebeck, and Penobscot.

NEW YORK,

Is bounded N. by Canada. E. New-England. S. Atlantic Ocean, and New Jersey. W. and N.W. Pennsylvania and Canada.—Counties and Towns; *New York:* New York (the capital of the province.—*Charlotte* and *Tryon* counties bordering upon the Iroquois.—*Albany:* Albany (an incorporated city, which carries a great trade with the Indians); Schonectad, or Schenectady (an incorporated town).—*Ulster.*—*Dutchess.*—*Orange:* Orange.—*Westchester:* Westchester (an incorporated town), Rye, Eastchester. The city of New-York is situated on the south point of Mahanatan Island, formed by Hudson's river. Ships of 500 tons may come up to the wharfs of the city, and be always afloat. New-York commands a fine prospect of waters, the Jerseys, Long and Staten Islands, &c. and contains near 3000 houses, divided into seven wards, and above 12,000 inhabitants. In the Broadway-street most of the houses have a row of trees before them; the generality of the other streets are narrow. One inconvenience is, the inhabitants being obliged to fetch their water from springs at a considerable distance from the town. Several islands belong to the Province of New-York; the two principal are *Long Island* and *Staten Island;* the first lies in length from East to West about 120 miles, and at a medium about 15 broad, it is divided into three counties, viz, King's Queen's, and Suffolk, and has no town of note. Staten Island, which makes one county, lies to the west of Long Island. Amongst the fortresses of the province are, Ticonderoga on Lake George, and Crown Point at the extremity of Lake Champlain, now in the hands of the Provincials.—*Capes* in New York are, May, Sandy-Hook, and Montock Points.—*Straits:* the Narrows and Hell-Gate; through the latter, about 80 yards wide, it is extremely dangerous sailing, on account of the different rapid currents; for if a vessel gets into any but the right one, she inevitably runs on a shoal of rocks on one side, or is whirled round and swallowed up by a dreadful vortex on the other.—*Rivers:* Hudson's or the North River (which runs through the whole province from North to South), Mohawk, and Schochery. On the Mohawk is a large cataract, called the Cohoes, whose perpendicular height is 70 feet.

NEW JERSEY, DIVIDED INTO EAST AND WEST,

Is bounded on the N. by New York. E. Atlantic Ocean. W. and S.W. Delaware River and Bay.—The counties and towns in the East District are, *Middlesex:* Perth-Amboy, New Brunswick, Woodbridge.—*Monmouth:* Freehold.—*Essex:* Elizabeth, Newark.—*Somerset.*—*Bergen:* Bergen.—Counties and towns in the West District; *Burlington:* Burlington, or Bridlington.—*Glocester:* Glocester.—*Salem:* Salem.—*Cumberland:* Hopewell.—*Cape May.*—*Hunterdon:* Trenton.—*Morris:* Morris.—*Sussex.*—Perth-Amboy, the provincial town of the East Jersey, is delightfully situated on a neck of land, included between the rivers Rariton and Amboy and a large open bay.—Burlington, the chief town of the West Jersey, stands on the Delaware. In these two towns the General Assembly of all the Jerseys sit alternately, and the distinct Provincial or Supreme Courts sit respectively.—Brunswick is remarkable for the number of its beautiful women. In this town, which is nearly the center of the East and West Jerseys, there was established, in 1746, a college for the instruction of youth, by a charter from Governor Belcher, with power to confer all degrees, as in the Universities of England.—Cape May is the chief Cape at the Entrance of Delaware Bay; Perth-Amboy the chief Harbour; Delaware, Rariton, and Pasaic, the principal Rivers.

PENNSYLVANIA, TOGETHER WITH THE COUNTIES ON DELAWARE,

Is bounded on the N. by part of New York. E. Delaware River, dividing it from New Jersey. S. Maryland. W. partly by Virginia, and partly by Canada.—The counties and towns are, *Philadelphia:* Philadelphia, Germantown, Dublin, Francfort.—*Chester:* Chester.—*Bucks:* Newtown, Bristol.—*Berks:* Reading.—*Northampton:* Easton.—*Lancaster:* Lancaster, a town of 500 houses.—*York:* York.—*Cumberland:* Carlisle, a town of 500 houses.—*Bedford.*—On Delaware; *Newcastle:* Newcastle.—*Kent:* Dover.—*Sussex:* Lewes.—The city of Philadelphia was planned by the exalted and benevolent genius of the famous William Penn. It is situated on a tongue of land, very near the confluence of the Delaware and Schuilkill Rivers, contains 3000 houses, and 18 or 20,000 inhabitants: it is disposed in the form of an oblong, designed to extend two miles from river to river. The streets are laid out in parallel lines, intersected by others at right angles, and are handsomely built, well lighted, and watched: a pavement of broad stones runs along each side for foot-passengers. The Quays are spacious and fine, the principal one is 200 feet wide, and to this a vessel of 500 tons may lay her broad-side.—Cape Hinlopen is the principal Cape of Pennsylvania, at the entrance of Delaware Bay.—The chief *Rivers* are, the Delaware, Susquehanna, and Schuilkill.

MARYLAND,

Is bounded on the N. by Pennsylvania. E. Counties of Delaware and Atlantic Ocean. S. and W. by the Patowmack River, which separates the Province from Virginia.—Its counties and towns are, in the East Division, *Worcester:* Princess Anne.—*Somerset:* Snow-hill.—*Dorset:* Dorset or Dorchester.—*Talbot:* Oxford.—*Cecil.*—*Queen-Anne's:* Queen's-*St. Mary's:* St. Mary's.—*Charles:* Bristol.—*Prince George:* Masterkout.—*Calvert:* Abingdon.—*Arundel:* Annapolis.—*Baltimore:* Baltimore.—*Frederic.*—Annapolis, the capital, is a small neat town, of 150 houses; the

the streets are irregular, and not paved. It is situated on a peninsula formed by the river Severn and two small creeks, affording a beautiful prospect of Cheasapeak-bay, and of the Eastern shore beyond it. The chief river, which is navigable, is Patowmack.—Cheasapeak-bay includes many creeks, which afford the Province great commercial advantages by the convenience of inland navigation.

VIRGINIA,

Is bounded on the N.E. by the River Patowmack, dividing it from Maryland. E. Atlantic Ocean. S. North-Carolina. W. and N.W. the Apalachean Mountains. The counties and towns are, Amherst, Henrico, Richmond, Williamsburg, Prince William, Spotsylvania, Charlotte; *James City*, chief towns, Williamsburg and James-Town; Northumberland, Nansemond, Buckingham, King and Queen, Stafford, Mecklenburg, Loudoun, Louisa, Dinwiddie, Essex or Rappahanock, York, Prince Edward, Lancaster, Fairfax, Goochland, Cumberland, Brunswick, Fauquier, Frederick, Middlesex, Northampton, Hampshire, Prince George, Augusta, Surry, Bedford, Isle of Wight, Hanover, King George, Glocester, Princess Ann, Warwick, Albemarle, Caroline, New Kent, Southampton, Lunenburgh, Culpeper, King William, Halifax, Sussex; *Norfolk*, chief town, Norfolk, now in ashes; Amelia; *Elizabeth*, chief town, Elizabeth; Chesterfield, Pitsylvania. Williamsburg, the capital town, situated between two creeks, the one falling into James, the other into York River, contains 200 houses. Here is a college, towards endowing which King William and Queen Mary gave 2000 l. and 2000 acres of land, with a duty of 1d. per pound on all tobacco exported to the other plantations.—The *Capes* of Virginia, called Henry and Charles, open a passage into the Bay of Cheasapeak, one of the largest and finest in the world, being 18 miles broad at its mouth, and 7 or 8 throughout a length of near 200 miles, which it runs N. up the country.—The chief *Rivers* are, James, York or Pamunky, Rappahanock, and Patowmack; they not only admit large ships into the very heart of the country, but abound with so many creeks, and receive such a multitude of inferior, yet navigable rivers, that Virginia seems unrivalled throughout the universe for convenience of inland navigation; indeed, it has been observed, and with reason, that every planter here has a river at his door.

CAROLINA, DIVIDED INTO NORTH AND SOUTH

Is bounded on the N. by Virginia. E. Atlantic Ocean. S. by Georgia and the Cherokees Indians. W. Apalachean Mountains and the Cherokees Indians. North Carolina is divided into the counties of Anson, Bladen, Beaufort, Brunswic, Bute, Cartaret, Carrituck, Craven, Chatham, Chowan, Dobbs, Duplin, Edgecumbe, Granville, Guilford, Hyde, Halifax, Johnston, Mecklenburgh, New Hanover, Northampton, Orange, Onslow, Pasquotank, Perquimous, Rowan, Surry, Tyrrel, Tryon, Pitt, Wake, Bertie, The principal Towns are, Bath, Brunswic, Edenton, Halifax, Hillsborough, Newbern, Salisbury, Wilmington, Edenton and Newbern are the capitals of the Province.—South Carolina contains the Counties and Towns of *Berkeley;* Charlestown, Dorchester, Shemtown.—*Colleton;* Jacksonburgh.—*Granville;* Beaufort, Port-Royal, Purrysburgh, New Radnor.—*Craven;* George-Town.— *Winyaw.*—Charles-Town is the capital and seat of government of South-Carolina, and for size, beauty, and trade, vies with the first towns in America; it is advantageously situated at the confluence of the two navigable rivers Ashley and Cowper, in a most delightful neigh-

bourhood: the streets are wide and straight, intersecting each other at right angles; and the houses, some of which are of brick, and others of wood, amounting to about 1000, are well and elegantly built: its harbour has a bar at the entrance, which excludes vessels of more than 200 tons.—The *Capes* are, Hatteras, Look-out, and Cape Fear, in North-Carolina; Cape Carteret, in South-Carolina.—The *Harbours* are, Roanoke, Pamtico, and Cape Fear, in North-Carolina; the two first do not admit vessels of above fourscore tons: Winyaw or George-Town, Charles-Town, and Port-Royal, in South-Carolina. Port-Royal, the best harbour in the Carolinas, is capable of receiving the largest fleets, both with respect to number, bulk, and burthen, with the utmost safety. The little town of Beaufort is built on an island of the same name, at the extremity of the harbour.—The *Rivers* are, Roanoke or Albemarle, Pamtico, Neus, Cape Fear, in North-Carolina; Pedee, Santee, and Savannah, in South-Carolina.

GEORGIA,

Is bounded on the E. and S.E. by the Savannah River, which divides it from South-Carolina, and by the Atlantic; on the S. by St. Mary's River; on the W. by the Creek Indians; and on the N. by the Cherokees. It is not yet divided into counties. Its chief town is Savannah, about 12 miles from the sea, upon the large river of the same name, navigable for boats 200 miles further to the second town Augusta, which stands upon a most fertile spot, and is very commodiously situated for the Indian trade. Between those two places, and on the same river, are the towns of New Gottingen, Ebenezer, Abercorn, &c. Frederica is built in one of the islands which divide the Eastern coast, and whole numerous channels are very favourable to the navigation of small vessels.— The *Rivers* of Georgia (besides the Savannah, already mentioned) are, the Little Hogohechee, Great Hogohechee, Alatamaha, Great Sitilla, &c. all navigable for boats a great way in the country.

FLORIDA, DIVIDED INTO EAST AND WEST.

By the Royal Proclamation of 1763, the following boundaries are annexed to those provinces, viz, East Florida is bounded to the Westward by the Gulf of Mexico and the Apalachicola River; to the Northward, by a Line drawn from that part of the said River where the Chatahooche and Flint Rivers meet, to the source of St. Mary's River, and by the Course of the said River to the Atlantic Ocean; and to the Eastward and Southward, by the Atlantic Ocean and the Gulf of Florida, including all islands within six leagues of the sea-coast.— St. Augustine, the chief town, is situated upon the Eastern shore, and contains 900 houses, mostly uninhabited. The River St. John, the principal of this province, in point of utility and beauty, is not inferior to any in America; vessels may go up the river almost as easy as down, for 200 miles.—West Florida is bounded to the Southward by the Gulf of Mexico, including all islands within six leagues of the coast from the River Apalachicola to Lake Ponchartrain; to the Westward, by the said Lake and the River Missisippi; to the Northward, by a Line drawn due East from that Part of the River Missisippi which lies in 31 degrees North latitude, to the confluence of the Rivers Flint and Chatahooche into the Apalachicola; and to the Eastward, by the said Apalachicola River. The chief town is Pensacola, built on the West side of a bay receiving several rivers, in which ships may lie safe from all winds: it is the best harbour on this coast. To the West of Pensacola is the great Bay Mobile, with several French settlements.

Index

NOTE:
Page numbers in roman type refer to the general text.
Page numbers in *italics* refer to the map commentaries.
Page numbers in **bold** type refer to maps.

D

E

F

G

M

P

List of Maps

Original Map Size is shown.
See back endsheet for map locations.

NEW SOUTH WALES

JAMES BAY

NEW B...

St. Anns Lake

Albany F.

Ft. Rupert

Henley Factory

Moose Fort

Perray R.

Abitibis

Nation of the Bear

Monsonis

Lake Alemipigon

L.S.te Pete

French Factory

PROVINCE

Little Algonquins

Rain L.

St. Peters R.

St. Peters Fort Destroy'd

L. Misisagan or Red Lake

Red Lake R.

C A N A D A

LAKE SUPERIOR

Algonquins

Mefsesagues

Amikoues

L. Nipifing

Horfeton

Machenoton

L. Tinten

Hinhaneton

R. St. Peter

Ajoues

Mjoues

Outagamis

Mafcoutens

LAKE HURONS

LAKE MICHIGAN

Fort Detroit

Fox R.

Quicapous

Parched Mds.

NEW YORK

LAKE ONTARIO

LAKE ERIE

SIX NATIONS

PENSILVANIA

MASSACHU...

Miffouri R.

Ofages

Ofages

Delawares

VIRGINIA

MARYLAND

L O U I S I A N A

Extensive Meadows

MISSISSIPI

Cherokees

NORTH CAROLINA

C. Hatteras

Chicafaws

Chacolaw

Chicasaws

Coufa

Creeks

Ockfuskee

Cowetas

Catawbas

SOUTH CAROLINA

C. Fear

Long Bay

GEORGIA

Chaetaws

Keeowe

Charles Town

Apalachicola Fort

WEST FLORIDA

Pensacola

St. Mark

EAST

St. Augustine

Bay of Mississipi

Apalaches

FLORIDA

Mouths of the Missisipi

C. Cannaveral

GULF OF MEXICO

THE WESTERN OR AT...

Shawano...

Twightwi or Piqu...

Wills Creek

WILLIAMSBURGH   281   77...

Winchester   194   97   8...

Showing th...

NB. The Dist...

from Boston to Willi...